# COMPENDIUM OF 1850 MODERN GREEK VERBS

set out in tabular form with a guide to the function and formation of tenses and moods

UNIVERSITY STUDIO PRESS

MARIA TSIOTSIOU-MOORE and MIKE HENSON

# COMPENDIUM OF 1850 MODERN GREEK VERBS

set out in tabular form with a guide to the function and formation of tenses and moods

**Part I**

The Three main types of verbs in all Tenses, mood and imperative forms

**Part II**

A. Tables of Greek verbs in English alphabetical order
B. Page index of verbs in Greek alphabetical order

UNIVERSITY STUDIO PRESS
Publishers of Academic Books and Journals
THESSALONIKI 2007

UNIVERSITY STUDIO PRESS
Publishers of Academic Books and Journals

**First published: Thessaloniki 2007** **ISBN 978-960-12-1617-1**



Printed and bound in Greece by the UNIVERSITY STUDIO PRESS



32, Armenopoulou Str., GR - 54635 THESSALONIKI - GREECE
Tel. +30 2310 208731, +30 2310 209637 • Fax +30 2310 216647
E-mail: info@universitystudiopress.gr • www.universitystudiopress.gr

# CONTENTS

**PART II**

# INTRODUCTION

This Compendium is a collection of Greek verbs used in spoken or written Modern Greek language. It is intended as a reference aid for establishing the various formations of tenses, moods and voices and to assist in the understanding of a Modern Greek text and in the use of correct forms when speaking or translating from one language to the other. Compound and idiomatic verbs were not chosen for inclusion in the list of verbs but rather single word verbs with a corresponding single word translation – even though many verbs have more than one commonly used meaning depending on the context. This is something not covered here but by presenting the various simple and compound tenses the Compendium provides a guide to situating events in time for clear and precise communication.

The first part of the book contains tables of verbs conjugated in all tenses both in the Active and Passive voices. These tables show examples which cover the conjugation pattern for each listed verb.

There are also pages where the meaning of each tense and the rules for forming the relevant endings are set out. The list of verbs should make it easier to understand and remember the variety of forms.

Other forms of speech with various verb constructions are also included, e.g. conditional and impersonal.

# MODERN GREEK VERBS

Verbs are parts of speech which indicate what a person does or feels or which describe his/her state, condition, intentions, wishes, obligations, etc. These verbal activities relate to events at different times in life, e.g. in the past, in the present, in the future or to some conditional situation.

Verbs inflect in their different **tenses** to express the time at which the action of the verb takes place and by means of **mood** indicate the attitude or viewpoint of the verb e.g. the **imperative mood,** used for an order or command. The **participle** of a verb indicates an action that occurs along with something else or a condition that something is in. A person, animal or an abstract noun which governs the meaning of a verb is known as the **subject.** The person, the animal or the abstract word or even a whole sentence which receives the action of the verb is called the **object**. All verbs have a subject, though some active verbs do not have an object. These are called **intransitive** verbs.

Greek verbs are inflected, which means that verbs have different endings depending on who or what the subject is. It is therefore not necessary in Greek to use the personal pronoun with the verb since the endings of the verb make it clear who or what the subject is.

Each tense of a verb has **six** different endings which are used to indicate the person (in the singular) or persons (in the plural) referred to e.g. first person singular (I), second person singular ( you ), third person singular (he, she, it), first person plural (we), second personal plural ( you ), third person plural (they).

Two categories used in Greek to describe verbs are: the **active voice** where a verb indicates an action carried out by the subject of the verb and the **passive voice** whereby the subject is the recipient of the action of the verb.

The passive voice comprises:

**Passive** verbs (διδάσκομαι – *I am taught),* where the subject is the receiver of the action.

**Deponent** verbs (έρχομαι – *I come),* which are verbs in passive form but their meaning is active.

**Reflexive** verbs (χτενίζομαι – *I comb my hair),* where the action is carried out by the subject of the verb on itself.

# PART I

The three main types of verbs in all tenses, moods and imperative forms

Meaning and formation of tenses

Active forms of verbs

Passive forms of verbs

# ACTIVE FORM (VOICE)
# (ΕΝΕΡΓΗΤΙΚΗ ΦΩΝΗ)

## 1.1 ΝΤΥΝΩ  I dress (somebody)

| Present | Imperfect | Past | Simple Future | Simple Subjunctive | Imperative Continuous | Imperative Simple |
|---|---|---|---|---|---|---|
| ντύνω | έντυνα | έντυσα | θα ντύσω | να ντύσω | | |
| ντύνεις | έντυνες | έντυσες | θα ντύσεις | να ντύσεις | ντύνε | ντύσε |
| ντύνει | έντυνε | έντυσε | θα ντύσει | να ντύσει | | |
| ντύνουμε | ντύναμε | ντύσαμε | θα ντύσουμε | να ντύσουμε | | |
| ντύνετε | ντύνατε | ντύσατε | θα ντύσετε | να ντύσετε | ντύνετε | ντύστε |
| ντύνουν | έντυναν | έντυσαν | θα ντύσουν | να ντύσουν | | |

| Continuous Future | Continuous Subjunctive | Present Perfect | Past Perfect | Future Perfect | Past Perfect Subjunctive |
|---|---|---|---|---|---|
| θα ντύνω | να ντύνω | έχω ντύσει | είχα ντύσει | θα έχω ντύσει | να είχα ντύσει |
| θα ντύνεις | να ντύνεις | έχεις ντύσει | είχες ντύσει | θα έχεις ντύσει | να είχες ντύσει |
| θα ντύνει | να ντύνει | έχει ντύσει | είχε ντύσει | θα έχει ντύσει | να είχε ντύσει |
| θα ντύνουμε | να ντύνουμε | έχουμε ντύσει | είχαμε ντύσει | θα έχουμε ντύσει | να είχαμε ντύσει |
| θα ντύνετε | να ντύνετε | έχετε ντύσει | είχατε ντύσει | θα έχετε ντύσει | νε είχατε ντύσει |
| θα ντύνουν | να ντύνουν | έχουν ντύσει | είχαν ντύσει | θα έχουν ντύσει | να είχαν ντύσει |

**Present Participle**: ντύνοντας

# PASSIVE FORM (VOICE)
# (ΠΑΘΗΤΙΚΗ ΦΩΝΗ)

## 1.2 NTYNOMAI I am (getting) dressed

| Present | Imperfect | Past | Simple Future | Simple Subjunctive | Imperative Continuous | Imperative Simple |
|---|---|---|---|---|---|---|
| ντύνομαι | ντυνόμουν | ντύθηκα | θα ντυθώ | να ντυθώ | | |
| ντύνεσαι | ντυνόσουν | ντύθηκες | θα ντυθείς | να ντυθείς | (να ντύνεσαι) | ντύσου |
| ντύνεται | ντυνόταν | ντύθηκε | θα ντυθεί | να ντυθεί | | |
| ντυνόμαστε | ντυνόμαστε/όμασταν | ντυθήκαμε | θα ντυθούμε | να ντυθούμε | | |
| ντύνεστε | ντυνόσαστε/όσασταν | ντυθήκατε | θα ντυθείτε | να ντυθείτε | ντύνεστε | ντυθείτε |
| ντύνονται | ντύνονταν/όντουσαν | ντύθηκαν | θα ντυθούν/ε | να ντυθούν | | |

| Continuous Future | Continuous Subjunctive | Present Perfect | Past Perfect | Future Perfect |
|---|---|---|---|---|
| θα ντύνομαι | να ντύνομαι | έχω ντυθεί | είχα ντυθεί | θα έχω ντυθεί |
| θα ντύνεσαι | να ντύνεσαι | έχεις ντυθεί | είχες ντυθεί | θα έχεις ντυθεί |
| θα ντύνεται | να ντύνεται | έχει ντυθεί | είχε ντυθεί | θα έχει ντυθεί |
| θα ντυνόμαστε | να ντυνόμαστε | έχουμε ντυθεί | έχουμε ντυθεί | θα έχουμε ντυθεί |
| θα ντύνεστε | να ντύνεστε | έχετε ντυθεί | έχετε ντυθεί | θα έχετε ντυθεί |
| θα ντύνονται | να ντύνονται | έχουν ντυθεί | έχουν ντυθεί | θα έχουν ντυθεί |

**Passive participle:** ντυμένος, ντυμένη, ντυμένο

# ACTIVE FORM (VOICE)
# (ΕΝΕΡΓΗΤΙΚΗ ΦΩΝΗ)

## 2.1 ΜΙΛΩ I speak

| Present | Imperfect | Past | Simple Future | Simple Subjunctive | Imperative Continuous | Imperative Simple |
|---|---|---|---|---|---|---|
| μιλώ (άω) | μιλούσα | μίλησα | θα μιλήσω | να μιλήσω | | |
| μιλάς | μιλούσες | μίλησες | θα μιλήσεις | να μιλήσεις | μίλα | μίλησε |
| μιλάει | μιλούσε | μίλησε | θα μιλήσει | να μιλήσει | | |
| μιλάμε | μιλούσαμε | μιλήσαμε | θα μιλήσουμε | να μιλήσουμε | | |
| μιλάτε | μιλούσατε | μιλήσατε | θα μιλήσετε | να μιλήσετε | μιλάτε | μιλήστε |
| μιλάν/ε | μιλούσαν/ε | μίλησαν | θα μιλήσουν | να μιλήσουν | | |

| Continuous Future | Continuous Subjunctive | Present Perfect | Past Perfect | Future Perfect | Past Perfect |
|---|---|---|---|---|---|
| θα μιλώ | να μιλώ | έχω μιλήσει | είχα μιλήσει | θα έχω μιλήσει | να είχα μιλήσει |
| θα μιλάς | να μιλάς | έχεις μιλήσει | είχες μιλήσει | θα έχεις μιλήσει | να είχες μιλήσει |
| θα μιλάει | να μιλάει | έχει μιλήσει | είχε μιλήσει | θα έχει μιλήσει | να είχε μιλήσει |
| θα μιλάμε | να μιλάμε | έχουμε μιλήσει | είχαμε μιλήσει | θα έχουμε μιλήσει | να είχαμε μιλήσει |
| θα μιλάτε | να μιλάτε | έχετε μιλήσει | είχατε μιλήσει | θα έχετε μιλήσει | να είχατε μιλήσει |
| θα μιλάνε | να μιλάν(ε) | έχουν μιλήσει | είχαν μιλήσει | θα έχουν μιλήσει | να είχαν μιλήσει |

**Active participle**: μιλώντας

# PASSIVE FORM (VOICE)
# (ΠΑΘΗΤΙΚΗ ΦΩΝΗ)

## 2.2 ΜΙΛΙΕΜΑΙ I am spoken to

| Present | Imperfect | Past | Simple Future | Simple Subjunctive | Imperative Continuous | Imperative Simple |
|---|---|---|---|---|---|---|
| μιλιέμαι | μιλιόμουν | μιλήθηκα | θα μιληθώ | να μιληθώ | | |
| μιλιέσαι | μιλιόσουν | μιλήθηκες | θα μιληθείς | να μιληθείς | (να μιλιέσαι) | μιλήσου |
| μιλιέται | μιλιόταν | μιλήθηκε | θα μιληθεί | να μιληθεί | | |
| μιλιόμαστε | μιλιόμαστε | μιληθήκαμε | θα μιληθούμε | να μιληθούμε | | |
| μιλιέστε | μιλιόσαστε | μιληθήκατε | θα μιληθείτε | να μιληθείτε | μιλιέστε | μιληθείτε |
| μιλιούνται | μιλιόνταν /ε | μιλήθηκαν /ήκανε | θα μιληθούν | να μιληθούν /ε | | |

| Continuous Future | Continuous Subjunctive | Present Perfect | Past Perfect | Future Perfect |
|---|---|---|---|---|
| θα μιλιέμαι | να μιλιέμαι | έχω μιληθεί | είχα μιληθεί | θα έχω μιληθεί |
| θα μιλιέσαι | να μιλιέσαι | έχεις μιληθεί | είχες μιληθεί | θα έχεις μιληθεί |
| θα μιλιέται | να μιλιέται | έχει μιληθεί | είχε μιληθεί | θα έχει μιληθεί |
| θα μιλιόμαστε | να μιλιόμαστε | έχουμε μιληθεί | είχαμε μιληθεί | θα έχουμε μιληθεί |
| θα μιλιέστε | να μιλιέστε | έχετε μιληθεί | είχατε μιληθεί | θα έχετε μιληθεί |
| θα μιλιούνται /ιόνται | να μιλιούνται | έχουν μιληθεί | είχαν μιληθεί | θα έχουν μιληθεί |

**Passive participle:** μιλημένος, μιλημένη, μιλημένο

# ACTIVE FORM (VOICE)
# (ΕΝΕΡΓΗΤΙΚΗ ΦΩΝΗ)

## 3.1 ΚΑΛΩ   I call (somebody)

| Present | Imperfect | Past | Simple Future | Simple Subjunctive | Imperative Continuous | Imperative Simple |
|---|---|---|---|---|---|---|
| καλώ (έω) | καλούσα | κάλεσα | θα καλέσω | να καλέσω | | |
| καλείς | καλούσες | κάλεσες | θα καλέσεις | να καλέσεις | να καλείς | κάλεσε |
| καλεί | καλούσε | κάλεσε | θα καλέσει | να καλέσει | | |
| καλούμε | καλούσαμε | καλέσαμε | θα καλέσουμε | να καλέσουμε | καλείτε | καλέστε |
| καλείτε | καλούσατε | καλέσατε | θα καλέσετε | να καλέσετε | | |
| καλούν | καλούσαν | κάλεσαν | θα καλέσουν | να καλέσουν | | |

| Contintinuous Future | Continuous Subjunctive | Present Perfect | Past Perfect | Future Perfect | Past Perfect Subjanctive |
|---|---|---|---|---|---|
| θα καλώ | να καλώ | έχω καλέσει | είχα καλέσει | θα έχω καλέσει | να είχα καλέσει |
| θα καλείς | να καλείς | έχεις καλέσει | είχες καλέσει | θε έχεις καλέσει | να είχες καλέσει |
| θα καλεί | να καλεί | έχει καλέσει | είχε καλέσει | θα έχει καλέσει | να είχε καλέσει |
| θα καλούμε | να καλούμε | έχουμε καλέσει | είχαμε καλέσει | θα έχουμε καλέσει | να είχαμε καλέσει |
| θα καλείτε | να καλείτε | έχετε καλέσει | είχατε καλέσει | θα έχετε καλέσει | να είχατε καλέσει |
| θα καλούν | να καλούν | έχουν καλέσει | είχαν καλέσει | θα έχουν καλέσει | να είχαν καλέσει |

**Active participle:** καλώντας

# PASSIVE FORM (VOICE)
# (ΠΑΘΗΤΙΚΗ ΦΩΝΗ)

## 3.2 ΚΑΛΟΥΜΑΙ I am called

| Present | Imperfect | Past | Simple Future | Simple Subjunctive | Imperative Continuous | Imperative Simple |
|---|---|---|---|---|---|---|
| καλούμαι | καλούμουν | καλέστηκα | θα καλεστώ | να καλεστώ | | |
| καλείσαι | καλούσουν | καλέστηκες | θα καλεστείς | να καλεστείς | (να καλείσαι) | καλέσου |
| καλείται | καλούνταν | καλέστηκε | θα καλεστεί | να καλεστεί | | |
| καλούμαστε | καλούμασταν/μαστε | καλεστήκαμε | θα καλεστούμε | να καλεστούμε | | |
| καλείστε | καλούσασταν/σαστε | καλεστήκατε | θα καλεστείτε | να καλεστείτε | καλείστε | καλεστείτε |
| καλούνται | καλούνταν/ε | καλέστηκαν | θα καλεστούν | να καλεστούν | | |

| Continuous Future | Continuous Subjunctive | Present Perfect | Past Perfect | Future Perfect |
|---|---|---|---|---|
| θα καλούμαι | να καλούμαι | έχω καλεστεί | είχα καλεστεί | θα έχω καλεστεί |
| θα καλείσαι | να καλείσαι | έχεις καλεστεί | είχες καλεστεί | θα έχεις καλεστεί |
| θα καλείται | να καλείται | έχει καλεστεί | είχε καλεστεί | θα έχει καλεστεί |
| θα καλούμαστε | να καλούμαστε | έχουμε καλεστεί | είχαμε καλεστεί | θα έχουμε καλεστεί |
| θα καλείστε | να καλείστε | έχετε καλεστεί | είχατε καλεστεί | θα έχετε καλεστεί |
| θα καλούνται | να καλούνται | έχουν καλεστεί | είχαν καλεστεί | θα έχουν καλεστεί |

**Passive participle:** καλεσμένος, καλεσμένη, καλεσμένο

# THE MEANING AND FORMATION OF TENSES IN THE ACTIVE FORM (VOICE)

## ACTIVE PRESENT (ΕΝΕΣΤΩΣ)

| | | | | | | |
|---|---|---|---|---|---|---|
| | | | Simple Future | Present Perfect | Simple Subjunctive | Simple Imperative |
| **PRESENT** | Imperfect | Past | | Past Perfect | Past Perfect Subj. | |
| | | | Continuous Future | Future Perfect | Continuous Subj. | Continuous Imp. |

A. **A. Meaning:**

a. **An action that is happening now**
- Διαβάζω τώρα *I am reading now*

b. **An action that happens regularly or constantly**
- Διαβάζω δύο ώρες κάθε μέρα *I read for two hours everyday*

c. **An action that started in the past and is still ongoing**
- Διαβάζω αυτό το βιβλίο από την περασμένη Κυριακή *I have been studying this book since last Sunday*

**B. Formation**:

**The present stem + the endings –ε, -εις, -ει,** and **-ουμε, -ετε, -ουν** in the six singular / plural forms. These endings will vary according to the type of verb being used. **The three types of verbs in the active voice are:**

| | | |
|---|---|---|
| γράφω ***I write*** | μιλώ (άω) ***I speak*** | καλώ (έω) ***I call*** |
| γράφ**εις** | μιλ**άς** | καλ**είς** |
| γράφ**ει** | μιλ**άει** | καλ**εί** |
| γράφ**ουμε** | μιλ**άμε** | καλ**ούμε** |
| γράφ**ετε** | μιλ**άτε** | καλ**είτε** |
| γράφ**ουν** | μιλ**άνε** | καλ**ούν** |

## NOTE

**Certain verbs however in Active Present tense are conjugated with different endings e.g.:**

| ακού**ω** *I hear I am listening* | κλαί**ω** *I cry I am crying* | φταί**ω** *I am to blame* | λέγ**ω** *I say I am saying* | πά**ω** *I go I am going* | τρώγ**ω** *I eat I am eating* |
|---|---|---|---|---|---|
| ακού**ς** | κλαί**ς** | φταί**ς** | λέγ**εις** | πα**ς** | τρω**ς** |
| ακού**ει** | κλαί**ει** | φταί**ει** | λέγ**ει** | πά**ει** | τρώ**ει** |
| ακού**με** | κλαί**με** | φταί**με** | λέ**με** | πά**με** | τρώ**με** |
| ακού**τε** | κλαί**τε** | φταί**τε** | λέ**τε** | πά**τε** | τρώ**τε** |
| ακού**ν (ε)** | κλαί**νε** | φταί**νε** | λέ**νε** | πά**νε** | τρώ**νε** |

# ACTIVE IMPERFECT (ΠΑΡΑΤΑΤΙΚΟΣ)

| Present | **IMPERFECT** | Past | Simple Future<br>Continuous Future | Present Perfect<br>Past Perfect<br>Future Perfect | Simple Subjunctive<br>Past Perfect Subj.<br>Continuous Subj. | Simple Imperative<br>Continuous Imp. |
|---|---|---|---|---|---|---|

**A. Meaning:**

**a. Something that used to happen in the past (but not any more)**

- Διάβαζα ποίηση όταν ήμουν στο Πανεπιστήμιο *I used to read poetry when I was at University*

**b. Something that was going on while something else happened at the same time**

- Διάβαζα την εφημερίδα όταν χτύπησε το τηλέφωνο *I was reading the newspaper when the telephone rang*
- Καθώς έφευγα από το σπίτι, ήρθε ο ταχυδρόμος *While I was leaving home, the postman appeared*
- Διάβαζε όταν μπήκα *She was reading when I came in*

**B. Formation:**

1. **Present stem + the endings -α, –ες, -ε, -αμε, -ατε, -αν**
2. **The accent moves to the third syllable from the end.**
3. **Add the prefix έ** if the verb has only two syllables. The **έ** is dropped in the first and second person plural since there are already three syllables. **Occasionally the prefix can be the letter ή.**
4. If the verb is stressed on the last syllable **(contracted verb)** then the endings are: **-ούσα, -ούσες,-ούσε, -ούσαμε, -ούσατε, -ούσαν.**

## NOTE

a) Verbs that start with a vowel keep the same vowel in the imperfect tense.
b) The verbs ξέρω (*I know*) and θέλω (*I want*) take the prefix **η** in the imperfect and past tenses: ήξερα (*I knew*), ήθελα (*I wanted*)

**Examples:**

| **Present: γράφω** *I write / I am writing* | **Present: μιλώ:** *I speak / I am speaking* | **Present: θέλω:** *I want / I am wanting* |
|---|---|---|
| **Imperfect** | **Imperfect** | **Imperfect** |
| έγραφ**α** *I used to write/ I was writing* | μιλ**ούσα** *I used to talk / I was talking* | ήθελ**α** *I used to want/ I was wanting* |
| έγραφ**ες** | μιλ**ούσες** | ήθελ**ες** |
| έγραφ**ε** | μιλ**ούσε** | ήθελ**ε** |
| γράφ**αμε** | μιλ**ούσαμε** | θέλ**αμε** |
| γράφ**ατε** | μιλ**ούσατε** | θέλ**ατε** |
| έγραφ**αν** (γράφανε) | μιλ**ούσαν (ε)** | ήθελ**αν** (θέλανε) |

# ACTIVE PAST (ΑΟΡΙΣΤΟΣ)

| Present | Imperfect | **PAST** | Simple Future<br>Continuous Future | Present Perfect<br>Past Perfect<br>Future Perfect | Simple Subjunctive<br>Past Perfect Subj.<br>Continuous Subj. | Simple Imperative<br>Continuous Imp. |
|---|---|---|---|---|---|---|

**A. Meaning:**

**An action that happened once at a certain time in the past**

- Διάβασα την εφημερίδα το πρωί *I read the newspaper in the morning*

**B. Formation:**

1. **Change the character and endings of the present tense into –σα, -σες, -σε, -σαμε, -σατε, -σαν (ε)**
2. **Move the accent to the third syllable from the end**
3. **Add the prefix έ** (or occasionally **ή**) **if the verb has only two syllables**

## NOTE

a) If the stem ends in **-γ, -κ, -χ, -χν, -ζ** the past endings are –**ξα, -ξες, -ξε, -ξαμε, -ξατε, -ξαν(ε)**
b) If the stem ends in **–π, –β, -φ,** or **ευ** the past endings are **–ψα, -ψες, -ψε, -ψαμε, -ψατε, -ψαν(ε)**
c) Contracted verbs end in –**ησα, -ησες, -ησε, -ήσαμε, -ήσατε, -ησαν(ε)**
**–ασα, -ασες, -ασε, -άσαμε –ασατε, -ασαν(ε)**
**–εσα, -εσες, -εσε, -έσαμε, -έσατε, -εσαν(ε)**

**Examples:**

| **Present: γράφω** *I write / I am writing* | **Present: ανοίγω** *I open / I am opening* | **Present: μιλ(ά)ω** *I speak / I am speaking* |
|---|---|---|
| **Past** | **Past** | **Past** |
| έγρα**ψα** ***I wrote*** | άνοι**ξα** ***I opened*** | μίλ**ησα** ***I talked*** |
| έγρα**ψες** | άνοι**ξες** | μίλ**ησες** |
| έγρα**ψε** | άνοι**ξε** | μίλη**σε** |
| γρά**ψαμε** | ανοί**ξαμε** | μιλ**ήσαμε** |
| γρά**ψατε** | ανοί**ξατε** | μιλ**ήσατε** |
| έγρα**ψαν** (γρά**ψανε**) | άνοι**ξαν** (ανοί**ξανε**) | μίλ**ησαν** (μιλ**ήσανε**) |

# ACTIVE SIMPLE FUTURE (ΑΠΛΟΣ ΜΕΛΛΟΝΤΑΣ)

| Present | Imperfect | Past | **SIMPLE FUTURE**<br>Continuous Future | Present Perfect<br>Past Perfect<br>Future Perfect | Simple Subjunctive<br>Past Perfect Subj.<br>Continuous Subj. | Simple Imperative<br>Continuous Imp. |
|---|---|---|---|---|---|---|

**A. Meaning:**

**An action in the future**

- Θα διαβάσω το γράμμα αύριο *I will read the letter tomorrow*

**B. Formation:**

**θα** + the endings **–σω, -σεις, -σει, -σουμε, -σετε, -σουν** if the last letter of the stem is **θ, ν, σ, τ,** ζ
**θα** + the endings **–ξω, -ξεις, -ξει, - ξουμε, -ξετε, -ξουν** if the last letter of the stem is **γ, κ, χ, χν** or **–αζω**
**θα** + the endings **–ψω, -ψεις,-ψει, -ψουμε, -ψετε, -ψουν** if the last letter of the stem is **π, β, φ** or the verb ends in **- εύω**
**θα** + the endings **–ήσω, -ήσεις, -ήσει, -ήσουμε, -ήσετε, -ήσουν** if the verbs are stressed on the last syllable (contracted verbs)
**–άσω, -άσεις, -άσει, -άσουμε, -άσετε, -άσουν**
**–έσω, -έσεις, -έσει, -έσουμε, -έσετε, -έσουν**

| **Present: γράφω** *I write / I am writing* | **μιλώ:** *I speak / I am speaking* | **θέλω:** *I want / I am wanting* |
|---|---|---|
| **Future** | **Future** | **Future** |
| θα γρά**ψω** *I will write* | θα μιλ**ήσω** *I will speak* | θα θελ**ήσω** *I will want* |
| θα γρά**ψεις** | θα μιλ**ήσεις** | θα θελ**ήσεις** |
| θα γρά**ψει** | θα μιλ**ήσει** | θα θελ**ήσει** |
| θα γρά**ψουμε** | θα μιλ**ήσουμε** | θα θελ**ήσουμε** |
| θα γρά**ψετε** | θα μιλ**ήσετε** | θα θελ**ήσετε** |
| θα γρά**ψουν** | θα μιλ**ήσουν** | θα θελ**ήσουν** |

# ACTIVE CONTINUOUS FUTURE (ΣΥΝΕΧΗΣ ΜΕΛΛΟΝΤΑΣ)

| Present | Imperfect | Past | Simple Future<br><br>**CONTINUOUS FUTURE** | Present Perfect<br>Past Perfect<br>Future Perfect | Simple Subjunctive<br>Past Perfect Subj.<br>Continuous Subj. | Simple Imperative<br><br>Continuous Imp. |
|---|---|---|---|---|---|---|

**A. Meaning:**

**An action that is repetitive or continuous in the future**

- Θα διαβάζω κάθε πρωί *I will be studying every morning*

**B. Formation:**

**The particle θα + Present tense**

**Examples:**

| **Present: γράφω** *I write / I am writing* | **μιλώ:** *I speak / I am speaking* | **θέλω:** *I want / I am wanting* |
|---|---|---|
| **Continuous Future** | **Continuous Future** | **Continuous Future** |
| θα γράφ**ω** *I will be writing* | θα μιλ**ώ** *I will be speaking* | θα θέλ**ω** *I will be wanting* |
| θα γράφ**εις** | θα μιλ**άς** | θα θέλ**εις** |
| θα γράφ**ει** | θα μιλ**άει** | θα θέλ**ει** |
| θα γράφ**ουμε** | θα μιλ**άμε** | θα θέλ**ουμε** |
| θα γράφ**ετε** | θα μιλ**άτε** | θα θέλ**ετε** |
| θα γράφ**ουν(ε)** | θα μιλ**άν(ε)** | θα θέλ**ουν(ε)** |

# ACTIVE PRESENT PERFECT (ΠΑΡΑΚΕΙΜΕΝΟΣ)

| Present | Imperfect | Past | Simple Future<br>Continuous Future | **PRESENT PERFECT**<br>Past Perfect<br>Future Perfect | Simple Subjunctive<br>Past Perfect Subj.<br>Continuous Subj. | Simple Imperative<br>Continuous Imp. |
|---|---|---|---|---|---|---|

**A. Meaning:**

**Something that has been completed in the past but is related to the present**

- Έχω γράψει το γράμμα πριν από πέντε μέρες — *I have written the letter five days ago*
- Έχουμε γράψει ήδη τις ασκήσεις — *We have already written the exercises*

**B. Formation:**

**Conjugate the verb έχω + 3rd person singular of the Simple Future tense** (without θα) **for all persons.**

**Example:**

**Present**: γράφω

**Present perfect**

**έχω γράψει**
**έχεις γράψει**
**έχει γράψει**
**έχουμε γράψει**
**έχετε γράψει**
**έχουν γράψει**

# ACTIVE PAST PERFECT (ΥΠΕΡΣΥΝΤΕΛΙΚΟΣ)

| Present | Imperfect | Past | Simple Future | Present Perfect | Simple Subjunctive | Simple Imperative |
|---|---|---|---|---|---|---|
| | | | | **PAST PERFECT** | Past Perfect Subj. | |
| | | | Continuous Future | Future Perfect | Continuous Subj. | Continuous Imp. |

**A. Meaning:**

**Something that had happened in the past before something else took place**

- Είχα διαβάσει το βιβλίο πριν να το δώσω πίσω *I had read the book before I gave it back*

**B. Formation:**

**Conjugate (the past tense of έχω) είχα + 3rd person singular of the Simple Future tense** (without θα) **for all persons**

**Example:**

**Present:** γράφω
**Simple Future:** θα γράψω

**Past perfect**

**είχα γράψει**
**είχες γράψει**
**είχε γράψει**
**είχαμε γράψει**
**είχατε γράψει**
**είχαν γράψει**

# ACTIVE FUTURE PERFECT (ΣΥΝΤΕΛΕΣΜΕΝΟΣ ΜΕΛΛΟΝΤΑΣ)

| Present | Imperfect | Past | Simple Future<br>Continuous Future | Present Perfect<br>Past Perfect<br>**FUTURE PERFECT** | Simple Subjunctive<br>Past Perfect Subj.<br>Continuous Subj. | Simple Imperative<br>Continuous Imp. |
|---|---|---|---|---|---|---|

**A. Meaning:**

**Something that will finish in the Future before another future action.**

- Θα έχω διαβάσει το βιβλίο πριν να φύγω *I will have read the book before I leave*

**B. Formation:**

**The particle θα + έχω + 3rd person singular of the Simple Future tense** (without θα) **for all persons**

**Example:**

**Present**: γράφ**ω**

**Future:** θα γρά**ψω**

**Future perfect**

**θα έχω γράψει**
**θα έχεις γράψει**
**θα έχει γράψει**
**θα έχουμε γράψει**
**θα έχετε γράψει**
**θα έχουν γράψει**

# ACTIVE SUBJUNCTIVE (ΥΠΟΤΑΚΤΙΚΗ)

**The Subjunctive mood in Greek occurs in sentences that depend on a main verb in whichever tense it may be.**
It is used after impersonal verbs and after conjunctions.
It is also used in Greek in a sentence where the subject of the main verb is different from the subject of the participle.
It is conjugated to indicate that its subject may differ from that of the main verb,
It describes situations we wish for, desire, request, suggest, or permit.
It is formed with the particle **να (να μην) + Present, the Future** (without θα), or **the Present Perfect** tense.

# ACTIVE CONTINUOUS SUBJUNCTIVE (ΥΠΟΤΑΚΤΙΚΗ ΕΝΕΣΤΩΤΑ)

| Present | Imperfect | Past | Simple Future<br><br>Continuous Future | Present Perfect<br>Past Perfect<br>Future Perfect | Simple Subjunctive<br>Past Perfect Subj.<br>**CONTINUOUS SUBJUNCTIVE** | Simple Imperative<br><br>Continuous Imp. |
|---|---|---|---|---|---|---|

**A. Meaning:**

**A wish, a demand or a suggestion that is constant or repetitive**

**B. Formation:**

να **+ Present tense**

- Ο γιατρός μου **είπε να πίνω** ένα ποτήρι κρασί κάθε μέρα — *My doctor told me to drink a glass of wine everyday*
- **Θέλω να γράφω** δέκα Ελληνικές λέξεις κάθε μέρα — *I want to write ten Greek words every day*

# ACTIVE SIMPLE SUBJUNCTIVE (ΑΠΛΗ ΥΠΟΤΑΚΤΙΚΗ)

| Present | Imperfect | Past | Simple Future<br>Continuous Future | Present Perfect<br>Past Perfect<br>Future Perfect | **SIMPLE SUBJUNCTIVE**<br>Past Perfect Subj.<br>Continuous Subj. | Simple Imperative<br>Continuous Imp. |
|---|---|---|---|---|---|---|

**A. Meaning:**

**A situation that occurs at the time of the main verb**

**B. Formation:**

**να + Simple Future** (but without the particle θα)

- **Θέλω να πιώ** μόνο νερό τώρα, όχι ούζο — *I want to drink only water now not ouzo*
- **Θέλω να γράψεις** το γράμμα τώρα — *I want you to write the letter now*
- **Πρέπει να φύγω** τώρα — *I must leave now*
- **Πρέπει να φύγετε** τώρα — *You must leave now*
- **Απαγορεύεται να καπνίσουμε** — *We are not allowed to smoke*
- **Προτιμώ να μην ταξιδέψετε** με αεροπλάνο — *I prefer you* [plural] *not to travel by aeroplane*

# ACTIVE PAST PERFECT SUBJUNCTIVE (ΥΠΟΤΑΚΤΙΚΗ ΥΠΕΡΣΥΝΤΕΛΙΚΟΥ)

| Present | Imperfect | Past | Simple Future<br>Continuous Future | Present Perfect<br>Past Perfect<br>Future Perfect | Simple Subjunctive<br>Continuous Subj.<br>**PAST PERFECT SUBJUNCTIVE** | Simple Imperative<br>Continuous Imp. |
|---|---|---|---|---|---|---|

**A. Meaning:**

**An action that failed to happen in the past**

**B. Formation**:

**Verb** + **να + Past Perfect**

- **Θα προτιμούσε να είχε σπουδάσει** Ιατρική — *He would have preferred tohave studied medicine*
- **Ήθελε να είχε γράψει** το γράμμα πριν να φύγει — *He would have liked to have written the letter before he went*

<u>NOTE</u>: **The negative form of the Subjunctive** is expressed by inserting **να μη(ν)** before the verb

- **Ελπίζω να μην μας έχουν δει** — *I hope they have not seen us*
- **Θα προτιμούσε να μην είχε μείνει** στο σπίτι — *He/she would have preferred not to have stayed at home*
- **Ήθελα να είχα μάθει** γαλλικά — *I wish i had learned French*
- **Ελπίζω να είχε τελειώσει** την δουλειά της πριν τις 12:00 — *I hope she had finished her work before 12:00 o'clock*

## NOTE

**The Simple Subjunctive is also used:**

1. **To indicate a) a polite question, b) a suggestion or c) a prohibition (as a negative Imperative)**

| | |
|---|---|
| • Να κλείσω το παράθυρο; | *Shall I close the window?* |
| • Να έρθω κι εγώ; | *Shall I come too?* |
| • Ναι, να κλείσεις το παράθυρο γιατί κάνει κρύο | *Yes, you should close the window because it is cold* |
| • Ναι, να έρθεις γιατί αλλιώς θα είσαι μόνη εδώ | *Yes, you should come because otherwise you will be here alone* |
| • Όχι, να μην κλείσεις το παράθυρο | *No, you should not close the window* |
| • Όχι, να μην έρθεις γιατί είναι αργά | *No, you should not come because it is too late* |

2. **After impersonal verbs**

| | |
|---|---|
| • Είναι πιθανόν να πάμε στο Λονδίνο αύριο | *It is possible that we may go to London tomorrow* |
| • Πρέπει να πάμε στο Λονδίνο αύριο | *We have to go to London tomorrow* |
| • Είναι δύσκολο να πάμε στο Λονδίνο αύριο | *It is difficult for us to go to London tomorrow* |
| • Πρέπει να ταξιδεύουμε στην Αγγλία συχνά | *We have to travel frequently to England* |
| • Είναι εύκολο να μάθουμε Ελληνικά | *It is easy for us to learn Greek* |

3. **After conjunctions as πριν** (before)**, χωρίς** (without) **ακόμα** (not yet)**, όταν** (when)**, πως** (how) **etc.**

| | |
|---|---|
| • Έφυγε πριν να την δω | *She left before I saw her* |
| • Έφυγε χωρίς να φάει τίποτα | *She left without eating anything* |
| • Ακόμα να τελειώσει! | *He still has not finished!* |
| • Η Ελένη έφυγε πριν να έρθει ο Νίκος | *Eleni left before Nikos came* |
| • Ακόμα να έρθει! | *He still has not come!* |
| • Όταν έρθει, να φύγουμε | *When he comes, we should leave* |
| • Πώς να πάω στο Λονδίνο; | *How can I go to London?* |

**The Continuous Subjunctive is used:**

1. **To indicate a polite request or a piece of advice** (used instead of the Imperative form of a verb)

| | |
|---|---|
| • Να πίνεις ένα ποτήρι κόκκινο κρασί κάθε μέρα | *You should drink a glass of red wine every day* |
| • Να γράφεις πιο καθαρά, δεν καταλαβαίνω | *You should write more clearly, I do not understand* |
| • Να έρχεσαι κάθε μέρα να με βλέπεις | *You should come to see me every day* |

2. **In sentences where an action is not being performed by the subject of the main verb** (in English a participle is used)

| | |
|---|---|
| • Τον είδα να τρέχει στον δρόμο | *I saw him running in the street* |
| • Τον είδαμε να έρχεται | *We saw him coming* |

# THE IMPERATIVE MOOD (ΠΡΟΣΤΑΚΤΙΚΗ)

**The Imperative form of the verb expresses a command, as well as a request.**
**It has two persons: 2nd person singular and 2nd person plural and it is formed from the stems of the Present and the Future tenses.**
**The negative Imperative (indicating prohibition) is expressed with the word μη(ν) in front of the Present or Future tense** (without θα).
**To form the Present Imperative of contracted verbs (i.e. verbs ending in –άω /ώ only):**

**Change the final –ώ of the Present tense into –α** when addressing one person
**Change the final –ώ of the Present tense into –άτε** when addressing more than one person or being polite

- **Μίλα** πιο αργά, παρακαλώ *Speak (sing.) more slowly, please*
- **Μιλάτε** πιο αργά, παρακαλώ *Speak* (plural) *more slowly, please*

## NOTE

Other contracted verbs (verbs ending in – έω / ώ) do not have the 2nd person singular form. If it is necessary to use a command or request using these verbs then use **να + second person singular of the Present tense.**

- Να καλείς τους φίλους σου τα Σαββατοκύριακα μόνο *Invite your friends at weekends only*

# ACTIVE CONTINUOUS IMPERATIVE (ΠΡΟΣΤΑΚΤΙΚΗ ΕΝΕΣΤΩΤΑ)

| Present | Imperfect | Past | Simple Future<br>Continuous Future | Present Perfect<br>Past Perfect<br>Future Perfect | Simple Subjunctive<br>Past Perfect Subj.<br>Continuous Subjunctive | Simple Imperative<br>**CONTINUOUS IMPERATIVE** |
|---|---|---|---|---|---|---|

A. **Meaning:**

**An order, a command or request that should be habitual or ongoing**

B. **Formation:**

**Change the final –ω of the Present tense into –ε** when addressing one person (2nd person sing.)
**Change the final –ω of the Present tense into –ετε** when addressing more than one person or being polite (2nd person plural)
(If the verb has more than two syllables the stress in the 2nd person singular moves back one syllable)

**<u>To form a prohibition</u> (negative Imperative) we use the particle μη (μην) in front of the 2nd personal singular or plural of the Present** tense.

| | |
|---|---|
| • **Μάθαινε** πέντε Ελληνικές λέξεις κάθε μέρα | *Learn (sing.) five words every day!* |
| • **Μαθαίνετε** πέντε Ελληνικές λέξεις κάθε μέρα | *Learn (plural) five words every day* |
| • **Μην πίνεις** τόσο πολύ | *Do not drink (sing.) so much* |
| • **Μην πίνετε** κρασί το πρωί | *Do not drink (plural) wine in the morning* |

# ACTIVE SIMPLE IMPERATIVE (ΠΡΟΣΤΑΚΤΙΚΗ ΜΕΛΛΟΝΤΑ)

| Present | Imperfect | Past | Simple Future<br>Continuous Future | Present Perfect<br>Past Perfect<br>Future Perfect | Simple Subjunctive<br>Past Perfect Subj.<br>Continuous Subj. | **SIMPLE IMPERATIVE**<br>Continuous Imp. |
|---|---|---|---|---|---|---|

**A. Meaning:**

**Something (an order or request) that must be done now**

**B. Formation:**

**Change the final –ω of the Future tense into –ε** when addressing one person
**Change the final –ω of the Future tense into –ετε** when adressing more than one person or being polite

- **Μάθε** επιτέλους το όνομά της! *Find out* [sing.] *her name after all this time!*
- **Μάθετε** επιτέλους το όνομά της! *Find out* [plural/polite] *her name after all this time!*

**To form the Simple Negative Imperative we use μη (μην) in front of the Future tense (without θα)**

- **Μη μάθεις** το όνομά της! *Do not find out her name!*

## NOTE

**To avoid using the Imperative for a demand or an order we often turn into a direct question or the use of the subjunctive mood.**

- Μαθαίνεις πέντε λέξεις κάθε μέρα, σε παρακαλώ; *Would you learn (keep on learning) five words every day, please?*
- Μπορείς να μαθαίνεις πέντε λέξεις κάθε μέρα; *Can you learn (keep on learning) five words every day?*
- Μπορείς να μάθεις πέντε λέξεις κάθε μέρα; *Can you learn ("learn-up") five words every day?*
- Θα μπορούσες να μαθαίνεις πέντε λέξεις κάθε μέρα; *Could you learn (keep on learning) five words every day?*
- Θα ήταν δυνατόν να μαθαίνεις πέντε λέξεις κάθε μέρα; *Would it be possible for you to learn five words every day?*

# NEGATIVE FORM OF VERBS

For the **negative** form the following words are used in front of the verb:

**δεν** **In front of any tense**

- Ο Νίκος δεν πίνει καφέ — *Nikos does not drink coffee*
- Δεν πήγαμε στο θέατρο χτες — *We did not go to the theatre yesterday*
- Δεν θα δουλέψω αύριο — *I will not work tomorrow*

**μη(ν)** **1. In the Subjunctive between the particle να and the verb**

- Ο Νίκος προτιμάει να μην μείνει πάλι εδώ — *Nikos prefers not to stay here again*

**2. With the Present or Future (without θα) tenses to express prohibition**

- Νίκο, μην πίνεις τόσο γρήγορα — *Niko, do not drink so quickly*
- Νίκο, μην πιείς άλλο κρασί, θα σε πειράξει — *Niko, do not drink any more wine; it will be bad for you*

**3. Before the Active Participle**

- Μην έχοντας χρόνο, δεν πήγα στην αγορά — *Not having any time, I did not go to the market*
- Περάσαμε όλο το βράδυ γελώντας με τα αστεία του — *We spent all the evening laughing at his jokes*

# THE INTERROGATIVE FORM OF VERBS

**When asking a question the voice is raised enquiringly at the beginning of the sentence. The structure and the form of the verb do not change.**

| | |
|---|---|
| • Θέλεις ένα καφέ; | *Do you want a coffee?* |
| • Τι θέλει; | *What does he (she/ it ) want?* |
| • Θέλετε να πάμε στο σινεμά; | *Do you* (plural) *want us to go the cinema?* |

## NOTE

There are various words we can use to make a polite question, a suggestion or to ask permission. The verb that follows these words can be in any tense or mood.

| | |
|---|---|
| • Μήπως θέλετε καφέ; | *Would you* (plural) *like some coffee?* |
| • Θα ήθελες ένα καφέ; | *Would you* (singular) *like a coffee?* |
| • Τι λες για ένα καφεδάκι? | *What about a coffee?* |
| • Άραγε θα φύγει; | *I wonder whether he will leave.* |
| • Λες να έφυγε; | *Do you think he has gone?* |
| • Να φύγουμε τώρα; | *Shall we go now?* |

# THE AUGMENT

In forming the Imperfect and the Past tenses (p. 21, 23) it was shown that when the verb has only two syllables, the Past and Imperfect tense is prefixed by adding the letter **έ** or occasionally **ή**. Some verbs in Modern Greek which survive from Ancient Greek, have a conjunction or a preposition prefixed. These verbs in their Imperfect and Past tense take the prefix **-έ** between the conjunction or the preposition and the main verb. Sometimes however the prepositional prefix is another word altogether and alters the meaning of the verb.

**Γράφω** συχνά στην Ελένη — *I often write to Eleni*
**Έγραψα** στην Ελένη χτες — *I wrote to Eleni yesterday*
**Ξαναέγραψα** στην Ελένη σήμερα το πρωί — *I wrote to Eleni again this morning*

**Δεν εγκρίνω** το καινούριο πρόγραμμα — *I do not approve of the new program*
(εν + κρίνω - the preposition **εν** changes into **εγ** before a consonant)
**Δεν ενέκρινα** το καινούριο πρόγραμμα — *I did not approve of the new program*
( εν + έκρινα)

**Αναλαμβάνω** καινούρια υπηρεσία — *I am taking up a new job*
(ανά +λαμβάνω)
**Ανέλαβα** υπηρεσία χτες — *I took up my job yesterday*
(ανά + έλαβα - the preposition **ανά** which ends at a vowel, looses this vowel before another vowel)

**Μας αντιγράφει σε όλα** — *He copies us in on everything*
(αντί+ γράφει)
**Αντέγραψε** το κείμενο από τον πίνακα — *He copied the text from the blackboard.*
(αντί+ έγραψε - the preposition **αντί** looses the vowel before the augment **έ**).

# THE INFINITIVE (ΑΠΑΡΕΜΦΑΤΟ)

Modern Greek has no unique form for the Infinitive as happens in Ancient Greek. Today it has been replaced by an appropriately conjugated form of the Subjunctive Mood (p. 30) e.g. I want to go *θέλω να πάω*. The 3rd person singular of the Simple Future (but without θα) of the Active or Passive form (Voice) is used together with the tenses of the verb to have (έχω – είχα – θα έχω) to form the Present, the Past, the Future Perfect tenses. Έχω – είχα – θα έχω are conjugated but the 3rd person singular of the Simple Future remains the same uninflected word for all persons.

- Έχω δώσει το βιβλίο πίσω — *I have given the book back*
- Είχαμε δώσει το βιβλίο πίσω — *We had given the book back*
- Θα έχουν δώσει το βιβλίο πίσω μέχρι αύριο — *They will have given the book back by tomorrow*
- Έχω κοιμηθεί 12 ώρες — *I have slept for 12 hours*
- Είχαμε ενδιαφερθεί για το ίδιο βιβλίο — *We had been interested in the same book*
- Θα έχουν κοιμηθεί μέχρι ώρα 10 το βράδυ — *They will have gone to sleep by 10 o'clock in the evening*

# ACTIVE PARTICIPLE (ΜΕΤΟΧΗ)

**A. Meaning:**

**The participle of active verbs indicates an action that occurs at the same time as the action of the main the verb. It follows a verb in any tense or mood and has one form for all persons - singular and plural. The subject of the participle is the same as that of the main verb.**

**B. Formation:**

**Replace the ending -ω – of the Present tense of the main verb with the ending - οντας** (for ordinary verbs) **or**

**- ώντας** (for contracted verbs)

- Γράφω **ακούοντας** μουσική — *I write while listening to music*
- Μπορείς να βρεις ό,τι θέλεις **ρωτώντας** — *You can find out whatever you want by asking*

# THE MEANING AND FORMATION OF TENSES AND MOODS IN THE PASSIVE FORM (VOICE)

## PASSIVE PRESENT (ΠΑΘΗΤΙΚΟΣ ΕΝΕΣΤΩΤΑΣ)

| | | | | | | |
|---|---|---|---|---|---|---|
| **PRESENT** | Imperfect | Past | Simple Future<br>Continuous Future | Present Perfect<br>Past Perfect<br>Future Perfect | Simple Subjunctive<br>Past Perfect Subj.<br>Continuous Subj. | Simple Imperative<br>Continuous Imp. |

**A. Meaning:**

**The same as in the active Present tense.**

**B. Formation:**

**Add the following endings to the stem of each category of active verb**

| | | |
|---|---|---|
| πληρών**ω** | (I pay) | **-ομαι, -εσαι, -εται, -όμαστε, -εστε,-ονται** |
| αγαπ**ώ (άω)** | (I love) | **-ιέμαι, -ιέσαι, -έται,, -ιόμαστε, -ιέστε, ιούνται** |
| στερ**ώ (έω)** | (I deprive) | **-ούμαι, -είσαι, -είται, -ούμαστε, - είστε, -ούνται** |

- πληρών**ομαι** *I am paid / I am being paid*
- αγαπ**ιέμαι** *I am loved / I am being loved*
- στερ**ούμαι** *I am deprived / I am being deprived*

## NOTE

1. **Some of the verbs which in active voice end in – ώνω may have different endings in the Present Passive tense**

Active voice Present tense: δικαι**ώνω** *I justify*
Passive voice Present tense: δικαι**ούμαι** *I am justified*

| | |
|---|---|
| δικαι**ούμαι** | δικαι**ούμεθα** |
| δικαι**ούσαι** | δικαι**ούσθε** |
| δικαι**ούται** | δικαι**ούνται** |

2. **Some other verbs ending in – ωμαι or -άμαι are conjugated differently in the Passive Present tense only**

| Passive Present tense: συσπ**ώμαι** *I winch* | κοιμ**άμαι** *I am asleep* |
|---|---|
| συσπ**ώμαι** | κοιμ**άμαι** |
| συσπ**άσαι** | κοιμ**άσαι** |
| συσπ**άται** | κοιμ**άται** |
| συσπ**ώμεθα** | κοιμ**ώμαστε** |
| συσπ**άσθε** | κοιμ**άστε** |
| συσπ**ώνται** | κοιμ**ούνται** |

3. **A few ancient Greek verbs survive in Modern Greek. They are mainly used in the Present tense and rarely in the Imperfect**

| **Present: επιτίθεμαι** *I attack* (somebody) | **Imperfect: επιτιθέμην** *I was attacking* (somebody) |
|---|---|
| **επιτίθεσαι** | **επιτίθεσο** |
| **επιτίθεται** | **επιτίθετο** |
| **επιτιθέμεθα** | **επιτιθέμεθα** |
| **επιτίθεσθε** | **επιτίθεσθε** |
| **επιτιθενται** | **επιτίθεντο** |

# PASSIVE IMPERFECT (ΠΑΘΗΤΙΚΟΣ ΠΑΡΑΤΑΤΙΚΟΣ)

| Present | **IMPERFECT** | Past | Simple Future<br>Continuous Future | Present Perfect<br>Past Perfect<br>Future Perfect | Simple Subjunctive<br>Past Perfect Subj.<br>Continuous Subj. | Simple Imperative<br>Continuous Imp. |
|---|---|---|---|---|---|---|

**A. Meaning:**

**The same as in active Imperfect tense**

**B. Formation:**

**Change the ending of the Passive Present into:**

| | **Passive Imperfect** | | **Passive Imperfect** | | **Passive Imperfect** |
|---|---|---|---|---|---|
| πληρών**ομαι** | πληρων**όμουν** | αγαπι**έμαι** | αγαπι**όμουν** | στερ**ούμαι** | στερ**ούμουν** |
| | πληρων**όσουν(α)** | | αγαπι**όσουν** | | στερ**ούσουν** |
| | πληρων**όταν(ε)** | | αγαπι**όταν** | | στερ**ούνταν** |
| | πληρων**όμασταν or–όμαστε** | | αγαπι**όμασταν, -ιόμαστε** | | στερ**ούμασταν, -ούμαστε** |
| | πληρων**όσασταν or –όσαστε** | | αγαπι**όσασταν, -ιόσαστε** | | στερού**σασταν**, **-ούσαστε** |
| | πληρών**ονταν or -όντουσαν** | | αγαπι**όνταν**,**-όντουσαν** | | στερού**νταν(ε)** |

- πληρω**νόμουν** *I was being paid* (Present tense: πληρώνομαι)
- αγαπ**ιόμουν** *I was being loved* (Present tense: αγαπιέμαι) [contracted verb]
- στερ**ούμουν** *I was being deprived* (Present tense: στερούμαι) [contracted verb]

# PASSIVE PAST (ΠΑΘΗΤΙΚΟΣ ΑΟΡΙΣΤΟΣ)

| Present | Imperfect | **PAST** | Simple Future<br>Continuous Future | Present Perfect<br>Past Perfect<br>Future Perfect | Simple Subjunctive<br>Past Perfect Subj.<br>Continuous Subj. | Simple Imperative<br>Continuous Imp. |
|---|---|---|---|---|---|---|

**A. Meaning:**

**The same as the active Past tense**

**B. Formation**

**Change the endings of the passive Present into:**

| Singular | Plural |
|---|---|
| **-ηκα** | **-ήκαμε** |
| **-ήκες** | **-ήκατε** |
| **-ηκε** | **-ηκαν** |

[Present: πληρώνωμαι]

πληρώθ**ηκα** *I was paid /I was being paid*
πληρώθ**ηκες**
πληρώθ**ηκε**
πληρωθ**ήκαμε**
πληρωθ**ήκατε**
πληρώθ**ηκαν**

## NOTE

Certain changes occur with the character of the stem. In the table of verbs you will be aware of these changes when you come across the Passive verbs in the Past tense.

| Passive verbs ending in: | in the Passive Past tense change into: |
|---|---|
| **- φομαι** | **- φτηκα** |
| **- φτομαι** | **- φτηκα** |
| **- νομαι** | **- ήθηκα or - θηκα or - στηκα** |
| **- θομαι** | **- στηκα** |
| **- ζομαι** | **- ήστηκα or - χτηκα** |
| **- ευομαι** | **- εύτηκα** |
| **- ιέμαι** | **- ήθηκα or - έθηκα or - άστηκα** |
| **- άμαι or - ούμαι** | **- ήθηκα or - έστηκα** |
| **- φομαι** | **- φτηκα** |

| **Present** | **Past** |
|---|---|
| γράφ**ομαι** | γρά**φτηκα** |
| σκέ**φτομαι** | σκέ**φτηκα** |
| ντύ**νομαι** | ντύ**θηκα** |
| κά**θομαι** | κά**θησα** |
| χτενί**ζομαι** | χτενί**στηκα** |
| ονειρ**εύομαι** | ονειρ**εύτηκα** |
| παραπον**ιέμαι** | παραπο**νέθηκα** |
| κοιμ**άμαι** | κοιμ**ήθηκα** |
| βά**φομαι** | βά**φτηκα** |

# PASSIVE SIMPLE FUTURE (ΠΑΘΗΤΙΚΟΣ ΑΠΛΟΣ ΜΕΛΛΟΝΤΑΣ)

| Present | Imperfect | Past | **SIMPLE FUTURE**<br>Continuous Future | Present Perfect<br>Past Perfect<br>Future Perfect | Simple Subjunctive<br>Past Perfect Subj.<br>Continuous Subj. | Simple Imperative<br>Continuous Imp. |
|---|---|---|---|---|---|---|

**A. Meaning:**

**The same as in the active Future tense**

**B. Formation:**

1. **Use the particle θα** and
2. **Change the Passive Past tense endings into: -ώ, -είς, -εί, -ούμε, -είτε, -ούν (ε)**
3. **Move the accent to the last syllable**

[Present: πληρ**ώνομαι**]

[Past: πληρ**ώθηκα**]

**Passive Future**

- **Θα πληρωθώ** *I will be paid*

**Passive Future**

**θα** πληρω**θώ**
**θα** πληρω**θείς**
**θα** πληρω**θεί**
**θα** πληρω**θούμε**
**θα** πληρω**θείτε**
**θα** πληρω**θούν**

# PASSIVE CONTINUOUS FUTURE (ΠΑΘΗΤΙΚΟΣ ΣΥΝΕΧΗΣ ΜΕΛΛΟΝΤΑΣ)

| Continuous | Imperfect | Past | Simple Future<br>**CONTINUOUS FUTURE** | Present Perfect<br>Past Perfect<br>Future Perfect | Simple Subjunctive<br>Past Perfect Subj.<br>Continuous Subj. | Simple Imperative<br>Continuous Imp. |
|---|---|---|---|---|---|---|

**A. Meaning:**

**The same as in active Continuous Future tense (This tense does not exist in English)**

**B. Formation:**

**θα + Passive Present**

- **θα πληρώνομαι** [κάθε εβδομάδα] *I will be paid [every week]*

**Continuous Future**

**θα** πληρών**ομαι**
**θα** πληρών**εσαι**
**θα** πληρών**εται**
**θα** πληρων**όμαστε**
**θα** πληρών**εστε**
**θα** πληρών**ονται**

# PASSIVE PRESENT PERFECT (ΠΑΘΗΤΙΚΟΣ ΠΑΡΑΚΕΙΜΕΝΟΣ)

| Present | Imperfect | Past | Simple Future<br>Continuous Future | **PRESENT PERFECT**<br>Past Perfect<br>Future Perfect | Simple Subjunctive<br>Past Perfect Subj.<br>Continuous Subj. | Simple Imperative<br>Continuous Imp. |
|---|---|---|---|---|---|---|

**A. Meaning:**

**The same as in the active Present Perfect tense**

**B. Formation:**

**Conjugate the verb έχω + 3rd person singular of the Passive Simple Future tense,** (without θα) **for all persons**

- **έχω πληρωθεί** *I have been paid*

**Passive Present Perfect**

**έχω πληρωθεί**
**έχεις πληρωθεί**
**έχει πληρωθεί**
**έχουμε πληρωθεί**
**έχετε πληρωθεί**
**έχουν πληρωθεί**

# PASSIVE PAST PERFECT (ΠΑΘΗΤΙΚΟΣ ΥΠΕΡΣΥΝΤΕΛΙΚΟΣ)

| Present | Imperfect | Past | Simple Future | Present Perfect | Simple Subjunctive | Simple Imperative |
|---|---|---|---|---|---|---|
| | | | | **PAST PERFECT** | Past Perfect Subjunctive | |
| | | | Continuous Future | Future Perfect | Continuous Subj. | Continuous Imp. |

**A. Meaning:**

**The same as the active Present Perfect tense**

**B. Formation:**

**Conjugate the verb είχα + 3rd person singular of the Passive Future tense** (without θα) **for all persons**

- **είχα πληρωθεί** *I had been paid*

**Passive Past Perfect**

**είχα πληρωθεί**
**είχες πληρωθεί**
**είχε πληρωθεί**
**είχαμε πληρωθεί**
**είχατε πληρωθεί**
**είχαν πληρωθεί**

# PASSIVE FUTURE PERFECT (ΠΑΘΗΤΙΚΟΣ ΣΥΝΤΕΛΕΣΜΕΝΟΣ ΜΕΛΛΟΝΤΑΣ)

| | | | | | | |
|---|---|---|---|---|---|---|
| Present | Imperfect | Past | Simple Future<br>Continuous Future | Present Perfect<br>Past Perfect<br>**FUTURE PERFECT** | Simple Subjunctive<br>Past Perfect Subj.<br>Continuous Subjunctive | Simple Imperative<br>Continuous Imp. |

**A. Meaning:**

**The same as the active Future tense**

**B. Formation:**

**Conjugate the verb θα έχω + 3rd person singular of the Passive Future tense** (without θα) **for all persons**

- **θα έχω πληρωθεί** *I will have been paid*

**Passive Future Perfect**

**θα έχω πληρωθεί**
**θα έχεις πληρωθεί**
**θα έχει πληρωθεί**
**θα έχουμε πληρωθεί**
**θα έχετε πληρωθεί**
**θα έχουν πληρωθεί**

# PASSIVE SUBJUNCTIVE (ΠΑΘΗΤΙΚΗ ΥΠΟΤΑΚΤΙΚΗ)

## PASSIVE CONTINUOUS SUBJUNCTIVE (ΠΑΘΗΤΙΚΗ ΣΥΝΕΧΗΣ ΥΠΟΤΑΚΤΙΚΗ)

| Present | Imperfect | Past | Simple Future<br>Continuous Future | Present Perfect<br>Past Perfect<br>Future Perfect | Simple Subjunctive<br>Past Perfect Subj.<br>**CONTINUOUS SUBJUNCTIVE** | Simple Imperative<br>Continuous Imp. |
|---|---|---|---|---|---|---|

**A. Meaning:**

**The same as in the active Continuous Subjunctive**

**B. Formation:**

**Verb + να + Passive Present tense**

- **θέλω να πληρώνομαι** [κάθε εβδομάδα] *I want to be paid [every week]*

# PASSIVE SIMPLE SUBJUNCTIVE (ΠΑΘΗΤΙΚΗ ΑΠΛΗ ΥΠΟΤΑΚΤΙΚΗ)

| Present | Imperfect | Past | Simple Future<br>Continuous Future | Present Perfect<br>Past Perfect<br>Future Perfect | **SIMPLE SUBJUNCTIVE**<br>Past Perfect Subj.<br>Continuous Subj. | Simple Imperative<br>Continuous Imp. |
|---|---|---|---|---|---|---|

**A. Meaning:**

**The same as in the active Simple Subjunctive**

**B. Formation:**

**Verb + να + Passive Simple Future tense** (without **θα**)

- **θέλω να πληρωθώ** *I want to be paid (i.e. now)*

**NOTE:** The Passive Simple Subjunctive is also used after the particles για να, όταν, αν, and impersonal verbs

- Για να έρθεις (έρχομαι) εδώ νωρίτερα πρέπει να πάρεις το πρωινό τραίνο — *To come here earlier you have to take the morning train*
- Όταν φύγουν, έλα αμέσως σπίτι — *When they leave, come home straight away*
- Αν έρθεις νωρίτερα, τηλεφώνησέ μου — *If you come earlier, ring me*
- Είναι εύκολο να έρθουμε με το τραίνο — *It is easy for us to come by train*
- Πρέπει να ερχόμαστε στην Αγγλία αρκετά συχνά — *We have to come to England quite often*

# PASSIVE IMPERATIVE (ΠΑΘΗΤΙΚΗ ΠΡΟΣΤΑΚΤΙΚΗ)

## PASSIVE CONTINUOUS IMPERATIVE (ΠΑΘΗΤΙΚΗ ΠΡΟΣΤΑΚΤΙΚΗ ΕΝΕΣΤΩΤΑ)

| Present | Imperfect | Past | Simple Future<br>Continuous Future | Present Perfect<br>Past Perfect<br>Future Perfect | Simple Subjunctive<br>Past Perfect Subj.<br>Continuous Subj. | Simple Imperative<br>**CONTINUOUS IMPERATIVE** |
|---|---|---|---|---|---|---|

**A. Meaning:**

**The same as the active Continuous Imperative.**

**B. Formation:**

**There is no 2nd person singular Imperative, but if needed, it can be expressed with the particle να + the form of the 2nd person singular:**

- **να πληρώνεσαι [δυό φορές παραπάνω]** *You should be paid [twice as much]*

**The 2nd person plural Imperative is formed from the 2nd person plural of the Present tense:**

- **πληρώνεστε [με τον μήνα]** *You are paid [monthly]*

**C. The negative Passive Present Imperative is formed with the particle:**

**μη(ν) + 2nd personal singular or plural of the Present tense**

# PASSIVE SIMPLE IMPERATIVE (ΑΠΛΗ ΠΑΘΗΤΙΚΗ ΠΡΟΣΤΑΚΤΙΚΗ)

| Present | Imperfect | Past | Simple Future<br>Continuous Future | Present Perfect<br>Past Perfect<br>Future Perfect | Simple Subjunctive<br>Past Perfect Subj.<br>Continuous Subj. | **SIMPLE IMPERATIVE**<br>Continuous Imp. |
|---|---|---|---|---|---|---|

**A. Meaning:**

**The same as the active Simple Imperative**

**B. Formation:**

1. **Active Future stem + ου** (θα πληρώσω) **for 2nd person singular**
   - **πληρώσου** *Be paid (now)* [singular]

2. **2nd person plural of the Passive Future tense without the particle θα** (θα πληρωθώ) **for the 2nd person plural**
   - **πληρωθείτε τώρα** *Be paid now* [plural]

# PASSIVE PARTICIPLES (ΠΑΘΗΤΙΚΕΣ ΜΕΤΟΧΕΣ)

## PASSIVE PRESENT PARTICIPLE (ΠΑΘΗΤΙΚΗ ΜΕΤΟΧΗ ΕΝΕΣΤΩΤΑ)

The Passive Present Participle shows the state or condition experienced by the subject of the main verb or the object of the verb. It exists in three genders and it is declined like an adjective.

**A. Meaning**:

**It is used as an adjective**

**B. Formation**:

**Replace the endings of the Passive Past tense as follows**:

| | | | |
|---|---|---|---|
| endings in | **-εύτηκα** | change into | **-μένος, -μένη, -μένο** |
| | **- θηκα** | | **-μενος, -μενη, -μενο** |
| | **- στηκα** | | **-σμένος, -σμένη, -σμένο** |
| | **- φτήκα** | | **-μμένος, -μμένη, -μμένο** |
| | **- χτήκα** | | **-γμένος, -γμένη, -γμένο** |

- Ο Γιώργος είναι παντρεμένος (παντρεύτηκα – I got married) *George is married*
- Η Ελένη επέστρεψε το κείμενο διορθωμένο ( διορθώθηκα - I was corrected) *Eleni returned the text corrected*
- Η Μαρία είναι κλεισμένη (κλείστηκα – I shut myself inside) στο γραφείο *Maria has shut herself in the study*
- Τα παιδιά είναι κουρασμένα (κουράστηκα – I was tired) *The children are tired*
- Θέλω τους ώμους μου καλυμμένους (καλύφτηκα – I was covered) *I want my shoulders covered*
- Η βάρκα είναι τραβηγμένη έξω από την θάλασσα (τραβήχτηκα – I was pulled) *The boat has been pulled out of the sea*

# PASSIVE PAST PARTICIPLE (ΠΑΘΗΤΙΚΗ ΜΕΤΟΧΗ ΑΟΡΙΣΤΟΥ)

The passive past participle is used as an adjective. The endings **- είς, - είσα, - έν** are hardly ever used orally, but they remain in the language and are common in legal or official documents, as well as in newspapers.

- Ο διορισθείς νέος υπουργός (διορίζομαι - *I am appointed*) *The newly appointed minister*
- Μίλησε για τους απολυθέντες υπαλλήλους (απολύθηκα - *I was dismissed*) *She talked about the dismissed civil servants*

# PARTICLES

These are auxiliary words which precede the verb and are used to form various kinds of expressions: **ας, θα, να**

## Ας

**The word ας is used with any tense and expresses a wish or it gives permition**

| | |
|---|---|
| Ας είχα κερδίσει το λαχείο | *I wish I had won the lottery* |
| Ας μην φάει, δεν με νοιάζει | *Let him not eat anything, I don't mind* |
| Ας διαβάζεις λίγο παραπάνω, αν θέλεις να περάσεις τις εξετάσεις | *You should study a little more if you want to pass your exams* |
| Ας ξέρει Αγγλικά καλά, δεν είναι καλός δάσκαλος | *No matter how well he knows English, he is not a good teacher* |
| Ας διάβαζα λίγο παραπάνω, όταν ήμουν μικρή | *I wish I had studied more when I was young* |
| Ας πάει ο Νίκος να αγοράσει εφημερίδα | *Let Nikos buy the newspaper* |
| Ας τον βοηθήσουμε | *Let's help him* |

## Θα

**Apart from the Future tense, θα is also used with other tenses to express a possibility** (conditional) (see Conditional structures page 61)

| | |
|---|---|
| Θα διαβάζει πολύ, φαντάζομαι, για τις εξετάσεις | *He must be studying a lot for his exams, I imagine* |
| Θα έμεινε στην δουλειά του αργά ψες το βράδυ, και δεν ήρθε | *He must have stayed late at work last night, as he did not come* |
| Θα πήγαινε στο πάρτυ χτες το βράδυ, αλλά δεν μπόρεσε | *He would have gone to the party last night but he could not make it* |
| Θα πήγαινε στο πάρτυ χτες, μου είπε | *He would have gone to the party yesterday, he told me* (indirect speech) |
| Θα πήγε στο πάρτυ, δεν είναι εδώ τώρα | *He must have gone to the party, he is not here now* |
| Θα έχει πάει στο πάρτυ, δεν είναι εδώ τώρα | *He may have gone to the party, he is not here now* |
| Θα είχε πάει στο πάρτυ, δεν ήταν στο σπίτι | *He might have gone to the party, he was not at home* |
| Θα καθυστέρησε κάπου | *He must have been delayed somewhere* |

**Να**

**In addition to using να with the Present or Future tense to form the Subjunctive, it is also used with other tenses to form various expressions:**

a) **Polite request** (simple subjunctive)

- Να φάμε κάτι; *Shall we eat something?*
- Να έρθω μαζί σας; *Shall I come with you?*

**b) A wish (**να + Imperfect tense or Present Perfect or Past perfect)

- Να πήγαινα στην Ελλάδα φέτος! *I wish I were going to Greece this year!*
- Αχ, να έβγαινε ο ήλιος λίγο! Oh, *I wish the sun would come out for a while!*
- Να είχα πάει κι εγώ στην Ελλάδα! *I wish I had gone to Greece as well*!
- Ελπίζω να έχω τελειώσει μέχρι τον Ιούλιο! *I hope that I will have finished by July!*

# IMPERSONAL VERBS

**These verbs are used only in the 3rd person singular or plural without a subject. They exist in all tenses and forms and are followed by a verb in the subjunctive mood. If the subject of the verb is in the plural form then these verbs take the 3rd person plural form. Verbs which indicate weather conditions are in 3rd person singular.**

| | |
|---|---|
| Πρέπει να είσαι προσεχτικός όταν οδηγείς | *You must be careful when driving* |
| Μπορεί να πάω στο Λονδίνο αύριο | *I may go to London tomorrow* |
| Αξίζει να δεις το μουσείο | *It is worth while to see the museum* |
| Αποκλείεται να πάμε με το αεροπλάνο | *It is not possible for us to go by air plane* |
| Μ' αρέσει να μαθαίνω ξένες γλώσσες | *I like learning foreign languages* |
| Μ' αρέσει το φόρεμα σου | *I like your dress* |
| Μ' αρέσουν τα γιαλιά σου | *I like your glasses* |
| Ξημερώνει νωρίς το καλοκαίρι | *The day breaks / dawns early in the summer* |
| Φυσάει πολύ σήμερα | *It is very windy today* |
| Χιονίζει συχνά στην Λαπωνία | *It snows often in Lapland* |
| Απαγορεύεται να καπνίζετε | *Smoking is not allowed* |
| Χρειάζεται να δείξεις περισσότερο ενδιαφέρον | *You need to show move interest* |

# IRREGULAR VERBS

Many verbs in all languages form their Future and Past tense and their Subjunctive with varying words:

**Βλέπω** τα πουλιά στον κήπο *I see the birds in the garden*
Χτες **είδα** μία αλεπού *Yesterday I saw a fox* .
Αύριο **θα δεις** τον σκύλο τους στον κήπο *Tomorrow you will see their dog in the garden*

**Many verbs are used with a conjunction or a preposition**

| | |
|---|---|
| Ενδιαφέρομαι για σας | *I am interested in you* |
| Λέω να αγοράσω ένα λεξικό | *I am thinking of buying a dictionary* |
| Λυπάμαι που άργησα | *I am sorry I was late* |
| Νομίζω ότι έχεις άδικο | *I think you are wrong* |
| Πιστεύω σε σένα | *I believe in you* |
| Πιστεύω ότι έφυγε νωρίτερα | *I believe( that) she left earlier* |
| Φοβάμαι μήπως δεν καταλαβαίνει | *I am afraid in case she does not understand* |
| Χαίρομαι που σε βλέπω | *I am glad to see you* |

# CONDITIONAL STRUCTURES

**The equivalent of the English active conditional is formed by combining the particle word θα with the Imperfect tense**

- Θα διάβαζα *I would read*
- Θα ήθελα *I would like*

Conditional sentences indicate actions or thoughts which may happen in the present or in the future under certain circumstances. Conditional structures consist of two clauses: a hypothetical clause introduced with the word **αν** (if) and another which is the possible result. The meaning depends on the tenses used.

## A. The open conditional

**1. αν + Present tense** — **Rresent tense**

Αν ξυπνώ αργά το πρωί....................... χάνω το τραίνο
*If I wake up late in the morning..............* *I miss the train*

**2. αν + Future form** (without θα ) — **Imperative**

Αν δεις την Ελένη.................................. πες της να περιμένει
*If you see Eleni........................................* *tell her to wait*

**3. αν + Future form** (without θα) — **Future tense**

Αν + αγοράσεις εισιτήρια..................... θα πάμε στο θέατρο
*If you buy tickets...................................* *we will go to the theatre*

**B. The hypothetical conditional**

| | |
|---|---|
| **1. αν + Imperfect tense** | **θα + Imperfect tense** |
| Αν ήξερα την διεύθυνσή της ........ | θα πήγαινα στο πάρτυ της |
| *If I knew her address* ........ | *I would go to her party* |
| **2. αν + Past Perfect** | **θα + Past Perfect** |
| Αν είχες αγοράσει εισιτήρια ........ | θα είχαμε πάει στο θέατρο |
| *If you had bought tickets* ........ | *we would have gone to the theatre* |

## 1. NOTE

All the tenses and forms illustrated above exist for the active, passive or deponent Greek verbs as well. Part 1 of the tables of verbs shows how they are conjugated and how they differ in all tenses, subjunctive moods and imperative forms

## 2. NOTE

An extensive selection of Greek verbs is clearly listed in the compendium of verbs. The numbers printed in the Present tense column refer to one of the model verb tables shown on pages 13–18, 20, 42.

# NOTES ON THE TABLES OF VERBS

The verb tables that follow show the 1st person singular of different tenses, the prefixes in the Imperfect and Past tense; the formation of the continuous and simple subjunctive and the continuous and simple Imperative forms which have two persons only.

**The tables do not contain the tenses and the Subjunctive which are formed on the basis of what has already been illustrated** (**see pages 13-18**). These are:

The **CONTINUOUS FUTURE:** formed with the particle **θα + Present tense** *θα τους γράφω κάθε μέρα* *I shall be writing to them every day*

The **CONTINUOUS SUBJUNCTIVE:** formed with the particle **να + Present tense** *θέλω να τους γράφω κάθε μέρα* *I want to write to them every day*

The **FUTURE PERFECT TENSE:** which is formed by conjugating the Future tense verb **θα έχω + 3rd person singular of the Simple Future tense** without θα) of the verb which stays the same for all persons *θα έχω γράψει το γράμμα μέχρι το βράδυ* *I will have written the letter by tonight*

The **PARTICIPLES OF ACTIVE AND PASSIVE VOICE VERBS**

## NOTE

In the tables, the Passive Forms of verbs are printed in italics.
All verbs have a number in the Present tense column which indicates that they are conjugated acording to the examples found in the corresponding pages.
Ordinary verbs with the number **13** are conjugated like the active verb **ντύνω** on page **13**
with the number **14** are conjugated like the passive voice verb **ντύνομαι** on page **14**

Contracted verbs with the number **15** indicate that the verb is conjugated like the contracted verb **μιλώ(-άω) on page 15**
the number **16** indicate that the verb is conjugated like the contracted verb **μιλιέμαι on page 16**
the number **17** indicate that the verb is conjugated like the contracted verb **καλώ(-έω) on page 17**
the number **18** indicate that the verb is conjugated like the contracted verb **καλούμαι(-έομαι) on page 18**
the number **20** indicate that the verb is conjugated **like the verbs on page 20**
the number **42** indicate that the verb is conjugated **like one of the verbs on page 42**

# PART II

A. Tables of Greek verbs in English alphabetical order

B. Pages index of verbs in Greek alphabetical order

| English Verb | Present | Imperfect | Past | Simple Future<br>Simple Subjunctive | Present Perfect<br>Past Perfect | Continuous Imperative | Simple Imperative |
|---|---|---|---|---|---|---|---|
| **I accuse** | κατηγορώ 17 | κατηγορούσα | κατηγόρησα | θα κατηγορήσω<br>να κατηγορήσω | έχω κατηγορήσει<br>είχα κατηγορήσει | να κατηγορείς<br>κατηγορείτε | κατηγόρησε<br>κατηγορήστε |
| **I ache** | πον(ά)ώ 15 | πονούσα | πόνεσα | θα πονέσω<br>να πονέσω | έχω πονέσει<br>είχα πονέσει | πόνα<br>πονάτε | πόνεσε<br>πονέστε |
| **I achieve** | επιτυγχάνω 13<br>επιτυχαίνω | επιτύγχανα<br>επιτύχαινα | επέτυχα | θα πετύχω<br>να πετύχω | έχω πετύχει<br>είχα πετύχει | πετύχαινε<br>πετυχαίνετε | πέτυχε<br>πετύχετε |
| **I acknowledge** (fact/situation) | *παραδέχομαι 14* | *παραδεχόμουν* | *παραδέχτηκα* | *θα παραδεχτώ*<br>*να παραδεχτώ* | *έχω παραδεχτεί*<br>*είχα παραδεχτεί* | *να παραδέχεσαι*<br>*παραδέχεστε* | *παραδέξου*<br>*παραδεχτείτε* |
| **I acquire** | αποχτώ 15 | αποχτούσα | απόχτησα | θα αποχτήσω<br>να αποχτήσω | έχω αποχτήσει<br>είχα αποχτήσει | απόχτα<br>αποχτάτε | απόχτησε<br>αποχτήστε |
| **I acquit** | αθωώνω 13 | αθώωνα | αθώωσα | θα αθωώσω<br>να αθωώσω | έχω αθωώσει<br>είχα αθωώσει | αθώωνε<br>αθωώνετε | αθώωσε<br>αθωώστε |
| **I act** | ενεργώ 17 | ενεργούσα | ενήργησα | θα ενεργήσω<br>να ενεργήσω | έχω ενεργήσει<br>είχα ενεργήσει | να ενεργείς<br>ενεργείτε | ενέργησε<br>ενεργήστε |
| **I act out** | αναπαρασταίνω 13 | αναπαράσταινα | αναπαράστησα | θα αναπαραστήσω<br>να αναπαραστήσω | έχω αναπαραστήσει<br>είχα αναπαραστήσει | αναπαράσταινε<br>αναπαρασταίνετε | αναπαράστησε<br>αναπαραστήστε |
| **I activate** | ενεργοποιώ 17 | ενεργοποιούσα | ενεργοποίησα | θα ενεργοποιήσω<br>να ενεργοποιήσω | έχω ενεργοποιήσει<br>είχα ενεργοποιήσει | να ενεργοποιείς<br>ενεργοποιείτε | ενεργοποίησε<br>ενεργοποιήστε |
| **I adapt** | διασκευάζω 13 | διασκεύαζα | διασκεύασα | θα διασκευάσω<br>να διασκευάσω | έχω διασκευάσει<br>είχα διασκευάσει | διασκεύαζε<br>διασκευάζετε | διασκεύαζε<br>διασκευάστε |
| **I add** | προσθέτω 13 | πρόσθετα | πρόσθεσα | θα προσθέσω<br>να προσθέσω | έχω προσθέσει<br>είχα προσθέσει | πρόσθετε<br>προσθέτετε | πρόσθεσε<br>προσθέστε |
| **I add up** | αθροίζω 13 | άθροιζα | άθροισα | θα αθροίσω<br>να αθροίσω | έχω αθροίσει<br>είχα αθροίσει | άθροιζε<br>αθροίζετε | άθροισε<br>αθροίστε |

| English Verb | Present | Imperfect | Past | Simple Future<br>Simple Subjunctive | Present Perfect<br>Past Perfect | Continuous Imperative | Simple Imperative |
|---|---|---|---|---|---|---|---|
| **I addict** | εθίζω 13 | έθιζα | έθισα | θα εθίσω<br>να εθίσω | έχω εθίσει<br>είχα εθίσει | έθιζε<br>εθίζετε | έθισε<br>εθίστε |
| **I address** | *απευθύνομαι 14* | *απευθυνόμουν* | *απευθύνθηκα* | *θα απευθυνθώ*<br>*να απευθυνθώ* | *έχω απευθυνθεί*<br>*είχα απευθυνθεί* | *να απευθύνεσαι*<br>*απευθύνεστε* | *απευθύνσου*<br>*απευθυνθείτε* |
| **I adhere** | τηρώ 17 | τηρούσα | τήρησα | θα τηρήσω<br>να τηρήσω | έχω τηρήσει<br>είχα τηρήσει | να τηρείς<br>τηρείτε | τήρησε<br>τηρήστε |
| **I adjust** (to rules) | *προσαρμόζομαι 14* | *προσαρμοζόμουν* | *προσαρμόστηκα* | *θα προσαρμοστώ*<br>*να προσαρμοστώ* | *έχω προσαρμοστεί*<br>*είχα προσαρμοστεί* | *να προσαρμόζεσαι*<br>*προσαρμόζεστε* | *προσαρμόσου*<br>*προσαρμοστείτε* |
| **I administer** | *διαχειρίζομαι 14* | *διαχειριζόμουν* | *διαχειρίστηκα* | *θα διαχειριστώ*<br>*να διαχειριστώ* | *έχω διαχειριστεί*<br>*είχα διαχειριστεί* | *να διαχειρίζεσαι*<br>*διαχειρίζεστε* | *διαχειρίσου*<br>*διαχειριστείτε* |
| **I admire** | θαυμάζω 13 | θαύμαζα | θαύμασα | θα θαυμάσω<br>να θαυμάσω | έχω θαυμάσει<br>είχα θαυμάσει | θαύμαζε<br>θαυμάζετε | θαύμασε<br>θαυμάστε |
| **I admit** | *αποδέχομαι 14* | *αποδεχόμουν* | *αποδέχτηκα* | *θα αποδεχτώ*<br>*να αποδεχτώ* | *έχω αποδεχτεί*<br>*είχα αποδεχτεί* | *να αποδέχεσαι*<br>*αποδέχεστε* | *αποδέξου*<br>*αποδεχτείτε* |
| **I adopt** | υιοθετώ 13 | υιοθετούσα | υιοθέτησα | θα υιοθετήσω<br>να υιοθετήσω | έχω υιοθετήσει<br>είχα υιοθετήσει | να υιοθετείς<br>υιοθετείτε | υιοθέτησε<br>υιοθετήστε |
| **I adore** | υπεραγαπώ 15 | υπεραγαπούσα | υπεραγάπησα | θα υπεραγαπήσω<br>να υπεραγαπήσω | έχω υπεραγαπήσει<br>είχα υπερεγαπήσει | υπεραγάπα<br>υπεραγαπάτε | υπεραγάπησε<br>υπεραγαπήστε |
| **I adorn** (with objects) | διακοσμώ 17 | διακοσμούσα | διακόσμησα | θα διακοσμήσω<br>να διακοσμήσω | έχω διακοσμήσει<br>είχα διακοσμήσει | να διακοσμείς<br>διακοσμείτε | διακόσμησε<br>διακοσμήστε |
| **I adulterate** | νοθεύω 13 | νόθευα | νόθεψα | θα νοθέψω<br>να νοθέψω | έχω νοθέψει<br>είχα νοθέψει | νόθευε<br>νοθεύετε | νόθεψε<br>νοθέψτε |
| **I advance** | *προάγομαι 14* | *προαγόμουν* | *προήχθηκα* | *έχω προαχθεί*<br>*είχα προαχθεί* | *θα προαχθώ*<br>*να προαχθώ* | *να προάγεσαι*<br>*προάγεστε* | *να προαχθείς*<br>*προαχθείτε* |

| English Verb | Present | Imperfect | Past | Simple Future<br>Simple Subjunctive | Present Perfect<br>Past Perfect | Continuous Imperative | Simple Imperative |
|---|---|---|---|---|---|---|---|
| **I advertise** | διαφημίζω 13 | διαφήμιζα | διαφήμισα | θα διαφημίσω<br>να διαφημίσω | έχω διαφημίσει<br>είχα διαφημίσει | διαφήμιζε<br>διαφημίζετε | διαφήμισε<br>διαφημίστε |
| **I advise** | συμβουλεύω 13 | συμβούλευα | συμβούλεψα | θα συμβουλέψω<br>να συμβουλέψω | έχω συμβουλέψει<br>είχα συμβουλέψει | συμβούλευε<br>συμβουλεύετε | συμβούλεψε<br>συμβουλέψτε |
| **I advocate** | συνηγορώ 17 | συνηγορούσα | συνηγόρησα | θα συνηγορήσω<br>να συνηγορήσω | έχω συνηγορήσει<br>είχα συνηγορήσει | να συνηγορείς<br>συνηγορείτε | συνηγόρησε<br>συνηγορήστε |
| **I affect**<br>(move deeply) | συγκινώ 17 | συγκινούσα | συγκίνησα | θα συγκινήσω<br>να συγκινήσω | έχω συγκινήσει<br>είχα συγκινήσει | να συγκινείς<br>συγκινείτε | συγκίνησε<br>συγκινήστε |
| **I affirm** | βεβαιώνω 13 | βεβαίωνα | βεβαίωσα | θα βεβαιώσω<br>να βεβαιώσω | έχω βεβαιώσει<br>είχα βεβαιώσει | βεβαίωνε<br>βεβαιώνετε | βεβαίωσε<br>βεβαιώστε |
| **I affix** | επισυνάπτω 13 | επισύναπτα | επισύναψα | θα επισυνάψω<br>να επισυνάψω | έχω επισυνάψει<br>είχα επισυνάψει | επισύναπτε<br>επισυνάπτετε | επισύναψε<br>επισυνάψτε |
| **I afford**<br>(time) | διαθέτω 13 | διέθετα | διέθεσα | θα διαθέσω<br>να διαθέσω | έχω διαθέσει<br>είχα διαθέσει | διάθετε<br>διαθέτετε | διάθεσε<br>διαθέστε |
| **I age** | γερν(ά)ώ 15 | γερνούσα | γέρασα | θα γεράσω<br>να γεράσω | έχω γεράσει<br>είχα γεράσει | γέρνα<br>γερνάτε | γέρασε<br>γεράστε |
| **I aggravate**<br>(situation) | επιδεινώνω 13 | επιδείνωνα | επιδείνωσα | θα επιδεινώσω<br>να επιδεινώσω | έχω επιδεινώσει<br>είχα επιδεινώσει | επιδείνωνε<br>επιδεινώνετε | επιδείνωσε<br>επιδεινώστε |
| **I agitate** | ανακινώ 17 | ανακινούσα | ανακίνησα | θα ανακινήσω<br>να ανακινήσω | έχω ανακινήσει<br>είχα ανακινήσει | να ανακινείς<br>ανακινείτε | ανακίνησε<br>ανακινήστε |
| **I agree** | συμφωνώ 17 | συμφωνούσα | συμφώνησα | θα συμφωνήσω<br>να συμφωνήσω | έχω συμφωνήσει<br>είχα συμφωνήσει | να συμφωνείς<br>συμφωνείτε | συμφώνησε<br>συμφωνήστε |
| **I aim** | σκοπεύω 13 | σκόπευα | σκόπευσα | θα σκοπεύσω<br>να σκοπεύσω | έχω σκοπεύσει<br>είχα σκοπεύσει | σκόπευε<br>σκοπεύετε | σκόπευσε<br>σκοπεύστε |

| English Verb | Present | Imperfect | Past | Simple Future<br>Simple Subjunctive | Present Perfect<br>Past Perfect | Continuous Imperative | Simple Imperative |
|---|---|---|---|---|---|---|---|
| **I aim** | κατευθύνω 13 | κατεύθυνα | κατεύθυνα | θα κατευθύνω<br>να κατευθύνω | έχω κατευθύνει<br>είχα κατευθύνει | να κατευθύνεις<br>κατευθύνετε | κατεύθυνε<br>κατευθύνετε |
| **I alarm** | ταράζω 13 | τάραζα | τάραξα | θα ταράξω<br>να ταράξω | έχω ταράξει<br>είχα ταράξει | τάραζε<br>ταράζετε | τάραξε<br>ταράξτε |
| **I alienate** | αποξενώνω 13 | αποξένωνα | αποξένωσα | θα αποξενώσω<br>να αποξενώσω | έχω αποξενώσει<br>είχα αποξενώσει | αποξένωνε<br>αποξενώνετε | αποξένωσε<br>αποξενώστε |
| **I alight** | *αποβιβάζομαι 14* | *αποβιβαζόμουν* | *αποβιβάστηκα* | *θα αποβιβαστώ*<br>*να αποβιβαστώ* | *έχω αποβιβαστεί*<br>*είχα αποβιβαστεί* | *να αποβιβάζεσαι*<br>*αποβιβάζεστε* | *αποβιβάσου*<br>*αποβιβαστείτε* |
| **I allege** | *ισχυρίζομαι 14* | *ισχυριζόμουν* | *ισχυρίστηκα* | *θα ισχυριστώ*<br>*να ισχυριστώ* | *έχω ισχυριστεί*<br>*είχα ισχυριστεί* | *να ισχυρίζεσαι*<br>*ισχυρίζεστε* | *ισχυρίσου*<br>*ισχυριστείτε* |
| **I allocate** | καταμερίζω 13 | καταμέριζα | καταμέρισα | θα καταμερίσω<br>να καταμερίσω | έχω καταμερίσει<br>είχα καταμερίσει | καταμέριζε<br>καταμερίζετε | καταμέρισε<br>καταμερίστε |
| **I allot** | παραχωρώ 17 | παροχωρούσα | παροχώρησα | θα παραχωρήσω<br>να παραχωρήσω | έχω παραχωρήσει<br>είχα παραχωρήσει | να παραχωρείς<br>παραχωρείτε | παραχώρησε<br>παραχωρήστε |
| **I alter** | μεταποιώ 17 | μεταποιούσα | μεταποίησα | θα μεταποιήσω<br>να μεταποιήσω | έχω μεταποιήσει<br>είχα μεταποιήσει | να μεταποιείς<br>μεταποιείτε | μεταποίησε<br>μεταποιήστε |
| **I alternate** | εναλλάσσω 13 | ενάλλασσα | ενάλλαξα | θα εναλλάξω<br>να εναλλάξω | έχω εναλλάξει<br>είχα εναλλάξει | ενάλλασσε<br>εναλλάσσετε | ενάλλαξε<br>εναλλάξτε |
| **I am ablaze** | *φλέγομαι 14* | *φλεγόμουν* | *εφλέγην* | *θα φλέγομαι*<br>*να φλέγομαι* | *έχω φλεγεί*<br>*είχα φλεγεί* | *να φλέγεσαι*<br>*φλέγεστε* | *φλέξου*<br>*φλεγείτε* |
| **I am absent** | απουσιάζω 13 | απουσίαζα | απουσίασα | θα απουσιάσω<br>να απουσιάσω | έχω απουσιάσει<br>είχα απουσιάσει | απουσίαζε<br>απουσιάζετε | απουσίασε<br>απουσιάστε |
| **I am absent** (missing) | λείπω 13 | έλειπα | έλειψα | θα λείψω<br>να λείψω | έχω λείψει<br>είχα λείψει | λείπε<br>λείπετε | λείψε<br>λείψτε |

| English Verb | Present | Imperfect | Past | Simple Future<br>Simple Subjunctive | Present Perfect<br>Past Perfect | Continuous Imperative | Simple Imperative |
|---|---|---|---|---|---|---|---|
| **I am acquainted** | *γνωρίζομαι 14* | *γνωριζόμουν* | *γνωρίστικα* | *θα γνωριστώ*<br>*να γνωσριστώ* | *έχω γνωριστεί*<br>*είχα γνωριστεί* | *να γνωρίζεσαι*<br>*γνωρίζεστε* | *γνωρίσου*<br>*γνωριστείτε* |
| **I am admired** | *θαυμάζομαι 14* | *θαυμαζόμουν* | *θαυμάστηκα* | *θα θαυμαστώ*<br>*να θαυμαστώ* | *έχω θαυμαστεί*<br>*είχα θαυμαστεί* | *να θαυμάζεσαι*<br>*θαυμάζεστε* | *θαυμάσου*<br>*θαυμαστείτε* |
| **I am ambitious** | φιλοδοξώ 17 | φιλοδοξούσα | φιλοδόξησα | θα φιλοδοξήσω<br>να φιλοδοξήσω | έχω φιλοδοξήσει<br>είχα φιλοδοξήσει | να φιλοδοξείς<br>φιλοδοξείτε | φιλοδόξησε<br>φιλοδοξήστε |
| **I am angry** | θυμώνω 13 | θύμωνα | θύμωσα | θα θυμώσω<br>να θυμώσω | έχω θυμώσει<br>είχα θυμώσει | θύμωνε<br>θυμώνετε | θύμωσε<br>θυμώστε |
| **I am ashamed** | *ντρέπομαι 14* | *ντρεπόμουν* | *ντράπηκα* | *θα ντραπώ*<br>*να ντραπώ* | *έχω ντραπεί*<br>*είχα ντραπεί* | *να ντρέπεσαι*<br>*ντρέπεστε* | *να ντραπείς*<br>*ντραπείτε* |
| **I am bored** | πλήττω 13 | έπληττα | έπληξα | θα πλήξω<br>να πλήξω | έχω πλήξει<br>είχα πλήξει | πλήττε<br>πλήττετε | πλήξε<br>πλήξτε |
| **I am cold** | κρυώνω 13 | κρύωνα | κρύωσα | θα κρυώσω<br>να κρυώσω | έχω κρυώσει<br>είχα κρυώσει | κρύωνε<br>κρυώνετε | κρύωσε<br>κρυώστε |
| **I am considered** | *θεωρούμαι 42* | *θεωρούμουν* | *θεωρήθηκα* | *θα θεωρηθώ*<br>*να θεωρηθώ* | *έχω θεωρηθεί*<br>*είχα θεωρηθεί* | *να θεωρείσαι*<br>*θεωρείστε* | *θεωρήσου*<br>*θεωρηθείτε* |
| **I am disobedient** | απειθώ 17 | απειθούσα | απείθησα | θα απειθήσω<br>να απειθήσω | έχω απειθήσει<br>είχα απειθήσει | να απειθείς<br>απειθείτε | απείθησε<br>απειθήστε |
| **I am enthusiastic** | ενθουσιάζομαι 14 | ενθουσιαζόμουν | ενθουσιάστηκα | θα ενθουσιαστώ<br>να ενθουσιαστώ | έχω ενθουσιαστεί<br>είχα ενθουσιαστεί | να ενθουσιάζεσαι<br>ενθουσιάζεστε | ενθουσιάσου<br>ενθουσιαστείτε |
| **I am found** | *βρίσκομαι 14* | *βρισκόμουν* | *βρέθηκα* | *θα βρεθώ*<br>*να βρεθώ* | *έχω βρεθεί*<br>*είχα βρεθεί* | *να βρίσκεσαι*<br>*βρίσκεστε* | *να βρεθείς*<br>*βρεθείτε* |
| **I am hungry** | πειν(ά)ώ 15 | πεινούσα | πείνασα | θα πεινάσω<br>να πεινάσω | έχω πεινάσει<br>είχα πεινάσει | πείνα<br>πεινάτε | πείνασε<br>πεινάστε |

| English Verb | Present | Imperfect | Past | Simple Future<br>Simple Subjunctive | Present Perfect<br>Past Perfect | Continuous Imperative | Simple Imperative |
|---|---|---|---|---|---|---|---|
| **I am taken ill** | αρρωσταίνω 13 | αρρώσταινα | αρρώστησα | θα αρρωστήσω<br>να αρρωστήσω | έχω αρρωστήσει<br>είχα αρρωστήσει | αρρώσταινε<br>αρρωσταίνετε | αρρώστησε<br>αρρωστήστε |
| **I am to blame** | φταίω 20 | έφταιγα | έφταιξα | θα φταίξω<br>να φταίξω | έχω φταίξει<br>είχα φταίξει | φταίγε<br>φταίγετε | φταίξε<br>φταίξτε |
| **I amaze** | εκθαμβώνω 13 | εκθάμβωνα | εκθάμβωσα | θα εκθαμβώσω<br>να εκθαμβώσω | έχω εκθαμβώσει<br>είχα εκθαμβώσει | εκθάμβωνε<br>εκθαμβώνετε | εκθάμβωσε<br>εκθαμβώστε |
| **I ambush** | αιφνιδιάζω 13 | αιφνιδίαζα | αιφνιδίασα | θα αιφνιδιάσω<br>να αιφνιδιάσω | έχω αιφνιδιάσει<br>είχα αιφνιδιάσει | αιφνιδίαζε<br>αιφνιδιάζετε | αιφνιδίασε<br>αιφνιδιάστε |
| **I amend** (text/laws) | τροποποιώ 17 | τροποποιούσα | τροποποίησα | θα τροποποιήσω<br>να τροποποιήσω | έχω τροποποιήσει<br>είχα τροποποιήσει | να τροποποιείς<br>τροποποιείτε | τροποποίησε<br>τροποποιήστε |
| **It amounts to** | *ανέρχεται 14* | *ανερχόταν* | *ανήλθε* | *θα ανέλθει*<br>*να ανέλθει* | *έχω ανέλθει*<br>*είχα ανέλθει* | *να ανέρχεσαι*<br>*ανέρχεστε* | *να ανέλθεις*<br>*ανέλθετε* |
| **I amplify** | ενισχύω 13 | ενίσχυα | ενίσχυσα | θα ενισχύσω<br>να ενισχύσω | έχω ενισχύσει<br>είχα ενισχύσει | ενίσχυε<br>ενισχύετε | ενίσχυσε<br>ενισχύστε |
| **I amputate** | ακρωτηριάζω 13 | ακρωτηρίαζα | ακρωτηρίασα | θα ακρωτηριάσω<br>να ακρωτηριάσω | έχω ακρωτηριάσει<br>είχα ακρωτηριάσει | ακρωτηρίαζε<br>ακρωτηριάζετε | ακρωτηρίασε<br>ακρωτηριάστε |
| **I anaesthetize** | ναρκώνω 13 | νάρκωνα | νάρκωσα | θα ναρκώσω<br>να ναρκώσω | έχω ναρκώσει<br>είχα ναρκώσει | νάρκωνε<br>ναρκώνετε | νάρκωσε<br>ναρκώστε |
| **I analyse** | αναλύω 13 | ανέλυα | ανέλυσα | θα αναλύσω<br>να αναλύσω | έχω αναλύσει<br>είχα αναλύσει | ανάλυε<br>αναλύετε | ανέλυσε<br>αναλύστε |
| **I anchor** | αγκυροβολώ 17 | αγκυροβολούσα | αγκυροβόλησα | θα αγκυροβολήσω<br>να αγκυροβολήσω | έχω αγκυροβολήσει<br>είχα αγκυροβολήσει | να αγκυροβολείς<br>αγκυροβολείτε | αγκυροβόλησε<br>αγκυροβολήστε |
| **I anger** (someone) | εξοργίζω 13 | εξόργιζα | εξόργησα | θα εξοργήσω<br>να εξοργήσω | έχω εξοργήσει<br>είχα εξοργήσει | εξόργιζε<br>εξοργίζετε | εξόργησε<br>εξοργήστε |

| English Verb | Present | Imperfect | Past | Simple Future<br>Simple Subjunctive | Present Perfect<br>Past Perfect | Continuous Imperative | Simple Imperative |
|---|---|---|---|---|---|---|---|
| **I anglicize** | αγγλοποιώ 17 | αγγλοποιούσα | αγγλοποίησα | θα αγγλοποιήσω<br>να αγγλοποιήσω | έχω αγγλοποιήσει<br>είχα αγγλοποιήσει | να αγγλοποιείς<br>αγγλοποιείτε | αγγλοποίησε<br>αγγλοποιήστε |
| **I animate** | εμψυχώνω 13 | εμψύχωνα | εμψύχωσα | θα εμψυχώσω<br>να εμψυχώσω | έχω εμψυχώσει<br>είχα εμψυχώσει | εμψύχωνε<br>εμψυχώνετε | εμψύχωσε<br>εμψυχώστε |
| **I annex** | προσαρτώ 15 | προσαρτούσα | προσάρτησα | θα προσαρτήσω<br>να προσαρτήσω | έχω προσαρτήσει<br>είχα προσαρτήσει | να προσαρτάς<br>προσαρτάτε | προσάρτησε<br>προσαρτήστε |
| **I annihilate** | εκμηδενίζω 13 | εκμηδένιζα | εκμηδένισα | θα εκμηδενίσω<br>να εκμηδενίσω | έχω εκμηδενίσει<br>είχα εκμηδενίσει | εκμηδένιζε<br>εκμηδενίζετε | εκμηδένισε<br>εκμηδενίστε |
| **I announce** | κηρύττω 13 | κήρυττα | κήρυξα | θα κηρύξω<br>να κηρύξω | έχω κηρύξει<br>είχα κηρύξει | κήρυττε<br>κηρύττετε | κήρυξε<br>κηρύξτε |
| **I announce** | αναγγέλλω 13 | ανάγγελλα | ανάγγειλα | θα αναγγείλω<br>να αναγγείλω | έχω αναγγείλει<br>είχα αναγγείλει | ανάγγελλε<br>αναγγέλλετε | ανάγγειλε<br>αναγγείλτε |
| **I annoy** | εκνευρίζω 13 | εκνεύριζα | εκνεύρισα | θα εκνευρίσω<br>να εκνευρίσω | έχω εκνευρίσει<br>είχα εκνευρίσει | εκνεύριζε<br>εκνευρίζετε | εκνεύρισε<br>εκνευρίστε |
| **I answer** | απαντ(ά)ώ 15 | απαντούσα | απήντησα | θα απαντήσω<br>να απαντήσω | έχω απαντήσει<br>είχα απαντήσει | απάντα<br>απαντάτε | απάντησε<br>απαντήστε |
| **I answer to** | *ανταποκρίνομαι 14* | *ανταποκρινόμουν* | *ανταποκρίθηκα* | *θα ανταποκριθώ*<br>*να ανταποκριθώ* | *έχω ανταποκριθεί*<br>*είχα ανταποκριθεί* | *να ανταποκρίνεσαι*<br>*ανταποκρίνεστε* | *ανταποκρίσου*<br>*ανταποκριθείτε* |
| **I appear** | *φαίνομαι 14* | *φαινόμουν* | *φάνηκα* | *θα φανώ*<br>*να φανώ* | *έχω φανεί*<br>*είχα φανεί* | *να φαίνεσαι*<br>*φαίνεστε* | *φανού*<br>*φανείτε* |
| **I appear** | *εμφανίζομαι 14* | *εμφανιζόμουν* | *εμφανίστηκα* | *θα εμφανιστώ*<br>*να εμφανιστώ* | *έχω εμφανιστεί*<br>*είχα εμφανιστεί* | *να εμφανίζεσαι*<br>*εμφανίζεστε* | *εμφανίσου*<br>*εμφανιστείτε* |
| **I apply for** (job/permit) | υποβάλλω 13 | υπέβαλλα | υπέβαλα | θα υποβάλω<br>να υποβάλω | έχω υποβάλει<br>είχα υποβάλει | υπόβαλλε<br>υποβάλλετε | υπόβαλε<br>υποβάλτε |

| English Verb | Present | Imperfect | Past | Simple Future<br>Simple Subjunctive | Present Perfect<br>Past Perfect | Continuous Imperative | Simple Imperative |
|---|---|---|---|---|---|---|---|
| **I appoint** | διορίζω 13 | διόριζα | διόρισα | θα διορίσω<br>να διορίσω | έχω διορίσει<br>είχα διορήσει | διόριζε<br>διορίζετε | διόρισε<br>διορίστε |
| **I apologize** | *απολογούμαι 18* | *απολογούμουν* | *απολογήθηκα* | *θα απολογηθώ*<br>*να απολογηθώ* | *έχω απολογηθεί*<br>*είχα απολογηθεί* | *να απολογείσαι*<br>*απολογείστε* | *απολογήσου*<br>*απολογηθείτε* |
| **I appreciate** | ανατιμ(ά)ώ 15 | ανατιμούσα | ανατίμησα | θα ανατιμήσω<br>να ανατιμήσω | έχω ανατιμήσει<br>είχα ανατιμήσει | ανατίμα<br>ανατιμάτε | ανατίμησε<br>ανατιμήστε |
| **I apprehend** | τσακώνω 13 | τσάκωνα | τσάκωσα | θα τσακώσω<br>να τσακώσω | έχω τσακώσει<br>είχα τσακώσει | τσάκωνε<br>τσακώνετε | τσάκωσε<br>τσακώστε |
| **I approach** | πλησιάζω 13 | πλησίαζα | πλησίασα | θα πλησιάσω<br>να πλησιάσω | έχω πλησιάσει<br>είχα πλησιάσει | πλησίαζε<br>πλησιάζετε | πλησίασε<br>πλησιάστε |
| **I approach** | ζυγώνω 13 | ζύγωνα | ζύγωσα | θα ζυγώσω<br>να ζυγώσω | έχω ζυγώσει<br>είχα ζυγώσει | ζύγωνε<br>ζυγώνετε | ζύγωσε<br>ζυγώστε |
| **I approve** | εγκρίνω 13 | έγκρινα | ενέκρινα | θα εγκρίνω<br>να εγκρίνω | έχω εγκρίνει<br>είχα εγκρίνει | έγκρινε<br>εγκρίνετε | έγκρινε<br>εγκρίνετε |
| **I argue** (quarrel) | φιλονικώ 17 | φιλονικούσα | φιλονίκησα | θα φιλονικήσω<br>να φιλονικήσω | έχω φιλονικήσει<br>είχα φιλονικήσει | να φιλονικείς<br>φιλονικείτε | φιλονίκησε<br>φιλονικήστε |
| **I argue** (reason) | επιχειρηματολογώ 17 | επιχειρημα-τολογούσα | επιχειρημα-τολόγησα | θα επιχειρημα-τολογήσω | έχω επιχειρημα-τολογήσει | να επιχειρημα-τολογείς | επιχειρημα-τολόγησε |
| | | | | να επιχειρημα-τολογήσω | είχα επιχειρημα-τολογήσει | επιχειρημα-τολογείτε | επιχειρημα-τολογήστε |
| **I arise** (difficulty) | ανακύπτω 13 | ανέκυπτα | ανέκυψα | θα ανακύψω<br>να ανακύψω | έχω ανακύψει<br>είχα ανακύψει | ανάκυπτε<br>ανακύπτετε | ανάκυψε<br>ανακύψτε |
| **I arm** | εξοπλίζω 13 | εξόπλιζα | εξόπλισα | θα εξοπλίσω<br>να εξοπλίσω | έχω εξοπλίσει<br>είχα εξοπλίσει | εξόπλιζε<br>εξοπλίζετε | εξόπλισε<br>εξοπλίστε |

| English Verb | Present | Imperfect | Past | Simple Future<br>Simple Subjunctive | Present Perfect<br>Past Perfect | Continuous Imperative | Simple Imperative |
|---|---|---|---|---|---|---|---|
| **I arouse** | αφυπνίζω 13 | αφύπνιζα | αφύπνισα | θα αφυπνίσω<br>να αφυπνίσω | έχω αφυπνίσει<br>είχα αφυπνίσει | αφύπνιζε<br>αφυπνίζετε | αφύπνισε<br>αφυπνίστε |
| **I arrange** | κανονίζω 13 | κανόνιζα | κανόνισα | θα κανονίσω<br>να κανονίσω | έχω κανονίσει<br>είχα κανονίσει | κανόνιζε<br>κανονίζετε | κανόνισε<br>κανονίστε |
| **I arrest** | συλλαμβάνω 13 | συλλάμβανα | συνέλαβα | θα συλλάβω<br>να συλλάβω | έχω συλλάβει<br>είχα συλλάβει | συλλάμβανε<br>συλλαμβάνετε | συνέλαβε<br>συλλάβετε |
| **I arrive** | φτάνω 13 | έφτανα | έφτασα | θα φτάσω<br>να φτάσω | έχω φτάσει<br>είχα φτάσει | φτάνε<br>φτάνετε | φτάσε<br>φτάστε |
| **I articulate** | εκφωνώ 17 | εκφωνούσα | εκφώνησα | θα εκφωνήσω<br>να εκφωνήσω | έχω εκφωνήσει<br>είχα εκφωνήσει | να εκφωνείς<br>εκφωνείτε | εκφώνησε<br>εκφωνήστε |
| **I ascend** | *ανέρχομαι 14* | *ανερχόμουν* | *ανήλθα* | *θα ανέλθω*<br>*να ανέλθω* | *έχω ανέλθει*<br>*είχα ανέλθει* | *να ανέρχεσαι*<br>*ανέρχεστε* | *άνελθε*<br>*ανέλθετε* |
| **I ascertain *(details/facts)*** | διαπιστώνω 13 | διαπίστωνα | διεπίστωσα | θα διαπιστώσω<br>να διαπιστώσω | έχω διαπιστώσει<br>είχα διαπιστώσει | διαπίστωνε<br>διαπιστώνετε | διαπίστωσε<br>διαπιστώστε |
| **I ascribe** | καταλογίζω 13 | καταλόγιζα | κατελόγισα | θα καταλογίσω<br>να καταλογίσω | έχω καταλογίσει<br>είχα καταλογίσει | καταλόγιζε<br>καταλογίζετε | καταλόγισε<br>καταλογίστε |
| **I ask** (a question) | ρωτ(ά)ώ 15 | ρωτούσα | ρώτησα | θα ρωτήσω<br>να ρωτήσω | έχω ρωτήσει<br>είχα ρωτήσει | ρώτα<br>ρωτάτε | ρώτησε<br>ρωτήστε |
| **I ask** (request) | ζητ(ά)ώ 15 | ζητούσα | ζήτησα | θα ζητήσω<br>να ζητήσω | έχω ζητήσει<br>είχα ζητήσει | ζήτα<br>ζητάτε | ζήτησε<br>ζητήστε |
| **I aspire** | αποβλέπω 13 | απέβλεπα | απέβλεψα | θα αποβλέψω<br>να αποβλέψω | έχω αποβλέψει<br>είχα αποβλέψει | απόβλεπε<br>αποβλέπετε | απόβλεψε<br>αποβλέψτε |
| **I assassinate** | δολοφονώ 17 | δολοφονούσα | δολοφόνησα | θα δολοφονήσω<br>να δολοφονήσω | έχω δολοφονήσει<br>είχα δολοφονήσει | να δολοφονείς<br>δολοφονείτε | δολοφόνησε<br>δολοφονήστε |

| English Verb | Present | Imperfect | Past | Simple Future<br>Simple Subjunctive | Present Perfect<br>Past Perfect | Continuous Imperative | Simple Imperative |
|---|---|---|---|---|---|---|---|
| **I assess** | αποτιμ(ά)ώ 15 | αποτιμούσα | αποτίμησα | θα αποτιμήσω<br>να αποτιμήσω | έχω αποτιμήσει<br>είχα αποτιμήσει | αποτίμα<br>αποτιμάτε | αποτίμησε<br>αποτιμήστε |
| **I assign** | αναθέτω 13 | ανέθετα | ανέθεσα | θα αναθέσω<br>να αναθέσω | έχω αναθέσει<br>είχα αναθέσει | ανάθετε<br>αναθέτετε | ανάθεσε<br>αναθέστε |
| **I assimilate** | αφομοιώνω 13 | αφομοίωνα | αφομοίωσα | θα αφομοιώσω<br>να αφομοιώσω | έχω αφομοιώσει<br>είχα αφομοιώσει | αφομοίωνε<br>αφομοιώνετε | αφομοίωσε<br>αφομοιώστε |
| **I assist** | συντρέχω 13 | συνέτρεχα | συνέτρεξα | θα συντρέξω<br>να συντρέξω | έχω συντρέξει<br>είχα συντρέξει | σύντρεχε<br>συντρέχετε | σύντρεξε<br>συντρέξτε |
| **I associate**<br>(link/connect) | *σχετίζομαι 14* | *σχετιζόμουν* | *σχετίστηκα* | *θα σχετιστώ*<br>*να σχετιστώ* | *έχω σχετιστεί*<br>*είχα σχετιστεί* | *να σχετίζεσαι*<br>*σχετίζεστε* | *σχετίσου*<br>*σχετιστείτε* |
| **I assure**<br>(convince) | διαβεβαιώνω 13 | διαβεβαίωνα | διαβεβαίωσα | θα διαβεβαιώσω<br>να διαβεβαιώσω | έχω διαβεβαιώσει<br>είχα διαβεβαιώσει | διαβεβαίωνε<br>διαβεβαιώνετε | διαβεβαίωσε<br>διαβεβαιώστε |
| **I assure**<br>(success) | κατοχυρώνω 13 | κατοχύρωνα | κατοχύρωσα | θα κατοχυρώσω<br>να κατοχυρώσω | έχω κατοχυρώσει<br>είχα κατοχυρώσει | κατοχύρωνε<br>κατοχυρώνετε | κατοχύρωσε<br>κατοχυρώστε |
| **I astonish** | καταπλήττω 13 | κατέπληττα | κατέπληξα | θα καταπλήξω<br>να καταπλήξω | έχω καταπλήξει<br>ειχα καταπλήξει | κατάπληττε<br>καταπλήττετε | κατάπληξε<br>καταπλήξτε |
| **I attach**<br>(importance) | προσδίδω 13 | προσέδιδα | προσέδωσα | θα προσδώσω<br>να προσδώσω | έχω προσδώσει<br>είχα προσδώσει | να προσδίδεις<br>προσδίδετε | πρόσδωσε<br>προσδώστε |
| **I attach** | προσκολλ(ά)ώ 15 | προσκολλούσα | προσκόλλησα | θα προσκολλήσω<br>να προσκολλήσω | έχω προσκολήσει<br>είχα προσκολήσει | προσκόλλα<br>προσκολλάτε | προσκόλλησε<br>προσκολλήστε |
| **I attack** | *επιτίθεμαι 42* | *επιτιθόμουν* | *επιτέθηκα* | *θα επιτεθώ*<br>*να επιτεθώ* | *έχω επιτεθεί*<br>*είχα επιτεθεί* | *να επιτίθεσαι*<br>*επιτίθεστε* | *να επιτεθείς*<br>*επιτεθείτε* |
| **I attain** | πραγματοποιώ 17 | πραγματοποιούσα | πραγματοποίησα | θα πραγματο-<br>ποιήσω | έχω πραγματο-<br>ποιήσει | να πραγματο-<br>ποιείς | πραγματο-<br>ποίησε |

| English Verb | Present | Imperfect | Past | Simple Future<br>Simple Subjunctive | Present Perfect<br>Past Perfect | Continuous Imperative | Simple Imperative |
|---|---|---|---|---|---|---|---|
| (realize) | | | | να πραγματο-<br>ποιήσω | είχα πραγματο-<br>ποιήσει | πραγματοποιείτε | πραγματο-<br>ποιήστε |
| **I attain**<br>(reach) | φθάνω 13 | έφτανα | έφτασα | θα φτάσω<br>να φτάσω | έχω φτάσει<br>είχα φτάσει | φτάνε<br>φτάνετε | φτάσε<br>φτάστε |
| **I attempt** | προσπαθώ 17 | προσπαθούσα | προσπάθησα | θα προσπαθήσω<br>να προσπαθήσω | έχω προσπαθήσει<br>είχα προσπαθήσει | να προσπαθείς<br>προσπαθείτε | προσπάθησε<br>προσπαθήστε |
| **I attend** | παρακολουθώ 17 | παρακολουθούσα | παρακολούθησα | θα παρακολουθήσω<br>να παρακολουθήσω | έχω παρακολουθήσει<br>είχα παρακολουθήσει | να παρακολουθείς<br>παρακολουθείτε | παρακολούθησε<br>παρακολουθήστε |
| **I attend to** | *περιποιούμαι 18* | *περιποιόμουν* | *περιποιήθηκα* | *θα περιποιηθώ*<br>*να περιποιηθώ* | *έχω περιποιηθεί*<br>*είχα περιποιηθεί* | *να περιποιείσαι*<br>*περιποιείστε* | *περιποιήσου*<br>*περιποιηθείτε* |
| **I attract**<br>(attention) | προσελκύω 13 | προσήλκυα | προσήλκυσα | θα προσελκύσω<br>να προσελκύσω | έχω προσελκύσει<br>είχα προσελκύσει | προσέλκυε<br>προσελκύετε | προσέλκυσε<br>προσελκύστε |
| **I attract** | γοητεύω 13 | γοήτευα | γοήτευσα | θα γοητεύσω<br>να γοητεύσω | έχω γοητεύσει<br>είχα γοητεύσει | γοήτευε<br>γοητεύετε | γοήτευσε<br>γοητεύστε |
| **I avert** | αποτρέπω 13 | απέτρεπα | απέτρεψα | θα αποτρέψω<br>να αποτρέψω | έχω αποτρέψει<br>είχα αποτρέψει | απότρεπε<br>αποτρέπετε | απότρεψε<br>αποτρέψτε |
| **I avoid** | αποφεύγω 13 | απέφευγα | απέφυγα | θα αποφύγω<br>να αποφύγω | έχω αποφύγει<br>είχα αποφύγει | απόφευγε<br>αποφεύγετε | απόφυγε<br>αποφύγετε |
| **I await** | αναμένω 13 | ανέμενα | ανέμεινα | θα αναμείνω<br>να αναμείνω | έχω αναμείνει<br>είχα αναμείνει | ανάμενε<br>αναμένετε | ανάμεινε<br>αναμείνετε |
| **I award** | απονέμω 13 | απένεμα | απένειμα | θα απονέμω<br>να απονέμω | έχω απονέμει<br>είχα απονέμει | απόνεμε<br>απονέμετε | απόνειμε<br>απονείμετε |
| **I babble** | ψελλίζω 13 | ψέλλιζα | ψέλλισα | θα ψελλίσω<br>να ψελλίσω | έχω ψελλίσει<br>είχα ψελλίσει | ψέλλιζε<br>ψελλίζετε | ψέλλισε<br>ψελλίστε |

| English Verb | Present | Imperfect | Past | Simple Future<br>Simple Subjunctive | Present Perfect<br>Past Perfect | Continuous Imperative | Simple Imperative |
|---|---|---|---|---|---|---|---|
| **I back** | στηρίζω 13 | στήριζα | στήριξα | θα στηρίξω<br>να στηρίξω | έχω στηρίξει<br>είχα στηρίξει | στήριζε<br>στηρίζετε | στήριξε<br>στηρίξτε |
| **I backslide** | ξανακυλώ 15 | ξανακυλούσα | ξανακύλησα | θα ξανακυλήσω<br>να ξανακυλήσω | έχω ξανακυλήσει<br>είχα ξανακυλήσει | ξανακύλα<br>ξανακυλάτε | ξανακύλησε<br>ξανακυλήστε |
| **I backtrack** | υποχωρώ 17 | υποχωρούσα | υποχώρησα | θα υποχωρήσω<br>να υποχωρήσω | έχω υποχωρήσει<br>είχα υποχωρήσει | να υποχωρείς<br>υποχωρείτε | υποχώρησε<br>υποχωρήστε |
| **I bake** | ψήνω 13 | έψηνα | έψησα | θα ψήσω<br>να ψήσω | έχω ψήσει<br>είχα ψήσει | ψήνε<br>ψήνετε | ψήσε<br>ψήστε |
| **I balance** | ισορροπώ 17 | ισορροπούσα | ισορρόπησα | θα ισορροπήσω<br>να ισορροπήσω | έχω ισορροπήσει<br>είχα ισορροπήσει | να ισορροπείς<br>ισορροπείτε | ισορρόπησε<br>ισορροπήστε |
| **I baptise** | βαφτίζω 13 | βάφτιζα | βάφτισα | θα βαφτίσω<br>να βαφτίσω | έχω βαφτίσει<br>είχα βαφτίσει | βάφτιζε<br>βαφτίζετε | βάφτισε<br>βαφτίστε |
| **I bar** | φράζω 13 | έφραζα | έφραξα | θα φράξω<br>να φράξω | έχω φράξει<br>είχα φράξει | φράζε<br>φράζετε | φράξε<br>φράξτε |
| **I bare** (reveal) | γυμνώνω 13 | γύμνωνα | γύμνωσα | θα γυμνώσω<br>να γυμνώσω | έχω γυμνώσει<br>είχα γυμνώσει | γύμνωνε<br>γυμνώνετε | γύμνωσε<br>γυμνώστε |
| **I bargain** | παζαρεύω 13 | παζάρευα | παζάρεψα | θα παζαρέψω<br>να παζαρέψω | έχω παζαρέψει<br>είχα παζαρέψει | παζάρευε<br>παζαρεύετε | παζάρεψε<br>παζαρέψτε |
| **I bark** | γαυγίζω 13 | γαύγιζα | γαύγισα | θα γαυγίσω<br>να γαυγίσω | έχω γαυγίσει<br>είχα γαυγίσει | γαύγιζε<br>γαυγίζετε | γαύγισε<br>γαυγίστε |
| **I barricade** | *ταμπουρώνομαι 14* | *ταμπουρωνόμουν* | *ταμπουρώθηκα* | *θα ταμπουρωθώ*<br>*να ταμπουρωθώ* | *έχω ταμπουρωθεί*<br>*είχα ταμπουρωθεί* | *να ταμπουρώνεσαι*<br>*ταμπουρώνεστε* | *ταμπουρώσου*<br>*ταμπουρωθείτε* |
| **I base** | βασίζω 13 | βάσιζα | βάσισα | θα βασίσω<br>να βασίσω | έχω βασίσει<br>είχα βασίσει | βάσιζε<br>βασίζετε | βάσισε<br>βασίστε |

| English Verb | Present | Imperfect | Past | Simple Future<br>Simple Subjunctive | Present Perfect<br>Past Perfect | Continuous Imperative | Simple Imperative |
|---|---|---|---|---|---|---|---|
| **I bash** | κοπανάω 15 | κοπανούσα | κοπάνησα | θα κοπανήσω<br>να κοπανήσω | έχω κοπανήσει<br>είχα κοπανήσει | κοπάνα<br>κοπανάτε | κοπάνησε<br>κοπανήστε |
| **I bask** | *λιάζομαι 14* | *λιαζόμουν* | *λιάστηκα* | *θα λιαστώ*<br>*να λιαστώ* | *έχω λιαστεί*<br>*είχα λιαστεί* | *να λιάζεσαι*<br>*λιάζεστε* | *λιάσου*<br>*λιαστείτε* |
| **I bathe** | λούζω 13 | έλουζα | έλουσα | θα λούσω<br>να λούσω | έχω λούσει<br>είχα λούσει | λούζε<br>λούζετε | λούσε<br>λούστε |
| **I batter** | δέρνω 13 | έδερνα | έδειρα | θα δείρω<br>να δείρω | έχω δείρει<br>είχα δείρει | δέρνε<br>δέρνετε | δείρε<br>δείρτε |
| **I battle** | *τσακώνομαι 14* | *τσακωνόμουν* | *τσακώθηκα* | *θα τσακωθώ*<br>*να τσακωθώ* | *έχω τσακωθεί*<br>*είχα τσακωθεί* | *να τσακώνεσαι*<br>*τσακώνεστε* | *τσακώσου*<br>*τσακωθείτε* |
| **I battle** | *αγωνίζομαι 14* | *αγωνιζόμουν* | *αγωνίστηκα* | *θα αγωνιστώ*<br>*να αγωνιστώ* | *έχω αγωνιστεί*<br>*είχα αγωνιστεί* | *να αγωνίζεσαι*<br>*αγωνίζεστε* | *αγωνίσου*<br>*αγωνιστείτε* |
| **I beam** | ακτινοβολώ 15 | ακτινοβολούσα | ακτινιβόλησα | θα ακτινοβολήσω<br>να ακτινοβολήσω | έχω ακτινοβολήσει<br>είχα ακτινοβολήσει | ακτινοβόλα<br>ακτινοβολάτε | ακτινοβόλησε<br>ακτινοβολήστε |
| **I bear** (tolerate) | *ανέχομαι 14* | *ανεχόμουν* | *ανέχτηκα* | *θα ανεχτώ*<br>*να ανεχτώ* | *έχω ανεχτεί*<br>*είχα ανεχτεί* | *να ανέχεσαι*<br>*ανέχεστε* | *ανέξου*<br>*ανεχτείτε* |
| **I beat** | χτυπ(ά)ώ 15 | χτυπούσα | χτύπησα | θα χτυπήσω<br>να χτυπήσω | έχω χτυπήσει<br>είχα χτυπήσει | χτύπα<br>χτυπάτε | χτύπησε<br>χτυπήστε |
| **I beautify** | ωραιοποιώ 17 | ωραιοποιούσα | ωραιωποίησα | θα ωραιοποιήσω<br>να ωραιοποιήσω | έχω ωραιοποιήσει<br>είχα ωραιοποιήσει | να ωραιοποιείς<br>ωραιοποιείτε | ωραιοποίησε<br>ωραιοποιήστε |
| **I beckon** | νεύω 13 | ένευα | ένευσα | θα νεύσω<br>να νεύσω | έχω νεύσει<br>είχα νεύσει | νεύε<br>νεύετε | νεύσε<br>νεύστε |
| **I become** | *γίνομαι 14* | *γινόμουν* | *έγινα* | *θα γίνω*<br>*να γίνω* | *έχω γίνει*<br>*είχα γίνει* | *να γίνεσαι*<br>*γίνεστε* | *γίνου*<br>*γίνετε* |

| English Verb | Present | Imperfect | Past | Simple Future<br>Simple Subjunctive | Present Perfect<br>Past Perfect | Continuous Imperative | Simple Imperative |
|---|---|---|---|---|---|---|---|
| **I become fat** | παχαίνω 14 | πάχαινα | πάχυνα | θα παχύνω<br>να παχύνω | έχω παχύνει<br>είχα παχύνει | πάχαινε<br>παχαίνετε | πάχυνε<br>παχύντε |
| **I become thin** | αδυνατίζω 13 | αδυνάτιζα | αδυνάτισα | θα αδυνατίσω<br>να αδυνατίσω | έχω αδυνατίσει<br>είχα αδυνατίσει | αδυνάτιζε<br>αδυνατίζετε | αδυνάτισε<br>αδυνατίστε |
| **I beg** | ζητιανεύω 13 | ζητιάνευα | ζητιάνεψα | θα ζητιανέψω<br>να ζητιανέψω | έχω ζητιανέψει<br>είχα ζητιανέψει | ζητιάνευε<br>ζητιανεύετε | ζητιάνεψε<br>ζητιανέψτε |
| **I beg** | επαιτώ 17 | επαιτούσα | επαίτησα | θα επαιτήσω<br>να επαιτήσω | έχω επαιτήσει<br>είχα επαιτήσει | να επαιτείς<br>επαιτείτε | επαίτησε<br>επαιτήστε |
| **I begin** | αρχίζω 13 | άρχιζα | άρχισα | θα αρχίσω<br>να αρχίσω | έχω αρχίσει<br>είχα αρχίσει | άρχιζε<br>αρχίζετε | άρχισε<br>αρχίστε |
| **I behave** | *φέρομαι 14* | *φερόμουν* | *φέρθηκα* | *θα φερθώ*<br>*να φερθώ* | *έχω φερθεί*<br>*είχα φερθεί* | *να φέρεσαι*<br>*φέρεστε* | *φέρσου*<br>*φερθείτε* |
| **I behead** | αποκεφαλίζω 13 | αποκεφάλιζα | αποκεφάλισα | θα αποκεφαλίσω<br>να αποκεφαλίσω | έχω αποκεφαλίσει<br>είχα αποκεφαλίσει | αποκεφάλιζε<br>αποκεφαλίζετε | αποκεφάλισε<br>αποκεφαλίστε |
| **I belie** (disprove) | διαψεύδω 13 | διέψευδα | διέψευσα | θα διαψεύσω<br>να διαψεύσω | έχω διαψεύσει<br>είχα διαψεύσει | διάψευδε<br>διαψεύδετε | διάψευσε<br>διαψεύστε |
| **I believe** | πιστεύω 13 | πίστευα | πίστεψα | θα πιστέψω<br>να πιστέψω | έχω πιστέψει<br>είχα πιστέψει | πίστευε<br>πιστεύετε | πίστεψε<br>πιστέψτε |
| **I bellow** | μουγκρίζω 13 | μούγκριζα | μούγκρισα | θα μουγκρίσω<br>να μουγκρίσω | έχω μουγκρίσει<br>είχα μουγκρίσει | μούγκριζε<br>μουγκρίζετε | μούγκρισε<br>μουγκρίστε |
| **I belong** | ανήκω 13 | ανήκα | ανήκα | θα ανήκω<br>να ανήκω | – | – | άνηκε<br>ανήκετε |
| **I belt** | ζώνω 13 | έζωνα | έζωσα | θα ζώσω<br>να ζώσω | έχω ζώσει<br>είχα ζώσει | ζώνε<br>ζώνετε | ζώσε<br>ζώστε |

| English Verb | Present | Imperfect | Past | Simple Future<br>Simple Subjunctive | Present Perfect<br>Past Perfect | Continuous Imperative | Simple Imperative |
|---|---|---|---|---|---|---|---|
| **I belt out** | ξεφωνίζω 13 | ξεφώνιζα | ξεφώνισα | θα ξεφωνίσω<br>να ξεφωνίσω | έχω ξεφωνίσει<br>είχα ξεφωνίσει | ξεφώνιζε<br>ξεφωνίζετε | ξεφώνισε<br>ξεφωνίστε |
| **I am silent** | σιωπώ 15 | σιωπούσα | σιώπησα | θα σιωπήσω<br>να σιωπήσω | έχω σιωπήσει<br>είχα σιωπήσει | σιώπα<br>σιωπάτε | σιώπησε<br>σιωπήστε |
| **I bemoan** | θρηνώ 17 | θρηνούσα | θρήνησα | θα θρηνήσω<br>να θρηνήσω | έχω θρηνήσει<br>είχα θρηνήσει | να θρηνείς<br>θρηνείτε | θρήνησε<br>θρηνήστε |
| **I bend** | λυγίζω 13 | λύγιζα | λύγισα | θα λυγίσω<br>να λυγίσω | έχω λυγίσει<br>είχα λυγίσει | λύγιζε<br>λυγίζετε | λύγισε<br>λυγίστε |
| **I bequeath** | κληροδοτώ 17 | κληροδοτούσα | κληροδότησα | θα κληροδοτήσω<br>να κληροδοτήσω | έχω κληροδοτήσει<br>είχα κληροδοτήσει | να κληροδοτείς<br>κληροδοτείτε | κληροδότησε<br>κληροδοτήστε |
| **I besiege** | πολιορκώ 17 | πολιορκούσα | πολιόρκησα | θα πολιορκήσω<br>να πολιορκήσω | έχω πολιορκήσει<br>είχα πολιορκήσει | να πολιορκείς<br>πολιορκείτε | πολιόρκησε<br>πολιορκήστε |
| **I bet** | στοιχηματίζω 13 | στοιχημάτιζα | στοιχημάτισα | θα στοιχηματίσω<br>να στοιχηματίσω | έχω στοιχηματίσει<br>είχα στοιχηματίσει | στοιχημάτιζε<br>στοιχηματίζετε | στοιχημάτισε<br>στοιχηματίστε |
| **I betray** | προδίδω 13 | πρόδιδα | πρόδωσα | θα προδώσω<br>να προδώσω | έχω προδώσει<br>είχα προδώσει | πρόδιδε<br>προδίδετε | πρόδωσε<br>προδώστε |
| **I bind** | δεσμεύω 13 | δέσμευα | δέσμευσα | θα δεσμεύσω<br>να δεσμεύσω | έχω δεσμεύσει<br>είχα δεσμεύσει | δέσμευε<br>δεσμεύετε | δέσμευσε<br>δεσμεύστε |
| **I bisect** | διχοτομώ 17 | διχοτομούσα | διχοτόμησα | θα διχοτομήσω<br>να διχοτομήσω | έχω διχοτομήσει<br>είχα διχοτομήσει | να διχοτομείς<br>διχοτομείτε | διχοτόμησε<br>διχοτομήστε |
| **I bite** | δαγκώνω 13 | δάγκωνα | δάγκωσα | θα δαγκώσω<br>να δαγκώσω | έχω δαγκώσει<br>είχα δαγκώσει | δάγκωνε<br>δαγκώνετε | δάγκωσε<br>δαγκώστε |
| **I blackmail** | εκβιάζω 13 | εκβίαζα | εκβίασα | θα εκβιάσω<br>να εκβιάσω | έχω εκβιάσει<br>είχα εκβιάσει | εκβίαζε<br>εκβιάζετε | εκβίασε<br>εκβιάστε |

| English Verb | Present | Imperfect | Past | Simple Future<br>Simple Subjunctive | Present Perfect<br>Past Perfect | Continuous Imperative | Simple Imperative |
|---|---|---|---|---|---|---|---|
| **I blame** | ψέγω 13 | έψεγα | έψεξα | θα ψέξω<br>να ψέξω | έχω ψέξει<br>είχα ψέξει | ψέγε<br>ψέγετε | ψέξε<br>ψέξτε |
| **I blaspheme** | βλαστημώ 15 | βλαστημούσα | βλαστήμησα | θα βλαστημήσω<br>να βλαστημήσω | έχω βλαστημήσει<br>είχα βλαστημήσει | βλαστήμα<br>βλαστημάτε | βλαστήμησε<br>βλαστημήστε |
| **I blast off**<br>(rocket) | *εκτοξεύομαι 14* | *εκτοξευόμουν* | *εκτοξεύτηκα* | *θα εκτοξευτώ*<br>*να εκτοξευτώ* | *έχω εκτοξευτεί*<br>*είχα εκτοξευτεί* | *να εκτοξεύεσαι*<br>*εκτοξεύεστε* | *εκτοξεύσου*<br>*εκτοξευτείτε* |
| **I bleed** | αιμορραγώ 17 | αιμορραγούσα | αιμορράγησα | θα αιμορραγήσω<br>να αιμορραγήσω | έχω αιμορραγήσει<br>είχα αιμορραγήσει | να αιμορραγείς<br>αιμορραγείτε | αιμορράγησε<br>αιμορραγήστε |
| **I bleed**<br>(nose) | ματώνω 13 | μάτωνα | μάτωσα | θα ματώσω<br>να ματώσω | έχω ματώσει<br>είχα ματώσει | μάτωνε<br>ματώνετε | μάτωσε<br>ματώστε |
| **I bless** | ευλογώ 17 | ευλογούσα | ευλόγησα | θα ευλογήσω<br>να ευλογήσω | έχω ευλογήσει<br>είχα ευλογήσει | ευλόγει<br>ευλογείτε | ευλόγησε<br>ευλογήστε |
| **I blind** | τυφλώνω 13 | τύφλωνα | τύφλωσα | θα τυφλώσω<br>να τυφλώσω | έχω τυφλώσει<br>είχα τυφλώσει | τύφλωνε<br>τυφλώνετε | τύφλωσε<br>τυφλώστε |
| **I blind** | στραβώνω 13 | στράβωνα | στράβωσα | θα στραβώσω<br>να στραβώσω | έχω στραβώσει<br>είχα στραβώσει | στράβωνε<br>στραβώνετε | στράβωσε<br>στραβώστε |
| **I blister** | φουσκαλιάζω 13 | φουσκάλιαζα | φουσκάλιασα | θα φουσκαλιάσω<br>να φουσκαλιάσω | έχω φουσκαλιάσει<br>είχα φουσκαλιάσει | φουσκάλιαζε<br>φουσκαλιάζετε | φουσκάλιασε<br>φουσκαλιάστε |
| **I block** | μπλοκάρω 13 | μπλόκαρα | μπλοκάρησα | θα μπλοκάρω<br>να μπλοκάρω | έχω μπλοκάρει<br>είχα μπλοκάρει | μπλόκαρε<br>μπλοκάρετε | μπλοκάρησε<br>μπλοκαρήστε |
| **I block up** | βουλώνω 13 | βούλωνα | βούλωσα | θα βουλώσω<br>να βουλώσω | έχω βουλώσει<br>είχα βουλώσει | βούλωνε<br>βουλώνετε | βούλωσε<br>βουλώστε |
| **I bloom** | ανθίζω 13 | άνθιζα | άνθισα | θα ανθίσω<br>να ανθίσω | έχω ανθίσει<br>είχα ανθίσει | άνθιζε<br>ανθίζετε | άνθισε<br>ανθίστε |

| English Verb | Present | Imperfect | Past | Simple Future<br>Simple Subjunctive | Present Perfect<br>Past Perfect | Continuous Imperative | Simple Imperative |
|---|---|---|---|---|---|---|---|
| **I blot** | στυπώνω 13 | στύπωνα | στύπωσα | θα στυπώσω<br>να στυπώσω | έχω στυπώσει<br>είχα στυπώσει | στύπωνε<br>στυπώνετε | στύπωσε<br>στυπώστε |
| **I blow** | φυσάω 15 | φυσούσα | φύσηξα | θα φυσήξω<br>να φυσήξω | έχω φυσήξει<br>είχα φυσήξει | φύσα<br>φυσάτε | φύσηξε<br>φυσήξτε |
| **I bluff** | μπλοφάρω 13 | μπλόφαρα | μπλοφάρησα | θα μπλοφάρω<br>να μπλοφάρω | έχω μπλοφάρει<br>είχα μπλοφάρει | μπλόφαρε<br>μπλοφάρετε | μπλοφάρησε<br>μπλοφαρήστε |
| **I blunt** | αμβλύνω 13 | άμβλυνα | άμβλυνα | θα αμβλύνω<br>να αμβλύνω | έχω αμβλύνει<br>είχα αμβλύνει | άμβλυνε<br>αμβλύνετε | άμβλυνε<br>αμβλύντε |
| **I blur** | βουρκώνω 13 | βούρκωνα | βούρκωσα | θα βουρκώσω<br>να βουρκώσω | έχω βουρκώσει<br>είχα βουρκώσει | βούρκωνε<br>βουρκώνετε | βούρκωσε<br>βουρκώστε |
| **I blurt out** | ξεφουρνίζω 13 | ξεφούρνιζα | ξεφούρνισα | θα ξεφουρνίσω<br>να ξεφουρνίσω | έχω ξεφουρνίσει<br>είχα ξεφουρνίσει | ξεφούρνιζε<br>ξεφουρνίζετε | ξεφούρνισε<br>ξεφουρνίστε |
| **I blush** | κοκκινίζω 13 | κοκκίνιζα | κοκκίνισα | θα κοκκινίσω<br>να κοκκινίσω | έχω κοκκινίσει<br>είχα κοκκινίσει | κοκκίνιζε<br>κοκκινίζετε | κοκκίνισε<br>κοκκινίστε |
| **I board** | *επιβιβάζομαι 14* | *επιβιβαζόμουν* | *επιβιβάστηκα* | *θα επιβιβαστώ*<br>*να επιβιβαστώ* | *έχω επιβιβαστεί*<br>*είχα επιβιβαστεί* | *να επιβιβάζεσαι*<br>*επιβιβάζεστε* | *επιβιβάσου*<br>*επιβιβαστείτε* |
| **I boast** | καυχιέμαι 16 | καυχιόμουν | καυχήθηκα | θα καυχηθώ<br>να καυχηθώ | έχω καυχηθεί<br>είχα καυχηθεί | να καυχιέσαι<br>καυχιέστε | *καυχήσου*<br>καυχηθείτε |
| **I boast** | κομπάζω 13 | κόμπαζα | κόμπασα | θα κομπάσω<br>να κομπάσω | έχω κομπάσει<br>είχα κομπάσει | κόμπαζε<br>κομπάζετε | κόμπασε<br>κομπάστε |
| **I boil** | βράζω 13 | έβραζα | έβρασα | θα βράσω<br>να βράσω | έχω βράσει<br>είχα βράσει | βράζε<br>βράζετε | βράσε<br>βράστε |
| **I bolt**<br>(door) | αμπαρώνω 13 | αμπάρωνα | αμπάρωσα | θα αμπαρώσω<br>να αμπαρώσω | έχω αμπαρώσει<br>είχα αμπαρώσει | αμπάρωνε<br>αμπαρώνετε | αμπάρωσε<br>αμπαρώστε |

| English Verb | Present | Imperfect | Past | Simple Future<br>Simple Subjunctive | Present Perfect<br>Past Perfect | Continuous Imperative | Simple Imperative |
|---|---|---|---|---|---|---|---|
| **I bomb** | βομβαρδίζω 13 | βομβάρδιζα | βομβάρδισα | θα βομβαρδίσω<br>να βομβαρδίσω | έχω βομβαρδίσει<br>είχα βομβαρδίσει | βομβάρδιζε<br>βομβαρδίζετε | βομβάρδισε<br>βομβαρδίστε |
| **I bone** | ξεκοκαλίζω 13 | ξεκοκάλιζα | ξεκοκάλισα | θα ξεκοκαλίσω<br>να ξεκοκαλίσω | έχω ξεκοκαλίσει<br>είχα ξεκοκαλίσει | ξεκοκάλιζε<br>ξεκοκαλίζετε | ξεκοκάλισε<br>ξεκοκαλίστε |
| **I boo** | γιουχαΐζω 13 | γιουχάιζα | γιουχάισα | θα γιουχαΐσω<br>να γιουχαΐσω | έχω γιουχαΐσει<br>είχα γιουχαΐσει | γιουχάιζε<br>γιουχαΐζετε | γιουχάισε<br>γιουχαΐστε |
| **I boost** | ανυψώνω 13 | ανύψωνα | ανύψωσα | θα ανυψώσω<br>να ανυψώσω | έχω ανυψώσει<br>είχα ανυψώσει | ανύψωνε<br>ανυψώνετε | ανύψωσε<br>ανυψώστε |
| **I booze** | μεθοκοπάω 15 | μεθοκοπούσα | μεθοκόπησα | θα μεθοκοπήσω<br>να μεθοκοπήσω | έχω μεθοκοπήσει<br>είχα μεθοκοπήσει | μεθοκόπα<br>μεθοκοπάτε | μεθοκόπησε<br>μεθοκοπήστε |
| **I border** | συνορεύω 13 | συνόρευα | συνόρεψα | θα συνορέψω<br>να συνορέψω | έχω συνορέψει<br>είχα συνορέψει | συνόρευε<br>συνορεύετε | συνόρεψε<br>συνορέψτε |
| **I bore** | διατρυπώ 15 | διατρυπούσα | διατρύπησα | θα διατρυπήσω<br>να διατρυπήσω | έχω διατρυπήσει<br>είχα διατρυπήσει | να διατρυπάς<br>διατρυπάτε | διατρύπησε<br>διατρυπήστε |
| **I borrow** | *δανείζομαι 14* | *δανειζόμουν* | *δανείστηκα* | *θα δανειστώ*<br>*να δανειστώ* | *έχω δανειστεί*<br>*είχα δανειστεί* | *να δανείζεσαι*<br>*δανείζεστε* | *δανείσου*<br>*δανειστείτε* |
| **I boss** | κουμαντάρω 13 | κουμάνταρα | κουμαντάρησα | θα κουμαντάρω<br>να κουμαντάρω | έχω κουμαντάρει<br>είχα κουμαντάρει | κουμάνταρε<br>κουμαντάρετε | κουμαντάρησε<br>κουμανταρήστε |
| **I bother** (about something) | *νοιάζομαι 14* | *νοιαζόμουν* | *νοιάστηκα* | *θα νοιαστώ*<br>*να νοιαστώ* | *έχω νοιαστεί*<br>*είχα νοιαστεί* | *να νοιάζεσαι*<br>*νοιάζεστε* | *νοιάσου*<br>*νοιαστείτε* |
| **I bother** (disturb) | ενοχλώ 17 | ενοχλούσα | ενόχλησα | θα ενοχλήσω<br>να ενοχλήσω | έχω ενοχλήσει<br>είχα ενοχλήσει | να ενοχλείς<br>ενοχλείτε | ενόχλησε<br>ενοχλήστε |
| **I bottle** | εμφιαλώνω 13 | εμφιάλωνα | εμφιάλωσα | θα εμφιαλώσω<br>να εμφιαλώσω | έχω εμφιαλώσει<br>είχα εμφιαλώσει | εμφιάλωνε<br>εμφιαλώνετε | εμφιάλωσε<br>εμφιαλώστε |

| English Verb | Present | Imperfect | Past | Simple Future<br>Simple Subjunctive | Present Perfect<br>Past Perfect | Continuous Imperative | Simple Imperative |
|---|---|---|---|---|---|---|---|
| **I bounce** | χοροπηδώ 15 | χοροπηδούσα | χοροπήδηξα | θα χοροπηδήξω<br>να χοροπηδήξω | έχω χοροπηδήξει<br>είχα χοροπηδήξει | χοροπήδα<br>χοροπηδάτε | χοροπήδηξε<br>χοροπηδήξτε |
| **I bound** | σκιρτώ 15 | σκιρτούσα | σκίρτησα | θα σκιρτήσω<br>να σκιρτήσω | έχω σκιρτήσει<br>είχα σκιρτήσει | σκίρτα<br>σκιρτάτε | σκίρτησε<br>σκιρτήστε |
| **I bow** (yield) | υποκύπτω 13 | υπέκυπτα | υπέκυψα | θα υποκύψω<br>να υποκύψω | έχω υποκύψει<br>είχα υποκύψει | υπόκυπτε<br>υποκύπτετε | υπόκυψε<br>υποκύψτε |
| **I bow** | *υποκλίνομαι 14* | *υποκλινόμουν* | *υποκλίθηκα* | *θα υποκλιθώ*<br>*να υποκλιθώ* | *έχω υποκλιθεί*<br>*είχα υποκλιθεί* | *να υποκλίνεσαι*<br>*υποκλίνεστε* | *υποκλίσου*<br>*υποκλιθείτε* |
| **I box** (sport) | πυγμαχώ 17 | πυχμαχούσα | πυγμάχησα | θα πυγμαχήσω<br>να πυγμαχήσω | έχω πυγμαχήσει<br>είχα πυγμαχήσει | να πυγμαχείς<br>πυγμαχείτε | πυγμάχησε<br>πυγμαχήστε |
| **I boycott** | μποϋκοτάρω 13 | μποϋκόταρα | μποϋκοτάρησα | θα μποϋκοτάρω<br>να μποϋκοτάρω | έχω μποϋκοτάρει<br>είχα μποϋκοτάρει | μποϋκόταρε<br>μποϋκοτάρετε | μποϋκοτάρησε<br>μποϋκοταρήστε |
| **I brace** (shoulders) | ισιώνω 13 | ίσιωνα | ίσιωσα | θα ισιώσω<br>να ισιώσω | έχω ισιώσει<br>είχα ισιώσει | ίσιωνε<br>ισιώνετε | ίσιωσε<br>ισιώστε |
| **I brag** | *κοκορεύομαι 14* | *κοκορευόμουν* | *κοκορεύτηκα* | *θα κοκορευτώ*<br>*να κοκορευτώ* | *έχω κοκορευτεί*<br>*είχα κοκορευτεί* | *να κοκορεύεσαι*<br>*κοκορεύεστε* | *κοκορέψου*<br>*κοκορευτείτε* |
| **I brag** | καμαρώνω 13 | καμάρωνα | καμάρωσα | θα καμαρώσω<br>να καμαρώσω | έχω καμαρώσει<br>είχα καμαρώσει | καμάρωνε<br>καμαρώνετε | καμάρωσε<br>καμαρώστε |
| **I brake** (slow down) | φρενάρω 13 | φρέναρα | φρενάρισα | θα φρενάρω<br>να φρενάρω | έχω φρενάρει<br>είχα φρενάρει | φρέναρε<br>φρενάρετε | φρενάρισε<br>φρεναρίστε |
| **I branch out** (expand) | *επεκτείνομαι 14* | *επεκτεινόμουν* | *επεκτάθηκα* | *θα επεκταθώ*<br>*να επεκταθώ* | *έχω επεκταθεί*<br>*είχα επεκταθεί* | *να επεκτείνεσαι*<br>*επεκτείνεστε* | *επεκτάσου*<br>*επεκταθείτε* |
| **I brandish** | σείω 13 | έσεια | έσεισα | θα σείσω<br>να σείσω | έχω σείσει<br>είχα σείσει | σείε<br>σείετε | σείσε<br>σείστε |

| English Verb | Present | Imperfect | Past | Simple Future<br>Simple Subjunctive | Present Perfect<br>Past Perfect | Continuous Imperative | Simple Imperative |
|---|---|---|---|---|---|---|---|
| **I brawl** | *διαπληκτίζομαι 14* | *διαπληκτιζόμουν* | *διαπληκτίστηκα* | *θα διαπληκτιστώ*<br>*να διαπληκτιστώ* | *έχω διαπληκτιστεί*<br>*είχα διαπληκτιστεί* | *να διαπληκτίζεσαι*<br>*διαπληκτίζεστε* | *διαπληκτίσου*<br>*διαπληκτιστείτε* |
| **I bray** | γκαρίζω 13 | γκάριζα | γκάρισα | θα γκαρίσω<br>να γκαρίσω | έχω γκαρίσει<br>είχα γκαρίσει | γκάριζε<br>γκαρίζετε | γκάρισε<br>γκαρίστε |
| **I breach** | διαρρηγνύω 13 | διαρρήγνυα | διέρρηξα | θα διαρρήξω<br>να διαρρήξω | έχω διαρρήξει<br>είχα διαρρήξει | διαρρήγνυε<br>διαρρηγνύετε | διάρρηξε<br>διαρρήξτε |
| **I break** | σπάζω 13 | έσπαζα | έσπασα | θα σπάσω<br>να σπάσω | έχω σπάσει<br>είχα σπάσει | σπάζε<br>σπάζετε | σπάσε<br>σπάστε |
| **I break down** (machine) | χαλώ 15 | χαλούσα | χάλασα | θα χαλάσω<br>να χαλάσω | έχω χαλάσει<br>είχα χαλάσει | χάλα<br>χαλάτε | χάλασε<br>χαλάστε |
| **I break down** | καταρρέω 13 | καττέρρεα | κατέρρευσα | θα καταρρεύσω<br>να καταρρεύσω | έχω καταρρεύσει<br>είχα καταρρεύσει | κατάρρεε<br>καταρρέετε | κατάρρευσε<br>καταρρεύστε |
| **I breathe** | αναπνέω 13 | ανέπνεα | ανέπνευσα | θα αναπνεύσω<br>να αναπνεύσω | έχω αναπνεύσει<br>είχα αναπνεύσει | ανάπνεε<br>αναπνέετε | ανάπνευσε<br>αναπνεύστε |
| **I breathe in** | εισπνέω 13 | εισέπνεα | εισέπνευσα | θα εισπνεύσω<br>να εισπνεύσω | έχω εισπνεύσει<br>είχα εισπνεύσει | είσπνεε<br>εισπνέετε | είσπνευσε<br>εισπνεύστε |
| **I breathe out** | εκπνέω 13 | εξέπνεα | εξέπνευσα | θα εκπνεύσω<br>να εκπνεύσω | έχω εκπνεύσει<br>είχα εκπνεύσει | έκπνεε<br>εκπνέετε | έκπνευσε<br>εκπνεύστε |
| **I breed** (animals) | εκτρέφω 13 | εξέτρεφα | εξέθρεψα | θα εκθρέψω<br>να εκθρέψω | έχω εκθρέψει<br>είχα εκθρέψει | έκτρεφε<br>εκτρέφετε | έκθρεψε<br>εκθρέψτε |
| **I brew** | αποστάζω 13 | απόσταζα | απόσταξα | θα αποστάξω<br>να αποστάξω | έχω αποστάξει<br>είχα αποστάξει | απόσταζε<br>αποστάζετε | απόσταξε<br>αποστάξτε |
| **I bribe** | δωροδοκώ 17 | δωροδοκούσα | δωροδόκησα | θα δωροδοκήσω<br>να δωροδοκήσω | έχω δωροδοκήσω<br>είχα δωροδοκήσει | να δωροδοκείς<br>δωροδοκείτε | δωροδόκησε<br>δωροδοκήστε |

| English Verb | Present | Imperfect | Past | Simple Future<br>Simple Subjunctive | Present Perfect<br>Past Perfect | Continuous Imperative | Simple Imperative |
|---|---|---|---|---|---|---|---|
| **I bribe** | εξαγοράζω 13 | εξαγόραζα | εξαγόρασα | θα εξαγοράσω<br>να εξαγοράσω | έχω εξαγοράσει<br>είχα εξαγοράσει | εξαγόραζε<br>εξαγοράζετε | εξαγόρασε<br>εξαγοράστε |
| **I bridge** | γεφυρώνω 13 | γεφύρωνα | γεφύρωσα | θα γεφυρώσω<br>να γεφυρώσω | έχω γεφυρώσει<br>είχα γεφυρώσει | γεφύρωνε<br>γεφυρώνετε | γεφύρωσε<br>γεφυρώστε |
| **I brief**<br>(prime/inform) | κατατοπίζω 13 | κατατόπιζα | κατατόπισα | θα κατατοπίσω<br>να κατατοπίσω | έχω κατατοπίσει<br>είχα κατατοπίσει | κατατόπιζε<br>κατατοπίζετε | κατατόπισε<br>κατατοπίστε |
| **I brighten up** | *βελτιώνομαι 14* | *βελτιωνόμουν* | *βελτιώθηκα* | *θα βελτιωθώ*<br>*να βελτιωθώ* | *έχω βελτιωθεί*<br>*είχα βελτιωθεί* | *να βελτιώνεσαι*<br>*βελτιώνεστε* | *βελτιώσου*<br>*βελτιωθείτε* |
| **I bring** | φέρνω 13 | έφερνα | έφερα | θα φέρω<br>να φέρω | έχω φέρει<br>είχα φέρει | φέρνε<br>φέρνετε | φέρε<br>φέρτε |
| **I bring back**<br>(restore) | επαναφέρω 13 | επανέφερα | επανέφερα | θα επαναφέρω<br>να επαναφέρω | έχω επαναφέρει<br>είχα επαναφέρει | επανάφερνε<br>επαναφέρνετε | επανάφερε<br>επαναφέρτε |
| **I bring up** | ανατρέφω 13<br>αναθρέφω | ανάτρεφα | ανάθρεψα | θα αναθρέψω<br>να αναθρέψω | έχω αναθρέψει<br>είχα αναθρέψει | ανάθρεφε<br>αναθρέφετε | ανάθρεψε<br>αναθρέψτε |
| **I broadcast** | εκπέμπω 13 | εξέπεμπα | εξέπεμψα | θα εκπέμψω<br>να εκπέμψω | έχω εκπέμψει<br>είχα εκπέμψει | έκπεμπε<br>εκπέμπετε | έκπεμψε<br>εκπέμψτε |
| **I broaden** | πλαταίνω 13 | πλάταινα | πλάτυνα | θα πλατύνω<br>να πλατύνω | έχω πλατύνει<br>είχα πλατύνει | πλάταινε<br>πλαταίνετε | πλάτυνε<br>πλατύνετε |
| **I broaden** | διευρύνω 13 | διεύρυνα | διεύρυνα | θα διευρύνω<br>να διευρύνω | έχω διευρύνει<br>είχα διευρύνει | διεύρυνε<br>διευρύνετε | διεύρυνε<br>διευρύνετε |
| **I brood**<br>(hen) | κλωσσάω 15 | κλωσσούσα | κλώσσησα | θα κλωσσήσω<br>να κλωσσήσω | έχω κλωσσήσει<br>είχα κλωσσήσει | κλώσσα<br>κλωσσάτε | κλώσσησε<br>κλωσσήστε |
| **I brood**<br>(person) | *αναλογίζομαι 14* | *αναλογιζόμουν* | *αναλογίστηκα* | *θα αναλογιστώ*<br>*να αναλογιστώ* | *έχω αναλογιστεί*<br>*είχα αναλογιστεί* | *να αναλογίζεσαι*<br>*αναλογίζεστε* | *αναλογίσου*<br>*αναλογιστείτε* |

| English Verb | Present | Imperfect | Past | Simple Future<br>Simple Subjunctive | Present Perfect<br>Past Perfect | Continuous Imperative | Simple Imperative |
|---|---|---|---|---|---|---|---|
| **I browbeat** | εκφοβίζω 13 | εκφόβιζα | εκφόβισα | θα εκφοβίσω<br>να εκφοβίσω | έχω εκφοβίσει<br>είχα εκφοβίσει | εκφόβιζε<br>εκφοβίζετε | εκφόβισε<br>εκφοβίστε |
| **I browse** | ξεφυλλίζω 13 | ξεφύλλιζα | ξεφύλλισα | θα ξεφυλλίσω<br>να ξεφυλλίσω | έχω ξεφυλλίσει<br>είχα ξεφυλλίσει | ξεφύλλιζε<br>ξεφυλλίζετε | ξεφύλλισε<br>ξεφυλλίστε |
| **I browse** | χαζεύω 13 | χάζευα | χάζεψα | θα χαζέψω<br>να χαζέψω | έχω χαζέψει<br>είχα χαζέψει | χάζευε<br>χαζεύετε | χάζεψε<br>χαζέψτε |
| **I bruise** | μελανιάζω 13 | μελάνιαζα | μελάνιασα | θα μελανιάσω<br>να μελανιάσω | έχω μελανιάσει<br>είχα μελανιάσει | μελάνιαζε<br>μελανιάζετε | μελάνιασε<br>μελανιάστε |
| **I bruise** | μωλοπίζω 13 | μωλόπιζα | μωλόπισα | θα μωλοπίσω<br>να μωλοπίσω | έχω μωλοπίσει<br>είχα μωλοπίσει | μωλόπιζε<br>μωλοπίζετε | μωλόπισε<br>μωλοπίστε |
| **I brush** | βουρτσίζω 13 | βούρτσιζα | βούρτσισα | θα βουρτσίσω<br>να βουρτσίσω | έχω βουρτσίσει<br>είχα βουρτσίσει | βούρτσιζε<br>βουρτσίζετε | βούρτσισε<br>βουρτσίστε |
| **I brush up** | φρεσκάρω 13 | φρέσκαρα | φρέσκαρα<br>(φρεσκάρισα) | θα φρεσκάρω<br>να φρεσκάρω | έχω φρεσκάρει<br>είχα φρεσκάρει | φρέσκαρε<br>φρεσκάρετε | φρεσκάρισε<br>φρεσκαρίστε |
| **I bubble** | χοχλάζω 13 | χόχλαζα | χόχλασα | θα χοχλάσω<br>να χοχλάσω | έχω χοχλάσει<br>είχα χοχλάσει | χόχλαζε<br>χοχλάζετε | χόχλασε<br>χοχλάστε |
| **I buckle** | κουμπώνω 13 | κούμπωνα | κούμπωσα | θα κουμπώσω<br>να κουμπώσω | έχω κουμπώσει<br>είχα κουμπώσει | κούμπωνε<br>κουμπώνετε | κούμπωσε<br>κουμπώστε |
| **I budget** | προϋπολογίζω 13 | προϋπολόγιζα | προϋπολόγισα | θα προϋπολογίσω<br>να προϋπολογίσω | έχω προϋπολογίσει<br>είχα προϋπολογίσει | προϋπολόγιζε<br>προϋπολογίζετε | προϋπολόγισε<br>προϋπολογίστε |
| **I build** | χτίζω 13 | έχτιζα | έχτισα | θα χτίσω<br>να χτίσω | έχω χτίσει<br>είχα χτίσει | χτίζε<br>χτίζετε | χτίσε<br>χτίστε |
| **I bulge** | εξογκώνω 13 | εξόγκωνα | εξόγκωσα | θα εξογκώσω<br>να εξογκώσω | έχω εξογκώσει<br>είχα εξογκώσει | εξόγκωνε<br>εξογκώνετε | εξόγκωσε<br>εξογκώστε |

| English Verb | Present | Imperfect | Past | Simple Future<br>Simple Subjunctive | Present Perfect<br>Past Perfect | Continuous Imperative | Simple Imperative |
|---|---|---|---|---|---|---|---|
| **I bully** | *κακομετα-<br>χειρίζομαι 14* | *κακομετα-<br>χειριζόμουν* | *κακομετα-<br>χειρίστηκα* | *θα κακομετα-<br>χειριστώ*<br>*να κακομετα-<br>χειριστώ* | *έχω κακομετα-<br>χειριστεί*<br>*είχα κακομετα-<br>χειριστεί* | *να κακομετα-<br>χειρίζεσαι*<br>*κακομετα-<br>χειρίζεστε* | *κακομετα-<br>χειρίσου*<br>*κακομετα-<br>χειριστείτε* |
| **I bum around** | αλητεύω 13 | αλήτευα | αλήτεψα | θα αλητέψω<br>να αλητέψω | έχω αλητέψει<br>είχα αλητέψει | αλήτευε<br>αλητεύετε | αλήτεψε<br>αλητέψτε |
| **I bump** | *τραντάζομαι 14* | *τρανταζόμουν* | *τραντάχτηκα* | *θα τρανταχτώ*<br>*να τρανταχτώ* | *έχω τρανταχτεί*<br>*είχα τρανταχτεί* | *να τραντάζεσαι*<br>*τραντάζεστε* | *τραντάξου*<br>*τρανταχτείτε* |
| **I burden**<br>(with problems) | επιβαραίνω 13 | επιβάραινα | επιβάρυνα | θα επιβαρύνω<br>να επιβαρύνω | έχω επιβαρύνει<br>είχα επιβαρύνει | επιβάραινε<br>επιβαραίνετε | επιβάρυνε<br>επιβαρύντε |
| **I burden** | βαραίνω 13 | βάραινα | βάρυνα | θα βαρύνω<br>να βαρύνω | έχω βαρύνει<br>είχα βαρύνει | βάραινε<br>βαραίνετε | βάρυνε<br>βαρύντε |
| **I burn** | καί(γ)ω 20 | έκαιγα | έκαψα | θα κάψω<br>να κάψω | έχω κάψει<br>είχα κάψει | καίγε<br>καίγετε | κάψε<br>κάψτε |
| **I burn out**<br>(by overworking) | *εξαντλούμαι 18* | *εξαντλούμουν* | *εξαντλήθηκα* | *θα εξαντληθώ*<br>*να εξαντληθώ* | *έχω εξαντληθεί*<br>*είχα εξαντληθεί* | *να εξαντλείσαι*<br>*εξαντλείστε* | *εξαντλήσου*<br>*εξαντληθείτε* |
| **I burp** | *ρεύομαι 13* | *ρευόμουν* | *ρεύτηκα* | *θα ρευτώ*<br>*να ρευτώ* | *έχω ρευτεί*<br>*είχα ρευτεί* | *να ρεύεσαι*<br>*ρεύεστε* | *ρεύσου*<br>*ρευτείτε* |
| **I burrow** | ξεσκαλίζω 13 | ξεσκάλιζα | ξεσκάλισα | θα ξεσκαλίσω<br>να ξεσκαλίσω | έχω ξεσκαλίσει<br>είχα ξεσκαλίσει | ξεσκάλιζε<br>ξεσκαλίζετε | ξεσκάλισε<br>ξεσκαλίστε |
| **I burst**<br>(tyre/pipe) | σκάζω 13 | έσκαζα | έσκασα | θα σκάσω<br>να σκάσω | έχω σκάσει<br>είχα σκάσει | σκάζε<br>σκάζετε | σκάσε<br>σκάστε |
| **I bury** | θάβω 13 | έθαβα | έθαψα | θα θάψω<br>να θάψω | έχω θάψει<br>είχα θάψει | θάβε<br>θάβετε | θάψε<br>θάψτε |

| English Verb | Present | Imperfect | Past | Simple Future Simple Subjunctive | Present Perfect Past Perfect | Continuous Imperative | Simple Imperative |
|---|---|---|---|---|---|---|---|
| **I butter** | βουτυρώνω 13 | βουτύρωνα | βουτύρωσα | θα βουτυρώσω<br>να βουτυρώσω | έχω βουτυρώσει<br>είχα βουτηρώσει | βουτύρωνε<br>βουτυρώνετε | βουτύρωσε<br>βουτυρώστε |
| **I buy** | αγοράζω 13 | αγόραζα | αγόρασα | θα αγοράσω<br>να αγοράσω | έχω αγοράσει<br>είχα αγοράσει | αγόραζε<br>αγοράζετε | αγόρασε<br>αγοράστε |
| **I form** | σχηματίζω 13 | σχημάτιζα | σχημάτισα | θα σχηματίσω<br>να σχηματίσω | έχω σχηματίσει<br>είχα σχηματίσει | σχημάτιζε<br>σχηματίζετε | σχημάτισε<br>σχηματίστε |
| **I give birth to** | γεννάω 15 | γεννούσα | γέννησα | θα γεννήσω<br>να γεννήσω | έχω γεννήσει<br>είχα γεννήσει | γέννα<br>γεννάτε | γέννησε<br>γεννήστε |
| **I buzz** | βουίζω 13 | βούιζα | βούιξα | θα βουίξω<br>να βουίξω | έχω βουίξει<br>είχα βουίξει | βούιζε<br>βουίζετε | βούιξε<br>βουίξτε |
| **I cable** | τηλεγραφώ 17 | τηλεγραφούσα | τηλεγράφησα | θα τηλεγραφήσω<br>να τηλεγραφήσω | έχω τηλεγραφήσει<br>είχα τηλεγραφήσει | να τηλεγραφείς<br>τηλεγραφείτε | τηλεγράφησε<br>τηλεγραφήστε |
| **I cajole** | τουμπάρω 13 | τούμπαρα | τουμπάρησα | θα τουμπάρω<br>να τουμπάρω | έχω τουμπάρει<br>είχα τουμπάρει | τούμπαρε<br>τουμπάρετε | τουμπάρησε<br>τουμπαρήστε |
| **I call** | αποκαλώ 17 | αποκαλούσα | αποκάλεσα | θα αποκαλέσω<br>να αποκαλέσω | έχω αποκαλέσει<br>είχα αποκαλέσει | να αποκαλείς<br>αποκαλείτε | αποκάλεσε<br>αποκαλέστε |
| **I calm/calm down** | ηρεμώ 17 | ηρεμούσα | ηρέμησα | θα ηρεμήσω<br>να ηρεμήσω | έχω ηρεμήσει<br>είχα ηρεμήσει | να ηρεμείς<br>ηρεμείτε | ηρέμησε<br>ηρεμήστε |
| **I camouflage** | καμουφλάρω 13 | καμουφλάριζα | καμουφλάρισα | θα καμουφλάρω<br>να καμουφλάρω | έχω καμουφλάρει<br>είχα καμουφλάρει | καμούφλαρε<br>καμουφλάρετε | καμουφλάρισε<br>καμουφλαρίστε |
| **I camp** | κατασκηνώνω 13 | κατασκήνωνα | κατασκήνωσα | θα κατασκηνώσω<br>να κατασκηνώσω | έχω κατασκηνώσει<br>είχα κατασκηνώσει | κατασκήνωνε<br>κατασκηνώνετε | κατασκήνωσε<br>κατασκηνώστε |
| **I campaign** | εκστρατεύω 13 | εκστράτευα | εκστράτευσα | θα εκστρατεύσω<br>να εκστρατεύσω | έχω εκστρατεύσει<br>είχα εκστρατεύσει | εκστράτευε<br>εκστρατεύετε | εκστράτευσε<br>εκστρατεύστε |

| English Verb | Present | Imperfect | Past | Simple Future<br>Simple Subjunctive | Present Perfect<br>Past Perfect | Continuous Imperative | Simple Imperative |
|---|---|---|---|---|---|---|---|
| **I can** | μπορώ 17 | μπορούσα | μπόρεσα | θα μπορέσω<br>να μπορέσω | έχω μπορέσει<br>είχα μπορέσει | να μπορείς<br>μπορείτε | μπόρεσε<br>μπορέστε |
| **I cancel** | ματαιώνω 13 | ματαίωνα | ματαίωσα | θα ματαιώσω<br>να ματαιώσω | έχω ματαιώσει<br>είχα ματαιώσει | ματαίωνε<br>ματαιώνετε | ματαίωσε<br>ματαιώστε |
| **I canonize** | αγιοποιώ 17 | αγιοποιούσα | αγιοποίησα | θα αγιοποιήσω<br>να αγιοποιήσω | έχω αγιοποιήσει<br>είχα αγιοποιήσει | να αγιοποιείς<br>αγιοποιείτε | αγιοποίησε<br>αγιοποιήστε |
| **I capitalize** | κεφαλαιοποιώ 17 | κεφαλαιοποιούσα | κεφαλαιοποίησα | θα κεφαλαιοποιήσω<br>να κεφαλαιοποιήσω | έχω κεφαλαιοποιήσει<br>είχα κεφαλαιοποιήσει | να κεφαλαιοποιείς<br>κεφαλαιοποιείτε | κεφαλαιοποίησε<br>κεφαλαιοποιήστε |
| **I captivate** | σαγηνεύω 13 | σαγήνευα | σαγήνευσα | θα σαγηνεύσω<br>να σαγηνεύσω | έχω σαγηνεύσει<br>είχα σαγηνεύσει | σαγήνευε<br>σαγηνεύετε | σαγήνευσε<br>σαγηνεύστε |
| **I capture** | αιχμαλωτίζω 13 | αιχμαλώτιζα | αιχμαλώτισα | θα αιχμαλωτίσω<br>να αιχμαλωτίσω | έχω αιχμαλωτίσει<br>είχα αιχμαλωτίσει | αιχμαλώτιζε<br>αιχμαλωτίζετε | αιχμαλώτισε<br>αιχμαλωτίστε |
| **I care for** | φροντίζω 13 | φρόντιζα | φρόντισα | θα φροντίσω<br>να φροντίσω | έχω φροντίσει<br>είχα φροντίσει | φρόντιζε<br>φροντίζετε | φρόντισε<br>φροντίστε |
| **I caress** | χαϊδεύω 13 | χάϊδευα | χάϊδεψα | θα χαϊδέψω<br>να χαϊδέψω | έχω χαϊδέψει<br>είχα χαϊδέψει | χάϊδευε<br>χαϊδεύετε | χάϊδεψε<br>χαϊδέψτε |
| **I carry** | κουβαλώ 15 | κουβαλούσα | κουβάλησα | θα κουβαλήσω<br>να κουβαλήσω | έχω κουβαλήσει<br>είχα κουβαλήσει | κουβάλα<br>κουβαλάτε | κουβάλησε<br>κουβαλήστε |
| **I carve** | λαξεύω 13 | λάξευα | λάξεψα | θα λαξέψω<br>να λαξέψω | έχω λαξέψει<br>είχα λαξέψει | λάξευε<br>λαξεύετε | λάξεψε<br>λαξέψτε |
| **I cascade** (water) | κατρακυλ(ά)ώ 15 | κατρακυλούσα | κατρακύλησα | θα κατρακυλήσω<br>να κατρακυλήσω | έχω κατρακυλήσει<br>είχα κατρακυλήσει | κατρακύλα<br>κατρακυλάτε | κατρακύλησε<br>κατρακυλήστε |
| **I cash** (a cheque) | εξαργυρώνω 13 | εξαργύρωνα | εξαργύρωσα | θα εξαργυρώσω<br>να εξαργυρώσω | έχω εξαργυρώσει<br>είχα εξαργυρώσει | εξαργύρωνε<br>εξαργυρώνετε | εξαργύρωσε<br>εξαργυρώστε |

| English Verb | Present | Imperfect | Past | Simple Future<br>Simple Subjunctive | Present Perfect<br>Past Perfect | Continuous Imperative | Simple Imperative |
|---|---|---|---|---|---|---|---|
| **I cast aside** | παραμερίζω 13 | παραμέριζα | παραμέρισα | θα παραμερίσω<br>να παραμερίσω | έχω παραμερίσει<br>είχα παραμερίσει | παραμέριζε<br>παραμερίζετε | παραμέρισε<br>παραμερίστε |
| **I cast off** (from shore) | σαλπάρω 13 | σάλπαρα | σαλπάρισα | θα σαλπάρω<br>να σαλπάρω | έχω σαλπάρει<br>είχα σαλπάρει | σάλπαρε<br>σαλπάρετε | σαλπάρισε<br>σαλπαρίστε |
| **I catapult** | εξακοντίζω 13 | εξακόντιζα | εξακόντισα | θα εξακοντίσω<br>να εξακοντίσω | έχω εξακοντίσει<br>είχα εξακοντίσει | εξακόντιζε<br>εξακοντίζετε | εξακόντισε<br>εξακοντίστε |
| **I catch** | πιάνω 13 | έπιανα | έπιασα | θα πιάσω<br>να πιάσω | έχω πιάσει<br>είχα πιάσει | πιάνε<br>πιάνετε | πιάσε<br>πιάστε |
| **I catch** | αρπάζω 13 | άρπαζα | άρπαξα | θα αρπάξω<br>να αρπάξω | έχω αρπάξει<br>είχα αρπάξει | άρπαζε<br>αρπάζετε | άρπαξε<br>αρπάξτε |
| **I catch cold** | κρυολογώ 17 | κρυολογούσα | κρυολόγησα | θα κρυολογήσω<br>να κρυολογήσω | έχω κρυολογήσει<br>είχα κρυολογήσει | να κρυολογείς<br>κρυολογείτε | κρυολόγησε<br>κρυολογήστε |
| **I catch up** | προλαβαίνω 13 | προλάβαινα | πρόλαβα | θα προλάβω<br>να προλάβω | έχω προλάβει<br>είχα προλάβει | προλάβαινε<br>προλαβαίνετε | πρόλαβε<br>προλάβετε |
| **I cater for** | τροφοδοτώ 17 | τροφοδοτούσα | τροφοδότησα | θα τροφοδοτήσω<br>να τροφοδοτήσω | έχω τροφοδοτήσει<br>είχα τροφοδοτήσει | να τροφοδοτείς<br>τροφοδοτείτε | τροφοδότησε<br>τροφοδοτήστε |
| **I cause** | προξενώ 17 | προξενούσα | προξένησα | θα προξενήσω<br>να προξενήσω | έχω προξενήσει<br>είχα προξενήσει | να προξενείς<br>προξενείτε | προξένησε<br>προξενήστε |
| **I cauterize** | καυτηριάζω 13 | καυτηρίαζα | καυτηρίασα | θα καυτηριάσω<br>να καυτηριάσω | έχω καυτηριάσει<br>είχα καυτηριάσει | καυτηρίαζε<br>καυτηριάζετε | καυτηρίασε<br>καυτηριάστε |
| **I celebrate** | γιορτάζω 13 | γιόρταζα | γιόρτασα | θα γιορτάσω<br>να γιορτάσω | έχω γιορτάσει<br>είχα γιορτάσει | γιόρταζε<br>γιορτάζετε | γιόρτασε<br>γιορτάστε |
| **I cement** | τσιμεντάρω 13 | τσιμένταρα | τσιμένταρα<br>τσιμεντάρισα | θα τσιμεντάρω<br>να τσιμεντάρω | έχω τσιμεντάρει<br>είχα τσιμεντάρει | τσιμένταρε<br>τσιμεντάρετε | τσιμεντάρισε<br>τσιμενταρίστε |

| English Verb | Present | Imperfect | Past | Simple Future<br>Simple Subjunctive | Present Perfect<br>Past Perfect | Continuous Imperative | Simple Imperative |
|---|---|---|---|---|---|---|---|
| **I censor** | λογοκρίνω 13 | λογόκρινα | λογόκρινα | θα λογοκρίνω<br>να λογοκρίνω | έχω λογοκρίνει<br>είχα λογοκρίνει | λογόκρινε<br>λογοκρίνετε | λογόκρινε<br>λογοκρίνετε |
| **I censure** | επικρίνω 13 | επέκρινα | επέκρινα | θα επικρίνω<br>να επικρίνω | έχω επικρίνει<br>είχα επικρίνει | επίκρινε<br>επικρίνετε | επίκρινε<br>επικρίνετε |
| **I centralize** | κεντράρω 13 | κέντραρα | κεντράρησα | θα κεντράρω<br>να κεντράρω | έχω κεντράρει<br>είχα κεντράρει | κέντραρε<br>κεντράρετε | κεντράρησε<br>κεντραρήστε |
| **I centre on** | εστιάζω 13 | εστίαζα | εστίασα | θα εστιάσω<br>να εστιάσω | έχω εστιάσει<br>είχα εστιάσει | εστίαζε<br>εστιάζετε | εστίασε<br>εστιάστε |
| **I certify** | πιστοποιώ 17 | πιστοποιούσα | πιστοποίησα | θα πιστοποιήσω<br>να πιστοποιήσω | έχω πιστοποιήσει<br>είχα πιστοποιήσει | πιστοποίει<br>πιστοποιείτε | πιστοποίησε<br>πιστοποιήστε |
| **I chain** | αλυσοδένω 13 | αλυσόδενα | αλυσόδεσα | θα αλυσοδέσω<br>να αλυσοδέσω | έχω αλυσοδέσει<br>είχα αλυσοδέσει | αλυσόδενε<br>αλυσοδένετε | αλυσόδεσε<br>αλυσοδέστε |
| **I chance** | διακινδυνεύω 13 | διακινδύνευα | διακινδύνεψα | θα διακινδυνέψω<br>να διακινδυνέψω | έχω διακινδυνέψει<br>είχα διακινδυνέψει | διακινδύνευε<br>διακινδυνεύετε | διακινδύνεψε<br>διακινδυνέψτε |
| **I change** | αλλάζω 13 | άλλαζα | άλλαξα | θα αλλάξω<br>να αλλάξω | έχω αλλάξει<br>είχα αλλάξει | άλλαζε<br>αλλάζετε | άλλαξε<br>αλλάξτε |
| **I change** | μεταβάλλω 13 | μετέβαλλα | μετέβαλα | θα μεταβάλω<br>να μεταβάλω | έχω μεταβάλλει<br>είχα μεταβάλλει | μετάβαλλε<br>μεταβάλλετε | μετάβαλε<br>μεταβάλτε |
| **I chant** | ψάλλω 13<br>ψέλνω 13 | έψελνα | έψαλα | θα ψάλλω<br>να ψάλλω | έχω ψάλλει<br>είχα ψάλλει | ψάλλε<br>ψάλλετε | ψάλε<br>ψάλτε |
| **I characterize** | χαρακτηρίζω 13 | χαρακτήριζα | χαρακτήρισα | θα χαρακτηρίσω<br>να χαρακτηρίσω | έχω χαρακτηρίσει<br>είχα χαρακτηρίσει | χαρακτήριζε<br>χαρακτηρίζετε | χαρακτήρισε<br>χαρακτηρίστε |
| **I charge** | χρεώνω 13 | χρέωνα | χρέωσα | θα χρεώσω<br>να χρεώσω | έχω χρεώσει<br>είχα χρεώσει | χρέωνε<br>χρεώνετε | χρέωσε<br>χρεώστε |

| English Verb | Present | Imperfect | Past | Simple Future<br>Simple Subjunctive | Present Perfect<br>Past Perfect | Continuous Imperative | Simple Imperative |
|---|---|---|---|---|---|---|---|
| **I charm** | θέλγω 13 | έθελγα | έθελξα | θα θέλξω<br>να θέλξω | έχω θέλξει<br>είχα θέλξει | θέλγε<br>θέλγετε | θέλξε<br>θέλξτε |
| **I chart** | χαρτογραφώ 17 | χαρτογραφούσα | χαρτογράφησα | θα χαρτογραφήσω<br>να χαρτογραφήσω | έχω χαρτογραφήσει<br>είχα χαρτογραφήσει | να χαρτογραφείς<br>χαρτογραφείτε | χαρτογράφησε<br>χαρτογραφήστε |
| **I chart** | καταγράφω 13 | κατέγραφα | κατέγραψα | θα καταγράψω<br>να καταγράψω | έχω καταγράψει<br>είχα καταγράψει | κατάγραφε<br>καταγράφετε | κατάγραψε<br>καταγράψτε |
| **I chase** | καταδιώκω 13 | κατεδίωκα | κατεδίωξα | θα καταδιώξω<br>να καταδιώξω | έχω καταδιώξει<br>είχα καταδιώξει | καταδίωκε<br>καταδιώκετε | καταδίωξε<br>καταδιώξτε |
| **I chat** | κουβεντιάζω 13 | κουβέντιαζα | κουβέντιασα | θα κουβεντιάσω<br>να κουβεντιάσω | έχω κουβεντιάσει<br>είχα κουβεντιάσει | κουβέντιαζε<br>κουβεντιάζετε | κουβέντιασε<br>κουβεντιάστε |
| **I chatter** | φλυαρώ 17 | φλυαρούσα | φλυάρησα | θα φλυαρήσω<br>να φλυαρήσω | έχω φλυαρήσει<br>είχα φλυαρήσει | να φλυαρείς<br>φλυαρείτε | φλυάρησε<br>φλυαρήστε |
| **I cheapen** | ξεπέφτω 13 | ξέπεφτα | ξέπεσα | θα ξεπέσω<br>να ξεπέσω | έχω ξεπέσει<br>είχα ξεπέσει | ξέπεφτε<br>ξεπέφτετε | ξέπεσε<br>ξεπέστε |
| **I cheat** | απατώ 15 | απατούσα | απάτησα | θα απατήσω<br>να απατήσω | έχω απατήσει<br>είχα απατήσει | απάτα<br>απατάτε | απάτησε<br>απατήστε |
| **I cheat** (at cards) | εξαπατώ 15 | εξαπατούσα | εξαπάτησα | θα εξαπατήσω<br>να εξαπατήσω | έχω εξαπατήσει<br>είχα εξαπατήσει | εξαπάτα<br>εξαπατάτε | εξαπάτησε<br>εξαπατήστε |
| **I check** | τσεκάρω 13 | τσέκαρα | τσέκαρα<br>τσεκάρισα | θα τσεκάρω<br>να τσεκάρω | έχω τσεκάρει<br>είχα τσεκάρει | τσέκαρε<br>τσεκάρετε | τσεκάρισε<br>τσεκαρίστε |
| **I check** | ανακόπτω 13 | ανάκοπτα | ανάκοψα | θα ανακόψω<br>να ανακόψω | έχω ανακόψει<br>είχα ανακόψει | ανάκοπτε<br>ανακόπτετε | ανάκοψε<br>ανακόψτε |
| **I check** | ελέγχω 13 | έλεγχα | ήλεγξα | θα ελέγξω<br>να ελέγξω | έχω ελέγξει<br>είχα ελέγξει | έλεγχε<br>ελέγχετε | έλεγξε<br>ελέγξτε |

| English Verb | Present | Imperfect | Past | Simple Future<br>Simple Subjunctive | Present Perfect<br>Past Perfect | Continuous Imperative | Simple Imperative |
|---|---|---|---|---|---|---|---|
| **I cheer** | ζητωκραυγάζω 13 | ζητωκραύγαζα | ζητωκραύγασα | θα ζητωκραυγάσω<br>να ζητωκραυγάσω | έχω ζητωκραυγάσει<br>είχα ζητωκραυγάσει | ζητωκραύγαζε<br>ζητωκραυγάζετε | ζητωκραύγασε<br>ζητωκραυγάστε |
| **I chew** | μασ(ά)ώ 15 | μασούσα | μάσησα | θα μασήσω<br>να μασήσω | έχω μασήσει<br>είχα μασήσει | μάσα<br>μασάτε | μάσησε<br>μασήστε |
| **I chide** | κατσαδιάζω 13 | κατσάδιαζα | κατσάδιασα | θα κατσαδιάσω<br>να κατσαδιάσω | έχω κατσαδιάσει<br>είχα κατσαδιάσει | κατσάδιαζε<br>κατσαδιάζετε | κατσάδιασε<br>κατσαδιάστε |
| **I chill** | καταψύχω 13 | κατέψυχα | κατέψυξα | θα καταψύξω<br>να καταψύξω | έχω καταψύξει<br>είχα καταψύξει | κατάψυχε<br>καταψύχετε | κατάψυξε<br>καταψύξτε |
| **I chip** | ραγίζω 13 | ράγιζα | ράγισα | θα ραγίσω<br>να ραγίσω | έχω ραγίσει<br>είχα ραγίσει | ράγιζε<br>ραγίζετε | ράγισε<br>ραγίστε |
| **I chip in** | τσοντάρω 13 | τσόνταρα | τσοντάρισα | θα τσοντάρω<br>να τσοντάρω | έχω τσοντάρει<br>είχα τσοντάρει | τσόνταρε<br>τσοντάρετε | τσοντάρισε<br>τσονταρίστε |
| **I chirp** | τιτιβίζω 13 | τιτίβιζα | τιτίβισα | θα τιτιβίσω<br>να τιτιβίσω | έχω τιτιβίσει<br>είχα τιτιβίσει | τιτίβεζε<br>τιτιβίζετε | τιτίβεσε<br>τιτιβίστε |
| **I choke**<br>(on food) | *πνίγομαι 13* | *πνιγόμουν* | *πνίχτηκα* | *θα πνιγώ*<br>*να πνιγώ* | *έχω πνιγεί*<br>*είχα πνιγεί* | *να πνίγεσαι*<br>*πνίγεστε* | *πνίξου*<br>*πνιχτείτε* |
| **I choose** | διαλέγω 13 | διάλεγα | διάλεξα | θα διαλέξω<br>να διαλέξω | έχω διαλέξει<br>είχα διαλέξει | διάλεγε<br>διαλέγετε | διάλεξε<br>διαλέξτε |
| **I chop down/off** | πελεκώ 15 | πελεκούσα | πελέκησα | θα πελεκήσω<br>να πελεκήσω | έχω πελεκήσει<br>είχα πελεκήσει | πελέκα<br>πελεκάτε | πελέκησε<br>πελεκήστε |
| **I chug along**<br>(vehicle/boat) | αγκομαχώ 15 | αγκομαχούσα | αγκομάχησα | θα αγκομαχήσω<br>να αγκομαχήσω | έχω αγκομαχήσει<br>είχα αγκομαχήσει | αγκομάχα<br>αγκομαχάτε | αγκομάχησε<br>αγκομαχήστε |
| **I circulate** | κυκλοφορώ 15 | κυκλοφορούσα | κυκλοφόρησα | θα κυκλοφορήσω<br>να κυκλοφορήσω | έχω κυκλοφορήσει<br>είχα κυκλοφορήσει | να κυκλοφορείς<br>κυκλοφορείτε | κυκλοφόρησε<br>κυκλοφορήστε |

| English Verb | Present | Imperfect | Past | Simple Future<br>Simple Subjunctive | Present Perfect<br>Past Perfect | Continuous Imperative | Simple Imperative |
|---|---|---|---|---|---|---|---|
| **I circumvent** | παρακάμπτω 13 | παρέκαμπτα | παρέκαμψα | θα παρακάμψω<br>να παρακάμψω | έχω παρακάμψει<br>είχα παρακάμψει | παράκαμπτε<br>παρακάμπτετε | παράκαμψε<br>παρακάμψτε |
| **I cite** | μνημονεύω 13 | μνημόνευα | μνημόνευσα | θα μνημονεύσω<br>να μνημονεύσω | έχω μνημονεύσει<br>είχα μνημονεύσει | μνημόνευε<br>μνημονεύετε | μνημόνευσε<br>μνημονεύστε |
| **I cite**<br>(in a legal action) | εγκαλώ 17 | εγκαλούσα | εγκάλεσα | θα εγκαλέσω<br>να εγκαλέσω | έχω εγκαλέσει<br>είχα εγκαλέσει | να εγκαλείς<br>εγκαλείτε | εγκάλεσε<br>εγκαλέστε |
| **I claim** | διεκδικώ 17 | διεκδικούσα | διεκδίκησα | θα διεκδικήσω<br>να διεκδικήσω | έχω διεκδικήσει<br>είχα διεκδικήσει | να διεκδικείς<br>διεκδικείτε | διεκδίκησε<br>διεκδικήστε |
| **I clap** | χειροκροτώ 15 | χειροκροτούσα | χειροκρότησα | θα χειροκροτήσω<br>να χειροκροτήσω | έχω χειροκροτήσει<br>είχα χειροκροτήσει | χειροκρότα<br>χειροκροτάτε | χειροκρότησε<br>χειροκροτήστε |
| **I clarify** | διευκρινίζω 13 | διευκρίνιζα | διευκρίνισα | θα διευκρινίσω<br>να διευκρινίσω | έχω διευκρινίσει<br>είχα διευκρινίσει | διευκρίνιζε<br>διευκρινίζετε | διευκρίνισε<br>διευκρινίστε |
| **I class** | κατατάσσω 13 | κατέτασσα | κατέταξα | θα κατατάξω<br>να κατατάξω | έχω κατατάξει<br>είχα κατατάξει | κατάτασσε<br>κατατάσσετε | κατάταξε<br>κατατάξτε |
| **I classify** | ταξινομώ 17 | ταξινομούσα | ταξινόμησα | θα ταξινομήσω<br>να ταξινομήσω | έχω ταξινομήσει<br>είχα ταξινομήσει | να ταξινομείς<br>ταξινομείτε | ταξινόμησε<br>ταξινομήστε |
| **I clean** | καθαρίζω 13 | καθάριζα | καθάρισα | θα καθαρίσω<br>να καθαρίσω | έχω καθαρίσει<br>είχα καθαρίσει | καθάριζε<br>καθαρίζετε | καθάρισε<br>καθαρίστε |
| **I cleanse**<br>(purify) | εξαγνίζω 13 | εξάγνιζα | εξάγνισα | θα εξαγνίσω<br>να εξαγνίσω | έχω εξαγνίσει<br>είχα εξαγνίσει | εξάγνιζε<br>εξαγνίζετε | εξάγνισε<br>εξαγνίστε |
| **I clear** | αποσαφηνίζω 13 | αποσαφήνιζα | αποσαφήνισα | θα αποσαφηνίσω<br>να αποσαφηνίσω | έχω αποσαφηνίσει<br>είχα αποσαφηνίσει | αποσαφήνιζε<br>αποσαφηνίζετε | αποσαφήνισε<br>αποσαφηνίστε |
| **I clear** | εκκαθαρίζω 13 | εκκαθάριζα | εκκαθάρισα | θα εκκαθαρίσω<br>να εκκαθαρίσω | έχω εκκαθαρίσει<br>είχα εκκαθαρίσει | εκκαθάριζε<br>εκκαθαρίζετε | εκκαθάρισε<br>εκκαθαρίστε |

| English Verb | Present | Imperfect | Past | Simple Future<br>Simple Subjunctive | Present Perfect<br>Past Perfect | Continuous Imperative | Simple Imperative |
|---|---|---|---|---|---|---|---|
| **I clear my throat** | ξεροβήχω 13 | ξερόβηχα | ξερόβηξα | θα ξεροβήξω<br>να ξεροβήξω | έχω ξεροβήξει<br>είχα ξεροβήξει | ξερόβηχε<br>ξεροβήχετε | ξερόβηξε<br>ξεροβήξτε |
| **I clear up** | συγυρίζω 13 | συγύριζα | συγύρισα | θα συγυρίσω<br>να συγυρίσω | έχω συγυρίσει<br>είχα συγυρίσει | συγύριζε<br>συγυρίζετε | συγύρισε<br>συγυρίστε |
| **I climb** | σκαρφαλώνω 13 | σκαρφάλωνα | σκαρφάλωσα | θα σκαρφαλώσω<br>να σκαρφαλώσω | έχω σκαρφαλώσει<br>είχα σκαρφαλώσει | σκαρφάλωνε<br>σκαρφαλώνετε | σκαρφάλωσε<br>σκαρφαλώστε |
| **I clinch** (a deal) | οριστοικοποιώ 17 | οριστικοποιούσα | οριστικοποίησα | θα οριστικοποιήσω<br>να οριστικοποιήσω | έχω οριστικοποιήσει<br>είχα οριστικοποιήσει | να οριστικοποιείς<br>οριστικοποιείτε | οριστικοποίησε<br>οριστικοποιήστε |
| **I clink** | τσουγκρίζω 13 | τσούγκριζα | τσούγκρισα | θα τσουγκρίσω<br>να τσουγκρίσω | έχω τσουγκρίσει<br>είχα τσουγκρίσει | τσούγκριζε<br>τσουγκρίζετε | τσούγκρισε<br>τσουγκρίστε |
| **I clip** (fasten to) | καρφιτσώνω 13 | καρφίτσωνα | καρφίτσωσα | θα καρφιτσώσω<br>να καρφιτσώσω | έχω καρφιτσώσει<br>είχα καρφιτσώσει | καρφίτσωνε<br>καρφιτσώνετε | καρφίτσωσε<br>καρφιτσώστε |
| **I clip** (hedges) | ψαλιδίζω 13 | ψαλίδιζα | ψαλίδισα | θα ψαλιδίσω<br>να ψαλιδίσω | έχω ψαλιδίσει<br>είχα ψαλιδίσει | ψαλίδιζε<br>ψαλιδίζετε | ψαλίδισε<br>ψαλιδίστε |
| **I close** | κλείνω 13 | έκλεινα | έκλεισα | θα κλείσω<br>να κλείσω | έχω κλείσει<br>είχα κλείσει | κλείνε<br>κλείνετε | κλείσε<br>κλείστε |
| **I clot** | σβωλιάζω 13 | σβώλιαζα | σβώλιασα | θα σβωλιάσω<br>να σβωλιάσω | έχω σβωλιάσει<br>είχα σβωλιάσει | σβώλιαζε<br>σβωλιάζετε | σβώλιασε<br>σβωλιάστε |
| **I cloud** | θολώνω 13 | θόλωνα | θόλωσα | θα θολώσω<br>να θολώσω | έχω θολώσει<br>είχα θολώσει | θόλωνε<br>θολώνετε | θόλωσε<br>θολώστε |
| **It clouds over** | συννεφιάζει 13 | συννέφιαζε | συννέφιασε | θα συννεφιάσει<br>να συννεφιάσει | έχει συννεφιάσει<br>είχε συννεφιάσει | συννέφιαζε<br>συννεφιάζετε | συννέφιασε<br>συννεφιάστε |
| **I clout** | καρπαζώνω 13 | καρπάζωνα | καρπάζωσα | θα καρπαζώσω<br>να καρπαζώσω | έχω καρπαζώσει<br>είχα καρπαζώσει | καρπάζωνε<br>καρπαζώνετε | καρπάζωσε<br>καρπαζώστε |

| English Verb | Present | Imperfect | Past | Simple Future<br>Simple Subjunctive | Present Perfect<br>Past Perfect | Continuous Imperative | Simple Imperative |
|---|---|---|---|---|---|---|---|
| **I cluck** | κακαρίζω 13 | κακάριζα | κακάρισα | θα κακαρίσω<br>να κακαρίσω | έχω κακαρίσει<br>είχα κακαρίσει | κακάριζε<br>κακαρίζετε | κακάρισε<br>κακαρίστε |
| **I clutch** | σφίγγω 13 | έσφιγγα | έσφιξα | θα σφίξω<br>να σφίξω | έχω σφίξει<br>είχα σφίξει | σφίγγε<br>σφίγγετε | σφίξε<br>σφίξτε |
| **I clutter** | παραφορτώνω 13 | παραφόρτωνα | παραφόρτωσα | θα παραφορτώσω<br>να παραφορτώσω | έχω παραφορτώσει<br>είχα παραφορτώσει | παραφόρτωνε<br>παραφορτώνετε | παραφόρτωσε<br>παραφορτώστε |
| **I coach** (athlete) | προπονώ 17 | προπονούσα | προπόνησα | θα προπονήσω<br>να προπονήσω | έχω προπονήσει<br>είχα προπονήσει | να προπονείς<br>προπονείτε | προπόνησε<br>προπονήστε |
| **I coach** (student) | προγυμνάζω 13 | προγύμναζα | προγύμνασα | θα προγυμνάσω<br>να προγυμνάσω | έχω προγυμνάσει<br>είχα προγυμνάσει | προγύμναζε<br>προγυμνάζετε | προγύμνασε<br>προγυμνάστε |
| **I coat** | καλύπτω 13 | κάλυπτα | κάλυψα | θα καλύψω<br>να καλύψω | έχω καλύψει<br>είχα καλύψει | κάλυπτε<br>καλύπτετε | κάλυψε<br>καλύψτε |
| **I coax** | καλοπιάνω 13 | καλόπιανα | καλόπιασα | θα καλοπιάσω<br>να καλοπιάσω | έχω καλοπιάσει<br>είχα καλοπιάσει | καλόπιανε<br>καλοπιάνετε | καλόπιασε<br>καλοπιάστε |
| **I cock** (rifle/gun) | οπλίζω 13 | όπλιζα | όπλισα | θα οπλίσω<br>να οπλίσω | έχω οπλίσει<br>είχα οπλίσει | όπλιζε<br>οπλίζετε | όπλισε<br>οπλίστε |
| **I codify** | κωδικοποιώ 17 | κωδικοποιούσα | κωδικοποίησα | θα κωδικοποιήσω<br>να κωδικοποιήσω | έχω κωδικοποιήσει<br>είχα κωδικοποιήσει | να κωδικοποιείς<br>κωδικοποιείτε | κωδικοποίησε<br>κωδικοποιήστε |
| **I coerce** | καταναγκάζω 13 | κατανάγκαζα | κατανάγκασα | θα καταναγκάσω<br>να καταναγκάσω | έχω καταναγκάσει<br>είχα καταναγκάσει | κατανάγκαζε<br>καταναγκάζετε | κατανάγκασε<br>καταναγκάστε |
| **I cohabit** | συζώ 17 | συζούσα | συνέζησα | θα συζήσω<br>να συζήσω | έχω συζήσει<br>είχα συζήσει | να συζείς<br>συζείτε | σύζησε<br>συζήστε |
| **I coil** | τυλίγω 13 | τύλιγα | τύλιξα | θα τυλίξω<br>να τυλίξω | έχω τυλίξει<br>είχα τυλίξει | τύλιγε<br>τυλίγετε | τύλιξε<br>τυλίξτε |

| English Verb | Present | Imperfect | Past | Simple Future<br>Simple Subjunctive | Present Perfect<br>Past Perfect | Continuous Imperative | Simple Imperative |
|---|---|---|---|---|---|---|---|
| **I coincide** | συμπίπτω 13 | συνέπιπτα | συνέπεσα | θα συμπέσω<br>να συμπέσω | έχω συμπέσει<br>είχα συμπέσει | να συμπίπτεις<br>συμπίπτετε | σύμπεσε<br>συμπέστε |
| **I collaborate** | συμπράττω 13 | συνέπραττα | συνέπραξα | θα συμπράξω<br>να συμπράξω | έχω συμπράξει<br>είχα συμπράξει | σύμπραττε<br>συμπράττετε | σύμπραξε<br>συμπράξτε |
| **I collapse** | *σωριάζομαι 14* | *σωριαζόμουν* | *σωριάστηκα* | *θα σωριαστώ*<br>*να σωριαστώ* | *έχω σωριαστεί*<br>*είχα σωριαστεί* | *να σωριάζεσαι*<br>*σωριάζεστε* | *σωριάσου*<br>*σωριαστείτε* |
| **I collect** | μαζεύω 13 | μάζευα | μάζεψα | θα μαζέψω<br>να μαζέψω | έχω μαζέψει<br>είχα μαζέψει | μάζευε<br>μαζεύετε | μάζεψε<br>μαζέψτε |
| **I collect**<br>(as hobby) | συλλέγω 13 | συνέλεγα | συνέλεξα | θα συλλέξω<br>να συλλέξω | έχω συλλέξει<br>είχα συλλέξει | σύλλεγε<br>συλλέγετε | σύλλεξε<br>συλλέξτε |
| **I collect**<br>(debts) | εισπράττω 13 | εισέπραττα | εισέπραξα | θα ειπράξω<br>να εισπράξω | έχω εισπράξει<br>είχα εισπράξει | είσπραττε<br>εισπράττετε | είσπραξε<br>εισπράξτε |
| **I colour**<br>(dye) | βάφω 13 | έβαφα | έβαψα | θα βάψω<br>να βάψω | έχω βάψει<br>είχα βάψει | βάφε<br>βάφετε | βάψε<br>βάψτε |
| **I colour in** | χρωματίζω 13 | χρωμάτιζα | χρωμάτισα | θα χρωματίσω<br>να χρωματίσω | έχω χρωματίσει<br>είχα χρωματίσει | χρωμάτιζε<br>χρωματίζετε | χρωμάτισε<br>χρωματίστε |
| **I comb** | χτενίζω 13 | χτένιζα | χτένισα | θα χτενίσω<br>να χτενίσω | έχω χτενίσει<br>είχα χτενίσει | χτένιζε<br>χτενίζετε | χτένισε<br>χτενίστε |
| **I combat** | καταπολεμώ 15 | καταπολεμούσα | καταπολέμησα | θα καταπολεμήσω<br>να καταπολεμήσω | έχω καταπολεμήσει<br>είχα καταπολεμήσει | καταπολέμα<br>καταπολεμάτε | καταπολέμησε<br>καταπολεμήστε |
| **I combine** | συνδυάζω 13 | συνδύαζα | συνδύασα | θα συνδυάσω<br>να συνδυάσω | έχω συνδυάσει<br>είχα συνδυάσει | συνδύαζε<br>συνδυάζετε | συνδύασε<br>συνδυάστε |
| **I come** | *έρχομαι 14* | *ερχόμουν* | *ήρθα* | *θα έρθω*<br>*να έρθω* | *έχω έρθει*<br>*είχα έρθει* | *να έρχεσαι*<br>*έρχεστε* | *έλα*<br>*ελάτε* |

| English Verb | Present | Imperfect | Past | Simple Future<br>Simple Subjunctive | Present Perfect<br>Past Perfect | Continuous Imperative | Simple Imperative |
|---|---|---|---|---|---|---|---|
| **I come apart** | *διαλύομαι 13* | *διαλυόμουν* | *διαλύθηκα* | *θα διαλυθώ*<br>*να διαλυθώ* | *έχω διαλυθεί*<br>*είχα διαλυθεί* | *να διαλύεσαι*<br>*διαλύεστε* | *διαλύσου*<br>*διαλυθείτε* |
| **I come back** | *ξανάρχομαι 13* | *ξαναρχόμουν* | *ξαναήρθα* | *θα ξανάρθω*<br>*να ξανάρθω* | *έχω ξανάρθει*<br>*είχα ξανάρθει* | *να ξανάρχεσαι*<br>*ξανάρχεστε* | *ξαναέλα*<br>*ξαναελάτε* |
| **I come from** | *προέρχομαι 13* | *προερχόμουν* | *προήλθα* | *θα προέλθω*<br>*να προέλθω* | *έχω προέλθει*<br>*είχα προέλθει* | *να προέρχεσαι*<br>*προέρχεστε* | *να προέλθεις*<br>*προέλθετε* |
| **I come out**<br>(appear) | *αποκαλύπτομαι 14* | *αποκαλυπτόμουν* | *αποκαλύφτηκα* | *θα αποκαλυφτώ*<br>*να αποκαλυφτώ* | *έχω αποκαλυφτεί*<br>*είχα αποκαλυφτεί* | *να αποκαλύπτεσαι*<br>*αποκαλύπτεστε* | *αποκαλύψου*<br>*αποκαλυφτείτε* |
| **I come round** | *συνέρχομαι 14* | *συνερχόμουν* | *συνήλθα* | *θα συνέλθω*<br>*να συνέλθω* | *έχω συνέλθει*<br>*είχα συνέλθει* | *να συνέρχεσαι*<br>*συνέρχεστε* | *σύνελθε*<br>*συνέλθετε* |
| **I come under** | *υπάγομαι 14* | *υπαγόμουν* | *υπάχθηκα* | *θα υπαχθώ*<br>*να υπαχθώ* | *έχω υπαχθεί*<br>*είχα υπαχθεί* | *να υπάγεσαι*<br>*υπάγεσθε* | *να υπαχθείς*<br>*υπαχθείτε* |
| **I come up**<br>(in conversation) | *αναφέρομαι 14* | *αναφερόμουν* | *αναφέρθηκα* | *θα αναφερθώ*<br>*να αναφερθώ* | *έχω αναφερθεί*<br>*είχα αναφερθεί* | *να αναφέρεστε*<br>*αναφέρεστε* | *αναφέρσου*<br>*αναφερθείτε* |
| **I comfort** | παρηγορώ 17 | παρηγορούσα | παρηγόρησα | θα παρηγορήσω<br>να παρηγορήσω | έχω παρηγορήσει<br>είχα παρηγορήσει | παρηγόρει<br>παρηγορείτε | παρηγόρησε<br>παρηγορήστε |
| **I command** | διατάζω 13 | διέταζα | διέταξα | θα διατάξω<br>να διατάξω | έχω διατάξει<br>είχα διατάξει | διάταζε<br>διατάζετε | διάταξε<br>διατάξτε |
| **I command** | διοικώ 17 | διοικούσα | διοίκησα | θα διοικήσω<br>να διοικήσω | έχω διοικήσει<br>είχα διοικήσει | να διοικείς<br>διοικείτε | διοίκησε<br>διοικήστε |
| **I commemorate** | μνημονεύω 13 | μνημόνευα | μνημόνευσα | θα μνημονεύσω<br>να μνημονεύσω | έχω μνημονεύσει<br>είχα μνημονεύσει | μνημόνευε<br>μνημονεύετε | μνημόνευσε<br>μνημονεύστε |
| **I commend**<br>(praise) | εγκωμιάζω 13 | εγκωμίαζα | εγκωμίασα | θα εγκωμιάσω<br>να εγκωμιάσω | έχω εγκωμιάσει<br>είχα εγκωμιάσει | εγκωμίαζε<br>εγκωμιάζετε | εγκωμίασε<br>εγκωμιάστε |

| English Verb | Present | Imperfect | Past | Simple Future<br>Simple Subjunctive | Present Perfect<br>Past Perfect | Continuous Imperative | Simple Imperative |
|---|---|---|---|---|---|---|---|
| **I comment** | σχολιάζω 13 | σχολίαζα | σχολίασα | θα σχολιάσω<br>να σχολιάσω | έχω σχολιάσει<br>είχα σχολιάσει | σχολίαζε<br>σχολιάζετε | σχολίασε<br>σχολιάστε |
| **I commit** (crime) | διαπράττω 13 | διέπραττα | διέπραξα | θα διαπράξω<br>να διαπράξω | έχω διαπράξει<br>είχα διαπράξει | διάπραττε<br>διαπράττετε | διάπραξε<br>διαπράξτε |
| **I commit myself** | *δεσμεύομαι 14* | *δεσμευόμουν* | *δεσμεύτηκα* | *θα δεσμευτώ*<br>*να δεσμευτώ* | *έχω δεσμευτεί*<br>*είχα δεσμευτεί* | *να δεσμεύεσαι*<br>*δεσμεύεστε* | *δεσμεύσου*<br>*δεσμευτείτε* |
| **I commit suicide** | αυτοκτονώ 17 | αυτοκτονούσα | αυτοκτόνησα | θα αυτοκτονήσω<br>να αυτοκτονήσω | έχω αυτοκτονήσει<br>είχα αυτοκτονήσει | να αυτοκτονείς<br>αυτοκτονείτε | αυτοκτόνησε<br>αυτοκτονήστε |
| **I communicate** | επικοινωνώ 17 | επικοινωνούσα | επικοινώνησα | θα επικοινωνήσω<br>να επικοινωνήσω | έχω επικοινωνήσει<br>είχα επικοινωνήσει | να επικοινωνείς<br>επικοινωνείτε | επικοινώνησε<br>επικοινωνήστε |
| **I compare** | συγκρίνω 13 | συνέκρινα | συνέκρινα | θα συγκρίνω<br>να συγκρίνω | έχω συγκρίνει<br>είχα συγκρίνει | σύγκρινε<br>συγκρίνετε | σύγκρινε<br>συγκρίνετε |
| **I compel** | αναγκάζω 13 | ανάγκαζα | ανάγκασα | θα αναγκάσω<br>να αναγκάσω | έχω αναγκάσει<br>είχα αναγκάσει | ανάγκαζε<br>αναγκάζετε | ανάγκασε<br>αναγκάστε |
| **I compensate** | αποζημιώνω 13 | αποζημίωνα | αποζημίωσα | θα αποζημιώσω<br>να αποζημιώσω | έχω αποζημιώσει<br>είχα αποζημιώσει | αποζημίωνε<br>αποζημιώνετε | αποζημίωσε<br>αποζημιώστε |
| **I compete** | *ανταγωνίζομαι 14* | *ανταγωνιζόμουν* | *ανταγωνίστηκα* | *θα ανταγωνιστώ*<br>*να ανταγωνιστώ* | *έχω ανταγωνιστεί*<br>*είχα ανταγωνιστεί* | *να ανταγωνίζεσαι*<br>*ανταγωνίζεστε* | *ανταγωνίσου*<br>*ανταγωνιστείτε* |
| **I complain** | *παραπονούμαι 18*<br>*παραπονιέμαι 16* | *παραπονούμουν*<br>*παραπονιόμουν* | *παραπονέθηκα* | *θα παραπονεθώ*<br>*να παραπονεθώ* | *έχω παραπονεθεί*<br>*είχα παραπονεθεί* | *να παραπονιέσαι*<br>*παραπονιέστε* | *παραπονέσου*<br>*παραπονεθείτε* |
| **I complement** | φιλοφρονώ 17 | φιλοφρονούσα | φιλοφρόνησα | θα φιλοφρονήσω<br>να φιλοφρονήσω | έχω φιλοφρονήσει<br>είχα φιλοφρονήσει | να φιλοφρονείς<br>φιλοφρονείτε | φιλοφρόνησε<br>φιλοφρονήστε |
| **I complete** (task) | ολοκληρώνω 13 | ολοκλήρωνα | ολοκλήρωσα | θα ολοκληρώσω<br>να ολοκληρώσω | έχω ολοκληρώσει<br>είχα ολοκληρώσει | ολοκλήρωνε<br>ολοκληρώνετε | ολοκλήρωσε<br>ολοκληρώστε |

| English Verb | Present | Imperfect | Past | Simple Future<br>Simple Subjunctive | Present Perfect<br>Past Perfect | Continuous Imperative | Simple Imperative |
|---|---|---|---|---|---|---|---|
| **I complete** (form) | συμπληρώνω 13 | συμπλήρωνα | συμπλήρωσα | θα συμπληρώσω<br>να συμπληρώσω | έχω συμπληρώσει<br>είχα συμπληρώσει | συμπλήρωνε<br>συμπληρώνετε | συμπλήρωσε<br>συμπληρώστε |
| **I complicate** | δυσκολεύω 13 | δυσκόλευα | δυσκόλεψα | θα δυσκολέψω<br>να δυσκολέψω | έχω δυσκολέψει<br>είχα δυσκολέψει | δυσκόλευε<br>δυσκολεύετε | δυσκόλεψε<br>δυσκολέψτε |
| **I complicate** | περιπλέκω 13 | περιέπλεκα | περιέπλεξα | θα περιπλέξω<br>να περιπλέξω | έχω περιπλέξει<br>είχα περιπλέξει | περίπλεκε<br>περιπλέκετε | περίπλεξε<br>περιπλέξτε |
| **I compliment** | κοπλιμεντάρω 13 | κοπλιμέντάρα | κοπλιμεντάρησα | θα κοπλιμε-<br>νταρήσω<br>να κοπλιμε-<br>νταρήσω | έχω κοπλιμε-<br>νταρήσει<br>είχα κοπλιμε-<br>νταρήσει | κοπλιμένταρε<br>κοπλιμεντάρετε | κοπλιμεντάρησε<br>κοπλιμενταρήστε |
| **I compose** (a letter) | συντάσσω 13 | συνέτασσα | συνέταξα | θα συντάξω<br>να συντάξω | έχω συντάξει<br>είχα συντάξει | σύντασσε<br>συντάσσετε | σύνταξε<br>συντάξτε |
| **I compose** (music) | συνθέτω 13 | συνέθετα | συνέθεσα | θα συνθέσω<br>να συνθέσω | έχω συνθέσει<br>είχα συνθέσει | σύνθετε<br>συνθέτετε | σύνθεσε<br>συνθέστε |
| **I comprehend** | κατανοώ 17 | κατανοούσα | κατανόησα | θα κατανοήσω<br>να κατανοήσω | έχω κατανοήσει<br>είχα κατανοήσει | να κατανοείς<br>κατανοείτε | κατανόησε<br>κατανοήστε |
| **I compress** | συμπιέζω 13 | συμπίεζα | συμπίεσα | θα συμπιέσω<br>να συμπιέσω | έχω συμπιέσει<br>είχα συμπιέσει | συμπίεζε<br>συμπιέζετε | συμπίεσε<br>συμπιέστε |
| **I compromise** | υπαναχωρώ 17 | υπαναχωρούσα | υπαναχώρεσα | θα υπαναχωρήσω<br>να υπαναχωρήσω | έχω υπαναχωρήσει<br>είχα υπαναχωρήσει | να υπαναχωρείς<br>υπαναχωρείτε | υπαναχώρησε<br>υπαναχωρήστε |
| **I compromise** | *συμβιβάζομαι 14* | *συμβιβαζόμουν* | *συμβιβάστηκα* | *θα συμβιβαστώ*<br>*να συμβιβαστώ* | *έχω συμβιβαστεί*<br>*είχα συμβιβαστεί* | *να συμβιβάζεσαι*<br>*συμβιβάζεστε* | *συμβιβάσου*<br>*συμβιβαστείτε* |
| **I conceal** | αποκρύβω 13 | απέκρυβα | απέκρυψα | θα αποκρύψω<br>να αποκρύψω | έχω αποκρύψει<br>είχα αποκρύψει | απόκρυβε<br>αποκρύβετε | απόκρυψε<br>αποκρύψτε |

| English Verb | Present | Imperfect | Past | Simple Future<br>Simple Subjunctive | Present Perfect<br>Past Perfect | Continuous Imperative | Simple Imperative |
|---|---|---|---|---|---|---|---|
| **I conceive** | *διανοούμαι 18* | *διανοούμουν* | *διανοήθηκα* | *θα διανοηθώ*<br>*να διανοηθώ* | *έχω διανοηθεί*<br>*είχα διανοηθεί* | *να διανοείσαι*<br>*διανοείστε* | *διανοήσου*<br>*διανοηθείτε* |
| **I concentrate** | *συγκεντρώνομαι 14* | *συγκεντρωνόμουν* | *συγκεντρώθηκα* | *θα συγκεντρωθώ*<br>*να συγκεντρωθώ* | *έχω συγκεντρωθεί*<br>*είχα συγκεντρωθεί* | *να συγκεντρώνεσαι*<br>*συγκεντρώνεστε* | *συγκεντρώσου*<br>*συγκεντρωθείτε* |
| **It concerns** | αφορά 15 | αφορούσε | αφορούσε | θα αφορά<br>να αφορά | – | – | – |
| **I conclude** | καταλήγω 13 | κατέληγα | κατέληξα | θα καταλήξω<br>να καταλήξω | έχω καταλήξει<br>είχα καταλήξει | κατάληγε<br>καταλήγετε | κατάληξε<br>καταλήξτε |
| **I conclude** (deduce) | συμπεραίνω 13 | συμπέραινα | συμπέρανα | θα συμπεράνω<br>να συμπεράνω | έχω συμπεράνει<br>είχα συμπεράνει | συμπέραινε<br>συμπεραίνετε | συμπέρανε<br>συμπεράνετε |
| **I concoct** | *μηχανεύομαι 14* | *μηχανευόμουν* | *μηχανεύτηκα* | *θα μηχανευτώ*<br>*να μηχανευτώ* | *έχω μηχανευτεί*<br>*είχα μηχανευτεί* | *να μηχανεύεσαι*<br>*μηχανεύεστε* | *μηχανεύσου*<br>*μηχανευτείτε* |
| **I condemn** | αποδοκιμάζω 13 | αποδοκίμαζα | αποδοκίμασα | θα αποδοκιμάσω<br>να αποδοκιμάσω | έχω αποδοκιμάσει<br>είχα αποδοκιμάσει | αποδοκίμαζε<br>αποδοκιμάζετε | αποδοκίμασε<br>αποδοκιμάστε |
| **I confer** (jury/panel) | *συσκέπτομαι 14* | *συσκεπτόμουν* | *συσκέφτηκα* | *θα συσκεφτώ*<br>*να συσκεφτώ* | *έχω συσκεφτεί*<br>*είχα συσκεφτεί* | *να συσκέπτεσαι*<br>*συσκέπτεστε* | *συσκέψου*<br>*συσκεφτείτε* |
| **I confess** | ομολογώ 17 | ομολογούσα | ομολόγησα | θα ομολογήσω<br>να ομολογήσω | έχω ομολογήσει<br>είχα ομολογήσει | να ομολογείς<br>ομολογείτε | ομολόγησε<br>ομολογήστε |
| **I am confined** | *περιορίζομαι 14* | *περιοριζόμουν* | *περιορίστηκα* | *θα περιοριστώ*<br>*να περιοριστώ* | *έχω περιοριστεί*<br>*είχα περιοριστεί* | *να περιορίζεσαι*<br>*περιορίζεστε* | *περιορίσου*<br>*περιοριστείτε* |
| **I confirm** | επιβεβαιώνω 13 | επιβεβαίωνα | επιβεβαίωσα | θα επιβεβαιώσω<br>να επιβεβαιώσω | έχω επιβεβαιώσει<br>είχα επιβεβαιώσει | επιβεβαίωνε<br>επιβεβαιώνετε | επιβεβαίωσε<br>επιβεβαιώστε |
| **I confiscate** | κατάσχω 13 | κατείσχα | κατάσχεσα | θα κατασχέσω<br>να κατασχέσω | έχω κατασχέσει<br>είχα κατασχέσει | κάτασχε<br>κατάσχετε | κατάσχεσε<br>κατασχέστε |

| English Verb | Present | Imperfect | Past | Simple Future<br>Simple Subjunctive | Present Perfect<br>Past Perfect | Continuous Imperative | Simple Imperative |
|---|---|---|---|---|---|---|---|
| **I conform** | *συμμορφώνομαι 14* | *συμμορφωνόμουν* | *συμμορφώθηκα* | *θα συμμορφωθώ*<br>*να συμμορφωθώ* | *έχω συμμορφωθεί*<br>*είχα συμμορφωθεί* | *να συμμορφώνεσαι*<br>*συμμορφώνεστε* | *συμμορφώσου*<br>*συμμορφωθείτε* |
| **I confuse** | σαστίζω 13 | σάστιζα | σάστισα | θα σαστίσω<br>να σαστίσω | έχω σαστίσει<br>είχα σαστίσει | σάστιζε<br>σαστίζετε | σάστισε<br>σαστίστε |
| **I confront** | αντιμετωπίζω 13 | αντιμετώπιζα | αντιμετώπισα | θα αντιμετωπίσω<br>να αντιμετωπίσω | έχω αντιμετωπίσει<br>είχα αντιμετωπίσει | αντιμετώπιζε<br>αντιμετωπίζετε | αντιμετώπισε<br>αντιμετωπίστε |
| **I congratulate** | συγχαίρω 13 | συνέχαιρα | συγχάρηκα | θα συγχαρώ<br>να συγχαρώ | έχω συγχαρεί<br>είχα συγχαρεί | σύγχαιρε<br>συγχαίρετε | σύγχαρε<br>συγχαρείτε |
| **I connect** | συνδέω 13 | σενέδεα | σενέδεσα | θα συνδέσω<br>να συνδέσω | έχω συνδέσει<br>είχα συνδέσει | σύνδεε<br>συνδέετε | σύνδεσε<br>συνδέστε |
| **I conquer** | κατακτώ 15 | κατακτούσα | κατάκτησα | θα κατακτήσω<br>να κατακτήσω | έχω κατακτήσει<br>είχα κατακτήσει | να κατακτάς<br>κατακτάτε | κατάκτησε<br>κατακτήστε |
| **I consent** | *συγκατατίθεμαι 13* | *συγκατετιθόμουν* | *συγκατατέθηκα* | *θα συγκατατεθώ*<br>*να συγκατατεθώ* | *έχω συγκατατεθεί*<br>*είχα συγκατατεθεί* | *να συγκατατίθεσαι*<br>*συγκατατίθεστε* | *συγκαταθέσου*<br>*συγκατατεθείτε* |
| **I conserve** (preserve) | διατηρώ 17 | διατηρούσα | διατήρησα | θα διατηρήσω<br>να διατηρήσω | έχω διατηρήσει<br>είχα διατηρήσει | να διατηρείς<br>διατηρείτε | διατήρησε<br>διατηρήστε |
| **I consider** | θεωρώ 17 | θεωρούσα | θεώρησα | θα θεωρήσω<br>να θεωρήσω | έχω θεωρήσει<br>είχα θεωρήσει | να θεωρείς<br>θεωρείτε | θεώρησε<br>θεωρήστε |
| **I consider** | *συλλογίζομαι 14* | *συλλογιζόμουν* | *συλλογίστηκα* | *θα συλλογιστώ*<br>*να συλλογιστώ* | *έχω συλλογιστεί*<br>*είχα συλλογιστεί* | *να συλλογίζεσαι*<br>*συλλογίζεστε* | *συλλογίσου*<br>*συλλογισθείτε* |
| **I consign** | αποστέλλω 13 | απόστελλα | απόστειλα | θα αποστείλω<br>να αποστείλω | έχω αποστείλει<br>είχα αποστείλει | απόστελλε<br>αποστέλλετε | απόστειλε<br>αποστείλτε |
| **It consists** | *αποτελείται 14* | *αποτελούταν* | *αποτελέστηκε* | *θα αποτελεστεί*<br>*να αποτελεστεί* | *έχει αποτελεστεί*<br>*είχε αποτελεστεί* | – | – |
| **I consolidate** | σταθεροποιώ 13 | σταθεροποιούσα | σταθεροποίησα | θα σταθεροποιήσω<br>να σταθεροποιήσω | έχω σταθεροποιήσει<br>είχα σταθεροποιήσει | να σταθεροποιείς<br>σταθεροποιείτε | σταθεροποίησε<br>σταθεροποιήστε |

| English Verb | Present | Imperfect | Past | Simple Future<br>Simple Subjunctive | Present Perfect<br>Past Perfect | Continuous Imperative | Simple Imperative |
|---|---|---|---|---|---|---|---|
| **I conspire** | συνωμοτώ 17 | συνωμοτούσα | συνωμότησα | θα συνωμοτήσω<br>να συνωμοτήσω | έχω συνωμοτήσει<br>είχα συνωμοτήσει | να συνωμοτείς<br>συνωμοτείτε | συνωμότησε<br>συνωμοτήστε |
| **I constitute** | συνιστώ 15 | συνιστούσα | συνέστησα | θα συνιστήσω<br>να συνιστήσω | έχω συνιστήσει<br>είχα συνιστήσει | συνίστα<br>συνιστάτε | συνίστησε<br>συνιστήστε |
| **I constrict** | συσφίγγω 13 | σύσφιγγα | σύσφιξα | θα συσφίξω<br>να συσφίξω | έχω συσφίξει<br>είχα συσφίξει | σύσφιγγε<br>συσφίγγετε | σύσφιξε<br>συσφίξτε |
| **I construct** | κατασκευάζω 13 | κατασκεύαζα | κατασκεύασα | θα κατασκευάσω<br>να κατασκευάσω | έχω κατασκευάσει<br>είχα κατασκευάσει | κατασκεύαζε<br>κατασκευάζετε | κατασκεύασε<br>κατασκευάστε |
| **I consult** | *συμβουλεύομαι 14* | *συμβουλευόμουν* | *συμβουλεύτηκα* | *θα συμβουλευτώ*<br>*να συμβουλευτώ* | *έχω συμβουλευτεί*<br>*είχα συμβουλευτεί* | *να συμβουλεύεσαι*<br>*συμβουλεύεστε* | *συμβουλεύσου*<br>*συμβουλευτείτε* |
| **I consume** | καταναλώνω 13 | κατανάλωνα | κατανάλωσα | θα καταναλώσω<br>να καταναλώσω | έχω καταναλώσει<br>είχα καταναλώσει | κατανάλωνε<br>καταναλώνετε | κατανάλωσε<br>καταναλώστε |
| **I consume** | αναλώνω 13 | ανάλωνα | ανάλωσα | θα αναλώσω<br>να αναλώσω | έχω αναλώσει<br>είχα αναλώσει | ανάλωνε<br>αναλώνετε | ανάλωσε<br>αναλώστε |
| **I contact** | *εφάπτομαι 14* | *εφαπτόμουν* | – | – | – | – | – |
| **I contain** | περιέχω 13 | περιείχα | περιείχα | θα περιέχω<br>να περιέχω | – | – | – |
| **I contain myself** | *συγκρατούμαι 18*<br>*συγκρατιέμαι 16* | *συγκρατούμουν*<br>*συγκρατιόμουν* | *συγκρατήθηκα* | *θα συγκρατηθώ*<br>*να συγκρατηθώ* | *έχω συγκρατηθεί*<br>*είχα συγκρατηθεί* | *να συγκρατείσαι*<br>*συγκρατείστε* | *συγκρατήσου*<br>*συγκρατηθείτε* |
| **I contemplate** | *στοχάζομαι 14* | *στοχαζόμουν* | *στοχάστηκα* | *θα στοχαστώ*<br>*να στοχαστώ* | *έχω στοχαστεί*<br>*είχα στοχαστεί* | *να στοχάζεσαι*<br>*στοχάζεστε* | *στοχάσου*<br>*στοχαστείτε* |
| **I contend** | *διατείνομαι 14* | *διατεινόμουν* | – | – | – | – | – |
| **I content myself** | *αρκούμαι 18* | *αρκούμουν* | *αρκέστηκα* | *θα αρκεστώ*<br>*να αρκεστώ* | *έχω αρκεστεί*<br>*είχα αρκεστεί* | *να αρκείσαι*<br>*αρκείστε* | *αρκέσου*<br>*αρκεστείτε* |

| English Verb | Present | Imperfect | Past | Simple Future<br>Simple Subjunctive | Present Perfect<br>Past Perfect | Continuous Imperative | Simple Imperative |
|---|---|---|---|---|---|---|---|
| **I contest** | αμφισβητώ 17 | αμφισβητούσα | αμφισβήτησα | θα αμφισβητήσω<br>να αμφισβητήσω | έχω αμφισβητήσει<br>είχα αμφισβητήσει | να αμφισβητείς<br>αμφισβητείτε | αμφισβήτησε<br>αμφισβητήστε |
| **I contest** | *διαγωνίζομαι 14* | *διαγωνιζόμουν* | *διαγωνίστηκα* | *θα διαγωνιστώ*<br>*να διαγωνιστώ* | *έχω διαγωνιστεί*<br>*είχα διαγωνιστεί* | *να διαγωνίζεσαι*<br>*διαγωνίζεστε* | *διαγωνίσου*<br>*διαγωνιστείτε* |
| **I contest** (decision) | αντικρούω 13 | αντέκρουα | αντέκρουσα | θα αντικρούσω<br>να αντικρούσω | έχω αντικρούσει<br>είχα αντικρούσει | αντίκρουε<br>αντικρούετε | αντίκρουσε<br>αντικρούστε |
| **I continue** | συνεχίζω 13 | συνέχιζα | συνέχισα | θα συνεχίσω<br>να συνεχίσω | έχω συνεχίσει<br>είχα συνεχίσει | συνέχιζε<br>συνεχίζετε | συνέχισε<br>συνεχίστε |
| **I contort** (face) | συστρέφω 13 | σύστρεφα | σύστρεψα | θα συστρέψω<br>να συστρέψω | έχω συστρέψει<br>είχα συστρέψει | σύστρεφε<br>συστρέφετε | σύστρεψε<br>συστρέψτε |
| **I contract** | *συστέλλομαι 14* | *συστελλόμουν* | *συστάλθηκα* | *θα συσταλθώ*<br>*να συσταλθώ* | *έχω συσταλθεί*<br>*είχα συσταλθεί* | *να συστέλλεσαι*<br>*συστέλλεστε* | *συστάλσου*<br>*συσταλθείτε* |
| **I contradict** | αντιφάσκω 13 | αντέφασκα | αντέφασκα | θα αντιφάσκω<br>να αντιφάσκω | – | – | αντίφασκε<br>αντιφάσκετε |
| **I contrast** | αντιπαραβάλλω 13 | αντιπαρέβαλλα | αντιπαρέβαλα | θα αντιπαραβάλω<br>να αντιπαραβάλω | έχω αντιπαραβάλει<br>είχα αντιπαραβάλει | αντιπαράβαλλε<br>αντιπαραβάλλετε | αντιπαράβαλε<br>αντιπαραβάλτε |
| **I contribute** | συνεισφέρω 13 | συνείσφερα | συνεισέφερα | θα συνεισφέρω<br>να συνεισφέρω | έχω συνεισφέρει<br>είχα συνεισφέρει | να συνεισφέρεις<br>συνεισφέρετε | συνείσφερε<br>συνεισφέρτε |
| **I contribute** | συμβάλλω 13 | συνέβαλλα | συνέβαλα | θα συμβάλω<br>να συμβάλω | έχω συμβάλει<br>είχα συμβάλει | σύμβαλλε<br>συμβάλλετε | σύμβαλε<br>συμβάλτε |
| **I contrive** | κατορθώνω 13 | κατόρθωνα | κατόρθωσα | θα κατορθώσω<br>να κατορθώσω | έχω κατορθώσει<br>είχα κατορθώσει | κατόρθωνε<br>κατορθώνετε | κατόρθωσε<br>κατορθώστε |
| **I control** (inflation) | συγκρατώ 15 | συγκρατούσα | συγκράτησα | θα συγκρατήσω<br>να συγκρατήσω | έχω συγκρατήσει<br>είχα συγκρατήσει | συγκράτα<br>συγκρατάτε | συγκράτησε<br>συγκρατήστε |

| English Verb | Present | Imperfect | Past | Simple Future<br>Simple Subjunctive | Present Perfect<br>Past Perfect | Continuous Imperative | Simple Imperative |
|---|---|---|---|---|---|---|---|
| **I convene** | συγκαλώ 17 | συγκαλούσα | συγκάλεσα | θα συγκαλέσω<br>να συγκαλέσω | έχω συγκαλέσει<br>είχα συγκαλέσει | να συγκαλείς<br>συγκαλείτε | συγκάλεσε<br>συγκαλέστε |
| **I converge** | συγκλίνω 13 | σύγκλινα | συνέκλινα | θα συγκλίνω<br>να συγκλίνω | έχω συγκλίνει<br>είχα συγκλίνει | σύγκλινε<br>συγκλίνετε | σύγκλινε<br>συγκλίνετε |
| **I converse** | συνομιλώ 17 | συνομιλούσα | συνομίλησα | θα συνομιλήσω<br>να συνομιλήσω | έχω συνομιλήσει<br>είχα συνομιλήσει | να συνομιλείς<br>συνομιλείτε | συνομίλησε<br>συνομιλήστε |
| **I convert** | μετατρέπω 13 | μετέτρεπα | μετέτρεψα | θα μετατρέψω<br>να μετατρέψω | έχω μετατρέψει<br>είχα μετατρέψει | μετάτρεπε<br>μετατρέπετε | μετάτρεψε<br>μετατρέψτε |
| **I convert**<br>(of religion) | προσηλυτίζω 13 | προσηλύτιζα | προσηλύτισα | θα προσηλυτίσω<br>να προσηλυτίσω | έχω προσηλυτίσει<br>είχα προσηλυτίσει | προσηλύτιζε<br>προσηλυτίζετε | προσηλύτισε<br>προσηλυτίστε |
| **I convince** | πείθω 13 | έπειθα | έπεισα | θα πείσω<br>να πείσω | έχω πείσει<br>είχα πείσει | πείθε<br>πείθετε | πείσε<br>πείστε |
| **I cook** | μαγειρεύω 13 | μαγείρευα | μαγείρεψα | θα μαγειρέψω<br>να μαγειρέψω | έχω μαγειρέψει<br>είχα μαγειρέψει | μαγείρευε<br>μαγειρεύετε | μαγείρεψε<br>μαγειρέψτε |
| **I cook up**<br>(makeup/think up) | σκαρώνω 13 | σκάρωνα | σκάρωσα | θα σκαρώσω<br>να σκαρώσω | έχω σκαρώσει<br>είχα σκαρώσει | σκάρωνε<br>σκαρώνετε | σκάρωσε<br>σκαρώστε |
| **I cool** | δροσίζω 13 | δρόσιζα | δρόσισα | θα δροσίσω<br>να δροσίσω | έχω δροσίσει<br>είχα δροσίσει | δρόσιζε<br>δροσίζετε | δρόσισε<br>δροσίστε |
| **I coop up** | μαντρώνω 13 | μάντρωνα | μάντρωσα | θα μαντρώσω<br>να μαντρώσω | έχω μαντρώσει<br>είχα μαντρώσει | μάντρωνε<br>μαντρώνετε | μάντρωσε<br>μαντρώστε |
| **I cooperate** | *συνεργάζομαι 14* | *συνεργαζόμουν* | *συνεργάστηκα* | *θα συνεργαστώ*<br>*να συνεργαστώ* | *έχω συνεργαστεί*<br>*είχα συνεργαστεί* | *να συνεργάζεσαι*<br>*συνεργάζεστε* | *συνεργάσου*<br>*συνεργαστείτε* |
| **I coordinate** | συντονίζω 13 | συντόνιζα | συντόνισα | θα συντονίσω<br>να συντονίσω | έχω συντονίσει<br>είχα συντονίσει | συντόνιζε<br>συντονίζετε | συντόνισε<br>συντονίστε |

| English Verb | Present | Imperfect | Past | Simple Future<br>Simple Subjunctive | Present Perfect<br>Past Perfect | Continuous Imperative | Simple Imperative |
|---|---|---|---|---|---|---|---|
| **I copy** | αντιγράφω 13 | αντέγραφα | αντέγραψα | θα αντιγράψω<br>να αντιγράψω | έχω αντιγράψει<br>είχα αντιγράψει | αντίγραφε<br>αντιγράφετε | αντίγραψε<br>αντιγράψτε |
| **I corner** | στριμώχνω 13 | στρίμωχνα | στρίμωξα | θα στριμώξω<br>να στριμώξω | έχω στριμώξει<br>είχα στριμώξει | στρίμωχνε<br>στριμώχνετε | στρίμωξε<br>στριμώξτε |
| **I correct** | διορθώνω 13 | διόρθωνα | διόρθωσα | θα διορθώσω<br>να διορθώσω | έχω διορθώσει<br>είχα διορθώσει | διόρθωνε<br>διορθώνετε | διόρθωσε<br>διορθώστε |
| **I correspond** | αλληλογραφώ 17 | αλληλογραφούσα | αλληλογράφησα | θα αλληλογραφήσω<br>να αλληλογραφήσω | έχω αλληλογραφήσει<br>είχα αλληλογραφήσει | να αλληλογραφείς<br>αλληλογραφείτε | αλληλογράφησε<br>αλληλογραφήστε |
| **I corrode**<br>(of metal) | *διαβρώνομαι 14* | *διαβρωνόμουν* | *διαβρώθηκα* | *θα διαβρωθώ*<br>*να διαβρωθώ* | *έχω διαβρωθεί*<br>*είχα διαβρωθεί* | *να διαβρώνεσαι*<br>*διαβρώνεστε* | *διαβρώσου*<br>*διαβρωθείτε* |
| **I corrupt**<br>(someone) | διαφθείρω 13 | διέφθειρα | διέφθειρα | θα διαφθείρω<br>να διαφθείρω | έχω διαφθείρει<br>είχα διαφθείρει | διάφθειρε<br>διαφθείρετε | διάφθειρε<br>διαφθείρτε |
| **I cost** | κοστίζω 13 | κόστιζα | κόστισα | θα κοστίσω<br>να κοστίσω | έχω κοστίσει<br>είχα κοστίσει | κόστιζε<br>κοστίζετε | κόστισε<br>κοστίστε |
| **I cough** | βήχω 13 | έβηχα | έβηξα | θα βήξω<br>να βήξω | έχω βήξει<br>είχα βήξει | βήχε<br>βήχετε | βήξε<br>βήξτε |
| **I count on** | *στηρίζομαι 14* | *στηριζόμουν* | *στηρίχτηκα* | *θα στηριχτώ*<br>*να στηριχτώ* | *έχω στηριχτεί*<br>*είχα στηριχτεί* | *να στηρίζεσαι*<br>*στηρίζεστε* | *στηρίξου*<br>*στηριχτείτε* |
| **I counterattack** | *αντεπιτίθεμαι 42* | *αντεπιτιθόμουν* | *αντεπιτέθηκα* | *θα αντεπιτεθώ*<br>*να αντεπιθετώ* | *έχω αντεπιτεθεί*<br>*είχα αντεπιτεθεί* | *να αντεπιτίθεσαι*<br>*αντεπιτίθεστε* | *αντεπιθέσου*<br>*αντεπιτεθείτε* |
| **I counterfeit** | παραχαράσσω 13 | παραχάρασσα | παραχάραξα | θα παραχαράξω<br>να παραχαράξω | έχω παραχαράξει<br>είχα παραχαράξει | παραχάρασσε<br>παραχαράσσετε | παραχάραξε<br>παραχαράξτε |
| **I countersign** | προσυπογράφω 13 | προσυπόγραφα | προσυπόγραψα | θα προσυπογράψω<br>να προσυπογράψω | έχω προσυπογράψει<br>είχα προσυπογράψει | προσυπόγραφε<br>προσυπογράφετε | προσυπόγραψε<br>προσυπογράψτε |

| English Verb | Present | Imperfect | Past | Simple Future<br>Simple Subjunctive | Present Perfect<br>Past Perfect | Continuous Imperative | Simple Imperative |
|---|---|---|---|---|---|---|---|
| **I cover** | σκεπάζω 13 | σκέπαζα | σκέπασα | θα σκεπάσω<br>να σκεπάσω | έχω σκεπάσει<br>είχα σκεπάσει | σκέπαζε<br>σκεπάζετε | σκέπασε<br>σκεπάστε |
| **I cover up** | συγκαλύπτω 13 | συγκάλυπτα | συγκάλυψα | θα συγκαλύψω<br>να συγκαλύψω | έχω συγκαλύψει<br>είχα συγκαλύψει | συγκάλυπτε<br>συγκαλύπτετε | συγκάλυψε<br>συγκαλύψτε |
| **I cower** | κουβαριάζω 13 | κουβάριαζα | κουβάριασα | θα κουβαριάσω<br>να κουβαριάσω | έχω κουβαριάσει<br>είχα κουβαριάσει | κουβάριαζε<br>κουβαριάζετε | κουβάριασε<br>κουβαριάστε |
| **I crackle** | τριζοβολάω 15 | τριζοβολούσα | τριζοβόλησα | θα τριζοβολήσω<br>να τριζοβολήσω | έχω τριζοβολήσει<br>είχα τριζοβολήσει | τριζοβόλα<br>τριζοβολάτε | τριζοβόλησε<br>τριζοβολήστε |
| **I cram** | παραγεμίζω 13 | παραγέμιζα | παραγέμισα | θα παραγεμίσω<br>να παραγεμίσω | έχω παραγεμίσει<br>είχα παραγεμίσει | παραγέμιζε<br>παραγεμίζετε | παραγέμισε<br>παραγεμίστε |
| **I crash** (collide) | *συγκρούομαι 14* | *συγκρουόμουν* | *συγκρούστηκα* | *θα συγκρουστώ*<br>*να συγκρουστώ* | *έχω συγκρουστεί*<br>*είχα συγκρουστεί* | *να συγκρούεσαι*<br>*συγκρούεστε* | *συγκρούσου*<br>*συγκρουστείτε* |
| **I crave** | λαχταρ(ά)ώ 15 | λαχταρούσα | λαχτάρησα | θα λαχταρήσω<br>να λαχταρήσω | έχω λαχταρήσει<br>είχα λαχταρήσει | λαχτάρα<br>λαχταράτε | λαχτάρησε<br>λαχταρήστε |
| **I crawl** | μπουσουλάω 15 | μπουσουλούσα | μπουσούλησα | θα μπουσουλήσω<br>να μπουσουλήσω | έχω μπουσουλήσει<br>είχα μπουσουλήσει | μπουσούλα<br>μπουσουλάτε | μπουσούλησε<br>μπουσουλήστε |
| **I crawl** (traffic) | τσουλάω 15 | τσουλούσα | τσούλησα | θα τσουλήσω<br>να τσουλήσω | έχω τσουλήσει<br>είχα τσουλήσει | τσούλα<br>τσουλάτε | τσούλησε<br>τσουλήστε |
| **I creak** | τρίζω 13 | έτριζα | έτριξα | θα τρίξω<br>να τρίξω | έχω τρίξει<br>είχα τρίξει | τρίζε<br>τρίζετε | τρίξε<br>τρίξτε |
| **I create** | δημιουργώ 17 | δημιουργούσα | δημιούργησα | θα δημιουργήσω<br>να δημιουργήσω | έχω δημιουργήσει<br>είχα δημιουργήσει | να δημιουργείς<br>δημιουργείτε | δημιούργησε<br>δημιουργήστε |
| **I credit** (finance) | πιστώνω 13 | πίστωνα | πίστωσα | θα πιστώσω<br>να πιστώσω | έχω πιστώσει<br>είχα πιστώσει | πίστωνε<br>πιστώνετε | πίστωσε<br>πιστώστε |

| English Verb | Present | Imperfect | Past | Simple Future<br>Simple Subjunctive | Present Perfect<br>Past Perfect | Continuous Imperative | Simple Imperative |
|---|---|---|---|---|---|---|---|
| **I creep** | *σέρνομαι 14* | *σερνόμουν* | *σύρθηκα* | *θα συρθώ*<br>*να συρθώ* | *έχω συρθεί*<br>*είχα συρθεί* | *να σέρνεσαι*<br>*σέρνεστε* | *σύρσου*<br>*συρθείτε* |
| **I cringe** | ζαρώνω 14 | ζάρωνα | ζάρωσα | θα ζαρώσω<br>να ζαρώσω | έχω ζαρώσει<br>είχα ζαρώσει | ζάρωνε<br>ζαρώνετε | ζάρωσε<br>ζαρώστε |
| **I crinkle** | τσαλακώνω 13 | τσαλάκωνα | τσαλάκωσα | θα τσαλακώσω<br>να τσαλακώσω | έχω τσαλακώσει<br>είχα τσαλακώσει | τσαλάκωνε<br>τσαλακώνετε | τσαλάκωσε<br>τσαλακώστε |
| **I cripple** | σακατεύω 13 | σακάτευα | σακάτεψα | θα σακατέψω<br>να σακατέψω | έχω σακατέψει<br>είχα σακατέψει | σακάτευε<br>σακατεύετε | σακάτεψε<br>σακατέψτε |
| **I criticize** | κριτικάρω 13 | κριτίκαρα | κριτίκαρα | θα κριτικάρω<br>να κριτικάρω | έχω κριτικάρει<br>είχα κριτικάρει | κριτίκαρε<br>κριτικάρετε | κριτίκαρε<br>κριτικάρτε |
| **I croak** | κοάζω 13 | κόαζα | κόαξα | θα κοάξει<br>να κοάξει | έχω κοάξει<br>είχα κοάξει | κόαζε<br>κοάζετε | κόαξε<br>κοάξτε |
| **I crop up** | ξεφυτρώνω 13 | ξεφύτρωνα | ξεφύτρωσα | θα ξεφυτρώσω<br>να ξεφυτρώσω | έχω ξεφυτρώσει<br>είχα ξεφυτρώσει | ξεφύτρωνε<br>ξεφυτρώνετε | ξεφύτρωσε<br>ξεφυτρώστε |
| **I cross** (street) | διασχίζω 13 | διέσχιζα | διέσχισα | θα διασχίσω<br>να διασχίσω | έχω διασχίσει<br>είχα διασχίσει | διάσχιζε<br>διασχίζετε | διάσχισε<br>διασχίστε |
| **I cross myself** | *σταυροκοπιέμαι 16* | *σταυροκοπιόμουν* | *σταυροκοπήθηκα* | *θα σταυροκοπηθώ*<br>*να σταυροκοπηθώ* | *έχω σταυροκοπηθεί*<br>*είχα σταυροκοπηθεί* | *να σταυροκοπιέσαι*<br>*σταυροκοπιέστε* | *σταυροκοπήσου*<br>*σταυροκοπηθείτε* |
| **I cross-check** | διασταυρώνω 13 | διεσταύρωνα | διεσταύρωσα | θα διασταυρώσω<br>να διασταυρώσω | έχω διασταυρώσει<br>είχα διασταυρώσει | διασταύρωνε<br>διασταυρώνετε | διασταύρωσε<br>διασταυρώστε |
| **I crowd** | *στριμώχνομαι 14* | *στριμωχνόμουν* | *στριμώχτηκα* | *θα στριμωχτώ*<br>*να στριμωχτώ* | *έχω στριμωχτεί*<br>*είχα στριμωχτεί* | *να στριμώχνεσαι*<br>*στριμώχνεστε* | *στριμώξου*<br>*στριμωχτείτε* |
| **I crown** | στέφω 13 | έστεφα | έστεψα | θα στέψω<br>να στέψω | έχω στέψει<br>είχα στέψει | στέφε<br>στέφετε | στέψε<br>στέψτε |

| English Verb | Present | Imperfect | Past | Simple Future<br>Simple Subjunctive | Present Perfect<br>Past Perfect | Continuous Imperative | Simple Imperative |
|---|---|---|---|---|---|---|---|
| **I crucify** | σταυρώνω 15 | σταύρωνα | σταύρωσα | θα σταυρώσω<br>να σταυρώσω | έχω σταυρώσει<br>είχα σταυρώσει | σταύρωνε<br>σταυρώνετε | σταύρωσε<br>σταυρώστε |
| **I crunch** | τραγανίζω 13 | τραγάνιζα | τραγάνισα | θα τραγανίσω<br>να τραγανίσω | έχω τραγανίσει<br>είχα τραγανίσει | τραγάνιζε<br>τραγανίζετε | τραγάνισε<br>τραγανίστε |
| **I crush** (ice) | θρυμματίζω 13 | θρυμμάτιζα | θρυμμάτισα | θα θρυμματίσω<br>να θρυμματίσω | έχω θρυμματίσει<br>είχα θρυμματίσει | θρυμμάτιζε<br>θρυμματίζετε | θρυμμάτισε<br>θρυμματίστε |
| **I crush** | τσακίζω 13 | τσάκιζα | τσάκισα | θα τσακίσω<br>να τσακίσω | έχω τσακίσει<br>είχα τσακίσει | τσάκιζε<br>τσακίζετε | τσάκισε<br>τσακίστε |
| **I cry** | κλαί(γ)ω 20 | έκλαιγα | έκλαψα | θα κλάψω<br>να κλάψω | έχω κλάψει<br>είχα κλάψει | κλαίγε<br>κλαίγετε | κλάψε<br>κλάψτε |
| **I crystalise** | αποκρυσταλλώνω 13 | αποκρυστάλλωνα | αποκρυστάλλωσα | θα απο-<br>κρυσταλλώσω | έχω απο-<br>κρυσταλλώσει | απο-<br>κρυστάλλωνε | απο-<br>κρυστάλλωσε |
| | | | | να απο-<br>κρυσταλλώσω | είχα απο-<br>κρυσταλλώσει | απο-<br>κρυσταλλώνετε | απο-<br>κρυσταλλώστε |
| **I cuckold** | κερατώνω 17 | κεράτωνα | κεράτωσα | θα κερατώσω<br>να κερατώσω | έχω κερατώσει<br>είχα κερατώσει | κεράτωνε<br>κερατώνετε | κεράτωσε<br>κερατώστε |
| **I cultivate** | καλλιεργώ 17 | καλλιεργούσα | καλλιέργησα | θα καλλιεργήσω<br>να καλλιεργήσω | έχω καλλιεργήσει<br>είχα καλλιεργήσει | να καλλιεργείς<br>καλλιεργείτε | καλλιέργησε<br>καλλιεργήστε |
| **I curb** | χαλιναγωγώ 17 | χαλιναγωγούσα | χαλιναγώγησα | θα χαλιναγωγήσω<br>να χαλιναγωγήσω | έχω χαλιναγωγήσει<br>είχα χαλιναγωγήσει | να χαλιναγωγείς<br>χαλιναγωγείτε | χαλιναγώγησε<br>χαλιναγωγήστε |
| **I cure** | θεραπεύω 13 | θεράπευα | θεράπευσα | θα θεραπεύσω<br>να θεραπεύσω | έχω θεραπεύσει<br>είχα θεραπεύσει | θεράπευε<br>θεραπεύετε | θεράπευσε<br>θεραπεύστε |
| **I curl** | κατσαρώνω 13 | κατσάρωνα | κατσάρωσα | θα κατσαρώσω<br>νά κατσαρώσω | έχω κατσαρώσει<br>είχα κατσαρώσει | κατσάρωνε<br>κατσαρώνετε | κατσάρωσε<br>κατσαρώστε |

| English Verb | Present | Imperfect | Past | Simple Future<br>Simple Subjunctive | Present Perfect<br>Past Perfect | Continuous Imperative | Simple Imperative |
|---|---|---|---|---|---|---|---|
| **I curl up** | *κουλουριάζομαι 14* | *κουλουριαζόμουν* | *κουλουριάστηκα* | *θα κουλουριαστώ*<br>*να κουλουριαστώ* | *έχω κουλουριαστεί*<br>*είχα κουλουριαστεί* | *να κουλουριάζεσαι*<br>*κουλουριάζεστε* | *κουλουριάσου*<br>*κουλουριαστείτε* |
| **I curse** | *καταριέμαι 16* | *καταριόμουν* | *καταράστηκα* | *θα καταραστώ*<br>*να καταραστώ* | *έχω καταραστεί*<br>*είχα καταραστεί* | *να καταριέσαι*<br>*καταριέστε* | *καταράσου*<br>*καταραστείτε* |
| **I curse** | αναθεματίζω 13 | αναθεμάτιζα | αναθεμάτισα | θα αναθεματίσω<br>να αναθεματίσω | έχω αναθεματίσει<br>είχα αναθεματίσει | αναθεμάτιζε<br>αναθεματίζετε | αναθεμάτισε<br>αναθεματίστε |
| **I cut** | κόβω 13 | έκοβα | έκοψα | θα κόψω<br>να κόψω | έχω κόψει<br>είχα κόψει | κόβε<br>κόβετε | κόψε<br>κόψτε |
| **I cease** | παύω 13 | έπαυα | έπαψα | θα πάψω<br>να πάψω | έχω πάψει<br>είχα πάψει | παύε<br>παύετε | πάψε<br>πάψτε |
| **I crack** | κροταλίζω 13 | κροτάλιζα | κροτάλισα | θα κροταλίσω<br>να κροταλίσω | έχω κροταλίσει<br>είχα κροταλίσει | κροτάλιζε<br>κροταλίζετε | κροτάλισε<br>κροταλίστε |
| **I damage** | βλάπτω 13 | έβλαπτα | έβλαψα | θα βλάψω<br>να βλάψω | έχω βλάψει<br>είχα βλάψει | βλάπτε<br>βλάπτετε | βλάψε<br>βλάψτε |
| **I damage** | ζημιώνω 13 | ζημίωνα | ζημίωσα | θα ζημιώσω<br>να ζημιώσω | έχω ζημιώσει<br>είχα ζημιώσει | ζημίωνε<br>ζημιώνετε | ζημίωσε<br>ζημιώστε |
| **I dampen** | υγραίνω 13 | ύγραινα | ύγρανα | θα υγράνω<br>να υγράνω | έχω υγράνει<br>είχα υγράνει | ύγραινε<br>υγραίνετε | ύγρανε<br>υγράντε |
| **I dance** | χορεύω 13 | χόρευα | χόρεψα | θα χορέψω<br>να χορέψω | έχω χορέψει<br>είχα χορέψει | χόρευε<br>χορεύετε | χόρεψε<br>χορέψτε |
| **I am in danger** | κινδυνεύω 13 | κινδύνευα | κινδύνεψα | θα κινδυνέψω<br>να κινδυνέψω | έχω κινδυνέψει<br>είχα κινδυνέψει | κινδύνευε<br>κινδυνεύετε | κινδύνεψε<br>κινδυνέψτε |
| **I dangle** | ταλαντεύω 13 | ταλάντευα | ταλάντευσα | θα ταλαντεύσω<br>να ταλαντεύσω | έχω ταλαντεύσει<br>είχα ταλαντεύσει | ταλάντευε<br>ταλαντεύετε | ταλάντευσε<br>ταλαντεύστε |

| English Verb | Present | Imperfect | Past | Simple Future<br>Simple Subjunctive | Present Perfect<br>Past Perfect | Continuous Imperative | Simple Imperative |
|---|---|---|---|---|---|---|---|
| **I dare** | τολμώ 15 | τολμούσα | τόλμησα | θα τολμήσω<br>να τολμήσω | έχω τολμήσει<br>είχα τολμήσει | τόλμα<br>τολμάτε | τόλμησε<br>τολμήστε |
| **I darn** | μαντάρω 13 | μάνταρα | μαντάρησα | θα μαντάρω<br>να μαντάρω | έχω μαντάρει<br>είχα μαντάρει | μάνταρε<br>μαντάρετε | μαντάρησε<br>μανταρήστε |
| **I date** (object) | χρονολογώ 17 | χρονολογούσα | χρονολόγησα | θα χρονολογήσω<br>να χρονολογήσω | έχω χρονολογήσει<br>είχα χρονολογήσει | να χρονολογείς<br>χρονολογείτε | χρονολόγησε<br>χρονολογήστε |
| **I daub** | πασαλείβω 13 | πασάλειβα | πασάλειψα | θα πασαλείψω<br>να πασαλείψω | έχω πασαλείψει<br>είχα πασαλέιψει | πασάλειβε<br>πασαλείβετε | πασάλειψε<br>πασαλείψτε |
| **I daunt** | πτοώ 17 | πτοούσα | πτόησα | θα πτοήσω<br>να πτοήσω | έχω πτοήσει<br>είχα πτοήσει | να πτοείς<br>πτοείτε | πτόησε<br>πτοήστε |
| **I dawdle** | χασομερώ 15 | χασομερούσα | χασομέρησα | θα χασομερήσω<br>να χασομερήσω | έχω χασομερήσει<br>είχα χασομερήσει | χασομέρα<br>χασομεράτε | χασομέρησε<br>χασομερήστε |
| **It dawns** | ξημερώνει 13 | ξημέρωνε | ξημέρωσε | θα ξημερώσει<br>να ξημερώσει | έχει ξημερώσει<br>είχε ξημερώσει | ξημέρωνε<br>ξημερώνετε | ξημέρωσε<br>ξημερώστε |
| **I daydream** | ονειροπολώ 17 | ονειροπολούσα | ονειροπόλησα | θα ονειροπολήσω<br>να ονειροπολήσω | έχω ονειροπολήσει<br>είχα ονειροπολήσει | να ονειροπολείς<br>ονειροπολείτε | ονειροπόλησε<br>ονειροπολήστε |
| **I daze** | ζαυλακώνω 13 | ζαυλάκωνα | ζαυλάκωσα | θα ζαυλακώσω<br>να ζαυλακώσω | έχω ζαυλακώσει<br>είχα ζαυλακώσει | ζαυλάκωνε<br>ζαυλακώνετε | ζαυλάκωσε<br>ζαυλακώστε |
| **I dazzle** | εκτυφλώνω 13 | εκτύφλωνα | εκτύφλωσα | θα εκτυφλώσω<br>να εκτυφλώσω | έχω εκτυφλώσει<br>είχα εκτυφλώσει | εκτύφλωνε<br>εκτυφλώνετε | εκτύφλωσε<br>εκτυφλώστε |
| **I dazzle** | θαμπώνω 13 | θάμπωνα | θάμπωσα | θα θαμπώσω<br>να θαμπώσω | έχω θαμπώσει<br>είχα θαμπώσει | θάμπωνε<br>θαμπώνετε | θάμπωσε<br>θαμπώστε |
| **I deaden** | επιβραδύνω 13 | επιβράδυνα | επιβράδυνα | θα επιβραδύνω<br>να επιβραδύνω | έχω επιβραδύνει<br>είχα επιβραδύνει | επιβράδυνε<br>επιβραδύνετε | επιβράδυνε<br>επιβραδύντε |

| English Verb | Present | Imperfect | Past | Simple Future<br>Simple Subjunctive | Present Perfect<br>Past Perfect | Continuous Imperative | Simple Imperative |
|---|---|---|---|---|---|---|---|
| **I deafen** | (ξε)κουφαίνω 13 | ξεκούφαινα | ξεκούφανα | θα ξεκουφάνω<br>να ξεκουφάνω | έχω ξεκουφάνει<br>είχα ξεκουφάνει | ξεκούφαινε<br>ξεκουφαίνετε | ξεκούφανε<br>ξεκουφάντε |
| **I deal with** | *πραγματεύομαι 14* | *πραγματευόμουν* | *πραγματεύτηκα* | *θα πραγματευτώ*<br>*να πραγματευτώ* | *έχω πραγματευτεί*<br>*είχα πραγματευτεί* | *να πραγματεύεσαι*<br>*πραγματεύεστε* | *πραγματεύσου*<br>*πραγματευτείτε* |
| **I debase** | υποβιβάζω 13 | υποβίβαζα | υποβίβασα | θα υποβιβάσω<br>να υποβιβάσω | έχω υποβιβάσει<br>είχα υποβιβάσει | υποβίβαζε<br>υποβιβάζετε | υποβίβασε<br>υποβιβάστε |
| **I decay** | *αποσαρθρώνομαι 14* | *αποσαρθρωνόμουν* | *αποσαρθρώθηκα* | *θα αποσαρθρωθώ*<br>*να αποσαρθρωθώ* | *έχω αποσαρθρωθεί*<br>*είχα αποσαρθρωθεί* | *να αποσαρθρώνεσαι*<br>*αποσαρθρώνεστε* | *αποσαρθρώσου*<br>*αποσαρθρωθείτε* |
| **I decen-tralise** | αποκεντρώνω 13 | αποκέντρωνα | αποκέντρωσα | θα αποκεντρώσω<br>να αποκεντρώσω | έχω αποκεντρώσει<br>είχα αποκεντρώσει | αποκέντρωνε<br>αποκεντρώνετε | αποκέντρωσε<br>αποκεντρώστε |
| **I decide** | αποφασίζω 13 | αποφάσιζα | αποφάσισα | θα αποφασίσω<br>να αποφασίσω | έχω αποφασίσει<br>είχα αποφασίσει | αποφάσιζε<br>αποφασίζετε | αποφάσισε<br>αποφασίστε |
| **I decipher** | αποκρυπτο-γραφώ 17 | αποκρυπτο-γραφούσα | αποκρυπτο-γράφησα | θα αποκρυπτο-γραφήσω<br>να αποκρυπτο-γραφήσω | έχω αποκρυπτο-γραφήσει<br>είχα αποκρυπτο-γραφήσει | να αποκρυπτο-γραφείς<br>αποκρυπτο-γραφείτε | αποκρυπτο-γράφησε<br>αποκρυπτο-γραφήστε |
| **I declare** (result) | ανακοινώνω 13 | ανακοίνωνα | ανακοίνωσα | θα ανακοινώσω<br>να ανακοινώσω | έχω ανακοινώσει<br>είχα ανακοινώσει | ανακοίνωνε<br>ανακοινώνετε | ανακοίνωσε<br>ανακοινώστε |
| **I declare** | δηλώνω 13 | δήλωνα | δήλωσα | θα δηλώσω<br>να δηλώσω | έχω δηλώσει<br>είχα δηλώσει | δήλωνε<br>δηλώνετε | δήλωσε<br>δηλώστε |
| **I declassify** | δημοσιοποιώ 17 | δημοσιοποιούσα | δημοσιοποίησα | θα δημοσιοποιήσω<br>να δημοσιοποιήσω | έχω δημοσιοποιήσει<br>είχα δημοσιοποιήσει | να δημοσιοποιείς<br>δημοσιοποιείτε | δημοσιοποίησε<br>δημοσιοποιήστε |
| **I decline** | παρακμάζω 13 | παρήκμαζα | παρήκμασα | θα παρακμάσω<br>να παρακμάσω | έχω παρακμάσει<br>είχα παρακμάσει | παράκμαζε<br>παρακμάζετε | παράκμασε<br>παρακμάστε |

| English Verb | Present | Imperfect | Past | Simple Future<br>Simple Subjunctive | Present Perfect<br>Past Perfect | Continuous Imperative | Simple Imperative |
|---|---|---|---|---|---|---|---|
| **I decorate** (adorn with) | στολίζω 13 | στόλιζα | στόλισα | θα στολίσω<br>να στολίσω | έχω στολίσει<br>είχα στολίσει | στόλιζε<br>στολίζετε | στόλισε<br>στολίστε |
| **I decry** | κατακρίνω 13 | κατέκρινα | κατέκρινα | θα κατακρίνω<br>να κατακρίνω | έχω κατακρίνει<br>είχα κατακρίνει | κατάκρινε<br>κατακρίνετε | κατάκρινε<br>κτακρίνετε |
| **I dedicate** | αφιερώνω 13 | αφιέρωνα | αφιέρωσα | θα αφιερώσω<br>να αφιερώσω | έχω αφιερώσει<br>είχα αφιερώσει | αφιέρωνε<br>αφιερώνετε | αφιέρωσε<br>αφιερώστε |
| **I deem** | φρονώ 17 | φρονούσα | φρόνησα | θα φρονήσω<br>να φρονήσω | έχω φρονήσει<br>είχα φρονήσει | να φρονείς<br>φρονείτε | φρόνησε<br>φρονήστε |
| **I deepen** | βαθαίνω 13 | βάθαινα | βάθυνα | θα βαθύνω<br>να βαθύνω | έχω βαθύνει<br>είχα βαθύνει | βάθαινε<br>βαθαίνετε | βάθυνε<br>βαθύντε |
| **I defend** | *υπερασπίζομαι 14* | *υπερασπιζόμουν* | *υπερασπίστηκα* | *θα υπερασπιστώ*<br>*να υπερασπιστώ* | *έχω υπερασπιστεί*<br>*είχα υπερασπιστεί* | *να υπερασπίζεσαι*<br>*υπερασπίζεστε* | *υπερασπίσου*<br>*υπερασπιστείτε* |
| **I defile** | βεβηλώνω 13 | βεβήλωνα | βεβήλωσα | θα βεβηλώσω<br>να βεβηλώσω | έχω βεβηλώσει<br>είχα βεβηλώσει | βεβήλωνε<br>βεβηλώνετε | βεβήλωσε<br>βεβηλώστε |
| **I define** | καθορίζω 13 | καθόριζα | καθόρισα | θα καθορίσω<br>να καθορίσω | έχω καθορίσει<br>είχα καθορίσει | καθόριζε<br>καθορίζετε | καθόρισε<br>καθορίστε |
| **I defuse** (crisis) | εκτονώνω 13 | εκτόνωνα | εκτόνωσα | θα εκτονώσω<br>να εκτονώσω | έχω εκτονώσει<br>είχα εκτονώσει | εκτόνωνε<br>εκτονώνετε | εκτόνωσε<br>εκτονώστε |
| **I defy** | *αντιτάσσομαι 14* | *αντιτασσόμουν* | *αντιτάχτηκα* | *θα αντιταχτώ*<br>*να αντιταχτώ* | *έχω αντιταχτεί*<br>*είχα αντιταχτεί* | *να αντιτάσσεσαι*<br>*αντιτάσσεστε* | *αντιτάξου*<br>*αντιταχτείτε* |
| **I defy** | αψηφώ 15 | αψηφούσα | αψήφησα | θα αψηφήσω<br>να αψηφήσω | έχω αψηφήσει<br>είχα αψηφήσει | αψήφα<br>αψηφάτε | αψήφησε<br>αψηφήστε |
| **I degrade** | εξευτελίζω 13 | εξευτέλιζα | εξευτέλισα | θα εξευτελίσω<br>να εξευτελίσω | έχω εξευτελίσει<br>είχα εξευτελίσει | εξευτέλιζε<br>εξευτελίζετε | εξευτέλισε<br>εξευτελίστε |

| English Verb | Present | Imperfect | Past | Simple Future<br>Simple Subjunctive | Present Perfect<br>Past Perfect | Continuous Imperative | Simple Imperative |
|---|---|---|---|---|---|---|---|
| **I delay** | καθυστερώ 17 | καθυστερούσα | καθυστέρησα | θα καθυστερήσω<br>να καθυστερήσω | έχω καθυστερήσει<br>είχα καθυστερήσει | να καθυστερείς<br>καθυστερείτε | καθυστέρησε<br>καθυστερήστε |
| **I delete** | διαγράφω 13 | διέγραφα | διέγραψα | θα διαγράψω<br>να διαγράψω | έχω διαγράψει<br>είχα διαγράψει | διάγραφε<br>διαγράφετε | διάγραψε<br>διαγράψτε |
| **I deliver**<br>(hand over) | παραδίδω 13 | παρέδιδα | παρέδωσα | θα παραδώσω<br>να παραδώσω | έχω παραδώσει<br>είχα παραδώσει | παράδιδε<br>παραδίδετε | παράδωσε<br>παραδώστε |
| **I deliver** | διανέμω 13 | διένεμα | διένειμα | θα διανείμω<br>να διανείμω | έχω διανείμει<br>είχα διανείμει | διάνεμε<br>διανέμετε | να διανέμεις<br>διανείμετε |
| **I delude** | παραπλανώ 15 | παραπλανούσα | παραπλάνησα | θα παραπλανήσω<br>να παραπλανήσω | έχω παραπλανήσει<br>είχα παραπλανήσει | παραπλάνα<br>παραπλανάτε | παραπλάνησε<br>παραπλανήστε |
| **I delude myself** | *γελιέμαι 16* | *γελιόμουν* | *γελάστηκα* | *θα γελαστώ*<br>*να γελαστώ* | *έχω γελαστεί*<br>*είχα γελαστεί* | *να γελιέσαι*<br>*γελιέστε* | *γελάσου*<br>*γελαστείτε* |
| **I demand** | απαιτώ 15 | απαιτούσα | απαίτησα | θα απαιτήσω<br>να απαιτήσω | έχω απαιτήσει<br>είχα απαιτήσει | να απαιτείς<br>απαιτείτε | απαίτησε<br>απαιτήστε |
| **I demolish** | κατεδαφίζω 13 | κατεδάφιζα | κατεδάφισα | θα κατεδαφίσω<br>να κατεδαφίσω | έχω κατεδαφίσει<br>είχα κατεδαφίσει | κατεδάφιζε<br>κατεδαφίζετε | κατεδάφισε<br>κατεδαφίστε |
| **I demonstrate** | εκδηλώνω 13 | εκδήλωνα | εκδήλωσα | θα εκδηλώσω<br>να εκδηλώσω | έχω εκδηλώσει<br>είχα εκδηλώσει | εκδήλωνε<br>εκδηλώνετε | εκδήλωσε<br>εκδηλώστε |
| **I demonstrate**<br>(protest) | διαδηλώνω 13 | διαδήλωνα | διαδήλωσα | θα διαδηλώσω<br>να διαδηλώσω | έχω διαδηλώσει<br>είχα διαδηλώσει | διαδήλωνε<br>διαδηλώνετε | διαδήλωσε<br>διαδηλώστε |
| **I demoralize** | αποκαρδιώνω 13 | αποκαρδίωνα | αποκαρδίωσα | θα αποκαρδιώσω<br>να αποκαρδιώσω | έχω αποκαρδιώσει<br>είχα αποκαρδιώσει | αποκαρδίωνε<br>αποκαρδιώνετε | αποκαρδίωσε<br>αποκαρδιώστε |

| English Verb | Present | Imperfect | Past | Simple Future<br>Simple Subjunctive | Present Perfect<br>Past Perfect | Continuous Imperative | Simple Imperative |
|---|---|---|---|---|---|---|---|
| **I denationalize** | αποκρατικο-ποιώ 17 | αποκρατικο-ποιούσα | αποκρατικο-ποίησα | θα αποκρατικο-ποιήσω | έχω αποκρατικο-ποιήσει | να αποκρατικο-ποιείς | αποκρατικο-ποίησε |
| | | | | να αποκρατικο-ποιήσω | είχα αποκρατικο-ποιήσει | αποκρατικο-ποιείτε | αποκρατικο-ποιήστε |
| **I denigrate** | δυσφημώ 17 | δυσφημούσα | δυσφήμησα | θα δυσφημήσω<br>να δυσφημήσω | έχω δυσφημήσει<br>είχα δυσφημήσει | να δυσφημείς<br>δυσφημείτε | δυσφήμησε<br>δυσφημήστε |
| **I denounce** | καταγγέλλω 13 | κατάγγελλα | κατάγγειλα | θα καταγγείλω<br>να καταγγείλω | έχω καταγγείλει<br>είχα καταγγείλει | κατάγγελλε<br>καταγγέλλετε | κατάγγειλε<br>καταγγείλτε |
| **I dent** | κοιλαίνω 13 | κοίλαινα | κοίλανα | θα κοιλάνω<br>να κοιλάνω | έχω κοιλάνει<br>είχα κοιλάνει | κοίλαινε<br>κοιλαίνετε | κοίλανε<br>κοιλάντε |
| **I deny** | *απαρνούμαι 18* | *απαρνούμουν* | *απαρνήθηκα* | *θα απαρνηθώ*<br>*να απαρνηθώ* | *έχω απαρνηθεί*<br>*είχα απαρνηθεί* | *να απαρνείσαι*<br>*απαρνείστε* | *απαρνήσου*<br>*απαρνηθείτε* |
| **I depart** | αναχωρώ 17 | αναχωρούσα | αναχώρησα | θα αναχωρήσω<br>να αναχωρήσω | έχω αναχωρήσει<br>είχα αναχωρήσει | να αναχωρείς<br>αναχωρείτε | αναχώρησε<br>αναχωρήστε |
| **I depend on** | *εξαρτώμαι 42* | *εξαρτόμουν* | *εξαρτήθηκα* | *θα εξαρτηθώ*<br>*να εξαρτηθώ* | *έχω εξαρτηθεί*<br>*είχα εξαρτηθεί* | *να εξαρτάσαι*<br>*εξαρτάστε* | *εξαρτήσου*<br>*εξαρτηθείτε* |
| **I depict** | παρασταίνω 13 | παράσταινα | παράστησα | θα παραστήσω<br>να παραστήσω | έχω παραστήσει<br>είχα παραστήσει | παράσταινε<br>παρασταίνετε | παράστησε<br>παραστήστε |
| **I depose** | εκθρονίζω 13 | εκθρόνιζα | εκθρόνισα | θα εκθρονίσω<br>να εκθρονίσω | έχω εκθρονίσει<br>είχα εκθρονίσει | εκθρόνιζε<br>εκθρονίζετε | εκθρόνισε<br>εκθρονίστε |
| **I deposit** | προκαταβάλλω 13 | προκατέβαλλα | προκατέβαλα | θα προκαταβάλω<br>να προκαταβάλω | έχω προκαταβάλει<br>είχα προκαταβάλει | προκατάβαλλε<br>προκαταβάλλετε | προκατάβαλε<br>προκαταβάλτε |
| **I depress** | καταθλίβω 13 | κατέθλιβα | κατέθλιψα | θα καταθλίψω<br>να καταθλίψω | έχω καταθλίψει<br>είχα καταθλίψει | κατάθλιβε<br>καταθλίβετε | κατάθλιψε<br>καταθλίψτε |

| English Verb | Present | Imperfect | Past | Simple Future<br>Simple Subjunctive | Present Perfect<br>Past Perfect | Continuous Imperative | Simple Imperative |
|---|---|---|---|---|---|---|---|
| **I deprive** | στερώ 17 | στερούσα | στέρησα | θα στερήσω<br>να στερήσω | έχω στερήσει<br>είχα στερήσει | να στερείς<br>στερείτε | στέρησε<br>στερήστε |
| **I deride** | περιγελώ 15 | περιγελούσα | περιγέλασα | θα περιγελάσω<br>να περιγελάσω | έχω περιγελάσει<br>είχα περιγελάσει | περιγέλα<br>περιγελάτε | περιγέλασε<br>πριγελάστε |
| **I descend** | κατεβαίνω 13 | κατέβαινα | κατέβηκα | θα κατέβω<br>να κατέβω | έχω κατέβει<br>είχα κατέβει | κατέβαινε<br>κατεβαίνετε | κατέβα<br>κατεβείτε |
| **I describe** | περιγράφω 13 | περιέγραφα | περιέγραψα | θα περιγράψω<br>να περιγράψω | έχω περιγράψει<br>είχα περιγράψει | περίγραφε<br>περιγράφετε | περίγραψε<br>περιγράψτε |
| **I desert** | λιποτακτώ 17 | λιποτακτούσα | λιποτάκτησα | θα λιποτακτήσω<br>να λιποτακτήσω | έχω λιποτακτήσει<br>είχα λιποτακτήσει | να λιποτακτείς<br>λιποτακτείτε | λιποτάκτησε<br>λιποτακτήστε |
| **I design** | σχεδιάζω 13 | σχεδίαζα | σχεδίασα | θα σχεδιάσω<br>να σχεδιάσω | έχω σχεδιάσει<br>είχα σχεδιάσει | σχεδίαζε<br>σχεδιάζετε | σχεδίασε<br>σχεδιάστε |
| **I designate** | ορίζω 13 | όριζα | όρισα | θα ορίσω<br>να ορίσω | έχω ορίσει<br>είχα ορίσει | όριζε<br>ορίζετε | όρισε<br>ορίστε |
| **I desire** | επιθυμώ 17 | επιθυμούσα | επιθύμησα | θα επιθυμήσω<br>να επιθυμήσω | έχω επιθυμήσει<br>είχα επιθυμήσει | να επιθυμείς<br>επιθυμείτε | επιθύμησε<br>επιθυμήστε |
| **I despise** | περιφρονώ 17 | περιφρονούσα | περιφρόνησα | θα περιφρονήσω<br>να περιφρονήσω | έχω περιφρονήσει<br>είχα περιφρονήσει | να περιφρονείς<br>περιφρονείτε | περιφρόνησε<br>περιφρονήστε |
| **I destroy** | καταστρέφω 13 | κατέστρεφα | κατέστρεψα | θα καταστρέψω<br>να καταστρέψω | έχω καταστρέψει<br>είχα καταστρέψει | κατάστρεφε<br>καταστρέφετε | κατάστρεψε<br>καταστρέψτε |
| **I detect** | ανιχνεύω 13 | ανίχνευα | ανίχνευσα | θα ανιχνεύσω<br>να ανιχνεύσω | έχω ανιχνεύσει<br>είχα ανιχνεύσει | ανίχνευε<br>ανιχνεύετε | ανίχνευσε<br>ανιχνεύστε |
| **I determine** | οροθετώ 17 | οροθετούσα | οροθέτησα | θα οροθετήσω<br>να οροθετήσω | έχω οροθετήσει<br>είχα οροθετήσει | να οροθετείς<br>οροθετείτε | οροθέτησε<br>οροθετήστε |

| English Verb | Present | Imperfect | Past | Simple Future<br>Simple Subjunctive | Present Perfect<br>Past Perfect | Continuous Imperative | Simple Imperative |
|---|---|---|---|---|---|---|---|
| **I detest** | *απεχθάνομαι 14* | *απεχθανόμουν* | *απεχθάνθηκα* | *θα απεχθανθώ*<br>*να απεχθανθώ* | *έχω απεχθανθεί*<br>*είχα απεχθανθεί* | *να απεχθάνεσαι*<br>*απεχθάνεστε* | *απεχθάνσου*<br>*απεχθανθείτε* |
| **I deviate** | *εκτρέπομαι 14* | *εκτρεπόμουν* | *εκτράπηκα* | *θα εκτραπώ*<br>*να εκτραπώ* | *έχω εκτραπεί*<br>*είχα εκτραπεί* | *να εκτρέπεσαι*<br>*εκτρέπεστε* | *εκτράπου*<br>*εκτραπείτε* |
| **I develop** | αναπτύσσω 13 | ανέπτυσσα | ανέπτυξα | θα αναπτύξω<br>να αναπτύξω | έχω αναπτύξει<br>είχα αναπτύξει | ανάπτυσσε<br>αναπτύσσετε | ανάπτυξε<br>αναπτύξτε |
| **I dictate** | υπαγορεύω 13 | υπαγόρευα | υπαγόρευσα | θα υπαγορεύσω<br>να υπαγορεύσω | έχω υπαγορεύσει<br>είχα υπαγορεύσει | υπαγόρευε<br>υπαγορεύετε | υπαγόρεψε<br>υπαγορέψτε |
| **I die** | πεθαίνω 13 | πέθαινα | πέθανα | θα πεθάνω<br>να πεθάνω | έχω πεθάνει<br>είχα πεθάνει | πέθαινε<br>πεθαίνετε | πέθανε<br>πεθάντε |
| **I differentiate** | διαφοροποιώ 17 | διαφοροποιούσα | διαφοροποίησα | θα διαφοροποιήσω<br>να διαφοροποιήσω | έχω διαφοροποιήσει<br>είχα διαφοροποιήσει | να διαφοροποιείς<br>διαφοροποιείτε | διαφοροποίησε<br>διαφοροποιήστε |
| **I dig** | σκάβω 13 | έσκαβα | έσκαψα | θα σκάψω<br>να σκάψω | έχω σκάψει<br>είχα σκάψει | σκάβε<br>σκάβετε | σκάψε<br>σκάψτε |
| **I dine** | δειπνώ 17 | δειπνούσα | δείπνησα | θα δειπνήσω<br>να δειπνήσω | έχω δειπνήσει<br>είχα δειπνήσει | δείπνα<br>δειπνάτε | δείπνησε<br>δειπνήστε |
| **I dip** | χαμηλώνω 13 | χαμήλωνα | χαμήλωσα | θα χαμηλώσω<br>να χαμηλώσω | έχω χαμηλώσει<br>είχα χαμηλώσει | χαμήλωνε<br>χαμηλώνετε | χαμήλωσε<br>χαμηλώστε |
| **I disagree** | διαφωνώ 17 | διαφωνούσα | διαφώνησα | θα διαφωνήσω<br>να διαφωνήσω | έχω διαφωνήσει<br>είχα διαφωνήσει | να διαφωνείς<br>διαφωνείτε | διαφώνησε<br>διαφωνήστε |
| **I disappear** | *εξαφανίζομαι 14* | *εξαφανιζόμουν* | *εξαφανίστηκα* | *θα εξαφανιστώ*<br>*να εξαφανιστώ* | *έχω εξαφανιστεί*<br>*είχα εξαφανιστεί* | *να εξαφανίζεσαι*<br>*εξαφανίζεστε* | *εξαφανίσου*<br>*εξαφανιστείτε* |
| **I disarm** | αφοπλίζω 13 | αφόπλιζα | αφόπλισα | θα αφοπλίσω<br>να αφοπλίσω | έχω αφοπλίσει<br>είχα αφοπλίσει | αφόπλιζε<br>αφοπλίζετε | αφόπλισε<br>αφοπλίστε |

| English Verb | Present | Imperfect | Past | Simple Future<br>Simple Subjunctive | Present Perfect<br>Past Perfect | Continuous Imperative | Simple Imperative |
|---|---|---|---|---|---|---|---|
| **I discourage** | αποθαρρύνω 13 | αποθάρρυνα | αποθάρρυνα | θα αποθαρρύνω<br>να αποθαρρύνω | έχω αποθαρρύνει<br>είχα αποθαρρύνει | αποθάρρυνε<br>αποθαρρύνετε | αποθάρρυνε<br>αποθαρρύντε |
| **I discover** | ανακαλύπτω 13 | ανακάλυπτα | ανακάλυψα | θα ανακαλύψω<br>να ανακαλύψω | έχω ανακαλύψει<br>είχα ανακαλύψει | ανακάλυπτε<br>ανακαλύπτετε | ανακάλυψε<br>ανακαλύψτε |
| **I discredit** | υποβαθμίζω 13 | υποβάθμιζα | υποβάθμισα | θα υποβαθμίσω<br>να υποβαθμίσω | έχω υποβαθμίσει<br>είχα υποβαθμίσει | υποβάθμιζε<br>υποβαθμίζετε | υποβάθμισε<br>υποβαθμίστε |
| **I discriminate** | διακρίνω 13 | διέκρινα | διέκρινα | θα διακρίνω<br>να διακρίνω | έχω διακρίνει<br>είχα διακρίνει | διάκρινε<br>διακρίνετε | διάκρινε<br>διακρίνετε |
| **I disconnect** | αποσυνδέω 13 | αποσύνδεα | αποσύνδεσα | θα αποσυνδέσω<br>να αποσυνδέσω | έχω αποσυνδέσει<br>είχα αποσυνδέσει | αποσύνδεε<br>αποσυνδέετε | αποσύνδεσε<br>αποσυνδέστε |
| **I discuss** | συζητώ 15 | συζητούσα | συζήτησα | θα συζητήσω<br>να συζητήσω | έχω συζητήσει<br>είχα συζητήσει | συζήτα<br>συζητάτε | συζήτησε<br>συζητήστε |
| **I disentangle** | ξεμπερδεύω 13 | ξεμπέρδευα | ξεμπέρδεψα | θα ξεμπερδέψω<br>να ξεμπερδέψω | έχω ξεμπερδέψει<br>είχα ξεμπερδέψει | ξεμπέρδευε<br>ξεμπερδεύετε | ξεμπέρδεψε<br>ξεμπερδέψτε |
| **I disgrace** | ντροπιάζω 13 | ντρόπιαζα | ντρόπιασα | θα ντροπιάσω<br>να ντροπιάσω | έχω ντροπιάσει<br>είχα ντροπιάσει | ντρόπιαζε<br>ντροπιάζετε | ντρόπιασε<br>ντροπιάστε |
| **I disinfect** | απολυμαίνω 13 | απολύμαινα | απολύμανα | θα απολυμάνω<br>να απολυμάνω | έχω απολυμάνει<br>είχα απολυμάνει | απολύμαινε<br>απολυμαίνετε | απολύμανε<br>απολυμάντε |
| **I dislocate** | εξαρθρώνω 13 | εξάρθρωνα | εξάρθρωσα | θα εξαρθρώσω<br>να εξαρθρώσω | έχω εξαρθρώσει<br>είχα εξαρθρώσει | εξάρθρωνε<br>εξαρθρώνετε | εξάρθρωσε<br>εξαρθρώστε |
| **I disobey** | παρακούω 13 | παράκουα | παράκουσα | θα παρακούσω<br>να παρακούσω | έχω παρακούσει<br>είχα παρακούσει | παράκουε<br>παρακούετε | παράκουσε<br>παρακούστε |
| **I disparage** | διασύρω 13 | διέσυρα | διέσυρα | θα διασύρω<br>να διασύρω | έχω διασύρει<br>είχα διασύρει | διάσυρε<br>διασύρετε | διάσυρε<br>διασύρτε |

| English Verb | Present | Imperfect | Past | Simple Future<br>Simple Subjunctive | Present Perfect<br>Past Perfect | Continuous Imperative | Simple Imperative |
|---|---|---|---|---|---|---|---|
| **I disperse** | διασκορπίζω 13 | διεσκόρπιζα | διεσκόρπισα | θα διασκορπίσω<br>να διασκορπίσω | έχω διασκορπίσει<br>είχα διασκορπίσει | διασκόρπιζε<br>διασκορπίζετε | διασκόρπισε<br>διασκορπίστε |
| **I displace** | εκτοπίζω 13 | εκτόπιζα | εκτόπισα | θα εκτοπίσω<br>να εκτοπίσω | έχω εκτοπίσει<br>είχα εκτοπίσει | εκτόπιζε<br>εκτοπίζετε | εκτόπισε<br>εκτοπίστε |
| **I displease** | δυσαρεστώ 17 | δυσαρεστούσα | δυσαρέστησα | θα δυσαρεστήσω<br>να δυσαρεστήσω | έχω δυσαρεστήσει<br>είχα δυσαρεστήσει | να δυσαρεστείς<br>δυσαρεστείτε | δυσαρέστησε<br>δυσαρεστήστε |
| **I dispute** | λογομαχώ 17 | λογομαχούσα | λογομάχησα | θα λογομαχήσω<br>να λογομαχήσω | έχω λογομαχήσει<br>είχα λογομαχήσει | να λογομαχείς<br>λογομαχείτε | λογομάχησε<br>λογομαχήστε |
| **I disappoint** | απογοητεύω 13 | απογοήτευα | απογοήτεψα | θα απογοητέψω<br>να απογοητέψω | έχω απογοητέψει<br>είχα απογοητέψει | απογοήτευε<br>απογοητεύετε | απογοήτεψε<br>απογοητέψτε |
| **I disrupt** | διασπώ 15 | διασπούσα | διέσπασα | θα διασπάσω<br>να διασπάσω | έχω διασπάσει<br>είχα διασπάσει | να διασπάς<br>διασπάτε | διάσπασε<br>διασπάστε |
| **I dissolve** | διαλύω 13 | διέλυα | διέλυσα | θα διαλύσω<br>να διαλύσω | έχω διαλύσει<br>είχα διαλύσει | διάλυε<br>διαλύετε | διάλυσε<br>διαλύστε |
| **I disarm** | αφοπλίζω 13 | αφόπλιζα | αφόπλισα | θα αφοπλίσω<br>να αφοπλίσω | έχω αφοπλίσει<br>είχα αφοπλίσει | αφόπλιζε<br>αφοπλίζετε | αφόπλισε<br>αφοπλίστε |
| **I distract** | αποσπώ 15 | αποσπούσα | απόσπασα | θα αποσπάσω<br>να αποσπάσω | έχω αποσπάσει<br>είχα αποσπάσει | να αποσπάς<br>αποσπάτε | απόσπασε<br>αποσπάστε |
| **I distress** | θλίβω 13 | έθλιβα | έθλιψα | θα θλίψω<br>να θλίψω | έχω θλίψει<br>είχα θλίψει | θλίβε<br>θλίβετε | θλίψε<br>θλίψτε |
| **I distribute** | μοιράζω 13 | μοίραζα | μοίρασα | θα μοιράσω<br>να μοιράσω | έχω μοιράσει<br>είχα μοιράσει | μοίραζε<br>μοιράζετε | μοίρασε<br>μοιράστε |
| **I disturb** | αναστατώνω 13 | αναστάτωνα | αναστάτωσα | θα αναστατώσω<br>να αναστατώσω | έχω αναστατώσει<br>είχα αναστατώσει | αναστάτωνε<br>αναστατώνετε | αναστάτωσε<br>αναστατώστε |

| English Verb | Present | Imperfect | Past | Simple Future<br>Simple Subjunctive | Present Perfect<br>Past Perfect | Continuous Imperative | Simple Imperative |
|---|---|---|---|---|---|---|---|
| **I dislike** | αντιπαθώ 17 | αντιπαθούσα | αντιπάθησα | θα αντιπαθήσω<br>να αντιπαθήσω | έχω αντιπαθήσει<br>είχα αντιπαθήσει | να αντιπαθείς<br>αντιπαθείτε | αντιπάθησε<br>αντιπαθήστε |
| **I dive** | βουτώ 15 | βουτούσα | βούτηξα | θα βουτήξω<br>να βουτήξω | έχω βουτήξει<br>είχα βουτήξει | βούτα<br>βουτάτε | βούτηξε<br>βουτήξτε |
| **I divide** | διαιρώ 17 | διαιρούσα | διαίρεσα | θα διαιρέσω<br>να διαιρέσω | έχω διαιρέσει<br>είχα διαιρέσει | διαίρει<br>διαιρείτε | διαίρεσε<br>διαιρέστε |
| **I divorce** | χωρίζω 13 | χώριζα | χώρισα | θα χωρίσω<br>να χωρίσω | έχω χωρίσει<br>είχα χωρίσει | χώριζε<br>χωρίζετε | χώρισε<br>χωρίστε |
| **I do** | κάνω 13 | έκανα | έκανα | θα κάνω<br>να κάνω | έχω κάνει<br>είχα κάνει | κάνε<br>κάνετε | κάνε<br>κάντε |
| **I dogmatize** | δογματίζω 13 | δογμάτιζα | δογμάτισα | θα δογματίσω<br>να δογματίσω | έχω δογματίσει<br>είχα δογματίσει | δογμάτιζε<br>δογματίζετε | δογμάτισε<br>δογματίστε |
| **I dominate** | κυριαρχώ 17 | κυριαρχούσα | κυριάρχησα | θα κυριαρχήσω<br>να κυριαρχήσω | έχω κυριαρχήσει<br>είχα κυριαρχήσει | να κυριαρχείς<br>κυριαρχείτε | κυριάρχησε<br>κυριαρχήστε |
| **I donate** | χαρίζω 13 | χάριζα | χάρισα | θα χαρίσω<br>να χαρίσω | έχω χαρίσει<br>είχα χαρίσει | χάριζε<br>χαρίζετε | χάρισε<br>χαρίστε |
| **I double** | διπλασιάζω 13 | διπλασίαζα | διπλασίασα | θα διπλασιάσω<br>να διπλασιάσω | έχω διπλασιάσει<br>είχα διπλασιάσει | διπλασίαζε<br>διπλασιάζετε | διπλασίασε<br>διπλασιάστε |
| **I doubt** | αμφιβάλλω 13 | αμφέβαλλα | αμφέβαλα | θα αμφιβάλω<br>να αμφιβάλω | έχω αμφιβάλει<br>είχα αμφιβάλει | αμφίβαλλε<br>αμφιβάλλετε | αμφίβαλε<br>αμφιβάλτε |
| **I doze** | *μισοκοιμάμαι 42*<br>*λαγοκοιμάμαι* | *μισοκοιμόμουν* | *μισοκοιμήθηκα* | *θα μισοκοιμηθώ*<br>*να μισοκοιμηθώ* | *έχω μισοκοιμηθεί*<br>*είχα μισοκοιμηθεί* | *να μισοκοιμάσαι*<br>*μισοκοιμάστε* | *μισοκοιμήσου*<br>*μισοκοιμηθείτε* |
| **I dramatize** | δραματοποιώ 17 | δραματοποιούσα | δραματοποίησα | θα δραματοποιήσω<br>να δραματοποιήσω | έχω δραματοποιήσει<br>είχα δραματοποιήσει | να δραματοποιείς<br>δραματοπιείτε | δραματοποίησε<br>δραματοποιήστε |

| English Verb | Present | Imperfect | Past | Simple Future<br>Simple Subjunctive | Present Perfect<br>Past Perfect | Continuous Imperative | Simple Imperative |
|---|---|---|---|---|---|---|---|
| **I draw** | σκιτσάρω 13 | σκίτσαρα | σκιτσάρισα | θα σκιτσάρω<br>να σκιτσάρω | έχω σκιτσάρει<br>είχα σκιτσάρει | σκίτσαρε<br>σκιτσάρετε | σκιτσάρισε<br>σκιτσαρίστε |
| **I dream** | *ονειρεύομαι 14* | *ονειρευόμουν* | *ονειρεύτηκα* | *θα ονειρευτώ*<br>*να ονειρευτώ* | *έχω ονειρευτεί*<br>*είχα ονειρευτεί* | *να ονειρεύσαι*<br>*ονειρεύεστε* | *ονειρέψου*<br>*ονειρευτείτε* |
| **I dream up** (contrive) | *σκαρφίζομαι 14* | *σκαρφιζόμουν* | *σκαρφίστηκα* | *θα σκαρφιστώ*<br>*να σκαρφιστώ* | *έχω σκαρφιστεί*<br>*είχα σκαρφιστεί* | *να σκαρφίζεσαι*<br>*σκαρφίζεστε* | *σκαρφίσου*<br>*σκαρφιστείτε* |
| **I dress** | ντύνω 13 | έντυνα | έντυσα | θα ντύσω<br>να ντύσω | έχω ντύσει<br>είχα ντύσει | ντύνε<br>ντύνετε | ντύσε<br>ντύστε |
| **I drink** | πίνω 13 | έπινα | ήπια | θα πιω<br>να πιω | έχω πιει<br>είχα πιει | πίνε<br>πίνετε | πιές<br>πιείτε |
| **I drive** | οδηγώ 17 | οδηγούσα | οδήγησα | θα οδήγησω<br>να οδήγησω | έχω οδηγήσει<br>είχα οδηγήσει | να οδηγείς<br>οδηγείτε | οδήγησε<br>οδηγήστε |
| **I drown** | πνίγω 13 | έπνιγα | έπνιξα | θα πνίξω<br>να πνίξω | έχω πνίξει<br>είχα πνίξει | πνίγε<br>πνίγετε | πνίξε<br>πνίξτε |
| **I dry** | στεγνώνω 13 | στέγνωνα | στέγνωσα | θα στεγνώσω<br>να στεγνώσω | έχω στεγνώσει<br>είχα στεγνώσει | στέγνωνε<br>στεγνώνετε | στέγνωσε<br>στεγνώστε |
| **I dump** | *ξεφορτώνομαι 14* | *ξεφορτωνόμουν* | *ξεφορτώθηκα* | *θα ξεφορτωθώ*<br>*να ξεφορτωθώ* | *έχω ξεφορτωθεί*<br>*είχα ξεφορτωθεί* | *να ξεφορτώνεσαι*<br>*ξεφορτώνεστε* | *ξεφορτώσου*<br>*ξεφορτωθείτε* |
| **I dust** | ξεσκονίζω 13 | ξεσκόνιζα | ξεσκόνισα | θα ξεσκονίσω<br>να ξεσκονίσω | έχω ξεσκονίσει<br>είχα ξεσκονίσει | ξεσκόνιζε<br>ξεσκονίζετε | ξεσκόνισε<br>ξεσκονίστε |
| **I dye** | μπογιατίζω 13 | μπογιάτιζα | μπογιάτισα | θα μπογιατίσω<br>να μπογιατίσω | έχω μπογιατίσει<br>είχα μπογιατίσει | μπογιάτιζε<br>μπογιατίζετε | μπογιάτισε<br>μπογιατίστε |
| **I am exempted** | *εξαιρούμαι 18* | *εξαιρούμουν* | *εξαιρέθηκα* | *θα εξαιρεθώ*<br>*να εξαιρεθώ* | *έχω εξαιρεθεί*<br>*είχα εξαιρεθεί* | *να εξαιρείσαι*<br>*εξαιρείστε* | *εξαιρέσου*<br>*εξαιρεθείτε* |

| English Verb | Present | Imperfect | Past | Simple Future<br>Simple Subjunctive | Present Perfect<br>Past Perfect | Continuous Imperative | Simple Imperative |
|---|---|---|---|---|---|---|---|
| **I earn** | *δικαιούμαι 42* | *δικαιούμουν* | *δικαιώθηκα* | *θα δικαιωθώ*<br>*να δικαιωθώ* | *έχω δικαιωθεί*<br>*είχα δικαιωθεί* | *να δικαιώνεσαι*<br>*δικαιώνεστε* | *δικαιώσου*<br>*δικαιωθείτε* |
| **I eat** | τρώ(γ)ω 20 | έτρωγα | έφαγα | θα φάω<br>να φάω | έχω φάει<br>είχα φάει | τρώ(γ)ε<br>τρώ(γ)ετε | φάε<br>φάτε |
| **I echo** | αντηχώ 17 | αντηχούσα | αντήχησα | θα αντηχήσω<br>να αντηχήσω | έχω αντηχήσει<br>είχα αντηχήσει | να αντηχείς<br>αντηχείτε | αντήχησε<br>αντηχήστε |
| **I edit** | *επιμελούμαι 18* | *επιμελούμουν* | *επιμεληθηκα* | *θα επιμεληθώ*<br>*να επιμεληθώ* | *έχω επιμεληθεί*<br>*είχα επιμεληθεί* | *να επιμελείσαι*<br>*επιμελείστε* | *επιμελήσου*<br>*επιμεληθείτε* |
| **I educate** | μορφώνω 13 | μόρφωνα | μόρφωσα | θα μορφώσω<br>να μορφώσω | έχω μορφώσει<br>είχα μορφώσει | μόρφωνε<br>μορφώνετε | μόρφωσε<br>μορφώστε |
| **I elaborate** | εκπονώ 17 | εκπονούσα | εκπόνησα | θα εκπονήσω<br>να εκπονήσω | έχω εκπονήσει<br>είχα εκπονήσει | να εκπονείς<br>εκπονείτε | εκπόνησε<br>εκπονήστε |
| **I elect** | εκλέγω 13 | εξέλεγα | εξέλεξα | θα εκλέξω<br>να εκλέξω | έχω εκλέξει<br>είχα εκλέξει | να εκλέγεις<br>εκλέγετε | έκλεξε<br>εκλέξτε |
| **I elevate** | εξυψώνω 13 | εξύψωνα | εξύψωσα | θα εξυψώσω<br>να εξυψώσω | έχω εξυψώσει<br>είχα εξυψώσει | εξύψωνε<br>εξυψώνετε | εξύψωσε<br>εξυψώστε |
| **I eliminate** | εξαλείφω 13 | εξάλειφα | εξάλειψα | θα εξαλείψω<br>να εξαλείψω | έχω εξαλείψει<br>είχα εξαλείψει | εξάλειφε<br>εξαλείφετε | εξάλειψε<br>εξαλείψτε |
| **I elucidate** | επεξηγώ 17 | επεξηγούσα | επεξήγησα | θα επεξηγήσω<br>να επεξηγήσω | έχω επεξηγήσει<br>είχα επεξηγήσει | επεξήγει<br>επεξηγείτε | επεξήγησε<br>επεξηγήστε |
| **I embezzle** | *καταχρώμαι 42* | *καταχρώμουν* | *καταχράστηκα* | *θα καταχραστώ*<br>*να καταχραστώ* | *έχω καταχραστεί*<br>*είχα καταχραστεί* | *να καταχράσαι*<br>*καταχράστε* | *καταχράσου*<br>*καταχραστείτε* |
| **I embrace** | αγκαλιάζω 13 | αγκάλιαζα | αγκάλιασα | θα αγκαλιάσω<br>να αγκαλιάσω | έχω αγκαλιάσει<br>είχα αγκαλιάσει | αγκάλιαζε<br>αγκαλιάζετε | αγκάλιασε<br>αγκαλιάστε |

| English Verb | Present | Imperfect | Past | Simple Future<br>Simple Subjunctive | Present Perfect<br>Past Perfect | Continuous Imperative | Simple Imperative |
|---|---|---|---|---|---|---|---|
| **I embroider** | κεντ(ά)ώ 15 | κεντούσα | κέντησα | θα κεντήσω<br>να κεντήσω | έχω κεντήσει<br>είχα κεντήσει | κέντα<br>κεντάτε | κέντησε<br>κεντήστε |
| **I emigrate** | μεταναστεύω 13 | μετανάστευα | μετανάστευσα | θα μεταναστεύσω<br>να μεταναστεύσω | έχω μεταναστεύσει<br>είχα μεταναστεύσει | μετανάστευε<br>μεταναστεύετε | μετανάστευσε<br>μεταναστεύστε |
| **I emphasize** | τονίζω 13 | τόνιζα | τόνισα | θα τονίσω<br>να τονίσω | έχω τονίσει<br>είχα τονίσει | τόνιζε<br>τονίζετε | τόνισε<br>τονίστε |
| **I employ** | απασχολώ 15 | απασχολούσα | απασχόλησα | θα απασχολήσω<br>να απασχολήσω | έχω απασχολήσει<br>είχα απασχολήσει | να απασχολείς<br>απασχολείτε | απασχόλησε<br>απασχολήστε |
| **I embody** | ενσωματώνω 13 | ενσωμάτωνα | ενσωμάτωσα | θα ενσωματώσω<br>να ενσωματώσω | έχω ενσωματώσει<br>είχα ενσωματώσει | ενσωμάτωνε<br>ενσωματώνετε | ενσωμάτωσε<br>ενσωματώστε |
| **I empty** | αδειάζω 13 | άδειαζα | άδειασα | θα αδειάσω<br>να αδειάσω | έχω αδειάσει<br>είχα αδειάσει | άδειαζε<br>αδειάζετε | άδειασε<br>αδειάστε |
| **I encircle** | τριγυρίζω 13<br>τριγυρν(ά)ώ 15 | τριγύριζα | τριγύρισα | θα τριγυρίσω<br>να τριγυρίσω | έχω τριγυρίσει<br>είχα τριγυρίσει | τριγύρνα<br>τριγυρνάτε | τριγύρισε<br>τριγυρίστε |
| **I encourage** | ενθαρρύνω 13 | ενθάρρυνα | ενθάρρυνα | θα ενθαρρύνω<br>να ενθαρρύνω | έχω ενθαρρύνει<br>είχα ενθαρρύνει | ενθάρρυνε<br>ενθαρρύνετε | ενθάρρυνε<br>ενθαρρύντε |
| **I enforce** | ισχυροποιώ 17 | ισχυροποιούσα | ισχυροποίησα | θα ισχυροποιήσω<br>να ισχυροποιήσω | έχω ισχυροποιήσει<br>είχα ισχυροποιήσει | να ισχυροποιείς<br>ισχυροποιείτε | ισχυροποίησε<br>ισχυροποιήστε |
| **I engage** | *ασχολούμαι 18* | *ασχολούμουν* | *ασχολήθηκα* | *θα ασχοληθώ*<br>*να ασχοληθώ* | *έχω ασχοληθεί*<br>*είχα ασχοληθεί* | *να ασχολείσαι*<br>*ασχολείσθε* | *ασχολήσου*<br>*ασχοληθείτε* |
| **I engrave** | χαράζω 13 | χάραζα | χάραξα | θα χαράξω<br>να χαράξω | έχω χαράξει<br>είχα χαράξει | χάραζε<br>χαράζετε | χάραξε<br>χαράξτε |
| **I enjoy** | απολαμβάνω 13 | απολάμβανα | απόλαυσα | θα απολαύσω<br>να απολαύσω | έχω απολαύσει<br>είχα απολαύσει | απολάμβανε<br>απολαμβάνετε | απόλαυσε<br>απολαύστε |

| English Verb | Present | Imperfect | Past | Simple Future<br>Simple Subjunctive | Present Perfect<br>Past Perfect | Continuous Imperative | Simple Imperative |
|---|---|---|---|---|---|---|---|
| **I enjoy myself** | διασκεδάζω 13 | διασκέδαζα | διασκέδασα | θα διασκεδάσω<br>να διασκεδάσω | έχω διασκεδάσει<br>είχα διασκεδάσει | διασκέδαζε<br>διασκεδάζετε | διασκέδασε<br>διασκεδάστε |
| **I enlarge** | μεγεθύνω 13 | μεγέθυνα | μεγέθυνα | θα μεγεθύνω<br>να μεγεθύνω | έχω μεγεθύνει<br>είχα μεγεθύνει | μεγέθυνε<br>μεγεθύνετε | μεγέθυνε<br>μεγεθύντε |
| **I enlighten** | διαφωτίζω 13 | διαφώτιζα | διαφώτισα | θα διαφωτίσω<br>να διαφωτίσω | έχω διαφωτίσει<br>είχα διαφωτίσει | διαφώτιζε<br>διαφωτίζετε | διαφώτισε<br>διαφωτίστε |
| **I enliven** | ζωηρεύω 13 | ζωήρευα | ζωήρεψα | θα ζωηρέψω<br>να ζωηρέψω | έχω ζωηρέψει<br>είχα ζωηρέψει | ζωήρευε<br>ζωηρεύετε | ζωήρεψε<br>ζωηρέψτε |
| **I enrage** | μανιάζω 13 | μάνιαζα | μάνιασα | θα μανιάσω<br>να μανιάσω | έχω μανιάσει<br>είχα μανιάσει | μάνιαζε<br>μανιάζετε | μάνιασε<br>μανιάστε |
| **I enrol** | καταχωρώ 17 | καταχωρούσα | καταχώρησα | θα καταχωρήσω<br>να καταχωρήσω | έχω καταχωρήσει<br>είχα καταχωρήσει | να καταχωρείς<br>καταχωρείτε | καταχώρησε<br>καταχωρήστε |
| **I enrol myself** | *γράφομαι 14* | *γραφόμουν* | *γράφτηκα* | *θα γραφτώ*<br>*να γραφτώ* | *έχω γραφτεί*<br>*είχα γραφτεί* | *να γράφεσαι*<br>*γράφεστε* | *γράψου*<br>*γραφτείτε* |
| **I enslave** | υποδουλώνω 13 | υποδούλωνα | υποδούλωσα | θα υποδουλώσω<br>να υποδουλώσω | έχω υποδουλώσει<br>είχα υποδουλώσει | υποδούλωνε<br>υποδουλώνετε | υποδούλωσε<br>υποδουλώστε |
| **I entangle** | μπερδεύω 13 | μπέρδευα | μπέρδεψα | θα μπερδέψω<br>να μπερδέψω | έχω μπερδέψει<br>είχα μπερδέψει | μπέρδευε<br>μπερδεύετε | μπέρδεψε<br>μπερδέψτε |
| **I enter** | μπαίνω 13 | έμπαινα | μπήκα | θα μπω<br>να μπω | έχω μπει<br>είχα μπει | μπαίνε<br>μπαίνετε | μπές<br>μπείτε |
| **I entertain** | *δεξιώνομαι 14* | *δεξιωνόμουν* | *δεξιώθηκα* | *θα δεξιωθώ*<br>*να δεξιωθώ* | *έχω δεξιωθεί*<br>*είχα δεξιωθεί* | *να δεξιώνεσαι*<br>*δεξιώνεστε* | *δεξιώσου*<br>*δεξιωθείτε* |
| **I envy** | ζηλεύω 13 | ζήλευα | ζήλεψα | θα ζηλέψω<br>να ζηλέψω | έχω ζηλέψει<br>είχα ζηλέψει | ζήλευε<br>ζηλεύετε | ζήλεψε<br>ζηλέψτε |

| English Verb | Present | Imperfect | Past | Simple Future<br>Simple Subjunctive | Present Perfect<br>Past Perfect | Continuous Imperative | Simple Imperative |
|---|---|---|---|---|---|---|---|
| **I equalize** | ισοφαρίζω 13 | ισοφάριζα | ισοφάρισα | θα ισοφαρίσω<br>να ισοφαρίσω | έχω ισοφαρίσει<br>είχα ισοφαρίσει | ισοφάριζε<br>ισοφαρίζετε | ισοφάρισε<br>ισοφαρίστε |
| **I equip** | αρματώνω 13 | αρμάτωνα | αρμάτωσα | θα αρματώσω<br>να αρματώσω | έχω αρματώσει<br>είχα αρματώσει | αρμάτωνε<br>αρματώνετε | αρμάτωσε<br>αρματώστε |
| **I erase** | αποσβήνω 13 | απόσβηνα | απόσβησα | θα αποσβήσω<br>να αποσβήσω | έχω αποσβήσει<br>είχα αποσβήσει | απόσβηνε<br>αποσβήνετε | απόσβησε<br>αποσβήστε |
| **I am in error** | σφάλλω 13 | έσφαλλα | έσφαλα | θα σφάλω<br>να σφάλω | έχω σφάλει<br>είχα σφάλει | σφάλλε<br>σφάλλετε | σφάλε<br>σφάλτε |
| **I erupt** (volcano) | *εκρήγνυμαι 42* | *εκρηγνυόμουν* | *εξεράγην* | *θα εκραγώ*<br>*να εκραγώ* | *έχω εκραγεί*<br>*είχα εκραγεί* | *να εκρήγνυσαι*<br>*εκρήγνυστε* | *εκράξου*<br>*εκραγείτε* |
| **I erupt** (riots/war) | ξεσπ(ά)ώ 15 | ξεσπούσα | ξέσπασα | θα ξεσπάσω<br>να ξεσπάσω | έχω ξεσπάσει<br>είχα ξεσπάσει | ξέσπα<br>ξεσπάτε | ξέσπασε<br>ξεσπάστε |
| **I escalate** | κλιμακώνω 13 | κλιμάκωνα | κλιμάκωσα | θα κλιμακώσω<br>να κλιμακώσω | έχω κλιμακώσει<br>είχα κλιμακώσει | κλιμάκωνε<br>κλιμακώνεστε | κλιμάκωσε<br>κλιμακώστε |
| **I escape** (from prison) | δραπετεύω 13 | δραπέτευα | δραπέτευσα | θα δραπετεύσω<br>να δραπετεύσω | έχω δραπετεύσει<br>είχα δραπετεύσει | δραπέτευε<br>δραπετεύετε | δραπέτευσε<br>δραπετεύστε |
| **I escape** | γλυτώνω 13 | γλύτωνα | γλύτωσα | θα γλυτώσω<br>να γλυτώσω | έχω γλυτώσει<br>είχα γλυτώσει | γλύτωνε<br>γλυτώνετε | γλύτωσε<br>γλυτώστε |
| **I escape** | ξεφεύγω 13 | ξέφευγα | ξέφυγα | θα ξεφύγω<br>να ξεφύγω | έχω ξεφύγει<br>είχα ξεφύγει | ξέφευγε<br>ξεφεύγετε | ξέφυγε<br>ξεφύγετε |
| **I escort** | συνοδεύω 13 | συνόδευα | συνόδεψα | θα συνοδέψω<br>να συνοδέψω | έχω συνοδέψει<br>είχα συνοδέψει | συνόδευε<br>συνοδεύετε | συνόδεψε<br>συνοδέψτε |
| **I establish** | εδραιώνω 13 | εδραίωνα | εδραίωσα | θα εδραιώσω<br>να εδραιώσω | έχω εδραιώσει<br>είχα εδραιώσει | εδραίωνε<br>εδραιώνετε | εδραίωσε<br>εδραιώστε |

| English Verb | Present | Imperfect | Past | Simple Future<br>Simple Subjunctive | Present Perfect<br>Past Perfect | Continuous Imperative | Simple Imperative |
|---|---|---|---|---|---|---|---|
| **I estimate** | υπολογίζω 13 | υπολόγιζα | υπολόγισα | θα υπολογίσω<br>να υπολογίσω | έχω υπολογίσει<br>είχα υπολογίσει | υπολόγιζε<br>υπολογίζετε | υπολόγισε<br>υπολογίστε |
| **I exaggerate** | υπερβάλλω 13 | υπέρβαλλα | υπέρβαλα | θα υπερβάλω<br>να υπερβάλω | έχω υπερβάλει<br>είχα υπερβάλει | υπέρβαλλε<br>υπερβάλλετε | υπέρβαλε<br>υπερβάλτε |
| **I exaggerate** | μεγαλοποιώ 17 | μεγαλοποιούσα | μεγαλοποίησα | θα μεγαλοποιήσω<br>να μεγαλοποιήσω | έχω μεγαλοποιήσει<br>είχα μεγαλοποιήσει | μεγαλοποίει<br>μεγαλοποιείτε | μεγαλοποίησε<br>μεγακοποιήστε |
| **I examine** | εξετάζω 13 | εξέταζα | εξέτασα | θα εξετάσω<br>να εξετάσω | έχω εξετάσει<br>είχα εξετάσει | εξέταζε<br>εξετάζετε | εξέτασε<br>εξετάστε |
| **I exceed** | υπερβαίνω 13 | υπέρβαινα | υπέρβηκα | θα υπερβώ<br>να υπερβώ | έχω υπερβεί<br>είχα υπερβεί | υπέρβαινε<br>υπερβαίνετε | υπέρβα<br>υπερβείτε |
| **I except** | εξαιρώ 17 | εξαιρούσα | εξαίρεσα | θα εξαιρέσω<br>να εξαιρέσω | έχω εξαιρέσει<br>είχα εξαιρέσει | να εξαιρείς<br>εξαιρείτε | εξαίρεσε<br>εξαιρέστε |
| **I exchange** | ανταλλάζω 13 | αντάλλασσα | αντάλλαξα | θα ανταλλάξω<br>να ανταλλάξω | έχω ανταλλάξει<br>είχα ανταλλάξει | αντάλλαζε<br>ανταλλάζετε | αντάλλαξε<br>ανταλλάξτε |
| **I excite** | εξάπτω 13 | εξήπτα | εξήψα | θα εξάψω<br>να εξάψω | έχω εξάψει<br>είχα εξάψει | έξαπτε<br>εξάπτετε | έξαψε<br>εξάψτε |
| **I exclaim** | αναφωνώ 17 | αναφωνούσα | αναφώνησα | θα αναφωνήσω<br>να αναφωνήσω | έχω αναφωνήσει<br>είχα αναφωνήσει | να αναφωνείς<br>αναφωνείτε | αναφώνησε<br>αναφωνήστε |
| **I exclude** | αποκλείω 13 | απέκλεια | απέκλεισα | θα αποκλείσω<br>να αποκλείσω | έχω αποκλείσει<br>είχα αποκλείσει | απόκλειε<br>αποκλείετε | απόκλεισε<br>αποκλείστε |
| **I excuse** | δικαιολογώ 17 | δικαιολογούσα | δικαιολόγησα | θα δικαιολογήσω<br>να δικαιολογήσω | έχω δικαιολογήσει<br>είχα δικαιολογήσει | δικαιολόγει<br>δικαιολογείτε | δικαιολόγησε<br>δικαιολογήστε |
| **I execute** | εκτελώ 17 | εκτελούσα | εκτέλεσα | θα εκτελέσω<br>να εκτελέσω | έχω εκτελέσει<br>είχα εκτελέσει | να εκτελείς<br>εκτελείτε | εκτέλεσε<br>εκτελέστε |

| English Verb | Present | Imperfect | Past | Simple Future<br>Simple Subjunctive | Present Perfect<br>Past Perfect | Continuous Imperative | Simple Imperative |
|---|---|---|---|---|---|---|---|
| **I exempt** | απαλλάσσω 13 | απάλλασσα | απάλλαξα | θα απαλλάξω<br>να απαλλάξω | έχω απαλλάξει<br>είχα απαλλάξει | απάλλασσε<br>απαλλάσσετε | απάλλαξε<br>απαλλάξτε |
| **I exert** | ασκώ 17 | ασκούσα | άσκησα | θα ασκήσω<br>να ασκήσω | έχω ασκήσει<br>είχα ασκήσει | να ασκείς<br>ασκείτε | άσκησε<br>ασκήστε |
| **I exhibit** | εκθέτω 13 | εξέθετα | εξέθεσα | θα εκθέσω<br>να εκθέσω | έχω εκθέσει<br>είχα εκθέσει | έκθετε<br>εκθέτετε | έκθεσε<br>εκθέστε |
| **I exile** | εξορίζω 13 | εξόριζα | εξόρισα | θα εξορίσω<br>να εξορίσω | έχω εξορίσει<br>είχα εξορίσει | εξόριζε<br>εξορίζετε | εξόρισε<br>εξορίστε |
| **I exist** | υπάρχω 13 | υπήρχα | υπήρξα | θα υπάρξω<br>να υπάρξω | έχω υπάρξει<br>είχα υπάρξει | να υπάρχεις<br>υπάρχετε | ύπαρξε<br>υπάρξτε |
| **I exit** | *εξέρχομαι 14* | *εξερχόμουν* | *εξήλθα* | *θα εξέλθω*<br>*να εξέλθω* | *έχω εξέλθει*<br>*είχα εξέλθει* | *να εξέρχεσαι*<br>*εξέρχεστε* | *έξελθε*<br>*εξέλθετε* |
| **I expatriate** | *ξενιτεύομαι 14* | *ξενιτευόμουν* | *ξενιτεύτηκα* | *θα ξενιτευτώ*<br>*να ξενιτευτώ* | *έχω ξενιτευτεί*<br>*είχα ξενιτευτεί* | *να ξενιτεύεσαι*<br>*ξενιτεύεστε* | *ξενιτεύσου*<br>*ξενιτευτείτε* |
| **I expect** | προσδοκώ 17 | προσδοκούσα | προσδόκησα | θα προσδοκήσω<br>να προσδοκήσω | έχω προσδοκήσει<br>είχα προσδικήσει | να προσδοκείς<br>προσδοκείτε | προσδόκησε<br>προσδοκήστε |
| **I expel** | αποβάλλω 13 | απέβαλλα | απέβαλα | θα αποβάλω<br>να αποβάλω | έχω αποβάλει<br>είχα αποβάλει | απόβαλλε<br>αποβάλλετε | απόβαλε<br>αποβάλτε |
| **I experiment** | *πειραματίζομαι 14* | *πειραματιζόμουν* | *πειραματίστηκα* | *θα πειραματιστώ*<br>*να πειραματιστώ* | *έχω πειραματιστεί*<br>*είχα πειραματιστεί* | *να πειραματίζεσαι*<br>*πειραματίζεστε* | *πειραματίσου*<br>*πειραματιστείτε* |
| **I expire** | εκπνέω 13 | εξέπνεα | εξέπνευσα | θα εκπνεύσω<br>να εκπνεύσω | έχω εκπνεύσει<br>είχα εκπνεύσει | έκπνεε<br>εκπνέετε | έκπνευσε<br>εκπνεύστε |
| **I explain** | εξηγώ 17 | εξηγούσα | εξήγησα | θα εξηγήσω<br>να εξηγήσω | έχω εξηγήσει<br>είχα εξηγήσει | να εξηγείς<br>εξηγείτε | εξήγησε<br>εξηγήστε |

| English Verb | Present | Imperfect | Past | Simple Future<br>Simple Subjunctive | Present Perfect<br>Past Perfect | Continuous Imperative | Simple Imperative |
|---|---|---|---|---|---|---|---|
| **I explain** | ερμηνεύω 13 | ερμήνευα | ερμήνευσα | θα ερμηνεύσω<br>να ερμηνεύσω | έχω ερμηνεύσει<br>είχα ερμηνεύσει | ερμήνευε<br>ερμηνεύετε | ερμήνευσε<br>ερμηνεύστε |
| **I explode** | ανατινάζω 13 | ανατίναζα | ανατίναξα | θα ανατινάξω<br>να ανατινάξω | έχω ανατινάξει<br>είχα ανατινάξει | ανατίναζε<br>ανατινάζετε | ανατίναξε<br>ανατινάξετε |
| **I exploit** | *εκμεταλλεύομαι 14* | *εκμεταλλευόμουν* | *εκμεταλλεύτηκα* | *θα εκμεταλλευτώ*<br>*να εκμεταλλευτώ* | *έχω εκμεταλλευτεί*<br>*είχα εκμεταλλευτεί* | *να εκμεταλλεύεσαι*<br>*εκμεταλλεύεστε* | *εκμεταλλεύσου*<br>*εκμεταλλευτείτε* |
| **I explore** | εξερευνώ 15 | εξερευνούσα | εξερεύνησα | θα εξερευνήσω<br>να εξερευνήσω | έχω εξερευνήσει<br>είχα εξερευνήσει | εξερεύνα<br>εξερευνάτε | εξερεύνησε<br>εξερευνήστε |
| **I export** | εξάγω 13 | εξήγα | εξήγαγα | θα εξαγάγω<br>να εξαγάγω | έχω εξαγάγει<br>είχα εξαγάγει | να εξάγεις<br>εξάγετε | εξάγαγε<br>εξαγάγετε |
| **I expose** | ξεσκεπάζω 13 | ξεσκέπαζα | ξεσκέπασα | θα ξεσκεπάσω<br>να ξεσκεπάσω | έχω ξεσκεπάσει<br>είχα ξεσκεπάσει | ξεσκέπαζε<br>ξεσκεπάζετε | ξεσκέπασε<br>ξεσκεπάστε |
| **I express** | εκφράζω 13 | εξέφραζα | εξέφρασα | θα εκφράσω<br>να εκφράσω | έχω εκφράσει<br>είχα εκφράσει | έκφραζε<br>εκφράζετε | έκφρασε<br>εκφράστε |
| **I express myself** | *εκφράζομαι 14* | *εκφραζόμουν* | *εκφράστηκα* | *θα εκφραστώ*<br>*να εκφραστώ* | *έχω εκφραστεί*<br>*είχα εκφραστεί* | *να εκφράζεσαι*<br>*εκφράζεστε* | *εκφράσου*<br>*εκφραστείτε* |
| **I extend** | παρατείνω 13 | παράτεινα | παρέτεινα | θα παρατείνω<br>να παρατείνω | έχω παρατείνει<br>είχα παρατείνει | παράτεινε<br>παρατείνετε | παράτεινε<br>παρατείντε |
| **I exterminate** | εξολοθρεύω 13 | εξολόθρευα | εξολόθρεψα | θα εξολοθρέψω<br>να εξολοθρέψω | έχω εξολοθρέψει<br>είχα εξολοθρέψει | εξολόθρευε<br>εξολοθρεύετε | εξολόθρεψε<br>εξολοθρέψτε |
| **I extinguish** | σβήνω 13 | έσβηνα | έσβησα | θα σβήσω<br>να σβήσω | έχω σβήσει<br>είχα σβήσει | σβήνε<br>σβήνετε | σβήσε<br>σβήστε |
| **I extract** | εξωρύσσω 13 | εξώρυσσα | εξώρυξα | θα εξωρύξω<br>να εξωρύξω | έχω εξωρύξει<br>είχα εξωρύξει | εξώρυσσε<br>εξωρύσσετε | εξώρυξε<br>εξωρύξτε |

| English Verb | Present | Imperfect | Past | Simple Future<br>Simple Subjunctive | Present Perfect<br>Past Perfect | Continuous Imperative | Simple Imperative |
|---|---|---|---|---|---|---|---|
| **I exasperate** | παροξύνω 13 | παρόξυνα | παρόξυνα | θα παροξύνω<br>να παροξύνω | έχω παροξύνει<br>είχα παροξύνει | παρόξυνε<br>παροξύνετε | παρόξυνε<br>παροξύντε |
| **I fabricate** | επινοώ 17 | επινοούσα | επινόησα | θα επινοήσω<br>να επινοήσω | έχω επινοήσει<br>είχα επινοήσει | να επινοείς<br>επινοείτε | επινόησε<br>επινοήστε |
| **I facilitate** | διευκολύνω 13 | διευκόλυνα | διευκόλυνα | θα διευκολύνω<br>να διευκολύνω | έχω διευκολύνει<br>είχα διευκολύνει | διευκόλυνε<br>διευκολύνετε | διευκόλυνε<br>διευκολύντε |
| **I fail** | αποτυγχάνω 13 | αποτύγχανα | απέτυχα | θα αποτύχω<br>να αποτύχω | έχω αποτύχει<br>είχα αποτύχει | αποτύγχανε<br>αποτυγχάνετε | απότυχε<br>αποτύχετε |
| **I faint** | λιποθυμώ 15 | λιποθυμούσα | λιποθύμησα | θα λιποθυμήσω<br>να λιποθυμήσω | έχω λιποθυμήσει<br>είχα λιποθυμήσει | λιποθύμα<br>λιποθυμάτε | λιποθύμησε<br>λιποθυμήστε |
| **I fake** (documents) | πλαστο-<br>γραφώ 17 | πλαστο-<br>γραφούσα | πλαστο-<br>γράφησα | θα πλαστο-<br>γραφήσω | έχω πλαστο-<br>γραφήσει | να πλαστο-<br>γραφείς | πλαστο-<br>γράφησε |
| | | | | να πλαστο-<br>γραφήσω | είχα πλαστο-<br>γραφήσει | πλαστο-<br>γραφείτε | πλαστο-<br>γραφήστε |
| **I fall** | πέφτω 13 | έπεφτα | έπεσα | θα πέσω<br>να πέσω | έχω πέσει<br>είχα πέσει | πέφτε<br>πέφτετε | πέσε<br>πέστε |
| **I falsify** | παραποιώ 17 | παραποιούσα | παραποίησα | θα παραποιήσω<br>να παραποιήσω | έχω παραποιήσει<br>είχα παραποιήσει | να παραποιείς<br>παραποιείτε | παραποίησε<br>παραποιήστε |
| **I falter** | κομπιάζω 13 | κόμπιαζα | κόμπιασα | θα κομπιάσω<br>να κομπιάσω | έχω κομπιάσει<br>είχα κομπιάσει | κόμπιαζε<br>κομπιάζετε | κόμπιασε<br>κομπιάστε |
| **I familiarize myself** | *εξοικιώνομαι 14* | *εξοικιωνόμουν* | *εξοικιώθηκα* | *θα εξοικιωθώ*<br>*να εξοικιωθώ* | *έχω εξοικιωθεί*<br>*είχα εξοικιωθεί* | *να εξοικιώνεσαι*<br>*εξοικιώνεστε* | *εξοικιώσου*<br>*εξοικιωθείτε* |

| English Verb | Present | Imperfect | Past | Simple Future<br>Simple Subjunctive | Present Perfect<br>Past Perfect | Continuous Imperative | Simple Imperative |
|---|---|---|---|---|---|---|---|
| **I fancy** | γουστάρω 13 | γούσταρα | γουστάρησα | θα γουστάρω<br>να γουστάρω | έχω γουστάρει<br>είχα γουστάρει | γούσταρε<br>γουστάρετε | γουστάρησε<br>γουσταρήστε |
| **I fantasize** | φαντασιοκοπώ 17 | φαντασιοκοπούσα | φαντασιοκόπησα | θα φαντασιοκοπήσω<br>να φαντασιοκοπήσω | έχω φαντασιοκοπήσει<br>είχα φαντασιοκοπήσει | να φαντασιοκοπείς<br>φαντασιοκοπείτε | φαντασιοκόπησε<br>φαντασιοκοπήστε |
| **I fascinate** | μαγεύω 13 | μάγευα | μάγεψα | θα μαγέψω<br>να μαγέψω | έχω μαγέψει<br>είχα μαγέψει | μάγευε<br>μαγεύετε | μάγεψε<br>μαγέψτε |
| **I fast** | νηστεύω 13 | νήστευα | νήστεψα | θα νηστέψω<br>να νηστέψω | έχω νηστέψει<br>είχα νηστέψει | νήστευε<br>νηστεύετε | νήστεψε<br>νηστέψτε |
| **I fasten** | προσδένω 13 | πρόσδενα | πρόσδεσα | θα προσδέσω<br>να προσδέσω | έχω προσδέσει<br>είχα προσδέσει | πρόσδενε<br>προσδένετε | πρόσδεσε<br>προσδέστε |
| **I fathom** | βυθομετρώ 15 | βυθομετρούσα | βυθομέτρησα | θα βυθομετρήσω<br>να βυθομετρήσω | έχω βυθομετρήσει<br>είχα βυθομετρήσει | βυθομέτρα<br>βυθομετράτε | βυθομέτρησε<br>βυθομετρήστε |
| **I favour** | ευνοώ 17 | ευνοούσα | ευνόησα | θα ευνοήσω<br>να ευνοήσω | έχω ευνοήσει<br>είχα ευνοήσει | να ευνοείς<br>ευνοείτε | ευνόησε<br>ευνοήστε |
| **I fear** | *φοβάμαι 42* | *φοβόμουν* | *φοβήθηκα* | *θα φοβηθώ*<br>*να φοβηθώ* | *έχω φοβηθεί*<br>*είχα φοβηθεί* | *να φοβάσαι*<br>*φοβάστε* | *φοβήσου*<br>*φοβηθήτε* |
| **I am fed up** | *βαριέμαι 14* | *βαριόμουν* | *βαρέθηκα* | *θα βαρεθώ*<br>*να βαρεθώ* | *έχω βαρεθεί*<br>*είχα βαρεθεί* | *να βαριέσαι*<br>*βαριέστε* | *να βαρεθείς*<br>*βαρεθείτε* |
| **I feed** | ταΐζω 13 | τάιζα | τάισα | θα ταΐσω<br>να ταΐσω | έχω ταΐσει<br>είχα ταΐσει | τάιζε<br>ταΐζετε | τάισε<br>ταΐστε |
| **I feel** | *αισθάνομαι 14* | *αισθανόμουν* | *αισθάνθηκα* | *θα αισθανθώ*<br>*να αισθανθώ* | *έχω αισθανθεί*<br>*είχα αισθανθεί* | *να αισθάνεσαι*<br>*αισθάνεστε* | *να αισθανθείς*<br>*αισθανθείτε* |

| English Verb | Present | Imperfect | Past | Simple Future<br>Simple Subjunctive | Present Perfect<br>Past Perfect | Continuous Imperative | Simple Imperative |
|---|---|---|---|---|---|---|---|
| **I feel** (consider) | νιώθω 13 | ένιωθα | ένιωσα | θα νιώσω<br>να νιώσω | έχω νιώσει<br>είχα νιώσει | νιώθε<br>νιώθετε | νιώσε<br>νιώστε |
| **I feel dizzy** | *ζαλίζομαι 14* | *ζαλιζόμουν* | *ζαλίστηκα* | *θα ζαλιστώ*<br>*να ζαλιστώ* | *έχω ζαλιστεί*<br>*είχα ζαλιστεί* | *να ζαλίζεσαι*<br>*ζαλίζεστε* | *ζαλίσου*<br>*ζαλιστείτε* |
| **I feel for** (sympathise with) | *συμμερίζομαι 14* | *συμμεριζόμουν* | *συμμερίστηκα* | *θα συμμεριστώ*<br>*να συμμεριστώ* | *έχω συμμεριστεί*<br>*είχα συμμεριστεί* | *να συμμερίζεσαι*<br>*συμμερίζεστε* | *συμμερίσου*<br>*συμμεριστείτε* |
| **I feel for** (emotionally) | *συναισθάνομαι 14* | *συναισθανόμουν* | *συναισθάνηκα* | *θα συναισθανώ*<br>*να συναισθανώ* | *έχω συναισθανεί*<br>*είχα συναισθανεί* | *να συναισθάνεσαι*<br>*συναισθάνεστε* | *συναισθάνσου*<br>*συναισθανθείτε* |
| **I feel sleepy** | νυστάζω 13 | νύσταζα | νύσταξα | θα νυστάξω<br>να νυστάξω | έχω νυστάξει<br>είχα νυστάξει | νύσταζε<br>νυστάζετε | νύσταξε<br>νυστάξτε |
| **I fiddle** | πασπατεύω 13 | πασπάτευα | πασπάτεψα | θα πασπατέψω<br>να πασπατέψω | έχω πασπατέψει<br>είχα πασπατέψει | πασπάτευε<br>πασπατεύετε | πασπάτεψε<br>πασπατέψτε |
| **I fidget** | νευριάζω 13 | νευρίαζα | νευρίασα | θα νευριάσω<br>να νευριάσω | έχω νευριάσει<br>είχα νευριάσει | νευρίαζε<br>νευριάζετε | νευρίασε<br>νευριάστε |
| **I fight** | πολεμώ 15 | πολεμούσα | πολέμησα | θα πολεμήσω<br>να πολεμήσω | έχω πολεμήσει<br>είχα πολεμήσει | πολέμα<br>πολεμάτε | πολέμησε<br>πολεμήστε |
| **I file** | αρχειοθετώ 17 | αρχειοθετούσα | αρχειοθέτησα | θα αρχειοθετήσω<br>να αρχειοθετήσω | έχω αρχειοθετήσει<br>είχα αρχειοθετήσει | να αρχειοθετείς<br>αρχειοθετείτε | αρχειοθέτησε<br>αρχειοθετήστε |
| **I filibuster** | κωλυσιεργώ 17 | κωλυσιεργούσα | κωλυσιέργησα | θα κωλυσιεργήσω<br>να κωλυσιεργήσω | έχω κωλυσιεργήσει<br>είχα κωλυσιεργήσει | να κωλυσιεργείς<br>κωλυσιεργείτε | κωλυσιέργησε<br>κωλυσιεργήστε |
| **I fill** | γεμίζω 13 | γέμιζα | γέμισα | θα γεμίσω<br>να γεμίσω | έχω γεμίσει<br>είχα γεμίσει | γέμιζε<br>γεμίζετε | γέμισε<br>γεμίστε |
| **I fill** | φουσκώνω 13 | φούσκωνα | φούσκωσα | θα φουσκώσω<br>να φουσκώσω | έχω φουσκώσει<br>είχα φουσκώσει | φούσκωνε<br>φουσκώνετε | φούσκωσε<br>φουσκώστε |

| English Verb | Present | Imperfect | Past | Simple Future<br>Simple Subjunctive | Present Perfect<br>Past Perfect | Continuous Imperative | Simple Imperative |
|---|---|---|---|---|---|---|---|
| **I film** | κινηματο-γραφώ 17 | κινηματο-γραφούσα | κινηματο-γράφησα | θα κινηματο-γραφήσω | έχω κινηματο-γραφήσει | να κινηματο-γραφείς | κινηματο-γράφησε |
| | | | | να κινηματο-γραφήσω | είχα κινηματο-γραφήσει | κινηματο-γραφείτε | κινηματο-γραφήστε |
| **I finance** | χρηματοδοτώ 17 | χρηματοδοτούσα | χρηματοδότησα | θα χρηματοδοτήσω<br>να χρηματοδοτήσω | έχω χρηματοδοτήσει<br>είχα χρηματοδοτήσει | να χρηματοδοτείς<br>χρηματοδοτείτε | χρηματοδότησε<br>χρηματοδοτήστε |
| **I find** | βρίσκω 13 | έβρισκα | βρήκα | θα βρω<br>να βρω | έχω βρει<br>είχα βρει | βρίσκε<br>βρίσκετε | βρες<br>βρείτε |
| **I find difficult** | *δυσκολεύομαι 14* | *δυσκολευόμουν* | *δυσκολεύτηκα* | *θα δυσκολευτώ*<br>*να δυσκολευτώ* | *έχω δυσκολευτεί*<br>*είχα δυσκολευτεί* | *να δυσκολεύεσαι*<br>*δυσκολεύεστε* | *δυσκολέψου*<br>*δυσκολευτείτε* |
| **I find out** | εξακριβώνω 13 | εξακρίβωνα | εξακρίβωσα | θα εξακριβώσω<br>να εξακριβώσω | έχω εξακριβώσει<br>είχα εξακριβώσει | εξακρίβωνε<br>εξακριβώνετε | εξακρίβωσε<br>εξακριβώστε |
| **I finish** | τελειώνω 13 | τελείωνα | τελείωσα | θα τελειώσω<br>να τελειώσω | έχω τελειώσει<br>είχα τελειώσει | τελείωνε<br>τελειώνετε | τελείωσε<br>τελειώστε |
| **I fish** | ψαρεύω 13 | ψάρευα | ψάρεψα | θα ψαρέψω<br>να ψαρέψω | έχω ψαρέψει<br>είχα ψαρέψει | ψάρευε<br>ψαρεύετε | ψάρεψε<br>ψαρέψτε |
| **I fit** | εφαρμόζω 13 | εφάρμοζα | εφάρμοσα | θα εφαρμόσω<br>να εφαρμόσω | έχω εφαρμώσει<br>είχα εφαρμώσει | εφάρμοζε<br>εφαρμόζετε | εφάρμοσε<br>εφαρμόστε |
| **I fix** | παγιώνω 13 | παγίωνα | παγίωσα | θα παγιώσω<br>να παγιώσω | έχω παγιώσει<br>είχα παγιώσει | παγίωνε<br>παγιώνετε | παγίωσε<br>παγιώστε |
| **I flash** | απαστράφτω 13 | απάστραφτα | απάστραψα | θα απαστράψω<br>να απαστράψω | έχω απαστράψει<br>είχα απαστράψει | απάστραφτε<br>απαστράφτετε | απάστραψε<br>απαστράψτε |
| **I flatten** | ισοπεδώνω 13 | ισοπέδωνα | ισωπέδωσα | θα ισοπεδώσω<br>να ισοπεδώσω | έχω ισοπεδώσει<br>είχα ισοπεδώσει | ισοπέδωνε<br>ισοπεδώνετε | ισοπέδωσε<br>ισοπεδώστε |

| English Verb | Present | Imperfect | Past | Simple Future<br>Simple Subjunctive | Present Perfect<br>Past Perfect | Continuous Imperative | Simple Imperative |
|---|---|---|---|---|---|---|---|
| **I flatter** | κολακεύω 13 | κολάκευα | κολάκεψα | θα κολακέψω<br>να κολακέψω | έχω κολακέψει<br>είχα κολακέψει | κολάκευε<br>κολακεύετε | κολάκεψε<br>κολακέψτε |
| **I flaunt** | επιδεικνύω 13 | επιδείκνυα | επέδειξα | θα επιδείξω<br>να επιδείξω | έχω επιδείξει<br>είχα επιδείξει | επιδείκνυε<br>επιδεικνύετε | επίδειξε<br>επιδείξτε |
| **I flee** | διαφεύγω 13 | διέφευγα | διέφυγα | θα διαφύγω<br>να διαφύγω | έχω διαφύγει<br>είχα διαφύγει | διάφευγε<br>διαφεύγετε | διάφυγε<br>διαφύγετε |
| **I flick** | τινάζω 13 | τίναζα | τίναξα | θα τινάξω<br>να τινάξω | έχω τινάξει<br>είχα τινάξει | τίναζε<br>τινάζετε | τίναξε<br>τινάξτε |
| **I flicker** (eyelids) | τρεμοπαίζω 13 | τρεμόπαιζα | τρεμόπαιξα | θα τρεμοπαίξω<br>να τρεμοπαίξω | έχω τρεμοπαίξει<br>είχα τρεμοπαίξει | τρεμόπαιζε<br>τρεμοπαίζετε | τρεμόπαιξε<br>τρεμοπαίξτε |
| **I fling** | εκσφενδονίζω 13 | εκσφενδόνιζα | εκσφενδόνισα | θα εκσφενδονίσω<br>να εκσφενδονίσω | έχω εκσφενδονίσει<br>είχα εκσφενδονίσει | εκσφενδόνιζε<br>εκσφενδονίζετε | εκσφενδόνισε<br>εκσφενδονίστε |
| **I flirt** | φλερτάρω 13 | φλέρταρα | φλερτάρησα | θα φλερτάρω<br>να φλερτάρω | έχω φλερτάρει<br>είχα φλερτάρει | φλέρταρε<br>φλερτάρετε | φλερτάρησε<br>φλερταρήστε |
| **I float** | επιπλέω 13 | επέπλεα | επέπλευσα | θα επιπλεύσω<br>να επιπλεύσω | έχω επιπλεύσει<br>είχα επιπλεύσει | επίπλεε<br>επιπλέετε | επίπλευσε<br>επιπλεύστε |
| **I flood** | πλημμυρίζω 13 | πλημμύριζα | πλημμύρισα | θα πλημμυρίσω<br>να πλημμυρίσω | έχω πλημμυρίσει<br>είχα πλημμυρίσει | πλημμύριζε<br>πλημμυρίζετε | πλημμύρισε<br>πλημμυρίστε |
| **I floodlight** | φωταγωγώ 17 | φωταγωγούσα | φωταγώγησα | θα φωταγωγήσω<br>να φωταγωγήσω | έχω φωταγωγήσει<br>είχα φωταγωγήσει | να φωταγωγείς<br>φωταγωγείτε | φωταγώγησε<br>φωταγωγήστε |
| **I fluctuate** | *κυμαίνομαι 14* | *κυμαινόμουν* | *κυμάνθηκα* | *θα κυμανθώ*<br>*να κυμανθώ* | *έχω κυμανθεί*<br>*είχα κυμανθεί* | *να κυμαίνεσαι*<br>*κυμαίνεστε* | *να κυμανθείς*<br>*κυμανθείτε* |
| **I flow** | διαρρέω 13 | διέρρεα | διέρρευσα | θα διαρρεύσω<br>να διαρρεύσω | έχω διαρρεύσει<br>είχα διαρρεύσει | διάρρεε<br>διαρρέετε | να διαρεύσεις<br>διαρεύστε |

| English Verb | Present | Imperfect | Past | Simple Future<br>Simple Subjunctive | Present Perfect<br>Past Perfect | Continuous Imperative | Simple Imperative |
|---|---|---|---|---|---|---|---|
| **I fly** | πετώ 15 | πετούσα | πέταξα | θα πετάξω<br>να πετάξω | έχω πετάξει<br>είχα πετάξει | πέτα<br>πετάτε | πέταξε<br>πετάξτε |
| **I fold** | διπλώνω 13 | δίπλωνα | δίπλωσα | θα διπλώσω<br>να διπλώσω | έχω διπλώσει<br>είχα διπλώσει | δίπλωνε<br>διπλώνετε | δίπλωσε<br>διπλώστε |
| **I follow** | ακολουθώ 17 | ακολουθούσα | ακολούθησα | θα ακολουθήσω<br>να ακολουθήσω | έχω ακολουθήσει<br>είχα ακολουθήσει | να ακολουθείς<br>ακολουθείτε | ακολούθησε<br>ακολουθήστε |
| **I fool** | ξεγελώ 15 | ξεγελούσα | ξεγέλασα | θα ξεγελάσω<br>να ξεγελάσω | έχω ξεγελάσει<br>είχα ξεγελάσει | ξεγέλα<br>ξεγελάτε | ξεγέλασε<br>ξεγελάστε |
| **I force** | εξαναγκάζω 13 | εξανάγκαζα | εξανάγκασα | θα εξαναγκάσω<br>να εξαναγκάσω | έχω εξαναγκάσει<br>είχα εξαναγκάσει | εξανάγκαζε<br>εξαναγκάζετε | εξανάγκασε<br>εξαναγκάστε |
| **I forget** | ξεχνώ 15 | ξεχνούσα | ξέχασα | θα ξεχάσω<br>να ξεχάσω | έχω ξεχάσει<br>είχα ξεχάσει | ξέχνα<br>ξεχνάτε | ξέχασε<br>ξεχάστε |
| **I forgive** | συγχωρώ 17 | συγχωρούσα | συγχώρησα | θα συγχωρήσω<br>να συγχωρήσω | έχω συγχωρήσει<br>είχα συγχωρήσει | να συγχωρείς<br>συγχωρείτε | συγχώρησε<br>συγχωρήστε |
| **I fork** | *διακλαδίζομαι 14* | *διακλαδιζόμουν* | *διακλαδίστηκα* | *θα διακλαδιστώ*<br>*να διακλαδιστώ* | *έχω διακλαδιστεί*<br>*είχα διακλαδιστεί* | *να διακλαδίζεσαι*<br>*διακλαδίζεστε* | *διακλαδίσου*<br>*διακλαδιστείτε* |
| **I form** | διαμορφώνω 13 | διαμόρφωνα | διαμόρφωσα | θα διαμορφώσω<br>να διαμορφώσω | έχω διαμορφώσει<br>είχα διαμορφώσει | διαμόρφωνε<br>διαμορφώνετε | διαμόρφωσε<br>διαμορφώστε |
| **I formulate** | τυποποιώ 17 | τυποποιούσα | τυποποίησα | θα τυποποιήσω<br>να τυποποιήσω | έχω τυποποιήσει<br>είχα τυποποιήσει | να τυποποιείς<br>τυποποιείτε | τυποποίησε<br>τυποποιήστε |
| **I fortify** | οχυρώνω 13 | οχύρωνα | οχύρωσα | θα οχυρώσω<br>να οχυρώσω | έχω οχυρώσει<br>είχα οχυρώσει | οχύρωνε<br>οχυρώνετε | οχύρωσε<br>οχυρώστε |
| **I found** | ιδρύω 13 | ίδρυα | ίδρυσα | θα ιδρύσω<br>να ιδρύσω | έχω ιδρύσει<br>είχα ιδρύσει | ίδρυε<br>ιδρύετε | ίδρυσε<br>ιδρύστε |

| English Verb | Present | Imperfect | Past | Simple Future<br>Simple Subjunctive | Present Perfect<br>Past Perfect | Continuous Imperative | Simple Imperative |
|---|---|---|---|---|---|---|---|
| **I frame** (picture) | κορνιζώνω 13 | κορνίζωνα | κορνίζωσα | θα κορνιζώσω<br>να κορνιζώσω | έχω κορνιζώσει<br>είχα κορνιζώσει | κορνίζωνε<br>κορνιζώνετε | κορνίζωσε<br>κορνιζώστε |
| **I free** | ελευθερώνω 13 | ελευθέρωνα | ελευθέρωσα | θα ελευθερώσω<br>να ελευθερώσω | έχω ελευθερώσει<br>είχα ελευθερώσει | ελευθέρωνε<br>ελευθερώνετε | ελευθέρωσε<br>ελευθερώστε |
| **I freeze** | παγώνω 13 | πάγωνα | πάγωσα | θα παγώσω<br>να παγώσω | έχω παγώσει<br>είχα παγώσει | πάγωνε<br>παγώνετε | πάγωσε<br>παγώστε |
| **I freight** | ναυλώνω 13 | ναύλωνα | ναύλωσα | θα ναυλώσω<br>να ναυλώσω | έχω ναυλώσει<br>είχα ναυλώσει | ναύλωνε<br>ναυλώνετε | ναύλωσε<br>ναυλώστε |
| **I frequent** | συχνάζω 13 | σύχναζα | σύχνασα | θα συχνάσω<br>να συχνάσω | έχω συχνάσει<br>είχα συχνάσει | σύχναζε<br>συχνάζετε | σύχνασε<br>συχνάστε |
| **I freshen up** | *φρεσκάρομαι 14* | *φρεσκαριζόμουν* | *φρεσκαρίστηκα* | *θα φρεσκαριστώ*<br>*να φρεσκαριστώ* | *έχω φρεσκαριστεί*<br>*είχα φρεσκαριστεί* | *να φρεσκάρεσαι*<br>*φρεσκάρεστε* | *φρεσκαρίσου*<br>*φρεσκαριστείτε* |
| **I frighten** | τρομάζω 13 | τρόμαζα | τρόμαξα | θα τρομάξω<br>να τρομάξω | έχω τρομάξει<br>είχα τρομάξει | τρόμαζε<br>τρομάζετε | τρόμαξε<br>τρομάξτε |
| **I frown** | κατσουφιάζω 13 | κατσούφιαζα | κατσούφιασα | θα κατσουφιάσω<br>να κατσουφιάσω | έχω κατσουφιάσει<br>είχα κατσουφιάσει | κατσούφιαζε<br>κατσουφιάζετε | κατσούφιασε<br>κατσουφιάστε |
| **I frown on** | στραβοκοιτάζω 13 | στραβοκοίταζα | στραβοκοίταξα | θα στραβοκοιτάξω<br>να στραβοκοιτάξω | έχω στραβοκοιτάξει<br>είχα στραβοκοιτάξει | στραβοκοίταζε<br>στραβοκοιτάζετε | στραβοκοίταξε<br>στραβοκοιτάξτε |
| **I fruit** (bear fruit) | καρποφορώ 17 | καρποφορούσα | καρποφόρησα | θα καρποφορήσω<br>να καρποφορήσω | έχω καρποφορήσει<br>είχα καρποφορήσει | να καρποφορείς<br>καρποφορείτε | καρποφόρησε<br>καρποφορήτε |
| **I fry** | τηγανίζω 13 | τηγάνιζα | τηγάνισα | θα τηγανίσω<br>να τηγανίσω | έχω τηγανίσει<br>είχα τηγανίσει | τηγάνιζε<br>τηγανίζετε | τηγάνισε<br>τηγανίστε |
| **I fulfil** | εκπληρώνω 13 | εκπλήρωνα | εκπλήρωσα | θα εκπληρώσω<br>να εκπληρώσω | έχω εκπληρώσει<br>είχα εκπληρώσει | εκπλήρωνε<br>εκπληρώνετε | εκπλήρωσε<br>εκπληρώστε |

| English Verb | Present | Imperfect | Past | Simple Future<br>Simple Subjunctive | Present Perfect<br>Past Perfect | Continuous Imperative | Simple Imperative |
|---|---|---|---|---|---|---|---|
| **I fumble** | ψαχουλεύω 13 | ψαχούλευα | ψαχούλεψα | θα ψαχουλέψω<br>να ψαχουλέψω | έχω ψαχουλέψει<br>είχα ψαχουλέψει | ψαχούλευε<br>ψαχουλεύετε | ψαχούλεψε<br>ψαχουλέψτε |
| **I function** | λειτουργώ 17 | λειτουργούσα | λειτούργησα | θα λειτουργήσω<br>να λειτουργήσω | έχω λειτουργήσει<br>είχα λειτουργήσει | να λειτουργείς<br>λειτουργείτε | λειτούργησε<br>λειτουργήστε |
| **I furnish** | επιπλώνω 13 | επίπλωνα | επίπλωσα | θα επιπλώσω<br>να επιπλώσω | έχω επιπλώσει<br>είχα επιπλώσει | επίπλωνε<br>επιπλώνετε | επίπλωσε<br>επιπλώστε |
| **I gag** | φιμώνω 13 | φίμωνα | φίμωσα | θα φιμώσω<br>να φιμώσω | έχω φιμώσει<br>είχα φιμώσει | φίμωνε<br>φιμώνετε | φίμωσε<br>φιμώστε |
| **I gain** | κερδίζω 13 | κέρδιζα | κέρδισα | θα κερδίσω<br>να κερδίσω | έχω κερδίσει<br>είχα κερδίσει | κέρδιζε<br>κερδίζετε | κέρδισε<br>κερδίστε |
| **I gallop** | καλπάζω 13 | κάλπαζα | κάλπασα | θα καλπάσω<br>να καλπάσω | έχω καλπάσει<br>είχα καλπάσει | κάλπαζε<br>καλπάζετε | κάλπασε<br>καλπάστε |
| **I gamble** | χαρτοπαίζω 13 | χαρτόπαιζα | χαρτόπαιξα | θα χαρτοπαίξω<br>να χαρτοπαίξω | έχω χαρτοπαίξει<br>είχα χαρτοπαίξει | χαρτόπαιζε<br>χαρτοπαίζετε | χαρτόπαιξε<br>χαρτοπαίξτε |
| **I gasp** | αγκομαχώ 15 | αγκομαχούσα | αγκομάχησα | θα αγκομαχήσω<br>να αγκομαχήσω | έχω αγκομαχήσει<br>είχα αγκομαχήσει | αγκομάχα<br>αγκομαχάτε | αγκομάχησε<br>αγκομαχήστε |
| **I gather** | συναθροίζω 13 | συνάθροιζα | συνάθροισα | θα συναθροίσω<br>να συναθροίσω | έχω συναθροίσει<br>είχα συναθροίσει | συνάθροιζε<br>συναθροίζετε | συνάθροισε<br>συναθροίστε |
| **I generalise** | γενικεύω 13 | γενίκευα | γενίκευσα | θα γενικεύσω<br>να γενικεύσω | έχω γενικεύσει<br>είχα γενικεύσει | γενίκευε<br>γενικεύετε | γενίκευσε<br>γενικεύστε |
| **It generates** | επιφέρει 13 | επέφερε | επέφερε | θα επιφέρει<br>να επιφέρει | έχω επιφέρει<br>είχα επιφέρει | επίφερε<br>επιφέρετε | επίφερε<br>επιφέρτε |
| **I gesticulate** | χειρονομώ 17 | χειρονομούσα | χειρονόμησα | θα χειρονομήσω<br>να χειρονομήσω | έχω χειρονομήσει<br>είχα χειρονομήσει | να χειρονομείς<br>χειρονομείτε | χειρονόμησε<br>χειρονομήστε |

| English Verb | Present | Imperfect | Past | Simple Future<br>Simple Subjunctive | Present Perfect<br>Past Perfect | Continuous Imperative | Simple Imperative |
|---|---|---|---|---|---|---|---|
| **I get caught** | *πιάνομαι 14* | *πιανόμουν* | *πιάστηκα* | *θα πιαστώ*<br>*να πιαστώ* | *έχω πιαστεί*<br>*είχα πιαστεί* | *να πιάνεσαι*<br>*πιάνεστε* | *πιάσου*<br>*πιαστείτε* |
| **I get dressed** | *ντύνομαι 14* | *ντυνόμουν* | *ντύθηκα* | *θα ντυθώ*<br>*να ντυθώ* | *έχω ντυθεί*<br>*είχα ντυθεί* | *να ντύνεσαι*<br>*ντύνεστε* | *ντύσου*<br>*ντυθείτε* |
| **I get drunk** | μεθ(ά)ώ 15 | μεθούσα | μέθυσα | θα μεθύσω<br>να μεθύσω | έχω μεθύσει<br>είχα μεθύσει | μέθα<br>μεθάτε | μέθυσε<br>μεθύστε |
| **I get nervous** | *εκνευρίζομαι 14* | *εκνευριζόμουν* | *εκνευρίστηκα* | *θα εκνευριστώ*<br>*να εκνευριστώ* | *έχω εκνευριστεί*<br>*είχα εκνευριστεί* | *να εκνευρίζεσαι*<br>*εκνευρίζεστε* | *εκνευρίσου*<br>*εκνευριστείτε* |
| **I get ready** | *προετοιμάζομαι 14* | *προετοιμαζόμουν* | *προετοιμάστηκα* | *θα προετοιμαστώ*<br>*να προετοιμαστώ* | *έχω προετοιμαστεί*<br>*είχα προετοιμαστεί* | *να προετοιμάζεσαι*<br>*προετοιμάζεστε* | *προετοιμάσου*<br>*προετοιμαστείτε* |
| **I get rid of** | *απαλάσσομαι 14* | *απαλασσόμουν* | *απαλάχτηκα* | *θα απαλαχτώ*<br>*να απαλαχτώ* | *έχω απαλαχτεί*<br>*είχα απαλαχτεί* | *να απαλάσσεσαι*<br>*απαλάσσεστε* | *απαλάξου*<br>*απαλαχτείτε* |
| **I get up** | *σηκώνομαι 14* | *σηκωνόμουν* | *σηκώθηκα* | *θα σηκωθώ*<br>*να σηκωθώ* | *έχω σηκωθεί*<br>*είχα σηκωθεί* | *να σηκώνεσαι*<br>*σηκώνεστε* | *σηκώσου*<br>*σηκωθείτε* |
| **I get upset** | *συγχύζομαι 14* | *συγχυζόμουν* | *συγχύστηκα* | *θα συγχυστώ*<br>*να συγχυστώ* | *έχω συγχυστεί*<br>*είχα συγχυστεί* | *να συγχύζεσαι*<br>*συγχύζεστε* | *συγχύσου*<br>*συγχυστείτε* |
| **I get used to** | συνηθίζω 13 | συνήθιζα | συνήθισα | θα συνηθίσω<br>να συνηθίσω | έχω συνηθίσει<br>είχα συνηθίσει | συνήθιζε<br>συνηθίζετε | συνήθισε<br>συνηθίστε |
| **I giggle** | χαχανίζω 13 | χαχάνιζα | χαχάνισα | θα χαχανίσω<br>να χαχανίσω | έχω χαχανίσει<br>είχα χαχανίσει | χαχάνιζε<br>χαχανίζετε | χαχάνισε<br>χαχανίστε |
| **I give** | δίνω 13 | έδινα | έδωσα | θα δώσω<br>να δώσω | έχω δώσει<br>είχα δώσει | δίνε<br>δίνετε | δώσε<br>δώστε |
| **I am glad** | *χαίρομαι 14* | *χαιρόμουν* | *χάρηκα* | *θα χαρώ*<br>*να χαρώ* | *έχω χαρεί*<br>*είχα χαρεί* | *να χαίρεσαι*<br>*χαίρετε* | *χαίρε*<br>*χαρείτε* |

| English Verb | Present | Imperfect | Past | Simple Future<br>Simple Subjunctive | Present Perfect<br>Past Perfect | Continuous Imperative | Simple Imperative |
|---|---|---|---|---|---|---|---|
| **I glare** | λαμποκοπώ 15 | λαμποκοπούσα | λαμποκόπησα | θα λαμποκοπήσω<br>να λαμποκοπήσω | έχω λαμποκοπήσει<br>είχα λαμποκοπήσει | λαμποκόπα<br>λαμποκοπάτε | λαμποκόπησε<br>λαμποκοπήστε |
| **I glitter** | λάμπω 13 | έλαμπα | έλαμψα | θα λάμψω<br>να λάμψω | έχω λάμψει<br>είχα λάμψει | λάμπε<br>λάμπετε | λάμψε<br>λάμψτε |
| **I glorify** | δοξάζω 13 | δόξαζα | δόξασα | θα δοξάσω<br>να δοξάσω | έχω δοξάσει<br>είχα δοξάσει | δόξαζε<br>δοξάζετε | δόξασε<br>δοξάστε |
| **I glower at** | αγριοκοιτάζω 13 | αγριοκοίταζα | αγριοκοίταξα | θα αγριοκοιτάξω<br>να αγριοκοιτάξω | έχω αγριοκοιτάξει<br>είχα αγριοκοιτάξει | αγριοκοίταζε<br>αγριοκοιτάζετε | αγριοκοίταξε<br>αγριοκοιτάξτε |
| **I go** | πηγαίνω 13 | πήγαινα | πήγα | θα πάω<br>να πάω | έχω πάει<br>είχα πάει | πήγαινε<br>πηγαίνετε | πάνε<br>πάτε |
| **I go bankrupt** | χρεοκοπώ 15 | χρεοκοπούσα | χρεοκόπησα | θα χρεοκοπήσω<br>να χρεοκοπήσω | έχω χρεοκοπήσει<br>είχα χρεοκοπήσει | χρεοκόπα<br>χρεοκοπάτε | χρεοκόπησε<br>χρεοκοπήστε |
| **I go broke** | φαλιρίζω 13 | φαλίριζα | φαλίρισα | θα φαλιρίσω<br>να φαλιρίσω | έχω φαλιρίσει<br>είχα φαλιρίσει | φαλίριζε<br>φαλιρίζετε | φαλίρισε<br>φαλιρίστε |
| **I go mad** | *τρελλαίνομαι 14* | *τρελλαινόμουν* | *τρελλάθηκα* | *θα τρελλαθώ*<br>*να τρελλαθώ* | *έχω τρελλαθεί*<br>*είχα τρελλαθεί* | *να τρελλαίνεσαι*<br>*τρελλαίνεστε* | *να τρελλαθείς*<br>*τρελλαθείτε* |
| **I go in for politics** | *πολιτεύομαι 14* | *πολιτευόμουν* | *πολιτεύτηκα* | *θα πολιτευτώ*<br>*να πολιτευτώ* | *έχω πολιτευτεί*<br>*είχα πολιτευτεί* | *να πολιτεύεσαι*<br>*πολιτεύεστε* | *πολιτεύσου*<br>*πολιτευτείτε* |
| **I go near** | σιμώνω 13 | σίμωνα | σίμωσα | θα σιμώσω<br>να σιμώσω | έχω σιμώσει<br>είχα σιμώσει | σίμωνε<br>σιμώνετε | σίμωσε<br>σιμώστε |
| **I go off** | εκπυρσο-<br>κροτώ 17 | εκπυρσο-<br>κροτούσα | εκπυρσο-<br>κρότησα | θα εκπυρσοκροτήσω<br>να εκπυρσοκροτήσω | έχω εκπυρσοκροτήσει<br>είχα εκπυρσοκροτήσει | να εκπυρσοκροτείς<br>εκπυρσοκροτείτε | εκπυρσοκρότησε<br>εκπυρσοκροτήστε |
| **I go out** | βγαίνω 13 | έβγαινα | βγήκα | θα βγω<br>να βγω | έχω βγει<br>είχα βγει | βγαίνε<br>βγαίνετε | βγες<br>βγείτε |

| English Verb | Present | Imperfect | Past | Simple Future<br>Simple Subjunctive | Present Perfect<br>Past Perfect | Continuous Imperative | Simple Imperative |
|---|---|---|---|---|---|---|---|
| **I go up** | ανεβαίνω 13 | ανέβαινα | ανέβηκα | θα ανεβώ<br>να ανεβώ | έχω ανεβεί<br>είχα ανεβεί | ανέβαινε<br>ανεβαίνετε | ανέβα<br>ανεβήτε |
| **I gossip** | κουτσο-<br>μπολεύω 13 | κουτσο-<br>μπόλευα | κουτσο-<br>μπόλεψα | θα κουτσομπολέψω<br>να κουτσομπολέψω | έχω κουτσομπολέψει<br>είχα κουτσομπολέψει | κουτσομπόλευε<br>κουτσομπολεύετε | κουτσομπόλεψε<br>κουτσομπολέψτε |
| **I govern** | κυβερνώ 15 | κυβερνούσα | κυβέρνησα | θα κυβερνήσω<br>να κυβερνήσω | έχω κυβερνήσει<br>είχα κυβερνήσει | κυβέρνα<br>κυβερνάτε | κυβέρνησε<br>κυβερνήστε |
| **I grab** | γραπώνω 13 | γράπωνα | γράπωσα | θα γραπώσω<br>να γραπώσω | έχω γραπώσει<br>είχα γραπώσει | γράπωνε<br>γραπώνετε | γράπωσε<br>γραπώστε |
| **I grant** | χορηγώ 17 | χορηγούσα | χορήγησα | θα χορηγήσω<br>να χορηγήσω | έχω χορηγήσει<br>είχα χορηγήσει | να χορηγείς<br>χορηγείτε | χορήγησε<br>χορηγήστε |
| **I grasp** | αδράχνω 13 | άδραχνα | άδραξα | θα αδράξω<br>να αδράξω | έχω αδράξει<br>είχα αδράξει | άδραχνε<br>αδράχνετε | άδραξε<br>αδράξτε |
| **I graze** | βόσκω 13 | έβοσκα | βόσκησα | θα βοσκήσω<br>να βοσκήσω | έχω βοσκήσει<br>είχα βοσκήσει | βόσκε<br>βόσκετε | βόσκησε<br>βοσκήστε |
| **I grease** (lubricate) | λαδώνω 13 | λάδωνα | λάδωσα | θα λαδώσω<br>να λαδώσω | έχω λαδώσει<br>είχα λαδώσει | λάδωνε<br>λαδώνετε | λάδωσε<br>λαδώστε |
| **I greet** | χαιρετώ 15 | χαιρετούσα | χαιρέτησα | θα χαιρετήσω<br>να χαιρετήσω | έχω χαιρετήσει<br>είχα χαιρετήσει | χαιρέτα<br>χαιρετάτε | χαιρέτησε<br>χαιρετήστε |
| **I grill** | καψαλίζω 13 | καψάλιζα | καψάλισα | θα καψαλίσω<br>να καψαλίσω | έχω καψαλίσει<br>είχα καψαλίσει | καψάλιζε<br>καψαλίζετε | καψάλισε<br>καψαλίστε |
| **I grind** | αλέθω 13 | άλεθα | άλεσα | θα αλέσω<br>να αλέσω | έχω αλέσει<br>είχα αλέσει | άλεθε<br>αλέθετε | άλεσε<br>αλέστε |
| **I groan** | γογγύζω 13 | γόγγυζα | γόγγυσα | θα γογγύσω<br>να γογγύσω | έχω γογγύσει<br>είχα γογγύσει | γόγγυζε<br>γογγύζετε | γόγγυσε<br>γογγύστε |

| English Verb | Present | Imperfect | Past | Simple Future<br>Simple Subjunctive | Present Perfect<br>Past Perfect | Continuous Imperative | Simple Imperative |
|---|---|---|---|---|---|---|---|
| **I grow** | ψηλώνω 13 | ψήλωνα | ψήλωσα | θα ψήλωσω<br>να ψηλώσω | έχω ψηλώσει<br>είχα ψηλώσει | ψήλωνε<br>ψηλώνετε | ψήλωσε<br>ψηλώστε |
| **I grow** (a business) | μεγαλώνω 13 | μεγάλωνα | μεγάλωσα | θα μεγαλώσω<br>να μεγαλώσω | έχω μεγαλώσει<br>είχα μεγαλώσει | μεγάλωνε<br>μεγαλώνετε | μεγάλωσε<br>μεγαλώστε |
| **I grumble** | γκρινιάζω 13 | γκρίνιαζα | γκρίνιασα | θα γκρινιάσω<br>να γκρινιάσω | έχω γκρινιάσει<br>είχα γκρινιάσει | γκρίνιαζε<br>γκρινιάζετε | γκρίνιασε<br>γκρινιάστε |
| **I grunt** | γρυλίζω 13 | γρύλιζα | γρύλισα | θα γρυλίσω<br>να γρυλίσω | έχω γρυλίσει<br>είχα γρυλίσει | γρύλιζε<br>γρυλίζετε | γρύλισε<br>γρυλίστε |
| **I guarantee** | *εγγυώμαι 42* | *εγγυόμουν* | *εγγυήθηκα* | *θα εγγυηθώ*<br>*να εγγυηθώ* | *έχω εγγυηθεί*<br>*είχα εγγυηθεί* | *να εγγυάσαι*<br>*εγγυάστε* | *εγγυήσου*<br>*εγγυηθείτε* |
| **I guard** | φρουρώ 17 | φρουρούσα | φρούρησα | θα φρουρήσω<br>να φρουρήσω | έχω φρουρήσει<br>είχα φρουρήσει | να φρουρείς<br>φρουρείτε | φρούρησε<br>φρουρήστε |
| **I guard** | φυλάω 15 | φύλαγα | φύλαξα | θα φυλάξω<br>να φυλάξω | έχω φυλάξει<br>είχα φυλάξει | φύλα<br>φυλάτε | φύλαξε<br>φυλάξτε |
| **I guess** | μαντεύω 13 | μάντευα | μάντεψα | θα μαντέψω<br>να μαντέψω | έχω μαντέψει<br>είχα μαντέψει | μάντευε<br>μαντεύετε | μάντεψε<br>μαντέψτε |
| **I guide** | ξεναγώ 17 | ξεναγούσα | ξενάγησα | θα ξεναγήσω<br>να ξεναγήσω | έχω ξεναγήσει<br>είχα ξεναγήσει | να ξεναγείς<br>ξεναγείτε | ξενάγησε<br>ξεναγήστε |
| **I gulp** | καταβροχθίζω 13 | καταβρόχθιζα | καταβρόχθισα | θα καταβροχθίσω<br>να καταβροχθίσω | έχω καταβροχθίσει<br>είχα καταβροχθίσει | καταβρόχθιζε<br>καταβροχθίζετε | καταβρόχθισε<br>καταβροχθίστε |
| **I gurgle** | γουργουρίζω 13 | γουργούριζα | γουργούρισα | θα γουργουρίσω<br>να γουργουρίσω | έχω γουργουρίσει<br>είχα γουργουρίσει | γουργούριζε<br>γουργουρίζετε | γουργούρισε<br>γουργουρίστε |
| **I handle** | *χειρίζομαι 14* | *χειριζόμουν* | *χειρίστηκα* | *θα χειριστώ*<br>*να χειριστώ* | *έχω χειριστεί*<br>*είχα χειριστεί* | *να χειρίζεσαι*<br>*χειρίζεστε* | *χειρίσου*<br>*χειριστείτε* |

| English Verb | Present | Imperfect | Past | Simple Future<br>Simple Subjunctive | Present Perfect<br>Past Perfect | Continuous Imperative | Simple Imperative |
|---|---|---|---|---|---|---|---|
| **I hang** (execute) | κρεμώ 15 | κρεμούσα | κρέμασα | θα κρεμάσω<br>να κρεμάσω | έχω κρεμάσει<br>είχα κρεμάσει | κρέμα<br>κρεμάτε | κρέμασε<br>κρεμάστε |
| **It happens** | συμβαίνει 13 | συνέβαινε | συνέβη | θα συμβεί<br>να συμβεί | έχει συμβεί<br>είχε συμβεί | – | – |
| **I harass** | παρενοχλώ 17 | παρενοχλούσα | παρενόχλησα | θα παρενοχλήσω<br>να παρενοχλήσω | έχω παρενοχλήσει<br>είχα παρενοχλήσει | να παρενοχλείς<br>παρενοχλείτε | παρενόχλησε<br>παρενοχλήστε |
| **I harm** | κακοποιώ 17 | κακοποιούσα | κακοποίησα | θα κακοποιήσω<br>να κακοποιήσω | έχω κακοποιήσει<br>είχα κακοποιήσει | να κακοποιείς<br>κακοποιείτε | κακοποίησε<br>κακοποιήστε |
| **I harvest** | θερίζω 13 | θέριζα | θέρισα | θα θερίσω<br>να θερίσω | έχω θερίσει<br>είχα θερίσει | θέριζε<br>θερίζετε | θέρισε<br>θερίστε |
| **I hasten** | σπεύδω 13 | έσπευδα | έσπευσα | θα σπεύσω<br>να σπεύσω | έχω σπεύσει<br>είχα σπεύσει | σπεύδε<br>σπεύδετε | σπεύσε<br>σπεύστε |
| **I hate** | μισώ 13 | μισούσα | μίσησα | θα μισήσω<br>να μισήσω | έχω μισήσει<br>είχα μισήσει | να μισείς<br>μισείτε | μίσησε<br>μισήστε |
| **I haunt** | στοιχειώνω 13 | στοίχειωνα | στοίχειωσα | θα στοιχειώσω<br>να στοιχειώσω | έχω στοιχειώσει<br>είχα στοιχειώσει | στοιχείωνε<br>στοιχειώνετε | στοίχειωσε<br>στοιχειώστε |
| **I have** | έχω 13 | είχα | είχα | θα έχω<br>να έχω | – | – | έχε<br>έχετε |
| **I have flu** | γριπιάζω 13 | γρίπιαζα | γρίπιασα | θα γριπιάσω<br>να γριπιάσω | έχω γριπιάσει<br>είχα γριπιάσει | γρίπιαζε<br>γριπιάζετε | γρίπιασε<br>γριπιάστε |
| **I have fun** | γλεντώ 15 | γλεντούσα | γλέντησα | θα γλεντήσω<br>να γλεντήσω | έχω γλεντήσει<br>είχα γλεντήσει | γλέντα<br>γλεντάτε | γλέντησε<br>γλεντήστε |
| **I have patience** | υπομένω 13 | υπέμενα | υπέμεινα | θα υπομείνω<br>να υπομείνω | έχω υπομείνει<br>είχα υπομείνει | υπόμενε<br>υπομένετε | υπόμεινε<br>υπομείντε |

| nglish Verb | Present | Imperfect | Past | Simple Future<br>Simple Subjunctive | Present Perfect<br>Past Perfect | Continuous Imperative | Simple Imperative |
|---|---|---|---|---|---|---|---|
| **I hazard** (a guess) | ριψοκινδυνεύω 13 | ριψοκινδύνευα | ριψοκινδύνεψα | θα ριψοκινδυνεύσω<br>να ριψοκινδυνεύσω | έχω ριψοκινδυνεύσει<br>είχα ριψοκινδυνεύσει | ριψοκινδύνευε<br>ριψοκινδυνεύετε | ριψοκινδύνεψε<br>ριψοκινδυνέψτε |
| **I heal** | γιατρεύω 13 | γιάτρευα | γιάτρεψα | θα γιατρέψω<br>να γιατρέψω | έχω γιατρέψει<br>είχα γιατρέψει | γιάτρευε<br>γιατρεύετε | γιάτρεψε<br>γιατρέψτε |
| **I hear** | ακούω 20 | άκουα | άκουσα | θα ακούσω<br>να ακούσω | έχω ακούσει<br>είχα ακούσει | άκουε<br>ακούτε | άκουσε<br>ακούστε |
| **I heat** | ζεσταίνω 13 | ζέσταινα | ζέστανα | θα ζεστάνω<br>να ζεστάνω | έχω ζεστάνει<br>είχα ζεστάνει | ζέσταινε<br>ζεσταίνετε | ζέστανε<br>ζεστάντε |
| **I help** | βοηθ(ά)ώ 15 | βοηθούσα | βοήθησα | θα βοηθήσω<br>να βοηθήσω | έχω βοηθήσει<br>είχα βοηθήσει | βοήθα<br>βοηθάτε | βοήθησε<br>βοηθήστε |
| **I herald** | προαναγγέλλω 13 | προανάγγελλα | προανάγγειλα | θα προαναγγείλω<br>να προαναγγείλω | έχω προαναγγείλει<br>είχα προαναγγείλει | προανάγγελλε<br>προαναγγέλλετε | προανάγγειλε<br>προαναγγείλτε |
| **I hesitate** | διστάζω 13 | δίσταζα | δίστασα | θα διστάσω<br>να διστάσω | έχω διστάσει<br>είχα διστάσει | δίσταζε<br>διστάζετε | δίστασε<br>διστάστε |
| **I hide** | κρύβω 13 | έκρυβα | έκρυψα | θα κρύψω<br>να κρύψω | έχω κρύψει<br>είχα κρύψει | κρύβε<br>κρύβετε | κρύψε<br>κρύψτε |
| **I highlight** | εξαίρω 13 | εξήρα | εξήρα | θα εξάρω<br>να εξάρω | έχω εξάρει<br>είχα εξάρει | να εξαίρεις<br>εξαίρετε | να εξάρεις<br>εξάρετε |
| **I hinder** | εμποδίζω 13 | εμπόδιζα | εμπόδισα | θα εμποδίσω<br>να εμποδίσω | έχω εμποδίσει<br>είχα εμποδίσει | εμπόδιζε<br>εμποδίζετε | εμπόδισε<br>εμποδίστε |
| **I hint** | υποδηλώνω 13 | υποδήλωνα | υποδήλωσα | θα υποδηλώσω<br>να υποδηλώσω | έχω υποδηλώσει<br>είχα υποδηλώσει | υποδήλωνε<br>υποδηλώνετε | υποδήλωσε<br>υποδηλώστε |
| **I hire** | νοικιάζω 13 | νοίκιαζα | νοίκιασα | θα νοικιάσω<br>να νοικιάσω | έχω νοικιάσει<br>είχα νοικιάσει | νοίκιαζε<br>νοικιάζετε | νοίκιασε<br>νοικιάστε |

| English Verb | Present | Imperfect | Past | Simple Future<br>Simple Subjunctive | Present Perfect<br>Past Perfect | Continuous Imperative | Simple Imperative |
|---|---|---|---|---|---|---|---|
| **I hire**<br>(employ) | προσλαμβάνω 13 | προσλάμβανα | προσέλαβα | θα προσλάβω<br>να προσλάβω | έχω προσλάβει<br>είχα προσλάβει | προσλάμβανε<br>προσλαμβάνετε | πρόσλαβε<br>προσλάβετε |
| **I hit** | βαρ(άω)ώ 15 | βαρούσα | βάρεσα | θα βαρέσω<br>να βαρέσω | έχω βαρέσει<br>είχα βαρέσει | βάρα<br>βαράτε | βάρεσε<br>βαρέστε |
| **I hoard**<br>(money/food) | αποθυσαυρίζω 13 | αποθυσαύριζα | αποθυσαύρισα | θα αποθυσαυρίσω<br>να αποθυσαυρίσω | έχω αποθυσαυρίσει<br>είχα αποθυσαυρίσει | αποθυσαύριζε<br>αποθυσαυρίζετε | αποθυσαύρισε<br>αποθυσαυρίστε |
| **I hold** | κρατ(άω)ώ 15 | κρατούσα | κράτησα | θα κρατήσω<br>να κρατήσω | έχω κρατήσει<br>είχα κρατήσει | κράτα<br>κρατάτε | κράτησε<br>κρατήστε |
| **I hold**<br>(support/bear) | βαστ(άω)ώ 15 | βαστούσα | βάστηξα | θα βαστήξω<br>να βαστήξω | έχω βαστήξει<br>είχα βαστήξει | βάστα<br>βαστάτε | βάστηξε<br>βαστήξτε |
| **I honour** | τιμ(άω)ώ 15 | τιμούσα | τίμησα | θα τιμήσω<br>να τιμήσω | έχω τιμήσει<br>είχα τιμήσει | τίμα<br>τιμάτε | τίμησε<br>τιμήστε |
| **I hook** | γαντζώνω 13 | γάντζωνα | γάντζωσα | θα γαντζώσω<br>να γαντζώσω | έχω γαντζώσει<br>είχα γαντζώσει | γάντζωνε<br>γαντζώνετε | γάντζωσε<br>γαντζώστε |
| **I hoot**<br>(car horn) | κορνάρω 13 | κόρναρα | κορνάρησα | θα κορνάρω<br>να κορνάρω | έχω κορνάρει<br>είχα κορνάρει | κόρναρε<br>κορνάρετε | κορνάρησε<br>κορναρήστε |
| **I hope** | ελπίζω 13 | ήλπιζα | ήλπισα | θα ελπίσω<br>να ελπίσω | έχω ελπίσει<br>είχα ελπίσει | έλπιζε<br>ελπίζετε | έλπισε<br>ελπίστε |
| **I hover** | *αιωρούμαι 18* | *αιωρούμουν* | *αιωρήθηκα* | *θα αιωρηθώ*<br>*να αιωρηθώ* | *έχω αιωρηθεί*<br>*είχα αιωρηθεί* | *να αιωρείσαι*<br>*αιωρείσθε* | *αιωρήσου*<br>*αιωρηθείτε* |
| **I howl**<br>(wind/animal) | ουρλιάζω 13 | ούρλιαζα | ούρλιαξα | θα ουρλιάξω<br>να ουρλιάξω | έχω ουρλιάξει<br>είχα ουρλιάξει | ούρλιαζε<br>ουρλιάζετε | ούρλιαξε<br>ουρλιάξτε |
| **I hum**<br>(tune) | σιγοτραγουδώ 15 | σιγοτραγουδούσα | σιγοτραγούδησα | θα σιγοτραγουδήσω<br>να σιγοτραγουδήσω | έχω σιγοτραγουδήσει<br>είχα σιγοτραγουδήσει | σιγοτραγούδα<br>σιγοτραγουδάτε | σιγοτραγούδησε<br>σιγοτραγουδήστε |

| English Verb | Present | Imperfect | Past | Simple Future<br>Simple Subjunctive | Present Perfect<br>Past Perfect | Continuous Imperative | Simple Imperative |
|---|---|---|---|---|---|---|---|
| **I humiliate** | ταπεινώνω 13 | ταπείνωνα | ταπείνωσα | θα ταπεινώσω<br>να ταπεινώσω | έχω ταπεινώσει<br>είχα ταπεινώσει | ταπείνωνε<br>ταπεινώνετε | ταπείνωσε<br>ταπεινώστε |
| **I hunt** | κυνηγώ 15 | κυνηγούσα | κυνήγησα | θα κυνηγήσω<br>να κυνηγήσω | έχω κυνηγήσει<br>είχα κυνηγήσει | κυνήγα<br>κυνηγάτε | κυνήγησε<br>κυνηγήστε |
| **I hurry** | *βιάζομαι 14* | *βιαζόμουν* | *βιάστηκα* | *θα βιαστώ*<br>*να βιαστώ* | *έχω βιαστεί*<br>*είχα βιαστεί* | *να βιάζεσαι*<br>*βιάζεστε* | *βιάσου*<br>*βιαστείτε* |
| **I hurt** | πληγώνω 13 | πλήγωνα | πλήγωσα | θα πληγώσω<br>να πληγώσω | έχω πληγώσει<br>είχα πληγώσει | πλήγωνε<br>πληγώνετε | πλήγωσε<br>πληγώστε |
| **I hush up** | αποσιωπώ 17 | αποσιωπούσα | αποσιώπησα | θα αποσιωπήσω<br>να αποσιωπήσω | έχω αποσιωπήσει<br>είχα αποσιωπήσει | να αποσιωπείς<br>αποσιωπείτε | αποσιώπησε<br>αποσιωπήστε |
| **I hush up** (scandal) | κουκουλώνω 13 | κουκούλωνα | κουκούλωσα | θα κουκουλώσω<br>να κουκουλώσω | έχω κουκουλώσει<br>είχα κουκουλώσει | κουκούλωνε<br>κουκουλώνετε | κουκούλωσε<br>κουκουλώστε |
| **I identify** (distinguish) | ταυτίζω 13 | ταύτιζα | ταύτισα | θα ταυτίσω<br>να ταυτίσω | έχω ταυτίσει<br>είχα ταυτίσει | ταύτιζε<br>ταυτίζετε | ταύτισε<br>ταυτίστε |
| **I idolize** | θεοποιώ 17 | θεοποιούσα | θεοποίησα | θα θεοποιήσω<br>να θεοποιήσω | έχω θεοποιήσει<br>είχα θεοποιήσει | να θεοποιείς<br>θεοποιείτε | θεοποίησε<br>θεοποιήστε |
| **I ignore** | αγνοώ 13 | αγνοούσα | αγνόησα | θα αγνοήσω<br>να αγνοήσω | έχω αγνοήσει<br>είχα αγνοήσει | να αγνοείς<br>αγνοείτε | αγνόησε<br>αγνοήστε |
| **I illuminate** | φωτίζω 13 | φώτιζα | φώτισα | θα φωτίσω<br>να φωτίσω | έχω φωτίσει<br>είχα φωτίσει | φώτιζε<br>φωτίζετε | φώτισε<br>φωτίστε |
| **I imagine** | *φαντάζομαι 14* | *φανταζόμουν* | *φαντάστηκα* | *θα φανταστώ*<br>*να φανταστώ* | *έχω φανταστεί*<br>*είχα φανταστεί* | *να φαντάζεσαι*<br>*φαντάζεστε* | *φαντάσου*<br>*φανταστείτε* |
| **I imitate** | *μιμούμαι 18* | *μιμούμουν* | *μιμήθηκα* | *θα μιμηθώ*<br>*να μιμηθώ* | *έχω μιμηθεί*<br>*είχα μιμηθεί* | *να μιμείσαι*<br>*μιμείστε* | *μιμήσου*<br>*μιμηθείτε* |

| English Verb | Present | Imperfect | Past | Simple Future<br>Simple Subjunctive | Present Perfect<br>Past Perfect | Continuous Imperative | Simple Imperative |
|---|---|---|---|---|---|---|---|
| **I immigrate** | μεταναστεύω 13 | ματανάστευα | μετανάστεψα | θα μεταναστέψω<br>να μεταναστέψω | έχω μεταναστέψει<br>είχα μεταναστέψει | μετανάστευε<br>μεταναστεύετε | μετανάστεψε<br>μεταναστέψτε |
| **I impel** | εξωθώ 17 | εξωθούσα | εξώθησα | θα εξωθήσω<br>να εξωθήσω | έχω εξωθήσει<br>είχα εξωθήσει | να εξωθείς<br>εξωθείτε | εξώθησε<br>εξωθήστε |
| **I impersonate** | παριστάνω 13 | παρίστανα | παράστησα | θα παραστήσω<br>να παραστήσω | έχω παραστήσει<br>είχα παραστήσει | παρίστανε<br>παριστάνετε | παράστησε<br>παραστήστε |
| **I impersonate** (mimic) | *υποδύομαι 14* | *υποδυόμουν* | *υποδύθηκα* | *θα υποδυθώ*<br>*να υποδυθώ* | *έχω υποδυθεί*<br>*είχα υποδυθεί* | *να υποδύεσαι*<br>*υποδύεστε* | *υποδύσου*<br>*υποδυθείτε* |
| **I implore** | ικετεύω 14 | ικέτευα | ικέτεψα | θα ικετέψω<br>να ικετέψω | έχω ικετέψει<br>είχα ικετέψει | ικέτευε<br>ικετεύετε | ικέτεψε<br>ικετέψτε |
| **I imply** | *υπαινίσσομαι 14* | *υπαινισσόμουν* | *υπαινίχτηκα* | *θα υπαινιχθώ*<br>*να υπαινιχθώ* | *έχω υπαινιχθεί*<br>*είχα υπαινιχθεί* | *να υπαινίσσεσαι*<br>*υπαινίσσεστε* | *υπαινίσου*<br>*υπαινιχθείτε* |
| **I import** | εισάγω 13 | εισήγα | εισήγαγα | θα εισαγάγω<br>να εισαγάγω | έχω εισαγάγει<br>είχα εισαγάγει | είσαγε<br>εισάγετε | εισήγαγε<br>εισαγάγετε |
| **I impose** | επιβάλλω 13 | επέβαλλα | επέβαλα | θα επιβάλλω<br>να επιβάλλω | έχω επιβάλλει<br>είχα επιβάλλει | επίβαλλε<br>επιβάλλετε | επίβαλε<br>επιβάλετε |
| **I impress** | εντυπωσιάζω 13 | εντυπωσίαζα | εντυπωσίασα | θα εντυπωσιάσω<br>να εντυπωσιάσω | έχω εντυπωσιάσει<br>είχα εντυπωσιάσει | εντυπωσίαζε<br>εντυπωσιάζετε | εντυπωσίασε<br>εντυπωσιάστε |
| **I imprison** | φυλακίζω 13 | φυλάκιζα | φυλάκισα | θα φυλακίσω<br>να φυλακίσω | έχω φυλακίσει<br>είχα φυλακίσει | φυλάκιζε<br>φυλακίζετε | φυλάκισε<br>φυλακίστε |
| **I improve** | βελτιώνω 13 | βελτίωνα | βελτίωσα | θα βελτιώσω<br>να βελτιώσω | έχω βελτιώσει<br>είχα βελτιώσει | βελτίωνε<br>βελτιώνετε | βελτίωσε<br>βελτιώστε |
| **I improvise** | αυτοσχεδιάζω 13 | αυτοσχεδίαζα | αυτοσχεδίασα | θα αυτοσχεδιάσω<br>να αυτοσχεδιάσω | έχω αυτοσχεδιάσει<br>είχα αυτοσχεδιάσει | αυτοσχεδίαζε<br>αυτοσχεδιάζετε | αυτοσχεδίασε<br>αυτοσχεδιάστε |

| English Verb | Present | Imperfect | Past | Simple Future<br>Simple Subjunctive | Present Perfect<br>Past Perfect | Continuous Imperative | Simple Imperative |
|---|---|---|---|---|---|---|---|
| **I inundate** | κατακλύζω 13 | κατάκλυζα | κατάκλυσα | θα κατακλύσω<br>να κατακλύσω | έχω κατακλύσει<br>είχα κατακλύσει | κατάκλυζε<br>κατακλύζετε | κατάκλυσε<br>κατακλύστε |
| **I inaugurate** | εγκαινιάζω 13 | εγκαινίαζα | εγκαινίασα | θα εγκαινιάσω<br>να εγκαινιάσω | έχω εγκαινιάσει<br>είχα εγκαινιάσει | εγκαινίαζε<br>εγκαινιάζετε | εγκαινίασε<br>εγκαινιάστε |
| **I incapacitate** | αχριστεύω 13 | αχρίστευα | αχρίστευσα | θα αχριστεύσω<br>να αχριστεύσω | έχω αχριστεύσει<br>είχα αχριστεύσει | αχρίστευε<br>αχριστεύετε | αχρίστεψε<br>αχριστέψτε |
| **I incarnate** | ενσαρκώνω 13 | ενσάρκωνα | ενσάρκωσα | θα ενσαρκώσω<br>να ενσαρκώσω | έχω ενσαρκώσει<br>είχα ενσαρκώσει | ενσάρκωνε<br>ενσαρκώνετε | ενσάρκωσε<br>ενσαρκώστε |
| **I incite** | ξεσηκώνω 13 | ξεσήκωνα | ξεσήκωσα | θα ξεσηκώσω<br>να ξεσηκώσω | έχω ξεσηκώσει<br>είχα ξεσηκώσει | ξεσήκωνε<br>ξεσηκώνετε | ξεσήκωσε<br>ξεσηκώστε |
| **I include** | περιλαμβάνω 13 | περιλάμβανα | περιέλαβα | θα περιλάβω<br>να περιλάβω | έχω περιλάβει<br>είχα περιλάβει | περιλάμβανε<br>περιλαμβάνετε | περίλαβε<br>περιλάβετε |
| **I increase** | αυξάνω 13<br>αυξαίνω 13 | αύξαινα | αύξησα | θα αυξήσω<br>να αυξήσω | έχω αυξήσει<br>είχα αυξήσει | αύξανε<br>αυξάνετε | αύξησε<br>αυξήστε |
| **I incubate** | εκκολάπτω 13 | εκκόλαπτα | εκκόλαψα | θα εκκολάψω<br>να εκκολάψω | έχω εκκολάψει<br>είχα εκκολάψει | εκκόλαπτε<br>εκκολάπτετε | εκκόλαψε<br>εκκολάψτε |
| **I indicate** | υποδεικνύω 13 | υποδείκνυα | υπέδειξα | θα υποδείξω<br>να υποδείξω | έχω υποδείξει<br>είχα υποδείξει | υποδείκνυε<br>υποδεικνύετε | υπόδειξε<br>υποδείξτε |
| **I am indifferent** | αδιαφορώ 17 | αδιαφορούσα | αδιαφόρησα | θα αδιαφορήσω<br>να αδιαφορήσω | έχω αδιαφορήσει<br>είχα αδιαφορήσει | να αδιαφορείς<br>αδιαφορείτε | αδιαφόρησε<br>αδιαφορήστε |
| **I am inspired** | *εμπνέομαι 14* | *εμπνεόμουν* | *εμπνεύστηκα* | *θα εμπνευστώ*<br>*να εμπνευστώ* | *έχω εμπνευστεί*<br>*είχα εμπνευστεί* | *να εμπνέεσαι*<br>*εμπνέεστε* | *εμπνεύσου*<br>*εμπνευστείτε* |
| **I am involved** | *μπλέκομαι 14* | *μπλεκόμουν* | *μπλέχτηκα* | *θα μπλεχτώ*<br>*να μπλεχτώ* | *έχω μπλεχτεί*<br>*είχα μπλεχτεί* | *να μπλέκεσαι*<br>*μπλέκεστε* | *μπλέξου*<br>*μπλεχτείτε* |

| English Verb | Present | Imperfect | Past | Simple Future<br>Simple Subjunctive | Present Perfect<br>Past Perfect | Continuous Imperative | Simple Imperative |
|---|---|---|---|---|---|---|---|
| **I infect** | μιαίωνω 13 | μίαινα | μίανα | θα μιάνω<br>να μιάνω | έχω μιάνει<br>είχα μιάνει | μίαινε<br>μιαίνετε | μίανε<br>μιάντε |
| **I am inflamed** | *ερεθίζομαι 14* | *ερεθιζόμουν* | *ερεθίστηκα* | *θα ερεθιστώ*<br>*να ερεθιστώ* | *έχω ερεθιστεί*<br>*είχα ερεθιστεί* | *να ερεθίζεσαι*<br>*ερεθίζεστε* | *ερεθίσου*<br>*ερεθιστείτε* |
| **I influence** | επηρεάζω 13 | επηρέαζα | επηρέασα | θα επηρεάσω<br>να επηρεάσω | έχω επηρεάσει<br>είχα επηρεάσει | επηρέαζε<br>επηρεάζετε | επηρέασε<br>επηρεάστε |
| **I inform** | πληροφορώ 17 | πληροφορούσα | πληροφόρησα | θα πληροφορήσω<br>να πληροφορήσω | έχω πληροφορήσει<br>είχα πληροφορήσει | να πληροφορείς<br>πληροφορείτε | πληροφόρησε<br>πληροφορήστε |
| **I inform** | καταδίδω 13 | κατέδιδα | κατέδωσα | θα καταδώσω<br>να καταδώσω | έχω καταδώσει<br>είχα καταδώσει | κατέδιδε<br>καταδίδετε | κατάδωσε<br>καταδώστε |
| **I infuriate** | βουρλίζω 13 | βούρλιζα | βούρλισα | θα βουρλίσω<br>να βουρλίσω | έχω βουρλίσει<br>είχα βουρλίσει | βούρλιζε<br>βουρλίζετε | βούρλισε<br>βουρλίστε |
| **I inhabit** | κατοικώ 17 | κατοικούσα | κατοίκησα | θα κατοικήσω<br>να κατοικήσω | έχω κατοικήσει<br>είχα κατοικήσει | να κατοικείς<br>κατοικείτε | κατοίκησε<br>κατοικήστε |
| **I inherit** | κληρονομώ 17 | κληρονομούσα | κληρονόμησα | θα κληρονομήσω<br>να κληρονομήσω | έχω κληρονομήσει<br>είχα κληρονομήσει | κληρονόμα<br>κληρονομάτε | κληρονόμησε<br>κληρονομήστε |
| **I inhibit** | αναχαιτίζω 13 | αναχαίτιζα | αναχαίτισα | θα αναχαιτίσω<br>να αναχαιτίσω | έχω αναχαιτίσει<br>είχα αναχαιτίσει | αναχαίτιζε<br>αναχαιτίζετε | αναχαίτισε<br>αναχαιτίστε |
| **I initiate** | μυώ 17 | μυούσα | μύησα | θα μυήσω<br>να μυήσω | έχω μυήσει<br>είχα μυήσει | να μυείς<br>μυείτε | μύησε<br>μυήστε |
| **I injure** | τραυματίζω 13 | τραυμάτιζα | τραυμάτισα | θα τραυματίσω<br>να τραυματίσω | έχω τραυματίσει<br>είχα τραυματίσει | τραυμάτιζε<br>τραυματίζετε | τραυμάτισε<br>τραυματίστε |
| **I innovate** | νεωτερίζω 13 | νεωτέριζα | νεωτέρισα | θα νεωτερίσω<br>να νεωτερίσω | έχω νεωτερίσει<br>είχα νεωτερίσει | νεωτέριζε<br>νεωτερίζετε | νεωτέρισε<br>νεωτερίστε |

| English Verb | Present | Imperfect | Past | Simple Future<br>Simple Subjunctive | Present Perfect<br>Past Perfect | Continuous Imperative | Simple Imperative |
|---|---|---|---|---|---|---|---|
| **I inquire into** | διερευν(ά)ώ 15 | διερευνούσα | διερεύνησα | θα διερευνήσω<br>να διερευνήσω | έχω διερευνήσει<br>είχα διερευνήσει | διερεύνα<br>διερευνάτε | διερεύνησε<br>διερευνήστε |
| **I insert** | παρεμβάλλω 13 | παρέμβαλλα | παρέμβαλα | θα παρεμβάλω<br>να παρεμβάλω | έχω παρεμβάλει<br>είχα παρεμβάλει | παρέμβαλλε<br>παρεμβάλλετε | παρέμβαλε<br>παρεμβάλτε |
| **I insist** | επιμένω 13 | επέμενα | επέμεινα | θα επιμείνω<br>να επιμείνω | έχω επιμείνει<br>είχα επιμείνει | επίμενε<br>επιμένετε | επίμεινε<br>επιμείνετε |
| **I insist** | αξιώ 15 | αξιούσα | αξίωσα | θα αξιώσω<br>να αξιώσω | έχω αξιώσει<br>είχα αξιώσει | να αξιείς<br>αξιείτε | αξίωσε<br>αξιώστε |
| **I inspect** | επιθεωρώ 17 | επιθεωρούσα | επιθεώρησα | θα επιθεωρήσω<br>να επιθεωρήσω | έχω επιθεωρήσει<br>είχα επιθεωρήσει | να επιθεωρείς<br>επιθεωρείτε | επιθεώρησε<br>επιθεωρήστε |
| **I inspire** | εμπνέω 13 | ενέπνεα | ενέπνευσα | θα εμπνεύσω<br>να εμπνεύσω | έχω εμπνεύσει<br>είχα εμπνεύσει | έμπνεε<br>εμπνέετε | ενέπνευσε<br>εμπνεύστε |
| **I install** | εγκαθιστώ 15 | εγκαθιστούσα | εγκατέστησα | θα εγκαταστήσω<br>να εγκαταστήσω | έχω εγκαταστήσει<br>είχα εγκαταστήσει | εγκαθίστα<br>εγκαθιστάτε | εγκατέστησε<br>εγκαταστήστε |
| **I instigate** | υποκινώ 17 | υποκινούσα | υποκίνησα | θα υποκινήσω<br>να υποκινήσω | έχω υποκινήσει<br>είχα υποκινήσει | να υποκινείς<br>υποκινείτε | υποκίνησε<br>υποκινήστε |
| **I institute** | καθιερώνω 13 | καθιέρωνα | καθιέρωσα | θα καθιερώσω<br>να καθιερώσω | έχω καθιερώσει<br>είχα καθιερώσει | καθιέρωνε<br>καθιερώνετε | καθιέρωσε<br>καθιερώστε |
| **I instruct** | καθοδηγώ 17 | καθοδηγούσα | καθοδήγησα | θα καθοδηγήσω<br>να καθοδηγήσω | έχω καθοδηγήσει<br>είχα καθοδηγήσει | να καθοδηγείς<br>καθοδηγείτε | καθοδήγησε<br>καθοδηγήστε |
| **I insulate** | μονώνω 13 | μόνωνα | μόνωσα | θα μονώσω<br>να μονώσω | έχω μονώσει<br>είχα μονώσει | μόνωνε<br>μονώνετε | μόνωσε<br>μονώστε |
| **I insult** | προσβάλλω 13 | πρόσβαλλα | προσέβαλα | θα προσβάλω<br>να προσβάλω | έχω προσβάλει<br>είχα προσβάλει | πρόσβαλλε<br>προσβάλλετε | πρόσβαλε<br>προσβάλτε |

| English Verb | Present | Imperfect | Past | Simple Future<br>Simple Subjunctive | Present Perfect<br>Past Perfect | Continuous Imperative | Simple Imperative |
|---|---|---|---|---|---|---|---|
| **I insure** | ασφαλίζω 13 | ασφάλιζα | ασφάλισα | θα ασφαλίσω<br>να ασφαλίσω | έχω ασφαλίσει<br>είχα ασφαλίσει | ασφάλιζε<br>ασφαλίζετε | ασφάλισε<br>ασφαλίστε |
| **I intensify** | εντείνω 13 | έντεινα | ενέτεινα | θα εντείνω<br>να εντείνω | έχω εντείνει<br>είχα εντείνει | έντεινε<br>εντείνετε | έντεινε<br>εντείντε |
| **I interest** | *ενδιαφέρομαι 14* | *ενδιαφερόμουν* | *ενδιαφέρθηκα* | *θα ενδιαφερθώ*<br>*να ενδιαφερθώ* | *έχω ενδιαφερθεί*<br>*είχα ενδιαφερθεί* | *να ενδιαφέρεσαι*<br>*ενδιαφέρεστε* | *ενδιαφέρσου*<br>*ενδιαφερθείτε* |
| **I interfere** | *ανακατεύομαι 14* | *ανακατευόμουν* | *ανακατεύτηκα* | *θα ανακατευτώ*<br>*να ανακατευτώ* | *έχω ανακατευτεί*<br>*είχα ανακατευτεί* | *να ανακατεύεσαι*<br>*ανακατεύεστε* | *ανακατέψου*<br>*ανακατευτείτε* |
| **I interpret** | διερμηνεύω 13 | διερμήνευα | διερμήνευσα | θα διερμηνεύσω<br>να διερμηνεύσω | έχω διερμηνεύσει<br>είχα διερμηνεύσει | διερμήνευε<br>διερμηνεύετε | διερμήνευσε<br>διερμηνεύστε |
| **I interrupt** | διακόπτω 13 | διέκοπτα | διέκοψα | θα διακόψω<br>να διακόψω | έχω διακόψει<br>είχα διακόψει | να διακόπτεις<br>διακόπτετε | διάκοψε<br>διακόψτε |
| **I intersect** (roads) | *διασταυρώνομαι 14* | *διεσταυρονόμουν* | *διεσταυρώθηκα* | *θα διασταυρωθώ*<br>*να διασταυρωθώ* | *έχω διασταυρωθεί*<br>*είχα διασταυρωθεί* | *να διασταυρώνεσαι*<br>*διασταυρώνεστε* | *διασταυρώσου*<br>*διασταυρωθείτε* |
| **I intervene** | παρεμβαίνω 13 | παρέμβαινα | παρέμβηκα | θα παρέμβω<br>να παρέμβω | έχω παρέμβει<br>είχα παρέμβει | παρέμβαινε<br>παρεμβαίνετε | να παρέμβεις<br>παρέμβετε |
| **I intervene** | μεσολαβώ 17 | μεσολαβούσα | μεσολάβησα | θα μεσολαβήσω<br>να μεσολαβήσω | έχω μεσολαβήσει<br>είχα μεσολαβήσει | να μεσολαβείς<br>μεσολαβείτε | μεσολάβησε<br>μεσολαβήστε |
| **I introduce** | συστήνω 13 | σύστηνα | σύστησα | θα συστήσω<br>να συστήσω | έχω συστήσει<br>είχα συστήσει | σύστηνε<br>συστήνετε | σύστησε<br>συστήστε |
| **I invade** | εισβάλλω 13 | εισέβαλλα | εισέβαλα | θα εισβάλω<br>να εισβάλω | έχω εισβάλλει<br>είχα εισβάλλει | να εισβάλλεις<br>εισβάλλετε | να εισβάλεις<br>εισβάλτε |
| **I invent** | εφευρίσκω 13 | εφεύρισκα | εφεύρα | θα εφεύρω<br>να εφεύρω | έχω εφεύρει<br>είχα εφεύρει | εφεύρισκε<br>εφευρίσκετε | να εφεύρεις<br>εφεύρετε |

| English Verb | Present | Imperfect | Past | Simple Future<br>Simple Subjunctive | Present Perfect<br>Past Perfect | Continuous Imperative | Simple Imperative |
|---|---|---|---|---|---|---|---|
| **I invest** | επενδύω 13 | επένδυα | επένδυσα | θα επενδύσω<br>να επενδύσω | έχω επενδύσει<br>είχα επενδύσει | επένδυε<br>επενδύετε | επένδυσε<br>επενδύστε |
| **I invite** | προσκαλώ 17 | προσκαλούσα | προσκάλεσα | θα προσκαλέσω<br>να προσκαλέσω | έχω προσκαλέσει<br>είχα προσκαλέσει | να προσκαλείς<br>προσκαλείτε | προσκάλεσε<br>προσκαλέστε |
| **I invoke** | *επικαλούμαι 18* | *επικαλούμουν* | *επικαλέστηκα* | *θα επικαλεστώ*<br>*να επικαλεστώ* | *έχω επικαλεστεί*<br>*είχα επικαλεστεί* | *να επικαλείσαι*<br>*επικαλείστε* | *επικαλέσου*<br>*επικαλεστείτε* |
| **I involve** | εμπλέκω 13 | έμπλεκα | έμπλεξα | θα εμπλέξω<br>να εμπλέξω | έχω εμπλέξει<br>είχα εμπλέξει | έμπλεκε<br>εμπλέκετε | μπλέξε<br>μπλέξτε |
| **I iron** | σιδερώνω 13 | σιδέρωνα | σιδέρωσα | θα σιδερώσω<br>να σιδερώσω | έχω σιδερώσει<br>είχα σιδερώσει | σιδέρωνε<br>σιδερώνετε | σιδέρωσε<br>σιδερώστε |
| **I irrigate** | αρδεύω 13 | άρδευα | άρδεψα | θα αρδέψω<br>να αρδέψω | έχω αρδέψει<br>είχα αρδέψει | άρδευε<br>αρδεύετε | άρδεψε<br>αρδέψτε |
| **I irritate** | εξαγριώνω 13 | εξαγρίωνα | εξαγρίωσα | θα εξαγριώσω<br>να εξαγριώσω | έχω εξαγριώσει<br>είχα εξαγριώσει | εξαγρίωνε<br>εξαγριώνετε | εξαγρίωσε<br>εξαγριώστε |
| **I isolate** | απομονώνω 13 | απομόνωνα | απομόνωσα | θα απομονώσω<br>να απομονώσω | έχω απομονώσει<br>είχα απομονώσει | απομόνωνε<br>απομονώνετε | απομόνωσε<br>απομονώστε |
| **I jam** | φρακάρω 13 | φράκαρα | φρακάρησα | θα φρακάρω<br>να φρακάρω | έχω φρακάρει<br>είχα φρακάρει | φράκαρε<br>φρακάρετε | φρακάρησε<br>φρακαρήστε |
| **I jeer** | καγχάζω 13 | κάγχαζα | κάγχαξα | θα καγχάξω<br>να καγχάξω | έχω καγχάξει<br>είχα καγχάξει | κάγχαζε<br>καγχάζετε | κάγχαξε<br>καγχάξτε |
| **I jingle** | κουδουνίζω 13 | κουδούνιζα | κουδούνισα | θα κουδουνίσω<br>να κουδουνίσω | έχω κουδουνίσει<br>είχα κουδουνίσει | κουδούνιζε<br>κουδουνίζετε | κουδούνισε<br>κουδουνίστε |
| **I jog** (someone's elbow) | σκουντ(ά)ώ 15 | σκουντούσα | σκούντηξα | θα σκουντήξω<br>να σκουντήξω | έχω σκουντήξει<br>είχα σκουντήξει | σκούντα<br>σκουντάτε | σκούντηξε<br>σκουντήξτε |

| English Verb | Present | Imperfect | Past | Simple Future<br>Simple Subjunctive | Present Perfect<br>Past Perfect | Continuous Imperative | Simple Imperative |
|---|---|---|---|---|---|---|---|
| **I join** | συνάπτω 13 | σύναπτα | σύναψα | θα συνάψω<br>να συνάψω | έχω συνάψει<br>είχα συνάψει | σύναπτε<br>συνάπτετε | σύναψε<br>συνάψτε |
| **I joke** | *αστειεύομαι 14* | *αστειευόμουν* | *αστειεύτηκα* | *θα αστειευτώ*<br>*να αστειευτώ* | *έχω αστειευτεί*<br>*είχα αστειευτεί* | *να αστειεύεσαι*<br>*αστειεύεστε* | *αστειεύσου*<br>*αστειευτείτε* |
| **I judge** | κρίνω 13 | έκρινα | έκρινα | θα κρίνω<br>να κρίνω | έχω κρίνει<br>είχα κρίνει | κρίνε<br>κρίνετε | κρίνε<br>κρίνετε |
| **I jumble** | ανακατώνω 13 | ανακάτωνα | ανακάτωσα | θα ανακατώσω<br>να ανακατώσω | έχω ανακατώσει<br>είχα ανακατώσει | ανακάτωνε<br>ανακατώνετε | ανακάτωσε<br>ανακατώστε |
| **I jump** | πηδ(άω)ώ 15 | πηδούσα | πήδηξα | θα πηδήξω<br>να πηδήξω | έχω πηδήξει<br>είχα πηδήξει | πήδα<br>πηδάτε | πήδησε<br>πηδήστε |
| **I keep** | *διατηρούμαι 18* | *διατηρούμουν* | *διατηρήθηκα* | *θα διατηρηθώ*<br>*να διατηρηθώ* | *έχω διατηρηθεί*<br>*είχα διατηρηθεί* | *να διατηρείσαι*<br>*διατηρείστε* | *διατηρήσου*<br>*διατηρηθείτε* |
| **I keep silent** | σωπαίνω 13 | σώπαινα | σώπασα | θα σωπάσω<br>να σωπάσω | έχω σωπάσει<br>είχα σωπάσει | σώπαινε<br>σωπαίνετε | σώπασε<br>σωπάστε |
| **I kick** | κλωτσ(άω)ώ 15 | κλωτσούσα | κλώτσησα | θα κλωτσήσω<br>να κλωτσήσω | έχω κλωτσήσει<br>είχα κλωτσήσει | κλώτσα<br>κλωτσάτε | κλώτσησε<br>κλωτσήστε |
| **I kidnap** | απαγάγω 13 | απήγαγα | απήγαγα | θα απαγάγω<br>να απαγάγω | έχω απαγάγει<br>είχα απαγάγει | απάγαγε<br>απαγάγετε | απάγαγε<br>απαγάγετε |
| **I kill** | σκοτώνω 13 | σκότωνα | σκότωσα | θα σκοτώσω<br>να σκοτώσω | έχω σκοτώσει<br>είχα σκοτώσει | σκότωνε<br>σκοτώνετε | σκότωσε<br>σκοτώστε |
| **I kiss** | φιλώ 15 | φιλούσα | φίλησα | θα φιλήσω<br>να φιλήσω | έχω φιλήσει<br>είχα φιλήσει | φίλα<br>φιλάτε | φίλησε<br>φιλήστε |
| **I knead** | ζυμώνω 13 | ζύμωνα | ζύμωσα | θα ζυμώσω<br>να ζυμώσω | έχω ζυμώσει<br>είχα ζυμώσει | ζύμωνε<br>ζυμώνετε | ζύμωσε<br>ζυμώστε |

| English Verb | Present | Imperfect | Past | Simple Future<br>Simple Subjunctive | Present Perfect<br>Past Perfect | Continuous Imperative | Simple Imperative |
|---|---|---|---|---|---|---|---|
| **I kneel** | γονατίζω 13 | γονάτιζα | γονάτισα | θα γονατίσω<br>να γονατίσω | έχω γονατίσει<br>είχα γονατίσει | γονάτιζε<br>γονατίζετε | γονάτισε<br>γονατίστε |
| **I knit** | πλέκω 13 | έπλεκα | έπλεξα | θα πλέξω<br>να πλέξω | έχω πλέξει<br>είχα πλέξει | πλέκε<br>πλέκετε | πλέξε<br>πλέξτε |
| **I knock** | κρούω 13 | έκρουα | έκρουσα | θα κρούσω<br>να κρούσω | έχω κρούσει<br>είχα κρούσει | κρούε<br>κρούετε | κρούσε<br>κρούστε |
| **I knock down** (building) | γκρεμίζω 13 | γκρέμιζα | γκρέμισα | θα γκρεμίσω<br>να γκρεμίσω | έχω γκρεμίσει<br>είχα γκρεμίσει | γκρέμιζε<br>γκρεμίζετε | γκρέμισε<br>γκρεμίστε |
| **I know** | ξέρω 13 | ήξερα | ήξερα | θα ξέρω<br>να ξέρω | – | ξέρε<br>ξέρετε | ξέρε<br>ξέρτε |
| **I know** | γνωρίζω 13 | γνώριζα | γνώρισα | θα γνωρίσω<br>να γνωρίσω | έχω γνωρίσει<br>είχα γνωρίσει | γνώριζε<br>γνωρίζετε | γνώρισε<br>γνωρίστε |
| **I labour** | *παιδεύομαι 14* | *παιδευόμουν* | *παιδεύτηκα* | *θα παιδευτώ*<br>*να παιδευτώ* | *έχω παιδευτεί*<br>*είχα παιδευτεί* | *να παιδεύομαι*<br>*παιδεύεστε* | *παιδεύσου*<br>*παιδευτείτε* |
| **I lack** | *στερούμαι 18* | *στερούμουν* | *στερήθηκα* | *θα στερηθώ*<br>*να στερηθώ* | *έχω στερηθεί*<br>*είχα στερηθεί* | *να στερείσαι*<br>*στερείστε* | *στερήσου*<br>*στερηθείτε* |
| **I lampoon** | γελοιοποιώ 17 | γελοιοποιούσα | γελοιοποίησα | θα γελοιοποιήσω<br>να γελοιοποιήσω | έχω γελοιοποιήσει<br>είχα γελοιοποιήσει | να γελοιοποιείς<br>γελοιοποιείτε | γελοιοποίησε<br>γελοιοποιήστε |
| **I languish** | μαραζώνω 13 | μαράζωνα | μαράζωσα | θα μαραζώσω<br>να μαραζώσω | έχω μαραζώσει<br>είχα μαραζώσει | μαράζωνε<br>μαραζώνετε | μαράζωσε<br>μαραζώστε |
| **I lap** | παφλάζω 13 | πάφλαζα | πάφλασα | θα παφλάσω<br>να παφλάσω | έχω παφλάσει<br>είχα παφλάσει | πάφλαζε<br>παφλάζετε | πάφλασε<br>παφλάστε |
| **I lapse** | παρεκλίνω 13 | παρέκλινα | παρέκλινα | θα παρεκλίνω<br>να παρεκλίνω | έχω παρεκλίνει<br>είχα παρεκλίνει | παρέκλινε<br>παρεκλίνετε | να παρεκλίνεις<br>παρεκλίνετε |

| English Verb | Present | Imperfect | Past | Simple Future<br>Simple Subjunctive | Present Perfect<br>Past Perfect | Continuous Imperative | Simple Imperative |
|---|---|---|---|---|---|---|---|
| **I last**<br>(keep going) | διαρκώ 17 | διαρκούσα | διήρκεσα | θα διαρκέσω<br>να διαρκέσω | έχω διαρκέσει<br>είχα διαρκέσει | να διαρκείς<br>διαρκείτε | διάρκησε<br>διαρκήστε |
| **I am late** | αργώ 17 | αργούσα | άργησα | θα αργήσω<br>να αργήσω | έχω αργήσει<br>είχα αργήσει | να αργείς<br>αργείτε | άργησε<br>αργήστε |
| **I laugh** | γελ(ά)ώ 15 | γελούσα | γέλασα | θα γελάσω<br>να γελάσω | έχω γελάσει<br>είχα γελάσει | γέλα<br>γελάτε | γέλασε<br>γελάστε |
| **I launch**<br>(ship) | καθελκύω 13 | καθέλκυα | καθέλκυσα | θα καθελκύσω<br>να καθελκύσω | έχω καθελκύσει<br>είχα καθελκύσει | καθέλκυε<br>καθελκύετε | καθέλκυσε<br>καθελκύστε |
| **I launch** | εκτοξεύω 13 | εκτόξευα | εκτόξευσα | θα εκτοξεύσω<br>να εκτοξεύσω | έχω εκτοξεύσει<br>είχα εκτοξεύσει | εκτόξευε<br>εκτοξεύετε | εκτόξευσε<br>εκτοξεύστε |
| **I launder** | μπουγαδιάζω 13 | μπουγάδιαζα | μπουγάδιασα | θα μπουγαδιάσω<br>να μπουγαδιάσω | έχω μπουγαδιάσει<br>είχα μπουγαδιάσει | μπουγάδιαζε<br>μπουγαδιάζετε | μπουγάδιασε<br>μπουγαδιάστε |
| **I lay** | θέτω 31 | έθετα | έθεσα | θα θέσω<br>να θέσω | έχω θέσει<br>είχα θέσει | να θέτεις<br>θέτετε | θέσε<br>θέστε |
| **I laze** | τεμπελιάζω 13 | τεμπέλιαζα | τεμπέλιασα | θα τεμπελιάσω<br>να τεμπελιάσω | έχω τεμπελιάσει<br>είχα τεμπελιάσει | τεμπέλιαζε<br>τεμπελιάζετε | τεμπέλιασε<br>τεμπελιάστε |
| **I lead** | *ηγούμαι 18* | *ηγούμουν* | *ηγήθηκα* | *θα ηγηθώ*<br>*να ηγηθώ* | *έχω ηγηθεί*<br>*είχα ηγηθεί* | *να ηγείσαι*<br>*ηγείστε* | *ηγήσου*<br>*ηγηθείτε* |
| **I leap** | αναπηδώ 15 | αναπηδούσα | αναπήδησα | θα αναπηδήσω<br>να αναπηδήσω | έχω αναπηδήσει<br>είχα αναπηδήσει | αναπήδα<br>αναπηδάτε | αναπήδησε<br>αναπηδήστε |
| **I learn** | μαθαίνω 13 | μάθαινα | έμαθα | θα μάθω<br>να μάθω | έχω μάθει<br>είχα μάθει | μάθαινε<br>μαθαίνετε | μάθε<br>μάθετε |
| **I leave** | φεύγω 13 | έφευγα | έφυγα | θα φύγω<br>να φύγω | έχω φύγει<br>είχα φύγει | φεύγα<br>φεύγετε | φύγε<br>φύγετε |

| English Verb | Present | Imperfect | Past | Simple Future<br>Simple Subjunctive | Present Perfect<br>Past Perfect | Continuous Imperative | Simple Imperative |
|---|---|---|---|---|---|---|---|
| **I leave** (abandon) | αφήνω 13 | άφηνα | άφησα | θα αφήσω<br>να αφήσω | έχω αφήσει<br>είχα αφήσει | άφηνε<br>αφήνετε | άφησε<br>αφήστε |
| **I legalize** | νομιμοποιώ 17 | νομιμοποιούσα | νομιμοποίησα | θα νομιμοποιήσω<br>να νομιμοποιήσω | έχω νομιμοποιήσει<br>είχα νομιμοποιήσει | να νομιμοποιείς<br>νομιμοποιείτε | νομιμοποίησε<br>νομιμοποιήστε |
| **I legislate** | νομοθετώ 17 | νομοθετούσα | νομοθέτησα | θα νομοθετήσω<br>να νομοθετήσω | έχω νομοθετήσει<br>είχα νομοθετήσει | να νομοθετείς<br>νομοθετείτε | νομοθέτησε<br>νομοθετήστε |
| **I lend** | δανείζω 13 | δάνειζα | δάνεισα | θα δανείσω<br>να δανείσω | έχω δανείσει<br>είχα δανείσει | δάνειζε<br>δανείζετε | δάνεισε<br>δανείστε |
| **I lengthen** | μακραίνω 13 | μάκραινα | μάκρυνα | θα μακρύνω<br>να μακρύνω | έχω μακρύνει<br>είχα μακρύνει | μάκραινε<br>μακραίνετε | μάκρυνε<br>μακρύντε |
| **I lessen** | λιγοστεύω 13 | λιγόστευα | λιγόστεψα | θα λιγοστέψω<br>να λιγοστέψω | έχω λιγοστέψει<br>είχα λιγοστέψει | λιγόστευε<br>λιγοστεύετε | λιγόστεψε<br>λιγοστέψτε |
| **I let** | εκμισθώνω 13 | εκμίσθωνα | εκμίσθωσα | θα εκμισθώσω<br>να εκμισθώσω | έχω εκμισθώσει<br>είχα εκμισθώσει | εκμίσθωνε<br>εκμισθώνετε | εκμίσθωσε<br>εκμισθώστε |
| **I liberate** | λυτρώνω 13 | λύτρωνα | λύτρωσα | θα λυτρώσω<br>να λυτρώσω | έχω λυτρώσει<br>είχα λυτρώσει | λύτρωνε<br>λυτρώνετε | λύτρωσε<br>λυτρώστε |
| **I lick** | γλείφω 13 | έγλειφα | έγλειψα | θα γλείψω<br>να γλείψω | έχω γλείψει<br>είχα γλείψει | γλείφε<br>γλείφετε | γλείψε<br>γλείψτε |
| **I lie** | *ψεύδομαι 14* | *ψευδόμουν* | *ψεύστηκα* | *θα ψευστώ*<br>*να ψευστώ* | *έχω ψευστεί*<br>*είχα ψευστεί* | *να ψεύδεσαι*<br>*ψεύδεστε* | *ψεύσου*<br>*ψευστείτε* |
| **I lie down** | ξαπλώνω 13 | ξάπλωνα | ξάπλωσα | θα ξαπλώσω<br>να ξαπλώσω | έχω ξαπλώσει<br>είχα ξαπλώσει | ξάπλωνε<br>ξαπλώνετε | ξάπλωσε<br>ξαπλώστε |
| **I lift (up)** | σηκώνω 13 | σήκωνα | σήκωσα | θα σηκώσω<br>να σηκώσω | έχω σηκώσει<br>είχα σηκώσει | σήκωνε<br>σηκώνετε | σήκωσε<br>σηκώστε |

| English Verb | Present | Imperfect | Past | Simple Future<br>Simple Subjunctive | Present Perfect<br>Past Perfect | Continuous Imperative | Simple Imperative |
|---|---|---|---|---|---|---|---|
| **I light** | ανάβω 13 | άναβα | άναψα | θα ανάψω<br>να ανάψω | έχω ανάψει<br>είχα ανάψει | άναβε<br>ανάβετε | άναψε<br>ανάψτε |
| **I lighten** | αστράφτω 13 | άστραφτα | άστραψα | θα αστράψω<br>να αστράψω | έχω αστράψει<br>είχα αστράψει | άστραφτε<br>αστράφτετε | άστραψε<br>αστράψτε |
| **I linger** | παραμένω 13 | παρέμενα | παρέμεινα | θα παραμείνω<br>να παραμείνω | έχω παραμείνει<br>είχα παραμείνει | παράμενε<br>παραμένετε | παράμεινε<br>παραμείντε |
| **I linger** | χρονοτριβώ 17 | χρονοτριβούσα | χρονοτρίβησα | θα χρονοτριβήσω<br>να χρονοτριβήσω | έχω χρονοτριβήσει<br>είχα χρονοτριβήσει | να χρονοτριβείς<br>χρονοτριβείτε | χρονοτρίβησε<br>χρονοτριβήστε |
| **I live**<br>(am alive) | ζω 17 | ζούσα | έζησα | θα ζήσω<br>να ζήσω | έχω ζήσει<br>είχα ζήσει | να ζείς<br>ζείτε | ζήσε<br>ζήστε |
| **I liquefy** | ρευστοποιώ 17 | ρευστοποιούσα | ρευστοποίησα | θα ρευστοποιήσω<br>να ρευστοποιήσω | έχω ρευστοποιήσει<br>είχα ρευστοποιήσει | να ρευστοποιείς<br>ρευστοποιείτε | ρευστοποίησε<br>ρευστοποιήστε |
| **I load** | φορτώνω 13 | φόρτωνα | φόρτωσα | θα φορτώσω<br>να φορτώσω | έχω φορτώσει<br>είχα φορτώσει | φόρτωνε<br>φορτώνετε | φόρτωσε<br>φορτώστε |
| **I loathe** | *σιχαίνομαι 14* | *σιχαινόμουν* | *σιχάθηκα* | *θα σιχαθώ*<br>*να σιχαθω* | *έχω σιχαθεί*<br>*είχα σιχαθεί* | *να σιχαίνεσαι*<br>*σιχαίνεστε* | *σιχάσου*<br>*σιχαθείτε* |
| **I locate** | εντοπίζω 13 | εντόπιζα | εντόπισα | θα εντοπίσω<br>να εντοπίσω | έχω εντοπίσει<br>είχα εντοπίσει | εντόπιζε<br>εντοπίζετε | εντόπισε<br>εντοπίστε |
| **I lock** | κλειδώνω 13 | κλείδωνα | κλείδωσα | θα κλειδώσω<br>να κλειδώσω | έχω κλειδώσει<br>είχα κλειδώσει | κλείδωνε<br>κλειδώνετε | κλείδωσε<br>κλειδώστε |
| **I log on**<br>(computer) | *συνδέομαι 14* | *συνδεόμουν* | *συνδέθηκα* | *θα συνδεθώ*<br>*να συνδεθώ* | *έχω συνδεθεί*<br>*είχα συνδεθεί* | *να συνδέεσαι*<br>*συνδέεστε* | *συνδέσου*<br>*συνδεθείτε* |
| **I look at** | κοιτάζω 13 | κοίταζα | κοίταξα | θα κοιτάξω<br>να κοιτάξω | έχω κοιτάξει<br>είχα κοιτάξει | κοίταζε<br>κοιτάζετε | κοίταξε<br>κοιτάξτε |

| English Verb | Present | Imperfect | Past | Simple Future<br>Simple Subjunctive | Present Perfect<br>Past Perfect | Continuous Imperative | Simple Imperative |
|---|---|---|---|---|---|---|---|
| **I loosen** (clothing) | ξεσφίγγω 13 | ξέσφιγγα | ξέσφιξα | θα ξεσφίξω<br>να ξεσφίξω | έχω ξεσφίξει<br>είχα ξεσφίξει | ξέσφιγγε<br>ξεσφίγγετε | ξέσφιξε<br>ξεσφίξτε |
| **I loot** (plunder) | κουρσεύω 13 | κούρσευα | κούρσεψα | θα κουρσέψω<br>να κουρσέψω | έχω κουρσέψει<br>είχα κουρσέψει | κούρσευε<br>κουρσεύετε | κούρσεψε<br>κουρσέψτε |
| **I lose** | χάνω 13 | έχανα | έχασα | θα χάσω<br>να χάσω | έχω χάσει<br>είχα χάσει | χάνε<br>χάνετε | χάσε<br>χάστε |
| **I am lost** | *χάνομαι 14* | *χανόμουν* | *χάθηκα* | *θα χαθώ*<br>*να χαθώ* | *έχω χαθεί*<br>*είχα χαθεί* | *να χάνεσαι*<br>*χάνεστε* | *χάσου*<br>*χαθείτε* |
| **I hesitate** | δειλιάζω 13 | δείλιαζα | δείλιασα | θα δειλιάσω<br>να δειλιάσω | έχω δειλιάσει<br>είχα δειλιάσει | δείλιαζε<br>δειλιάζετε | δείλιασε<br>δειλιάστε |
| **I love** | αγαπώ 15 | αγαπούσα | αγάπησα | θα αγαπήσω<br>να αγαπήσω | έχω αγαπήσει<br>είχα αγαπήσει | αγάπα<br>αγαπάτε | αγάπησε<br>αγαπήστε |
| **I lower** (price) | ρίχνω 13 | έριχνα | έριξα | θα ρίξω<br>να ρίξω | έχω ρίξει<br>είχα ρίξει | ρίχνε<br>ρίχνετε | ρίξε<br>ρίξτε |
| **I lubricate** | λιπαίνω 13 | λίπαινα | λίπανα | θα λιπάνω<br>να λιπάνω | έχω λιπάνει<br>είχα λιπάνει | λίπαινε<br>λιπαίνετε | λίπανε<br>λιπάντε |
| **I lunch** | γευματίζω 13 | γευμάτιζα | γευμάτισα | θα γευματίσω<br>να γευματίσω | έχω γευματίσει<br>είχα γευματίσει | γευμάτιζε<br>γευματίζετε | γευμάτισε<br>γευματίστε |
| **I lure** (entice) | παρασέρνω 13 | παράσερνα | παρέσυρα | θα παρασύρω<br>να παρασύρω | έχω παρασύρει<br>είχα παρασύρει | παράσερνε<br>παρασέρνετε | παράσυρε<br>παρασύρτε |
| **I lurk** | παραμονεύω 13 | παραμόνευα | παραμόνευσα | θα παραμονεύσω<br>να παραμονεύσω | έχω παραμονεύσει<br>είχα παραμονεύσει | παραμόνευε<br>παραμονεύετε | παραμόνευσε<br>παραμονεύστε |
| **I lust** | ποθώ 13 | ποθούσα | πόθησα | θα ποθήσω<br>να ποθήσω | έχω ποθήσει<br>είχα ποθήσει | να ποθείς<br>ποθείτε | πόθησε<br>ποθήστε |

| English Verb | Present | Imperfect | Past | Simple Future<br>Simple Subjunctive | Present Perfect<br>Past Perfect | Continuous Imperative | Simple Imperative |
|---|---|---|---|---|---|---|---|
| **I lynch** | λιντσάρω 13 | λίντσαρα | λιντσάρισα | θα λιντσάρω<br>να λιντσάρω | έχω λιντσάρει<br>είχα λιντσάρει | λίντσαρε<br>λιντσάρετε | λιντσάρισε<br>λιντσαρίστε |
| **I maintain** | διαφυλάττω 13 | διεφύλαττα | διεφύλαξα | θα διαφυλάξω<br>να διαφυλάξω | έχω διαφυλάξει<br>είχα διαφυλάξει | διαφύλαττε<br>διαφυλάτεττε | διαφύλαξε<br>διαφυλάξτε |
| **I make** | φτιάχνω 13 | έφτιαχνα | έφτιαξα | θα φτιάξω<br>να φτιάξω | έχω φτιάξει<br>είχα φτιάξει | φτιάχνε<br>φτιάχνετε | φτιάξε<br>φτιάξτε |
| **I make an appearance** | *παρουσιάζομαι 14* | *παρουσιαζόμουν* | *παρουσιάστηκα* | *θα παρουσιαστώ*<br>*να παρουσιαστώ* | *έχω παρουσιαστεί*<br>*είχα παρουσιαστεί* | *να παρουσιάζεσαι*<br>*παρουσιάζεστε* | *παρουσιάσου*<br>*παρουσιαστείτε* |
| **I make certain** | *βεβαιώνομαι 14* | *βεβαιωνόμουν* | *βεβαιώθηκα* | *θα βεβαιωθώ*<br>*να βεβαιωθώ* | *έχω βεβαιωθεί*<br>*είχα βεβαιωθεί* | *να βεβαιώνεσαι*<br>*βεβαιώνεστε* | *βεβαιώσου*<br>*βεβαιωθείτε* |
| **I make sure** | *σιγουρεύομαι 14* | *σιγουρευόμουν* | *σιγουρεύτηκα* | *θα σιγουρευτώ*<br>*να σιγουρευτώ* | *έχω σιγουρευτεί*<br>*είχα σιγουρευτεί* | *να σιγουρεύεσαι*<br>*σιγουρεύεστε* | *σιγουρέψου*<br>*σιγουρευτείτε* |
| **I manage** | καταφέρνω 13 | κατάφερνα | κατάφερα | θα καταφέρω<br>να καταφέρω | έχω καταφέρει<br>είχα καταφέρει | κατάφερνε<br>καταφέρνετε | κατάφερε<br>καταφέρτε |
| **I manifest** | εμφανίζω 13 | εμφάνιζα | εμφάνισα | θα εμφανίσω<br>να εμφανίσω | έχω εμφανίσει<br>είχα εμφανίσει | εμφάνιζε<br>εμφανίζετε | εμφάνισε<br>εμφανίστε |
| **I march** | βαδίζω 13 | βάδιζα | βάδισα | θα βαδίσω<br>να βαδίσω | έχω βαδίσει<br>είχα βαδίσει | βάδιζε<br>βαδίζετε | βάδισε<br>βαδίστε |
| **I mark** (indicate) | σημειώνω 13 | σημείωνα | σημείωσα | θα σημειώσω<br>να σημειώσω | έχω σημειώσει<br>είχα σημειώσει | σημείωνε<br>σημειώνετε | σημείωσε<br>σημειώστε |
| **I mark** | βαθμολογώ 17 | βαθμολογούσα | βαθμολόγησα | θα βαθμολογήσω<br>να βαθμολογήσω | έχω βαθμολογήσει<br>είχα βαθμολογήσει | να βαθμολογείς<br>βαθμολογείτε | βαθμολόγησε<br>βαθμολογήστε |
| **I marry** (join together) | παντρεύω 13 | πάντρευα | πάντρεψα | θα παντρέψω<br>να παντρέψω | έχω παντρέψει<br>είχα παντρέψει | πάντρευε<br>παντρεύετε | πάντρεψε<br>παντρέψτε |

| English Verb | Present | Imperfect | Past | Simple Future<br>Simple Subjunctive | Present Perfect<br>Past Perfect | Continuous Imperative | Simple Imperative |
|---|---|---|---|---|---|---|---|
| **I marry** | *παντρεύομαι 14* | *παντρευόμουν* | *παντρεύτηκα* | *θα παντρευτώ*<br>*να παντρευτώ* | *έχω παντρευτεί*<br>*είχα παντρευτεί* | *να παντρεύεσαι*<br>*παντρεύεστε* | *παντρέψου*<br>*παντρευτείτε* |
| **I match** (materials) | ταιριάζω 13 | ταίριαζα | ταίριαξα | θα ταιριάξω<br>να ταιριάξω | έχω ταιριάξει<br>είχα ταιριάξει | ταίριαζε<br>ταιριάζετε | ταίριαξε<br>ταιριάξτε |
| **I mature** | *αναπτύσσομαι 14* | *αναπτυσσόμουν* | *αναπτύχθηκα* | *θα αναπτυχθώ*<br>*να αναπτυχθώ* | *έχω αναπτυχθεί*<br>*είχα αναπτυχθεί* | *να αναπτύσσεσαι*<br>*αναπτύσσεστε* | *αναπτύξου*<br>*αναπτυχτείτε* |
| **I mean** | εννοώ 17 | εννοούσα | εννόησα | θα εννοήσω<br>να εννοήσω | έχω εννοήσει<br>είχα εννοήσει | εννόει<br>εννοείτε | εννόησε<br>εννοήστε |
| **I measure** | μετρ(ά)ώ 15 | μετρούσα | μέτρησα | θα μετρήσω<br>να μετρήσω | έχω μετρήσει<br>είχα μετρήσει | μέτρα<br>μετράτε | μέτρησε<br>μετρήστε |
| **I meet** | συναντ(ά)ώ 15 | συναντούσα | συνάντησα | θα συναντήσω<br>να συναντήσω | έχω συναντήσει<br>είχα συναντήσει | συνάντα<br>συναντάτε | συνάντησε<br>συναντήστε |
| **I meet** | ανταμώνω 13 | αντάμωνα | αντάμωσα | θα ανταμώσω<br>να ανταμώσω | έχω ανταμώσει<br>είχα ανταμώσει | αντάμωνε<br>ανταμώνετε | αντάμωσε<br>ανταμώστε |
| **I melt** | λιώνω 13 | έλιωνα | έλιωσα | θα λιώσω<br>να λιώσω | έχω λιώσει<br>είχα λιώσει | λιώνε<br>λιώνετε | λιώσε<br>λιώστε |
| **I memorize** | αποστηθίζω 13 | αποστήθιζα | αποστήθισα | θα αποστηθίσω<br>να αποστηθίσω | έχω αποστηθίσει<br>είχα αποστηθίσει | αποστήθιζε<br>αποστηθίζετε | αποστήθισε<br>αποστηθίστε |
| **I mesmerize** | υπνωτίζω 13 | υπνώτιζα | υπνώτισα | θα υπνωτίσω<br>να υπνωτίσω | έχω υπνωτίσει<br>είχα υπνωτίσει | υπνώτιζε<br>υπνωτίζετε | υπνώτισε<br>υπνωτίστε |
| **I milk** | αρμέγω 13 | άρμεγα | άρμεξα | θα αρμέξω<br>να αρμέξω | έχω αρμέξει<br>είχα αρμέξει | άρμεγε<br>αρμέγετε | άρμεξε<br>αρμέξτε |
| **I mirror** | καθρεφτίζω 13 | καθρέφτιζα | καθρέφτισα | θα καθρεφτίσω<br>να καθρεφτίσω | έχω καθρεφτίσει<br>είχα καθρεφτίσει | καθρέφτιζε<br>καθρεφτίζετε | καθρέφτισε<br>καθρεφτίστε |

| English Verb | Present | Imperfect | Past | Simple Future<br>Simple Subjunctive | Present Perfect<br>Past Perfect | Continuous Imperative | Simple Imperative |
|---|---|---|---|---|---|---|---|
| **I misbehave** | ατακτώ 15 | ατακτούσα | ατάκτησα | θα ατακτήσω<br>να ατακτήσω | έχω ατακτήσει<br>είχα ατακτήσει | να ατακτείς<br>ατακτείτε | ατάκτησε<br>ατακτήστε |
| **I misfire** | αστοχώ 17 | αστοχούσα | αστόχησα | θα αστοχήσω<br>να αστοχήσω | έχω αστοχήσει<br>είχα αστοχήσει | να αστοχείς<br>αστοχείτε | αστόχησε<br>αστοχήστε |
| **I am mistaken** | *απατώμαι 42* | *απατόμουν* | *απατήθηκα* | *θα απατηθώ*<br>*να απατηθώ* | *έχω απατηθεί*<br>*είχα απατηθεί* | *να απατάσαι*<br>*απατάστε* | *να απατηθείς*<br>*απατηθείτε* |
| **I am mistaken** | λαθεύω 13 | λάθευα | λάθεψα | θα λαθέψω<br>να λαθέψω | έχω λαθέψει<br>είχα λαθέψει | λάθευε<br>λαθεύετε | λάθεψε<br>λαθέψτε |
| **I misunderstand** | παρεξηγώ 17 | παρεξηγούσα | παρεξήγησα | θα παρεξηγήσω<br>να παρεξηγήσω | έχω παρεξηγήσει<br>είχα παρεξηγήσει | να παρεξηγείς<br>παρεξηγείτε | παρεξήγησε<br>παρεξηγήστε |
| **I mix** | ανακατεύω 13 | ανακάτευα | ανακάτεψα | θα ανακατέψω<br>να ανακατέψω | έχω ανακατέψει<br>είχα ανακατέψει | ανακάτευε<br>ανακατεύετε | ανακάτεψε<br>ανακατέψτε |
| **I moan** | βογκώ 15 | βογκούσα | βόγκηξα | θα βογκήξω<br>να βογκήξω | έχω βογκήξει<br>είχα βογκήξει | βόγκα<br>βογκάτε | βόγκηξε<br>βογκήξτε |
| **I ridicule** | *ειρωνεύομαι 14* | *ειρωνευόμουν* | *ειρωνεύτηκα* | *θα ειρωνευτώ*<br>*να ειρωνευτώ* | *έχω ειρωνευτεί*<br>*είχα ειρωνευτεί* | *να ειρωνεύεσαι*<br>*ειρωνεύεστε* | *ειρωνέψου*<br>*ειρωνευτείτε* |
| **I mock** | κοροϊδεύω 13 | κορόϊδευα | κορόϊδεψα | θα κοροϊδέψω<br>να κοροϊδέψω | έχω κοροϊδέψει<br>είχα κοροϊδέψει | κορόϊδευε<br>κοροϊδεύετε | κορόϊδεψε<br>κοροϊδέψτε |
| **I mop** | σφουγγαρίζω 13 | σφουγγάριζα | σφουγγάρισα | θα σφουγγαρίσω<br>να σφουγγαρίσω | έχω σφουγγαρίσει<br>είχα σφουγγαρίσει | σφουγγάριζε<br>σφουγγαρίζετε | σφουγγάρισε<br>σφουγγαρίστε |
| **I mortgage** | υποθηκεύω 13 | υποθήκευα | υποθήκευσα | θα υποθηκεύσω<br>να υποθηκεύσω | έχω υποθηκεύσει<br>είχα υποθηκεύσει | υποθήκευε<br>υποθηκεύετε | υποθήκευσε<br>υποθηκεύστε |
| **I mourn** | πενθώ 17 | πενθούσα | πένθησα | θα πενθήσω<br>να πενθήσω | έχω πενθήσει<br>είχα πενθήσει | να πενθείς<br>πενθείτε | πένθησε<br>πενθήστε |

| English Verb | Present | Imperfect | Past | Simple Future<br>Simple Subjunctive | Present Perfect<br>Past Perfect | Continuous Imperative | Simple Imperative |
|---|---|---|---|---|---|---|---|
| **I mow down** (decimate) | αποδεκατίζω 13 | αποδεκάτιζα | αποδεκάτισα | θα αποδεκατίσω<br>να αποδεκατίσω | έχω αποδεκατίσει<br>είχα αποδεκατίσει | αποδεκάτιζε<br>αποδεκατίζετε | αποδεκάτισε<br>αποδεκατίστε |
| **I muddle** | θαλασσώνω 13 | θαλάσσωνα | θαλάσσωσα | θα θαλασσώσω<br>να θαλασσώσω | έχω θαλασσώσει<br>είχα θαλασσώσει | θαλάσσωνε<br>θαλασσώνετε | θαλάσσωσε<br>θαλασσώστε |
| **I multiply** | πολλαπλασιάζω 13 | πολλαπλασίαζα | πολλαπλασίασα | θα πολλαπλασιάσω<br>να πολλαπλασιάσω | έχω πολλαπλασιάσει<br>είχα πολλαπλασιάσει | πολλαπλασίαζε<br>πολλαπλασιάζετε | πολλαπλασίασε<br>πολλαπλασιάστε |
| **I murder** | φονεύω 13 | φόνευα | φόνευσα | θα φονεύσω<br>να φονεύσω | έχω φονεύσει<br>είχα φονεύσει | φόνευε<br>φονεύετε | φόνευσε<br>φονεύστε |
| **I murmur** | μουρμουρίζω 13 | μουρμούριζα | μουρμούρισα | θα μουρμουρίσω<br>να μουρμουρίσω | έχω μουρμουρίσει<br>είχα μουρμουρίσει | μουρμούριζε<br>μουρμουρίζετε | μουρμούρισε<br>μουρμουρίστε |
| **I nag** | γλωσσοτρώγω 13 | γλωσσότρωγα | γλωσσόφαγα | θα γλωσσοφάγω<br>να γλωσσοφάγω | έχω γλωσσοφάγει<br>είχα γλωσσοφάγει | γλωσσότρωγε<br>γλωσσοτρώγετε | γλωσσόφαγε<br>γλωσσοφά(γε)τε |
| **I nail** | καρφώνω 13 | κάρφωνα | κάρφωσα | θα καρφώσω<br>να καρφώσω | έχω καρφώσει<br>είχα καρφώσει | κάρφωνε<br>καρφώνετε | κάρφωσε<br>καρφώστε |
| **I name** | ονομάζω 13 | ονόμαζα | ονόμασα | θα ονομάσω<br>να ονομάσω | έχω ονομάσει<br>είχα ονομάσει | ονόμαζε<br>ονομάζετε | ονόμασε<br>ονομάστε |
| **I narrate** | *διηγούμαι 18* | *διηγούμουν* | *διηγήθηκα* | *θα διηγηθώ*<br>*να διηγηθώ* | *έχω διηγηθεί*<br>*είχα διηγηθεί* | *να διηγείσαι*<br>*διηγείστε* | *διηγήσου*<br>*διηγηθείτε* |
| **I narrate** | *αφηγούμαι 18* | *αφηγούμην* | *αφηγήθηκα* | *θα αφηγηθώ*<br>*να αφηγηθώ* | *έχω αφηγηθεί*<br>*είχα αφηγηθεί* | *να αφηγείσαι*<br>*αφηγείστε* | *αφηγήσου*<br>*αφηγηθείτε* |
| **I narrow** | στενεύω 13 | στένευα | στένεψα | θα στενέψω<br>να στενέψω | έχω στενέψει<br>είχα στενέψει | στένευε<br>στενεύετε | στένεψε<br>στενέψτε |
| **I naturalize** | πολιτογραφώ 17 | πολιτογραφούσα | πολιτογράφησα | θα πολιτογραφήσω<br>να πολιτογραφήσω | έχω πολιτογραφήσει<br>είχα πολιτογραφήσει | να πολιτογραφείς<br>πολιτογραφείτε | πολιτογράφησε<br>πολιτογραφήστε |

| English Verb | Present | Imperfect | Past | Simple Future<br>Simple Subjunctive | Present Perfect<br>Past Perfect | Continuous Imperative | Simple Imperative |
|---|---|---|---|---|---|---|---|
| **I nauseate** | αναγουλιάζω 13 | αναγούλιαζα | αναγούλιασα | θα αναγουλιάσω<br>να αναγουλιάσω | έχω αναγουλιάσει<br>είχα αναγουλιάσει | αναγούλιαζε<br>αναγουλιάζετε | αναγούλιασε<br>αναγουλιάστε |
| **I navigate** | πιλοτάρω 13 | πιλόταρα | πιλοτάρησα | θα πιλοτάρω<br>να πιλοτάρω | έχω πιλοτάρει<br>είχα πιλοτάρει | πιλόταρε<br>πιλοτάρετε | πιλοτάρησε<br>πιλοταρήστε |
| **I need** | *χρειάζομαι 14* | *χρειαζόμουν* | *χρειάστηκα* | *θα χρειαστώ*<br>*να χρειαστώ* | *έχω χρειαστεί*<br>*είχα χρειαστεί* | *να χρειάζεσαι*<br>*χρειάζεστε* | *χρειάσου*<br>*χρειαστείτε* |
| **I neglect** | παραμελώ 17 | παραμελούσα | παραμέλησα | θα παραμελήσω<br>να παραμελήσω | έχω παραμελήσει<br>είχα παραμελήσει | να παραμελείς<br>παραμελείτε | παραμέλησε<br>παραμελήστε |
| **I negotiate**<br>(contract) | *διαπραγμα-*<br>*τεύομαι 14* | *διαπραγμα-*<br>*τευόμουν* | *διαπραγμα-*<br>*τεύτηκα* | *θα διαπραγμα-*<br>*τευτώ* | *έχω διαπραγμα-*<br>*τευτεί* | *να διαπραγμα-*<br>*τεύεσαι* | *διαπραγμα-*<br>*τεύσου* |
| | | | | *να διαπραγμα-*<br>*τευτώ* | *είχα διαπραγμα-*<br>*τευτεί* | *διαπραγμα-*<br>*τεύεστε* | *διαπραγμα-*<br>*τευτείτε* |
| **I nest** | φωλιάζω 13 | φώλιαζα | φώλιασα | θα φωλιάσω<br>να φωλιάσω | έχω φωλιάσει<br>είχα φωλιάσει | φώλιαζε<br>φωλιάζετε | φώλιασε<br>φωλιάστε |
| **I neutralize** | εξουδετερώνω 13 | εξουδετέρωνα | εξουδετέρωσα | θα εξουδετερώσω<br>να εξουδετερώσω | έχω εξουδετερώσει<br>είχα εξουδετερώσει | εξουδετέρωνε<br>εξουδετερώνετε | εξουδετέρωσε<br>εξουδετερώστε |
| **I nibble** | τσιμπολογώ 15 | τσιμπολογούσα | τσιμπολόγησα | θα τσιμπολογήσω<br>να τσιμπολογήσω | έχω τσιμπολογήσει<br>είχα τσιμπολογήσει | τσιμπολόγα<br>τσιμπολογάτε | τσιμπολόγησε<br>τσιμπολογήστε |
| **I nod**<br>(with head) | γνέφω 13 | έγνεφα | έγνεψα | θα γνέψω<br>να γνέψω | έχω γνέψει<br>είχα γνέψει | γνέφε<br>γνέφετε | γνέψε<br>γνέψτε |
| **I nod off** | *αποκοιμιέμαι 16* | *αποκοιμιόμουν* | *αποκοιμήθηκα* | *θα αποκοιμηθώ*<br>*να αποκοιμηθώ* | *έχω αποκοιμηθεί*<br>*είχα αποκοιμηθεί* | *να αποκοιμιέσαι*<br>*αποκοιμιέστε* | *αποκοιμήσου*<br>*αποκοιμηθείτε* |
| **I nominate** | ανακηρύσσω 13 | ανακήρυσσα | ανακήρυξα | θα ανακηρύξω<br>να ανακηρύξω | έχω ανακηρύξει<br>είχα ανακηρύξει | ανακήρυσσε<br>ανακηρύσσετε | ανακήρυξε<br>ανακηρύξτε |

| English Verb | Present | Imperfect | Past | Simple Future<br>Simple Subjunctive | Present Perfect<br>Past Perfect | Continuous Imperative | Simple Imperative |
|---|---|---|---|---|---|---|---|
| **I notice** | προσέχω 13 | πρόσεχα | πρόσεξα | θα προσέξω<br>να προσέξω | έχω προσέξει<br>είχα προσέξει | πρόσεχε<br>προσέχετε | πρόσεξε<br>προσέξτε |
| **I notify** | ειδοποιώ 17 | ειδοποιούσα | ειδοποίησα | θα ειδοποιήσω<br>να ειδοποιήσω | έχω ειδοποιήσει<br>είχα ειδοποιήσει | να ειδοποιείς<br>ειδοποιείτε | ειδοποίησε<br>ειδοποιήστε |
| **I nourish** | τρέφω 13 | έτρεφα | έθρεψα | θα θρέψω<br>να θρέψω | έχω θρέψει<br>είχα θρέψει | τρέφε<br>τρέφετε | θρέψε<br>θρέψτε |
| **I nurture** | γαλουχώ 17 | γαλουχούσα | γαλούχησα | θα γαλουχήσω<br>να γαλουχήσω | έχω γαλουχήσει<br>είχα γαλουχήσει | να γαλουχείς<br>γαλουχείτε | γαλούχησε<br>γαλουχήστε |
| **I obey** | υπακούω 13 | υπάκουα | υπάκουσα | θα υπακούσω<br>να υπακούσω | έχω υπακούσει<br>είχα υπακούσει | υπάκουε<br>υπακούετε | υπάκουσε<br>υπακούστε |
| **I object** | *αντιτίθεμαι 42* | *αντετιθόμουν* | *αντιτέθηκα* | *θα αντιτεθώ*<br>*να αντιτεθώ* | *έχω αντιτεθεί*<br>*είχα αντιτεθεί* | *να αντιτίθεσαι*<br>*αντιτίθεστε* | *να αντιτεθείς*<br>*αντιτεθείτε* |
| **I oblige** | υποχρεώνω 13 | υποχρέωνα | υποχρέωσα | θα υποχρεώσω<br>να υποχρεώσω | έχω υποχρεώσει<br>είχα υποχρεώσει | υποχρέωνε<br>υποχρεώνετε | υποχρέωσε<br>υποχρεώστε |
| **I am obliged** | *υποχρεώνομαι 14* | *υποχρεωνόμουν* | *υποχρεώθηκα* | *θα υποχρεωθώ*<br>*να υποχρεωθώ* | *έχω υποχρεωθεί*<br>*είχα υποχρεωθεί* | *να υποχρεώνεσαι*<br>*υποχρεώνεστε* | *υποχρεώσου*<br>*υποχρεωθείτε* |
| **I am obliged** | οφείλω 13 | όφειλα | όφειλα | θα οφείλω<br>να οφείλω | έχω οφείλει<br>είχα οφείλει | να οφείλεις<br>οφείλετε | όφειλε<br>οφείλτε |
| **I obscure** | συσκοτίζω 13 | συσκότιζα | συσκότισα | θα συσκοτίσω<br>να συσκοτίσω | έχω συσκοτίσει<br>είχα συσκοτίσει | συσκότιζε<br>συσκοτίζετε | συσκότισε<br>συσκοτίστε |
| **I observe** | παρατηρώ 17 | παρατηρούσα | παρατήρησα | θα παρατηρήσω<br>να παρατηρήσω | έχω παρατηρήσει<br>είχα παρατηρήσει | να παρατηρείς<br>παρατηρείτε | παρατήρησε<br>παρατηρήστε |
| **I obstruct** | παρεμποδίζω 13 | παρεμπόδιζα | παρεμπόδισα | θα παρεμποδίσω<br>να παρεμποδίσω | έχω παρεμποδίσει<br>είχα παρεμποδίσει | παρεμπόδιζε<br>παρεμποδίζετε | παρεμπόδισε<br>παρεμποδίστε |

| English Verb | Present | Imperfect | Past | Simple Future<br>Simple Subjunctive | Present Perfect<br>Past Perfect | Continuous Imperative | Simple Imperative |
|---|---|---|---|---|---|---|---|
| **I obtain** | *προμηθεύομαι 14* | *προμηθευόμουν* | *προμηθεύτηκα* | *θα προμηθευτώ*<br>*να προμηθευτώ* | *έχω προμηθευτεί*<br>*είχα προμηθευτεί* | *να προμηθεύσαι*<br>*προμηθεύεστε* | *προμηθεύσου*<br>*προμηθευτείτε* |
| **I occupy** | καταλαμβάνω 13 | καταλάμβανα | κατέλαβα | θα καταλάβω<br>να καταλάβω | έχω καταλάβει<br>είχα καταλάβει | καταλάμβανε<br>καταλαμβάνετε | κατάλαβε<br>καταλάβετε |
| **I offend** | θίγω 13 | έθιγα | έθιξα | θα θίξω<br>να θίξω | έχω θίξει<br>είχα θίξει | θίγε<br>θίγετε | θίξε<br>θίξτε |
| **I offer** | προσφέρ(ν)ω 13 | πρόσφερνα | πρόσφερα | θα προσφέρω<br>να προσφέρω | έχω προσφέρει<br>είχα προσφέρει | πρόσφερνε<br>προσφέρνετε | πρόσφερε<br>προσφέρτε |
| **I officiate** | χοροστατώ 17 | χοροστατούσα | χοροστάτησα | θα χοροστατήσω<br>να χοροστατήσω | έχω χοροστατήσει<br>είχα χοροστατήσει | να χοροστατείς<br>χοροστατείτε | χοροστάτησε<br>χοροστατήστε |
| **I offset** | ισοσταθμίζω 13 | ισοστάθμιζα | ισοστάθμισα | θα ισοσταθμίσω<br>να ισοσταθμίσω | έχω ισοσταθμίσει<br>είχα ισοσταθμίσει | ισοστάθμιζε<br>ισοσταθμίζετε | ισοστάθμισε<br>ισοσταθμίστε |
| **I omit** | παραλείπω 13 | παράλειπα | παράλειψα | θα παραλείψω<br>να παραλείψω | έχω παραλείψει<br>είχα παραλείψει | παράλειπε<br>παραλείπετε | παράλειψε<br>παραλείψτε |
| **I ooze** | αναβλύζω 13 | ανάβλυζα | ανάβλυσα | θα αναβλύσω<br>να αναβλύσω | έχω αναβλύσει<br>είχα αναβλύσει | ανάβλυζε<br>αναβλύζετε | ανάβλυσε<br>αναβλύστε |
| **I open** | ανοίγω 13 | άνοιγα | άνοιξα | θα ανοίξω<br>να ανοίξω | έχω ανοίξει<br>είχα ανοίξει | άνοιγε<br>ανοίγετε | άνοιξε<br>ανοίξτε |
| **I operate** | χειρουργώ 17 | χειρουργούσα | χειρούργησα | θα χειρουργήσω<br>να χειρουργήσω | έχω χειρουργήσει<br>είχα χειρουργήσει | να χειρουργείς<br>χειρουργείτε | χειρούργησε<br>χειρουργήστε |
| **I order** | παραγγέλλω 13 | παράγγελλα | παράγγειλα | θα παραγγείλω<br>να παραγγείλω | έχω παραγγείλει<br>είχα παραγγείλει | παράγγελλε<br>παραγγέλλετε | παράγγειλε<br>παραγγείλτε |
| **I organise** | οργανώνω 13 | οργάνωνα | οργάνωσα | θα οργανώσω<br>να οργανώσω | έχω οργανώσει<br>είχα οργανώσει | οργάνωνε<br>οργανώνετε | οργάνωσε<br>οργανώστε |

| English Verb | Present | Imperfect | Past | Simple Future<br>Simple Subjunctive | Present Perfect<br>Past Perfect | Continuous Imperative | Simple Imperative |
|---|---|---|---|---|---|---|---|
| **I orientate** | προσανατολίζω 13 | προσανατόλιζα | προσανατόλισα | θα προσανατολίσω<br>να προσανατολίσω | έχω προσανατολίσει<br>είχα προσανατολίσει | προσανατόλιζε<br>προσανατολίζετε | προσανατόλισε<br>προσανατολίστε |
| **I outshine** (surpass) | επισκιάζω 13 | επισκίαζα | επισκίασα | θα επισκιάσω<br>να επισκιάσω | έχω επισκιάσει<br>είχα επισκιάσει | επισκίαζε<br>επισκιάζετε | επισκίασε<br>επισκιάστε |
| **I am outvoted** | *καταψηφίζομαι 14* | *καταψηφιζόμουν* | *καταψηφίστηκα* | *θα καταψηφιστώ*<br>*να καταψηφιστώ* | *έχω καταψηφιστεί*<br>*είχα καταψηφιστεί* | *να καταψηφίζεσαι*<br>*καταψηφίζεστε* | *καταψηφίσου*<br>*καταψηφιστείτε* |
| **I overesti-mate** | υπερεκτιμώ 15 | υπερεκτιμούσα | υπερεκτίμησα | θα υπερεκτιμήσω<br>να υπερεκτιμήσω | έχω υπερεκτιμήσει<br>είχα υπερεκτιμήσει | υπερεκτίμα<br>υπερεκτιμάτε | υπερεκτίμησε<br>υπερεκτιμήστε |
| **I overprice** | υπερτιμώ 15 | υπερτιμούσα | υπερτίμησα | θα υπερτιμήσω<br>να υπερτιμήσω | έχω υπερτιμήσει<br>είχα υπερτιμήσει | υπερτίμα<br>υπερτιμάτε | υπερτίμησε<br>υπερτιμήστε |
| **I overhear** | κρυφακούω 13 | κρυφάκουα | κρυφάκουσα | θα κρυφακούσω<br>να κρυφακούσω | έχω κρυφακούσει<br>είχα κρυφακούσει | κρυφάκουε<br>κρυφακούετε | κρυφάκουσε<br>κρυφακούστε |
| **I overheat** | *υπερθερμαίνομαι 14* | *υπερθερμενόμουν* | *υπερθερμάνθηκα* | *θα υπερθερμανθώ*<br>*να υπερθερμανθώ* | *έχω υπερθερμανθεί*<br>*είχα υπερθερμανθεί* | *να υπερθερμαίνεσαι*<br>*υπερθερμαίνεστε* | *υπερθερμάνσου*<br>*υπερθερμανθείτε* |
| **I overlook** | παραβλέπω 13 | παρέβλεπα | παρέβλεψα | θα παραβλέψω<br>να παραβλέψω | έχω παραβλέψει<br>είχα παραβλέψει | παράβλεπε<br>παραβλέπετε | παράβλεψε<br>παραβλέψτε |
| **I overnight** | διανυκτερεύω 13 | διανυκτέρευα | διανυκτέρευσα | θα διανυκτερεύσω<br>να διανυκτερεύσω | έχω διανυκτερεύσει<br>είχα διανυκτερεύσει | διανυκτέρευε<br>διανυκτερεύετε | διανυκτέρεψε<br>διανυκτερέψτε |
| **I over-power** | καταβάλλω 13 | κατέβαλλα | κατέβαλα | θα καταβάλλω<br>να καταβάλλω | έχω καταβάλλει<br>είχα καταβάλλει | κατάβαλλε<br>καταβάλλετε | κατάβαλε<br>καταβάλτε |
| **I override** | υπερπηδώ 15 | υπερπηδούσα | υπερπήδηξα | θα υπερπηδήξω<br>να υπερπηδήξω | έχω υπερπηδήξει<br>είχα υπερπηδήξει | υπερπήδα<br>υπερπηδάτε | υπερπήδηξε<br>υπερπηδήξτε |
| **I overrule** | ανατρέπω 13 | ανέτρεπα | ανέτρεψα | θα ανατρέψω<br>να ανατρέψω | έχω ανατρέψει<br>είχα ανατρέψει | ανάτρεπε<br>ανατρέπετε | ανάτρεψε<br>ανατρέψτε |

| English Verb | Present | Imperfect | Past | Simple Future<br>Simple Subjunctive | Present Perfect<br>Past Perfect | Continuous Imperative | Simple Imperative |
|---|---|---|---|---|---|---|---|
| **I oversee** | επιβλέπω 13 | επέβλεπα | επέβλεψα | θα επιβλέψω<br>να επιβλέψω | έχω επιβλέψει<br>είχα επιβλέψει | επίβλεπε<br>επιβλέπετε | επίβλεψε<br>επιβλέψτε |
| **I oversleep** | *παρακοιμάμαι 42* | *παρακοιμόμουν* | *παρακοιμήθηκα* | *θα παρακοιμηθώ*<br>*να παρακοιμηθώ* | *έχω παρακοιμηθεί*<br>*είχα παρακοιμηθεί* | *να παρακοιμάσαι*<br>*παρακοιμάστε* | *παρακοιμήσου*<br>*παρακοιμηθείτε* |
| **I overtake** | προσπερνώ 15 | προσπερνούσα | προσπέρασα | θα προσπεράσω<br>να προσπεράσω | έχω προσπεράσει<br>είχα προσπεράσει | προσπέρνα<br>προσπερνάτε | προσπέρασε<br>προσπεράστε |
| **I overturn** | αναποδογυρίζω 13 | αναποδογύριζα | αναποδογύρισα | θα αναποδογυρίσω<br>να αναποδογυρίσω | έχω αναποδογυρίσει<br>είχα αναποδογυρίσει | αναποδογύριζε<br>αναποδογυρίζετε | αναποδογύρισε<br>αναποδογυρίστε |
| **I owe** | χρωστ(ά)ώ 15 | χρωστούσα | χρώσταγα | – | – | χρώστα<br>χρωστάτε | χρώσταγε<br>χρωστάτε |
| **I pace** | βηματίζω 13 | βημάτιζα | βημάτισα | θα βηματίσω<br>να βηματίσω | έχω βηματίσει<br>είχα βηματίσει | βημάτιζε<br>βηματίζετε | βημάτισε<br>βηματίστε |
| **I pack** | πακετάρω 13 | πακέταρα | πακετάρησα | θα πακετάρω<br>να πακετάρω | έχω πακετάρει<br>είχα πακετάρει | πακέταρε<br>πακετάρετε | πακετάρησε<br>πακεταρήστε |
| **I cram** | στοιβάζω 13 | στοίβαζα | στοίβασα | θα στοιβάσω<br>να στοιβάσω | έχω στοιβάσει<br>είχα στοιβάσει | στοίβαζε<br>στοιβάζετε | στοίβασε<br>στοιβάστε |
| **I paddle** | πλατσουλίζω 13 | πλατσούλιζα | πλατσούλισα | θα πλατσουλίσω<br>να πλατσουλίσω | έχω πλατσουλίσει<br>είχα πλατσουλίσει | πλατσούλιζε<br>πλατσουλίζετε | πλατσούλισε<br>πλατσουλίστε |
| **I paint** | ζωγραφίζω 13 | ζωγράφιζα | ζωγράφισα | θα ζωγραφίσω<br>να ζωγραφίσω | έχω ζωγραφίσει<br>είχα ζωγραφίσει | ζωγράφιζε<br>ζωγραφίζετε | ζωγράφισε<br>ζωγραφίστε |
| **I pale** | χλωμιάζω 13 | χλώμιαζα | χλώμιασα | θα χλωμιάσω<br>να χλωμιάσω | έχω χλωμιάσει<br>είχα χλωμιάσει | χλώμιαζε<br>χλωμιάζετε | χλώμιασε<br>χλωμιάστε |
| **I pamper** | κακομαθαίνω 13 | κακομάθαινα | κακόμαθα | θα κακομάθω<br>να κακοιμάθω | έχω κακομάθει<br>είχα κακομάθει | κακομάθαινε<br>κακομαθαίνετε | κακόμαθε<br>κακομάθετε |

| English Verb | Present | Imperfect | Past | Simple Future<br>Simple Subjunctive | Present Perfect<br>Past Perfect | Continuous Imperative | Simple Imperative |
|---|---|---|---|---|---|---|---|
| **I pamper** | κανακεύω 13 | κανάκευα | κανάκεψα | θα κανακέψω<br>να κανακέψω | έχω κανακέψει<br>είχα κανακέψει | κανάκευε<br>κανακεύετε | κανάκεψε<br>κανακέψτε |
| **I panic** | *πανικοβάλλομαι 14* | *πανικοβαλλόμουν* | *πανικοβλήθηκα* | *θα πανικοβληθώ*<br>*να πανικοβληθώ* | *έχω πανικοβληθεί*<br>*είχα πανικοβληθεί* | *να πανικοβάλλεσαι*<br>*πανικοβάλλεστε* | *να πανικοβληθείς*<br>*πανικοβληθείτε* |
| **I pant** | λαχανιάζω 13 | λαχάνιαζα | λαχάνιασα | θα λαχανιάσω<br>να λαχανιάσω | έχω λαχανιάσει<br>είχα λαχανιάσει | λαχάνιαζε<br>λαχανιάζετε | λαχάνιασε<br>λαχανιάστε |
| **I parade** | παρελαύνω 13 | παρέλαυνα | παρέλασα | θα παρελάσω<br>να παρελάσω | έχω παρελάσει<br>είχα παρελάσει | παρέλαυνε<br>παρελαύνετε | παρέλασε<br>παρελάστε |
| **I paralyse** | παραλύω 13 | παρέλυα | παρέλυσα | θα παραλύσω<br>να παραλύσω | έχω παραλύσει<br>είχα παραλύσει | παράλυε<br>παραλύετε | παράλυσε<br>παραλύστε |
| **I park** | παρκάρω 13 | πάρκαρα | παρκάρησα | θα παρκάρω<br>να παρκάρω | έχω παρκάρει<br>είχα παρκάρει | πάρκαρε<br>παρκάρετε | παρκάρησε<br>παρκαρήστε |
| **I participate** | συμμετέχω 13 | συμμετείχα | συμμετείχα | θα συμμετάσχω<br>να συμμετάσχω | έχω συμμετάσχει<br>είχα συμμετάσχει | συμμέτεχε<br>συμμετέχετε | να συμμετάσχεις<br>συμμετάσχετε |
| **I pass by** | περν(ά)ώ 15 | περνούσα | πέρασα | θα περάσω<br>να περάσω | έχω περάσει<br>είχα περάσει | πέρνα<br>περνάτε | πέρασε<br>περάστε |
| **I patrol** | περιπολώ 17 | περιπολούσα | περιπόλησα | θα περιπολήσω<br>να περιπολήσω | έχω περιπολήσει<br>είχα περιπολήσει | να περιπολείς<br>περιπολείτε | περιπόλησε<br>περιπολήστε |
| **I pause** | *κοντοστέκομαι 14* | *κοντοστεκόμουν* | *κοντοστάθηκα* | *θα κοντοσταθώ*<br>*να κοντοσταθώ* | *έχω κοντοσταθεί*<br>*είχα κοντοσταθεί* | *να κοντοστέκεσαι*<br>*κοντοστέκεστε* | *κοντοστάσου*<br>*κοντοσταθείτε* |
| **I pay** | πληρώνω 13 | πλήρωνα | πλήρωσα | θα πληρώσω<br>να πληρώσω | έχω πληρώσει<br>είχα πληρώσει | πλήρωνε<br>πληρώνετε | πλήρωσε<br>πληρώστε |
| **I am taxed** | *φορολογούμαι 18* | *φορολογούμουν* | *φορολογήθηκα* | *θα φορολογηθώ*<br>*να φορολογηθώ* | *έχω φορολογηθεί*<br>*είχα φορολογηθεί* | *να φορολογείσαι*<br>*φορολογείστε* | *φορολογήσου*<br>*φορολογηθείτε* |

| English Verb | Present | Imperfect | Past | Simple Future<br>Simple Subjunctive | Present Perfect<br>Past Perfect | Continuous Imperative | Simple Imperative |
|---|---|---|---|---|---|---|---|
| **I peep** | κρυφοκοιτάζω 13 | κρυφοκοίταζα | κρυφοκοίταξα | θα κρυφοκοιτάξω<br>να κρυφοκοιτάξω | έχω κρυφοκοιτάξει<br>είχα κρυφοκοιτάξει | κρυφοκοίταζε<br>κρυφοκοιτάζετε | κρυφοκοίταξε<br>κρυφοκοιτάξτε |
| **I pension off** | συνταξιοδοτώ 17 | συνταξιοδοτούσα | συνταξιοδότησα | θα συνταξιοδοτήσω<br>να συνταξιοδοτήσω | έχω συνταξιοδοτήσει<br>είχα συνταξιοδοτήσει | να συνταξιοδοτείς<br>συνταξιοδοτείτε | συνταξιοδότησε<br>συνταξιοδοτήστε |
| **I perfect** | τελειοποιώ 17 | τελειοποιούσα | τελειοποίησα | θα τελειοποιήσω<br>να τελειοποιήσω | έχω τελειοποιήσει<br>είχα τελειοποιήσει | να τελειοποιείς<br>τελειοποιείτε | τελειοποίησε<br>τελειοποιήστε |
| **I perform** | επιτελώ 17 | επιτελούσα | επιτέλεσα | θα επιτελέσω<br>να επιτελέσω | έχω επιτελέσει<br>είχα επιτελέσει | να επιτελείς<br>επιτελείτε | επιτέλεσε<br>επιτελέστε |
| **I perish** | *αφανίζομαι 14* | *αφανιζόμουν* | *αφανίστηκα* | *θα αφανιστώ*<br>*να αφανιστώ* | *έχω αφανιστεί*<br>*είχα αφανιστεί* | *να αφανίζεσαι*<br>*αφανίζεστε* | *αφανίσου*<br>*αφανιστείτε* |
| **I permeate** | εισχωρώ 17 | εισχωρούσα | εισχώρησα | θα εισχωρήσω<br>να εισχωρήσω | έχω εισχωρήσει<br>είχα εισχωρήσει | να εισχωρείς<br>εισχωρείτε | εισχώρησε<br>εισχωρήστε |
| **I permit** | επιτρέπω 13 | επέτρεπα | επέτρεψα | θα επιτρέψω<br>να επιτρέψω | έχω επιτρέψει<br>είχα επιτρέψει | επίτρεπε<br>επιτρέπετε | επίτρεψε<br>επιτρέψτε |
| **I perpetuate** | διαιωνίζω 13 | διαιώνιζα | διαιώνισα | θα διαιωνίσω<br>να διαιωνίσω | έχω διαιωνίσει<br>είχα διαιωνίσει | διαιώνιζε<br>διαιωνίζετε | διαιώνισε<br>διαιωνίστε |
| **I pester** | ταλαιπωρώ 17 | ταλαιπωρούσα | ταλαιπώρησα | θα ταλαιπωρήσω<br>να ταλαιπωρήσω | έχω ταλαιπωρήσει<br>είχα ταλαιπωρήσει | να ταλαιπωρείς<br>ταλαιπωρείτε | ταλαιπώρησε<br>ταλαιπωρήστε |
| **I pester** | σκοτίζω 13 | σκότιζα | σκότισα | θα σκοτίσω<br>να σκοτίσω | έχω σκοτίσει<br>είχα σκοτίσει | σκότιζε<br>σκοτίζετε | σκότισε<br>σκοτίστε |
| **I photograph** | φωτογραφίζω 13 | φωτογράφιζα | φωτογράφισα | θα φωτογραφίσω<br>να φωτογραφίσω | έχω φωτογραφίσει<br>είχα φωτογραφίσει | φωτογράφιζε<br>φωτογραφίζετε | φωτογράφισε<br>φωτογραφίστε |
| **I phrase** (verbally) | διατυπώνω 13 | διετύπωνα | διετύπωσα | θα διατυπώσω<br>να διατυπώσω | έχω διατυπώσει<br>είχα διατυπώσει | διατύπωνε<br>διατυπώνετε | διατύπωσε<br>διατυπώστε |

| English Verb | Present | Imperfect | Past | Simple Future<br>Simple Subjunctive | Present Perfect<br>Past Perfect | Continuous Imperative | Simple Imperative |
|---|---|---|---|---|---|---|---|
| **I pierce** | εισδύω 13 | είσδυα | είσδυσα | θα εισδύσω<br>να εισδύσω | έχω εισδύσει<br>είχα εισδύσει | είσδυε<br>εισδύετε | είσδυσε<br>εισδύστε |
| **I pierce** | τρυπάω 15 | τρυπούσα | τρύπησα | θα τρυπήσω<br>να τρυπήσω | έχω τρυπήσει<br>είχα τρυπήσει | τρύπα<br>τρυπάτε | τρύπησε<br>τρυπήστε |
| **I pilfer** | σουφρώνω 13 | σούφρωνα | σούφρωσα | θα σουφρώσω<br>να σουφρώσω | έχω σουφρώσει<br>είχα σουφρώσει | σούφρωνε<br>σουφρώνετε | σούφρωσε<br>σουφρώστε |
| **I pillage** | λεηλατώ 17 | λεηλατούσα | λεηλάτησα | θα λεηλατήσω<br>να λεηλατήσω | έχω λεηλατήσει<br>είχα λεηλατήσει | να λεηλατείς<br>λεηλατείτε | λεηλάτησε<br>λεηλατήστε |
| **I pillory** | διαπομπεύω 13 | διαπόμπευα | διαπόμπεψα | θα διαπομπέψω<br>να διαπομπέψω | έχω διαπομπέψει<br>είχα διαπομπέψει | διαπόμπευε<br>διαπομπεύετε | διαπόμπεψε<br>διαπομπέψτε |
| **I pinch**<br>(filch / pilfer) | τσιμπώ 15 | τσιμπούσα | τσίμπησα | θα τσιμπήσω<br>να τσιμπήσω | έχω τσιμπήσει<br>είχα τσιμπήσει | τσίμπα<br>τσιμπάτε | τσίμπησε<br>τσιμπήστε |
| **I pity** | οικτίρω 13 | οίκτιρα | οίκτιρα | θα οικτίρω<br>να οικτίρω | έχω οικτίρει<br>είχα οικτίρει | οίκτιρε<br>οικτίρετε | οίκτιρε<br>οικτίρτε |
| **I place** | τοποθετώ 17 | τοποθετούσα | τοποθέτησα | θα τοποθετήσω<br>να τοποθετήσω | έχω τοποθετήσει<br>είχα τοποθετήσει | να τοποθετείς<br>τοποθετείτε | τοποθέτησε<br>τοποθετήστε |
| **I plane** | ροκανίζω 13 | ροκάνιζα | ροκάνισα | θα ροκανίσω<br>να ροκανίσω | έχω ροκανίσει<br>είχα ροκανίσει | ροκάνιζε<br>ροκανίζετε | ροκάνισε<br>ροκανίστε |
| **I plant** | φυτεύω 13 | φύτευα | φύτεψα | θα φυτέψω<br>να φυτέψω | έχω φυτέψει<br>είχα φυτέψει | φύτευε<br>φυτεύετε | φύτεψε<br>φυτέψτε |
| **I play** | παίζω 13 | έπαιζα | έπαιξα | θα παίξω<br>να παίξω | έχω παίξει<br>είχα παίξει | παίζε<br>παίζετε | παίξε<br>παίξτε |
| **I play-act** | *υποκρίνομαι 14* | *υποκρινόμουν* | *υποκρίθηκα* | *θα υποκριθώ*<br>*να υποκριθώ* | *έχω υποκριθεί*<br>*είχα υποκριθεί* | *να υποκρίνεσαι*<br>*υποκρίνεστε* | *υποκρίσου*<br>*υποκριθείτε* |

| English Verb | Present | Imperfect | Past | Simple Future<br>Simple Subjunctive | Present Perfect<br>Past Perfect | Continuous Imperative | Simple Imperative |
|---|---|---|---|---|---|---|---|
| **I plead** | *προφασίζομαι 14* | *προφασιζόμουν* | *προφασίστηκα* | *θα προφασιστώ*<br>*να προφασιστώ* | *έχω προφασιστεί*<br>*είχα προφασιστεί* | *να προφασίζεσαι*<br>*προφασίζεστε* | *προφασίσου*<br>*προφασιστείτε* |
| **I am pleased** | *ευχαριστιέμαι 16* | *ευχαριστιόμουν* | *ευχαριστήθηκα* | *θα ευχαριστηθώ*<br>*να ευχαριστηθώ* | *έχω ευχαριστηθεί*<br>*είχα ευχαριστηθεί* | *να ευχαριστιέσαι*<br>*ευχαριστιέστε* | *ευχαριστήσου*<br>*ευχαριστηθείτε* |
| **I promise** | *υπόσχομαι 14* | *υποσχόμουν* | *υποσχέθηκα* | *θα υποσχεθώ*<br>*να υποσχεθώ* | *έχω υποσχεθεί*<br>*είχα υποσχεθεί* | *να υπόσχεσαι*<br>*υπόσχεστε* | *υποσχέσου*<br>*υποσχεθείτε* |
| **I plot** | μηχανοραφώ 17 | μηχανοραφούσα | μηχανοράφησα | θα μηχανοραφήσω<br>να μηχανοραφήσω | έχω μηχανοραφήσει<br>είχα μηχανοραφήσει | να μηχανοραφείς<br>μηχανοραφείτε | μηχανοράφησε<br>μηχανοραφήστε |
| **I plunge** | βυθίζω 13 | βύθιζα | βύθισα | θα βυθίσω<br>να βυθίσω | έχω βυθίσει<br>είχα βυθίσει | βύθιζε<br>βυθίζετε | βύθισε<br>βυθίστε |
| **I ponder** | *διαλογίζομαι 14* | *διαλογιζόμουν* | *διαλογίστηκα* | *θα διαλογιστώ*<br>*να διαλογιστώ* | *έχω διαλογιστεί*<br>*είχα διαλογιστεί* | *να διαλογίζεσαι*<br>*διαλογίζεστε* | *διαλογίσου*<br>*διαλογιστείτε* |
| **I poin out** | επισημαίνω 13 | επισήμαινα | επισήμανα | θα επισημάνω<br>να επισημάνω | έχω επισημάνει<br>είχα επισημάνει | επισήμαινε<br>επισημαίνετε | επισήμανε<br>επισημάντε |
| **I poison** | δηλητηριάζω 13 | δηλητηρίαζα | δηλητηρίασα | θα δηλητηριάσω<br>να δηλητηριάσω | έχω δηλητηριάσει<br>είχα δηλητηριάσει | δηλητηρίαζε<br>δηλητηριάζετε | δηλητηρίασε<br>δηλητηριάστε |
| **I polish** | λουστράρω 13 | λούστραρα | λουστράρησα | θα λουστραρήσω<br>να λουστραρήσω | έχω λουστραρήσει<br>είχα λουστραρήσει | λούστραρε<br>λουστράρετε | λουστράρησε<br>λουστραρήστε |
| **I pollute** | μολύνω 13 | μόλυνα | μόλυνα | θα μολύνω<br>να μολύνω | έχω μολύνει<br>είχα μολύνει | μόλυνε<br>μολύνετε | μόλυνε<br>μολύντε |
| **I predominate** | υπερισχύω 13 | υπερίσχυα | υπερίσχυσα | θα υπερισχύσω<br>να υπερισχύσω | έχω υπερισχύσει<br>είχα υπερισχίσει | υπερίσχυε<br>υπερισχύετε | υπερίσχυσε<br>υπερισχύστε |
| **I portray** | απεικονίζω 13 | απεικόνιζα | απεικόνισα | θα απεικονίσω<br>να απεικονίσω | έχω απεικονίσει<br>είχα απεικονίσει | απεικόνιζε<br>απεικονίζετε | απεικόνισε<br>απεικονίστε |

| English Verb | Present | Imperfect | Past | Simple Future<br>Simple Subjunctive | Present Perfect<br>Past Perfect | Continuous Imperative | Simple Imperative |
|---|---|---|---|---|---|---|---|
| **I pose** | ποζάρω 13 | πόζαρα | ποζάρισα | θα ποζάρω<br>να ποζάρω | έχω ποζάρει<br>είχα ποζάρει | πόζαρε<br>ποζάρετε | πόζαρε<br>ποζάρετε |
| **I post** | ταχυδρομώ 17 | ταχυδρομούσα | ταχυδρόμησα | θα ταχυδρομήσω<br>να ταχυδρομήσω | έχω ταχυδρομήσει<br>είχα ταχυδρομήσει | να ταχυδρομείς<br>ταχυδρομείτε | ταχυδρόμησε<br>ταχυδρομήστε |
| **I postpone** | αναβάλλω 13 | ανέβαλλα | ανέβαλα | θα αναβάλω<br>να αναβάλω | έχω αναβάλει<br>είχα αναβάλει | ανάβαλλε<br>αναβάλλετε | ανάβαλε<br>αναβάλτε |
| **I pour** | χύνω 13 | έχυνα | έχυσα | θα χύσω<br>να χύσω | έχω χύσει<br>είχα χύσει | χύνε<br>χύνετε | χύσε<br>χύστε |
| **I practise** | *προπονούμαι 18*<br>*προπονιέμαι 16* | *προπονούμουν*<br>*προπονιόμουν* | *προπονήθηκα* | *θα προπονηθώ*<br>*να προπονηθώ* | *έχω προπονηθεί*<br>*είχα προπονηθεί* | *να προπονείσαι*<br>*προπονείστε* | *προπονήσου*<br>*προπονηθείτε* |
| **I praise** | επαινώ 17 | επαινούσα | επαίνεσα | θα παινέσω<br>να παινέσω | έχω παινέσει<br>είχα παινέσει | να επαινείς<br>επαινείτε | παίνεσε<br>παινέστε |
| **I pray** | *προσεύχομαι 14* | *προσευχόμουν* | *προσευχήθηκα* | *θα προσευχηθώ*<br>*να προσευχηθώ* | *έχω προσευχηθεί*<br>*είχα προσευχηθεί* | *να προσεύχεσαι*<br>*προσεύχεστε* | *προσευχήσου*<br>*προσευχηθείτε* |
| **I predict** | προβλέπω 13 | προέβλεπα | προείδα | θα προβλέψω<br>να προβλέψω | έχω προβλέψει<br>είχα προβλέψει | πρόβλεπε<br>προβλέπετε | πρόβλεψε<br>προβλέψτε |
| **I prefer** | προτιμώ 15 | προτιμούσα | προτίμησα | θα προτιμήσω<br>να προτιμήσω | έχω προτιμήσει<br>είχα προτιμήσει | προτίμα<br>προτιμάτε | προτίμησε<br>προτιμήστε |
| **I prejudge** | προδικάζω 13 | προδίκαζα | προδίκασα | θα προδικάσω<br>να προδικάσω | έχω προδικάσει<br>είχα προδικάσει | προδίκαζε<br>προδικάζετε | προδίκασε<br>προδικάστε |
| **I prejudice** | προκαταλαμβάνω 13 | προκαταλάμβανα | προκατέλαβα | θα προκαταλάβω<br>να προκαταλάβω | έχω προκαταλάβει<br>είχα προκαταλάβει | προκαταλάμβανε<br>προκαταλαμβάνετε | προκατάλαβε<br>προκαταλάβετε |
| **I prepare** | ετοιμάζω 13 | ετοίμαζα | ετοίμασα | θα ετοιμάσω<br>να ετοιμάσω | έχω ετοιμάσει<br>είχα ετοιμάσει | ετοίμαζε<br>ετοιμάζετε | ετοίμασε<br>ετοιμάστε |

| English Verb | Present | Imperfect | Past | Simple Future<br>Simple Subjunctive | Present Perfect<br>Past Perfect | Continuous Imperative | Simple Imperative |
|---|---|---|---|---|---|---|---|
| **I present** (introduce) | παρουσιάζω 13 | παρουσίαζα | παρουσίασα | θα παρουσιάσω<br>να παρουσιάσω | έχω παρουσιάσει<br>είχα παρουσιάσει | παρουσίαζε<br>παρουσιάζετε | παρουσίασε<br>παρουσιάστε |
| **I preserve** | συντηρώ 17 | συντηρούσα | συντήρησα | θα συντηρήσω<br>να συντηρήσω | έχω συντηρήσει<br>είχα συντηρήσει | να συντηρείς<br>συντηρείτε | συντήρησε<br>συντηρήστε |
| **I preside** | προεδρεύω 13 | προέδρευα | προέδρευσα | θα προεδρεύσω<br>να προεδρεύσω | έχω προεδρεύσει<br>είχα προεδρεύσει | προέδρευε<br>προεδρεύετε | προέδρευσε<br>προεδρεύστε |
| **I press** | πιέζω 13 | πίεζα | πίεσα | θα πιέσω<br>να πιέσω | έχω πιέσει<br>είχα πιέσει | πίεζε<br>πιέζετε | πίεσε<br>πιέστε |
| **I presume** | προϋποθέτω 13 | προϋπέθετα | προϋπέθεσα | θα προϋποθέσω<br>να προϋποθέσω | έχω προϋποθέσει<br>είχα προϋποθέσει | προϋπόθετε<br>προϋποθέτετε | προϋπόθεσε<br>προϋποθέστε |
| **I pretend** | *προσποιούμαι 18* | *προσποιούμουν* | *προσποιήθηκα* | *θα προσποιηθώ*<br>*να προσποιηθώ* | *έχω προσποιηθεί*<br>*είχα προσποιηθεί* | *να προσποιείσαι*<br>*προσποιείστε* | *προσποιήσου*<br>*προσποιηθείτε* |
| **I prevail** | επικρατώ 17 | επικρατούσα | επικράτησα | θα επικρατήσω<br>να επικρατήσω | έχω επικρατήσει<br>είχα επικρατήσει | να επικρατείς<br>επικρατείτε | επικράτησε<br>επικρατήστε |
| **I prevent** | παρακωλύω 13 | παρακώλυα | παρακώλυσα | θα παρακωλύσω<br>να παρακωλύσω | έχω παρακωλύσει<br>είχα παρακωλύσει | παρακώλυε<br>παρακωλύετε | παρακώλυσε<br>παρακωλύστε |
| **I prick** | αγκυλώνω 13 | αγκύλωνα | αγκύλωσα | θα αγκυλώσω<br>να αγκυλώσω | έχω αγκυλώσει<br>είχα αγκυλώσει | αγκύλωνε<br>αγκυλώνετε | αγκύλωσε<br>αγκυλώστε |
| **I print** | τυπώνω 13 | τύπωνα | τύπωσα | θα τυπώσω<br>να τυπώσω | έχω τυπώσει<br>είχα τυπώσει | τύπωνε<br>τυπώνετε | τύπωσε<br>τυπώστε |
| **I privatise** | ιδιωτικοποιώ 17 | ιδιωτικοποιούσα | ιδιωτικοποίησα | θα ιδιωτικοποιήσω<br>να ιδιωτικοποιήσω | έχω ιδιωτικοποιήσει<br>είχα ιδιωτικοποιήσει | να ιδιωτικοποιείς<br>ιδιωτικοποιείτε | ιδιωτικοποίησε<br>ιδιωτικοποιήστε |
| **I proceed** | προχωρώ 15 | προχωρούσα | προχώρησα | θα προχωρήσω<br>να προχωρήσω | έχω προχωρήσει<br>είχα προχωρήσει | προχώρα<br>προχωράτε | προχώρησε<br>προχωρήστε |

| English Verb | Present | Imperfect | Past | Simple Future<br>Simple Subjunctive | Present Perfect<br>Past Perfect | Continuous Imperative | Simple Imperative |
|---|---|---|---|---|---|---|---|
| **I proclaim** | προκηρύσσω 13<br>προκηρύττω | προκήρυσσα | προκήρυξα | θα προκηρύξω<br>να προκηρύξω | έχω προκηρύξει<br>είχα προκηρύξει | προκήρυσσε<br>προκηρύσσετε | προκήρυξε<br>προκηρύξτε |
| **I produce** | παράγω 13 | παρήγα | παρήγαγα | θα παράγω<br>να παράγω | έχω παράγει<br>είχα παράγει | να παράγεις<br>παράγετε | παράγε<br>παραγάγετε |
| **I profit** | *ωφελούμαι 18* | *ωφελούμουν* | *ωφελήθηκα* | *θα ωφελήθώ*<br>*να ωφεληθώ* | *έχω ωφεληθεί*<br>*είχα ωφεληθεί* | *να ωφελείσαι*<br>*ωφελείστε* | *ωφελήσου*<br>*ωφεληθείτε* |
| **I profit by** | *επωφελούμαι 18* | *επωφελούμουν* | *επωφελήθηκα* | *θα επωφεληθώ*<br>*να επωφεληθώ* | *έχω επωφεληθεί*<br>*είχα επωφεληθεί* | *να επωφελείσαι*<br>*επωφελείστε* | *επωφελήσου*<br>*επωφεληθείτε* |
| **I progress** | προοδεύω 13 | προόδευα | προόδευσα | θα προοδεύσω<br>να προοδεύσω | έχω προοδεύσει<br>είχα προοδεύσει | προόδευε<br>προοδεύετε | προόδευσε<br>προοδεύστε |
| **I prohibit** | απαγορεύω 13 | απαγόρευα | απαγόρευσα | θα απαγορεύσω<br>να απαγορεύσω | έχω απαγορεύσει<br>είχα απαγορεύσει | απαγόρευε<br>απαγορεύετε | απαγόρευσε<br>απαγορεύστε |
| **I project** | προβάλλω 13 | πρόβαλλα | πρόβαλα | θα προβάλω<br>να προβάλω | έχω προβάλει<br>είχα προβάλει | πρόβαλλε<br>προβάλλετε | πρόβαλε<br>προβάλτε |
| **I promise** | *υπόσχομαι 14* | *υποσχόμουν* | *υποσχέθηκα* | *θα υποσχεθώ*<br>*να υποσχεθώ* | *έχω υποσχεθεί*<br>*είχα υποσχεθεί* | *να υπόσχεσαι*<br>*υπόσχεστε* | *υποσχέσου*<br>*υποσχεθείτε* |
| **I promote** | προάγω 13 | προήγα | προήγαγα | θα προαγάγω<br>να προαγάγω | έχω προαγάγει<br>είχα προαγάγει | να προάγεις<br>προάγετε | να προαγάγεις<br>προαγάγετε |
| **I promote** | προβιβάζω 13 | προβίβαζα | προβίβασα | θα προβιβάσω<br>να προβιβάσω | έχω προβιβάσει<br>είχα προβιβάσει | προβίβαζε<br>προβιβάζετε | προβίβασε<br>προβιβάστε |
| **I prompt** | παροτρύνω 13 | παρότρυνα | παρότρυνα | θα παροτρύνω<br>να παροτρύνω | έχω παροτρύνει<br>είχα παροτρύνει | να παροτρύνεις<br>παροτρύνετε | παρότρυνε<br>παροτρύνετε |
| **I pronounce** | προφέρω 13 | πρόφερα | πρόφερα | θα προφέρω<br>να προφέρω | έχω προφέρει<br>είχα προφέρει | να προφέρεις<br>προφέρετε | πρόφερε<br>προφέρτε |

| English Verb | Present | Imperfect | Past | Simple Future<br>Simple Subjunctive | Present Perfect<br>Past Perfect | Continuous Imperative | Simple Imperative |
|---|---|---|---|---|---|---|---|
| **I prop up** | στερεώνω 13 | στερέωνα | στερέωσα | θα στερεώσω<br>να στερεώσω | έχω στερεώσει<br>είχα στερεώσει | στερέωνε<br>στερεώνετε | στερέωσε<br>στερεώστε |
| **I prophesy** | προφητεύω 13 | προφήτευα | προφήτευσα | θα προφητεύσω<br>να προφητεύσω | έχω προφητεύσει<br>είχα προφητεύσει | προφήτευε<br>προφητεύετε | προφήτευσε<br>προφητεύστε |
| **I propose** | *εισηγούμαι 18* | *εισηγούμουν* | *εισηγήθηκα* | *θα εισηγηθώ*<br>*να εισηγηθώ* | *έχω εισηγηθεί*<br>*είχα εισηγηθεί* | *να εισηγείσαι*<br>*εισηγείστε* | *εισηγήσου*<br>*εισηγηθείτε* |
| **I prosper** | ευημερώ 18 | ευημερούσα | ευημέρησα | θα ευημερήσω<br>να ευημερήσω | έχω ευημερήσει<br>είχα ευημερήσει | να ευημερείς<br>ευημερείτε | ευημέρησε<br>ευημερήστε |
| **I prosper** | ακμάζω 13 | ήκμαζα | ήκμασα | θα ακμάσω<br>να ακμάσω | έχω ακμάσει<br>είχα ακμάσει | άκμαζε<br>ακμάζετε | άκμασε<br>ακμάστε |
| **I protect** | προστατεύω 13 | προστάτευα | προστάτεψα | θα προστατέψω<br>να προστατέψω | έχω προστατέψει<br>είχα προστατέψει | προστάτευε<br>προστατεύετε | προστάτεψε<br>προστατέψτε |
| **I protect** | περιφρουρώ 17 | περιφρουρούσα | περιφρούρησα | θα περιφρουρήσω<br>να περιφρουρήσω | έχω περιφρουρήσει<br>είχα περιφρουρήσει | να περιφρουρείς<br>περιφρουρείτε | περιφρούρησε<br>περιφρουρήστε |
| **I protest** | *διαμαρτύρομαι 14* | *διαμαρτυρόμουν* | *διαμαρτυρήθηκα* | *θα διαμαρτυρηθώ*<br>*να διαμαρτυρηθώ* | *έχω διαμαρτυρηθεί*<br>*είχα διαμαρτυρηθεί* | *να διαμαρτύρεσαι*<br>*διαμαρτύρεστε* | *διαμαρτυρήσου*<br>*διαμαρτυρηθείτε* |
| **I protrude** | προεξέχω 13 | προεξείχα | προεξείχα | θα προεξέχω<br>να προεξέχω | — | — | — |
| **I am proud** | *περηφανεύομαι 14* | *περηφανευόμουν* | *περηφανεύτηκα* | *θα περηφανευτώ*<br>*να περηφανευτώ* | *έχω περηφανευτεί*<br>*είχα περηφανευτεί* | *να περηφανεύεσαι*<br>*περηφανεύεστε* | *περηφανεύσου*<br>*περηφανευτείτε* |
| **I prove** | αποδεικνύω 13 | αποδείκνυα | απόδειξα | θα αποδείξω<br>να αποδείξω | έχω αποδείξει<br>είχα αποδείξει | αποδείκνυε<br>αποδεικνύετε | απόδειξε<br>αποδείξτε |
| **I provide** | παρέχω 13 | παρείχα | παρείχα | θα παρέχω<br>να παρέχω | — | να παρέχεις<br>παρέχετε | — |

| English Verb | Present | Imperfect | Past | Simple Future<br>Simple Subjunctive | Present Perfect<br>Past Perfect | Continuous Imperative | Simple Imperative |
|---|---|---|---|---|---|---|---|
| **I provoke** | προκαλώ 17 | προκαλούσα | προκάλεσα | θα προκαλέσω<br>να προκαλέσω | έχω προκαλέσει<br>είχα προκαλέσει | να προκαλείς<br>προκαλείτε | προκάλεσε<br>προκαλέστε |
| **I publish** | εκδίδω 13 | εξέδιδα | εξέδωσα | θα εκδώσω<br>να εκδώσω | έχω εκδώσει<br>είχα εκδώσει | έκδιδε<br>εκδίδετε | έκδωσε<br>εκδώστε |
| **I publish** | δημοσιεύω 13 | δημοσίευα | δημοσίευσα | θα δημοσιεύσω<br>να δημοσιεύσω | έχω δημοσιεύσει<br>είχα δημοσιεύσει | δημοσίευε<br>δημοσιεύετε | δημοσίευσε<br>δημοσιεύστε |
| **I puff** | ξεφυσώ 15 | ξεφυσούσα | ξεφύσησα | θα ξεφυσήσω<br>να ξεφυσήσω | έχω ξεφυσήσει<br>είχα ξεφυσήσει | ξεφύσα<br>ξεφυσάτε | ξεφύσηξε<br>ξεφυσήστε |
| **I pull** | τραβ(ά)ώ 15 | τραβούσα | τράβηξα | θα τραβήξω<br>να τραβήξω | έχω τραβήξει<br>είχα τραβήξει | τράβα<br>τραβάτε | τράβηξε<br>τραβήξτε |
| **I pull** | σέρνω 13 | έσερνα | έσυρα | θα σύρω<br>να σύρω | έχω σύρει<br>είχα σύρει | σέρνε<br>σέρνετε | σύρε<br>σύρτε |
| **I pump** | αντλώ 17 | αντλούσα | άντλησα | θα αντλήσω<br>να αντλήσω | έχω αντλήσει<br>είχα αντλήσει | να αντλείς<br>αντλείτε | άντλησε<br>αντλήστε |
| **I punch** | γρονθοκοπώ 15 | γρονθοκοπούσα | γρονθοκόπησα | θα γρονθοκοπήσω<br>να γρονθοκοπήσω | έχω γρονθοκοπήσει<br>είχα γρονθοκοπήσει | γρονθοκόπα<br>γρονθοκοπάτε | γρονθοκόπησε<br>γρονθοκοπήστε |
| **I punish** | τιμωρώ 17 | τιμωρούσα | τιμώρησα | θα τιμωρήσω<br>να τιμωρήσω | έχω τιμωρήσει<br>είχα τιμωρήσει | να τιμωρείς<br>τιμωρείτε | τιμώρησε<br>τιμωρήστε |
| **I pursue** | επιδιώκω 13 | επιδίωκα | επιδίωξα | θα επιδιώξω<br>να επιδιώξω | έχω επιδιώξει<br>είχα επιδιώξει | επιδίωκε<br>επιδιώκετε | επιδίωξε<br>επιδιώξτε |
| **I push** | σπρώχνω 13 | έσπρωχνα | έσπρωξα | θα σπρώξω<br>να σπρώξω | έχω σπρώξει<br>είχα σπρώξει | σπρώχνε<br>σπρώχνετε | σπρώξε<br>σπρώξτε |
| **I put** | βάζω 13 | έβαζα | έβαλα | θα βάλω<br>να βάλω | έχω βάλει<br>είχα βάλει | βάζε<br>βάζετε | βάλε<br>βάλτε |

| English Verb | Present | Imperfect | Past | Simple Future<br>Simple Subjunctive | Present Perfect<br>Past Perfect | Continuous Imperative | Simple Imperative |
|---|---|---|---|---|---|---|---|
| **I put in order** | τακτοποιώ 17 | τακτοποιούσα | τακτοποίησα | θα τακτοποιήσω<br>να τακτοποιήσω | έχω τακτοποιήσει<br>είχα τακτοποιήσει | να τακτοποιείς<br>τακτοποιείτε | τακτοποίησε<br>τακτοποιήστε |
| **I put on**<br>(wear) | φορώ 15 | φορούσα | φόρεσα | θα φορέσω<br>να φορέσω | έχω φορέσει<br>είχα φορέσει | φόρα<br>φοράτε | φόρεσε<br>φορέστε |
| **I puzzle** | προβληματίζω 13 | προβλημάτιζα | προβλημάτισα | θα προβληματίσω<br>να προβληματίσω | έχω προβληματίσει<br>είχα προβληματίσει | προβλημάτιζε<br>προβληματίζετε | προβλημάτισε<br>προβληματίστε |
| **I quarrel** | μαλώνω 13 | μάλωνα | μάλωσα | θα μαλώσω<br>να μαλώσω | έχω μαλώσει<br>είχα μαλώσει | μάλωνε<br>μαλώνετε | μάλωσε<br>μαλώστε |
| **I quarrel** | *τσακώνομαι 14* | *τσακωνόμουν* | *τσακώθηκα* | *θα τσακωθώ*<br>*να τσακωθώ* | *έχω τσακωθεί*<br>*είχα τσακωθεί* | *να τσακώνεσαι*<br>*τσακώνεστε* | *τσακώσου*<br>*τσακωθείτε* |
| **I question** | ανακρίνω 13 | ανάκρινα | ανέκρινα | θα ανακρίνω<br>να ανακρίνω | έχω ανακρίνει<br>είχα ανακρίνει | ανάκρινε<br>ανακρίνετε | ανάκρινε<br>ανακρίντε |
| **I quibble** | λεπτολογώ 17 | λεπτολογούσα | λεπτολόγησα | θα λεπτολογήσω<br>να λεπτολογήσω | έχω λεπτολογήσει<br>είχα λεπτολογήσει | να λεπτολογείς<br>λεπτολογείτε | λεπτολόγησε<br>λεπτολογήστε |
| **I quieten**<br>(down) | ησυχάζω 13 | ησύχαζα | ησύχασα | θα ησυχάσω<br>να ησυχάσω | έχω ησυχάσει<br>είχα ησυχάσει | ησύχαζε<br>ησυχάζετε | ησύχασε<br>ησυχάστε |
| **I quit** | παρατ(ά)ώ 15 | παρατούσα | παράτησα | θα παρατήσω<br>να παρατήσω | έχω παρατήσει<br>είχα παρατήσει | παράτα<br>παρατάτε | παράτησε<br>παρατήστε |
| **I quote**<br>(politician/poet) | παραθέτω 13 | παρέθετα | παρέθεσα | θα παραθέσω<br>να παραθέσω | έχω παραθέσει<br>είχα παραθέσει | παράθετε<br>παραθέτετε | παράθεσε<br>παραθέστε |
| **I rage** | *μαίνομαι 14* | *μαινόμουν* | – | – | – | – | – |
| **It rains** | βρέχει 13 | έβρεχε | έβρεξε | θα βρέξει<br>να βρέξει | έχει βρέξει<br>είχε βρέξει | βρέχε<br>βρέχετε | βρέξε<br>βρέξτε |

| English Verb | Present | Imperfect | Past | Simple Future<br>Simple Subjunctive | Present Perfect<br>Past Perfect | Continuous Imperative | Simple Imperative |
|---|---|---|---|---|---|---|---|
| **I raise** | ανορθώνω 13 | ανώρθωνα | ανώρθωσα | θα ανορθώσω<br>να ανορθώσω | έχω ανορθώσει<br>είχα ανορθώσει | ανόρθωνε<br>ανορθώνετε | ανόρθωσε<br>ανορθώστε |
| **I raise** (elevate) | υψώνω 13 | ύψωνα | ύψωσα | θα υψώσω<br>να υψώσω | έχω υψώσει<br>είχα υψώσει | ύψωνε<br>υψώνετε | ύψωσε<br>υψώστε |
| **I raise** | αναπτερώνω 13 | αναπτέρωνα | αναπτέρωσα | θα αναπτερώσω<br>να αναπτερώσω | έχω αναπτερώσει<br>είχα αναπτερώσει | αναπτέρωνε<br>αναπτερώνετε | αναπτέρωσε<br>αναπτερώστε |
| **I rape** | βιάζω 13 | βίαζα | βίαζα | θα βιάσω<br>να βιάσω | έχω βιάσει<br>είχα βιάσει | βίαζε<br>βιάζετε | βίασε<br>βιάστε |
| **I rake** | ανασκαλεύω 13 | ανασκάλευα | ανασκάλεψα | θα ανασκαλέψω<br>να ανασκαλέψω | έχω ανασκαλέψει<br>είχα ανασκαλέψει | ανασκάλευε<br>ανασκαλεύετε | ανασκάλεψε<br>ανασκαλέψτε |
| **I ratify** | κυρώνω 13 | κύρωνα | κύρωσα | θα κυρώσω<br>να κυρώσω | έχω κυρώσει<br>είχα κυρώσει | κύρωνε<br>κυρώνετε | κύρωσε<br>κυρώστε |
| **I rationalize** | αιτιολογώ 17 | αιτιολογούσα | αιτιολόγησα | θα αιτιολογήσω<br>να αιτιολογήσω | έχω αιτιολογήσει<br>είχα αιτιολογήσει | να αιτιολογείς<br>αιτιολογείτε | αιτιολόγησε<br>αιτιολογήστε |
| **I reach** | εκτείνω 13 | έκτεινα | εξέτεινα | θα εκτείνω<br>να εκτείνω | έχω εκτείνει<br>είχα εκτείνει | να εκτείνεις<br>εκτείνετε | έκτεινε<br>εκτείνετε |
| **I react** | αντιδρώ 15 | αντιδρούσα | αντέδρασα | θα αντιδράσω<br>να αντιδράσω | έχω αντιδράσει<br>είχα αντιδράσει | να αντιδράς<br>αντιδράτε | αντίδρασε<br>αντιδράστε |
| **I read** | διαβάζω 13 | διάβαζα | διάβασα | θα διαβάσω<br>να διαβάσω | έχω διαβάσει<br>είχα διαβάσει | διάβαζε<br>διαβάζετε | διάβασε<br>διαβάστε |
| **I realise** | *αντιλαμβάνομαι 14* | *αντιλαμβανόμουν* | *αντελήφθηκα* | *θα αντιληφθώ*<br>*να αντιληφθώ* | *έχω αντιληφθεί*<br>*είχα αντιληφθεί* | *να αντιλαμβάνεσαι*<br>*αντιλαμβάνεστε* | *αντιλήψου*<br>*αντιληφθείτε* |
| **I reason** | *λογικεύομαι 14* | *λογικευόμουν* | *λογικεύτηκα* | *θα λογικευτώ*<br>*να λογικευτώ* | *έχω λογικευτεί*<br>*είχα λογικευτεί* | *να λογικεύεσαι*<br>*λογικεύεστε* | *λογικέψου*<br>*λογικευτείτε* |

| English Verb | Present | Imperfect | Past | Simple Future<br>Simple Subjunctive | Present Perfect<br>Past Perfect | Continuous Imperative | Simple Imperative |
|---|---|---|---|---|---|---|---|
| **I rebuke** | επιπλήττω 13 | επέπληττα | επέπληξα | θα επιπλήξω<br>να επιπλήξω | έχω επιπλήξει<br>είχα επιπλήξει | επίπληττε<br>επιπλήττετε | επίπληξε<br>επιπλήξτε |
| **I recede** | ξεμακραίνω 13 | ξεμάκραινα | ξέμακρυνα | θα ξεμακρύνω<br>να ξεμακρύνω | έχω ξεμακρύνει<br>είχα ξεμακρύνει | ξεμάκραινε<br>ξεμακραίνετε | ξεμάκρυνε<br>ξεμακρύντε |
| **I receive** | *υποδέχομαι 14* | *υποδεχόμουν* | *υποδέχτηκα* | *θα υποδεχτώ*<br>*να υποδεχτώ* | *έχω υποδεχτεί*<br>*είχα υποδεχτεί* | *να υποδέχεσαι*<br>*υποδέχεστε* | *υποδέξου*<br>*υποδεχτείτε* |
| **I receive** | λαμβάνω 13 | λάμβανα | έλαβα | θα λάβω<br>να λάβω | έχω λάβει<br>είχα λάβει | λάμβανε<br>λαμβάνετε | λάβε<br>λάβετε |
| **I reckon** | λογαριάζω 13 | λογάριαζα | λογάριασα | θα λογαριάσω<br>να λογαριάσω | έχω λογαριάσει<br>είχα λογαριάσει | λογάριαζε<br>λογαριάζετε | λογάριασε<br>λογαριάστε |
| **I recognise** | αναγνωρίζω 13 | αναγνώριζα | αναγνώρισα | θα αναγνωρίσω<br>να αναγνωρίσω | έχω αναγνωρίσει<br>είχα αναγνωρίσει | αναγνώριζε<br>αναγνωρίζετε | αναγνώρισε<br>αναγνωρίστε |
| **I recollect** | αναπολώ 17 | αναπολούσα | αναπόλησα | θα αναπολήσω<br>να αναπολήσω | έχω αναπολήσει<br>είχα αναπολήσει | να αναπολείς<br>αναπολείτε | αναπόλησε<br>αναπολήστε |
| **I reconsider** | επανεξετάζω 13 | επανεξέταζα | επανεξέτασα | θα επανεξετάσω<br>να επανεξετάσω | έχω επανεξετάσει<br>είχα επανεξετάσει | επανεξέταζε<br>επανεξετάζετε | επανεξέτασε<br>επανεξετάστε |
| **I record** | ηχογραφώ 17 | ηχογραφούσα | ηχογράφησα | θα ηχογραφήσω<br>να ηχογραφήσω | έχω ηχογραφήσει<br>είχα ηχογραφήσει | να ηχογραφείς<br>ηχογραφείτε | ηχογράφησε<br>ηχογραφήστε |
| **I recover** | ξαναβρίσκω 13 | ξανάβρισκα | ξαναβρήκα | θα ξαναβρώ<br>να ξαναβρώ | έχω ξαναβρεί<br>είχα ξαναβρεί | ξανάβρισκε<br>ξαναβρίσκετε | ξαναβρές<br>ξαναβρείτε |
| **I recruit** | στρατολογώ 17 | στρατολογούσα | στρατολόγησα | θα στρατολογήσω<br>να στρατολογήσω | έχω στρατολογήσει<br>είχα στρατολογήσει | να στρατολογείς<br>στρατολογείτε | στρατολόγησε<br>στρατολογήστε |
| **I reduce** | ελαττώνω 13 | ελάττωνα | ελάττωσα | θα ελαττώσω<br>να ελαττώσω | έχω ελαττώσει<br>είχα ελαττώσει | ελάττωνε<br>ελαττώνετε | ελάττωσε<br>ελαττώστε |

| nglish Verb | Present | Imperfect | Past | Simple Future<br>Simple Subjunctive | Present Perfect<br>Past Perfect | Continuous Imperative | Simple Imperative |
|---|---|---|---|---|---|---|---|
| **I reduce** | περικόβω 13 | περιέκοβα | περιέκοψα | θα περικόψω<br>να περικόψω | έχω περικόψει<br>είχα περικόψει | περίκοβε<br>περικόβετε | περίκοψε<br>περικόψτε |
| **I reform** | αναμορφώνω 13 | αναμόρφωνα | αναμόρφωσα | θα αναμορφώσω<br>να αναμορφώσω | έχω αναμορφώσει<br>είχα αναμορφώσει | αναμόρφωνε<br>αναμορφώνετε | αναμόρφωσε<br>αναμορφώστε |
| **I reflect** | αντανακλώ 15 | αντανακλούσα | αντανάκλασα | θα αντανακλάσω<br>να αντανακλάσω | έχω αντανακλάσει<br>είχα αντανακλάσει | αντανάκλα<br>αντανακλάτε | αντανάκλασε<br>αντανακλάστε |
| **I refuse** | *αρνούμαι 18* | *αρνούμουν* | *αρνήθηκα* | *θα αρνηθώ*<br>*να αρνηθώ* | *έχω αρνηθεί*<br>*είχα αρνηθεί* | *να αρνείσαι*<br>*αρνείστε* | *αρνήσου*<br>*αρνηθείτε* |
| **I regenerate** | αναγεννώ 15 | αναγεννούσα | αναγέννησα | θα αναγεννήσω<br>να αναγεννήσω | έχω αναγεννήσει<br>είχα αναγεννήσει | αναγγέννα<br>αναγεννάτε | αναγέννησε<br>αναγεννήστε |
| **I regard**<br>(consider) | ατενίζω 13 | ατένιζα | ατένισα | θα ατενίσω<br>να ατενίσω | έχω ατενίσει<br>είχα ατενίσει | ατένιζε<br>ατενίζετε | ατένισε<br>ατενίστε |
| **I regret** | μετανιώνω 13 | μετάνιωνα | μετάνιωσα | θα μετανιώσω<br>να μετανιώσω | έχω μετανιώσει<br>είχα μετανιώσει | μετάνιωνε<br>μετανιώνετε | μετάνιωσε<br>μετανιώστε |
| **I rehearse** | προβάρω 13 | πρόβαρα | προβάρησα | θα προβάρω<br>να προβάρω | έχω προβάρει<br>είχα προβάρει | πρόβαρε<br>προβάρετε | προβάρησε<br>προβαρήστε |
| **I reject** | απορρίπτω 13 | απέρριπτα | απέρριψα | θα απορρίψω<br>να απορρίψω | έχω απορρίψει<br>είχα απορρίψει | απόρριπτε<br>απορρίπτετε | απόρριψε<br>απορρίψτε |
| **I reject**<br>(push back) | αποκρούω 13 | απέκρουα | απέκρουσα | θα αποκρούσω<br>να αποκρούσω | έχω αποκρούσει<br>είχα αποκρούσει | απόκρουε<br>αποκρούετε | απόκρουσε<br>αποκρούστε |
| **I rejoice** | αναγαλλιάζω 13 | αναγαλλίαζα | αναγαλλίασα | θα αναγαλλιάσω<br>να αναγαλλιάσω | έχω αναγαλλιάσει<br>είχα αναγαλλιάσει | αναγαλλίαζε<br>αναγαλλιάζετε | αναγαλλίασε<br>αναγαλλιάστε |
| **I relate** | σχετίζω 13 | σχέτιζα | σχέτισα | θα σχετίσω<br>να σχετίσω | έχω σχετίσει<br>είχα σχετίσει | σχέτιζε<br>σχετίζετε | σχέτισε<br>σχετίστε |

| English Verb | Present | Imperfect | Past | Simple Future<br>Simple Subjunctive | Present Perfect<br>Past Perfect | Continuous Imperative | Simple Imperative |
|---|---|---|---|---|---|---|---|
| **I relax** | χαλαρώνω 13 | χαλάρωνα | χαλάρωσα | θα χαλαρώσω<br>να χαλαρώσω | έχω χαλαρώσει<br>είχα χαλαρώσει | χαλάρωνε<br>χαλαρώνετε | χαλάρωσε<br>χαλαρώστε |
| **I relax** | *εκτονώνομαι 14* | *εκτονωνόμουν* | *εκτονώθηκα* | *θα εκτονωθώ*<br>*να εκτονωθώ* | *έχω εκτονωθεί*<br>*είχα εκτονωθεί* | *να εκτονώνεσαι*<br>*εκτονώνεστε* | *εκτονώσου*<br>*εκτονωθείτε* |
| **I relieve** | ανακουφίζω 13 | ανακούφιζα | ανακούφισα | θα ανακουφίσω<br>να ανακουφίσω | έχω ανακουφίσει<br>είχα ανακουφίσει | ανακούφιζε<br>ανακουφίζετε | ανακούφισε<br>ανακουφίστε |
| **I rely** | *βασίζομαι 14* | *βασιζόμουν* | *βασίστηκα* | *θα βασιστώ*<br>*να βασιστώ* | *έχω βασιστεί*<br>*είχα βασιστεί* | *να βασίζεσαι*<br>*βασίζεστε* | *βασίσου*<br>*βασιστείτε* |
| **I remain** | μένω 13 | έμενα | έμεινα | θα μείνω<br>να μείνω | έχω μείνει<br>είχα μείνει | μένε<br>μένετε | μείνε<br>μείνετε |
| **I remember** | *θυμάμαι 42* | *θυμόμουν* | *θυμήθηκα* | *θα θυμηθώ*<br>*να θυμηθώ* | *έχω θυμηθεί*<br>*είχα θυμηθεί* | *να θυμάσαι*<br>*θυμάστε* | *θυμήσου*<br>*θυμηθείτε* |
| **I remind** | θυμίζω 13 | θύμιζα | θύμισα | θα θυμίσω<br>να θυμίσω | έχω θυμίσει<br>είχα θυμίσει | θύμιζε<br>θυμίζετε | θύμισε<br>θυμίστε |
| **I remove** | απομακρύνω 13 | απομάκρυνα | απομάκρυνα | θα απομακρύνω<br>να απομακρύνω | έχω απομακρύνει<br>είχα απομακρύνει | απομάκρυνε<br>απομακρύνετε | απομάκρυνε<br>απομακρύντε |
| **I render** | ανταποδίδω 13 | ανταπέδιδα | ανταπέδωσα | θα ανταποδώσω<br>να ανταποδώσω | έχω ανταποδώσει<br>είχα ανταποδώσει | ανταπόδιδε<br>ανταποδίδετε | ανταπόδωσε<br>ανταποδώστε |
| **I renew** | ανανεώνω 13 | ανανέωνα | ανανέωσα | θα ανανεώσω<br>να ανανεώσω | έχω ανανεώσει<br>είχα ανανεώσει | ανανέωνε<br>ανανεώνετε | ανανέωσε<br>ανανεώστε |
| **I renovate** | ανακαινίζω 13 | ανακαίνιζα | ανακαίνισα | θα ανακαινίσω<br>να ανακαινίσω | έχω ανακαινίσει<br>είχα ανακαινίσει | ανακαίνιζε<br>ανακαινίζετε | ανακαίνισε<br>ανακαινίστε |
| **I rent** | νοικιάζω 13 | νοίκιαζα | νοίκιασα | θα νοικιάσω<br>να νοικιάσω | έχω νοικιάσει<br>είχα νοικιάσει | νοίκιαζε<br>νοικιάζετε | νοίκιασε<br>νοικιάστε |

| English Verb | Present | Imperfect | Past | Simple Future<br>Simple Subjunctive | Present Perfect<br>Past Perfect | Continuous Imperative | Simple Imperative |
|---|---|---|---|---|---|---|---|
| **I reorganise** | αναδιοργανώνω 13 | αναδιοργάνωνα | αναδιοργάνωσα | θα αναδιοργανώσω<br>να αναδιοργανώσω | έχω αναδιοργανώσει<br>είχα αναδιοργανώσει | αναδιοργάνωνε<br>αναδιοργανώνετε | αναδιοργάνωσε<br>αναδιοργανώστε |
| **I repair** | επισκευάζω 13 | επισκεύαζα | επισκεύασα | θα επισκευάσω<br>να επισκευάσω | έχω επισκευάσει<br>είχα επισκευάσει | επισκεύαζε<br>επισκευάζετε | επισκεύασε<br>επισκευάστε |
| **I repay** | εξοφλώ 17 | εξοφλούσα | εξόφλησα | θα εξοφλήσω<br>να εξοφλήσω | έχω εξοφλήσει<br>είχα εξοφλήσει | να εξοφλείς<br>εξοφλείτε | εξόφλησε<br>εξοφλήστε |
| **I repay** | ξεπληρώνω 13 | ξεπλήρωνα | ξεπλήρωσα | θα ξεπληρώσω<br>να ξεπληρώσω | έχω ξεπληρώσει<br>είχα ξεπληρώσει | ξεπλήρωνε<br>ξεπληρώνετε | ξεπλήρωσε<br>ξεπληρώστε |
| **I repeat** | επαναλαμβάνω 13 | επαναλάμβανα | επανέλαβα | θα επαναλάβω<br>να επαναλάβω | έχω επαναλάβει<br>είχα επαναλάβει | επαναλάμβανε<br>επαναλαμβάνετε | επανάλαβε<br>επαναλάβετε |
| **I repent** | μετανοώ 17 | μετανοούσα | μετανόησα | θα μετανοήσω<br>να μετανοήσω | έχω μετανοήσει<br>είχα μετανοήσει | να μετανοείς<br>μετανοείτε | μετανόησε<br>μετανοήστε |
| **I replace** | αντικαθιστώ 15 | αντικαθιστούσα | αντικατέστησα | θα αντικαταστήσω<br>να αντικαταστήσω | έχω αντικαταστήσει<br>είχα αντικαταστήσει | αντικαθίστα<br>αντικαθιστάτε | αντικατάστησε<br>αντικαταστήστε |
| **I replace** | αναπληρώνω 13 | αναπλήρωνα | αναπλήρωσα | θα αναπληρώσω<br>να αναπληρώσω | έχω αναπληρώσει<br>είχα αναπληρώσει | αναπλήρωνε<br>αναπληρώνετε | αναπλήρωσε<br>αναπληρώστε |
| **I reply** | *αποκρίνομαι 14* | *αποκρινόμουν* | *αποκρίθηκα* | *θα αποκριθώ*<br>*να αποκριθώ* | *έχω αποκριθεί*<br>*είχα αποκριθεί* | *να αποκρίνεσαι*<br>*αποκρίνεστε* | *αποκρίσου*<br>*αποκριθείτε* |
| **I report** | αναφέρω 13 | ανάφερα | ανέφερα | θα αναφερθώ<br>να αναφερθώ | έχω αναφερθεί<br>είχα αναφερθεί | να αναφέρεις<br>αναφέρετε | ανάφερε<br>αναφέρτε |
| **I represent** | αντιπροσωπεύω 14 | αντιπροσώπευα | αντιπροσώπευσα | θα αντιπροσωπεύσω<br>να αντιπροσωπεύσω | έχω αντιπροσωπεύσει<br>είχα αντιπροσωπεύσει | αντιπροσώπευε<br>αντιπροσωπεύετε | αντιπροσώπευσε<br>αντιπροσωπεύστε |
| **I repulse** | απωθώ 17 | απωθούσα | απώθησα | θα απωθήσω<br>να απωθήσω | έχω απωθήσει<br>είχα απωθήσει | να απωθείς<br>απωθείτε | απώθησε<br>απωθήστε |

| English Verb | Present | Imperfect | Past | Simple Future<br>Simple Subjunctive | Present Perfect<br>Past Perfect | Continuous Imperative | Simple Imperative |
|---|---|---|---|---|---|---|---|
| **I request** | *αιτούμαι 18* | *αιτούμουν* | *αιτήθηκα* | *θα αιτηθώ*<br>*να αιτηθώ* | *έχω αιτηθεί*<br>*είχα αιτηθεί* | *να αιτείσαι*<br>*αιτείστε* | *αιτήσου*<br>*αιτηθείτε* |
| **I rescue** | διασώζω 13 | διέσωζα | διέσωσα | θα διασώσω<br>να διασώσω | έχω διασώσει<br>είχα διασώσει | διάσωζε<br>διασώζετε | διάσωσε<br>διασώστε |
| **I research** | ερευνώ 15 | ερευνούσα | ερεύνησα | θα ερευνήσω<br>να ερευνήσω | έχω ερευνήσει<br>είχα ερευνήσει | ερεύνα<br>ερευνάτε | ερεύνησε<br>ερευνήστε |
| **I resemble** | μοιάζω 13 | έμοιαζα | έμοιασα | θα μοιάσω<br>να μοιάσω | έχω μοιάσει<br>είχα μοιάσει | να μοιάζεις<br>μοιάζετε | μοιάσε<br>μοιάστε |
| **I reside** | διαμένω 13 | διέμενα | διέμεινα | θα διαμείνω<br>να διαμείνω | έχω διαμείνει<br>είχα διαμείνει | διάμενε<br>διαμένετε | διάμεινε<br>διαμείνετε |
| **I resign** | *παραιτούμαι 18* | *παραιτούμουν* | *παραιτήθηκα* | *θα παραιτηθώ*<br>*να παραιτηθώ* | *έχω παραιτηθεί*<br>*είχα παραιτηθεί* | *να παραιτείσαι*<br>*παραιτείστε* | *παραιτήσου*<br>*παραιτηθείτε* |
| **I resist** | *αντιστέκομαι 14* | *αντιστεκόμουν* | *αντιστάθηκα* | *θα αντισταθώ*<br>*να αντισταθώ* | *έχω αντισταθεί*<br>*είχα αντισταθεί* | *να αντιστέκεσαι*<br>*αντιστέκεστε* | *αντιστάσου*<br>*αντισταθείτε* |
| **I respect** | *σέβομαι 14* | *σεβόμουν* | *σεβάστηκα* | *θα σεβαστώ*<br>*να σεβαστώ* | *έχω σεβαστεί*<br>*είχα σεβαστεί* | *να σέβεσαι*<br>*σέβεστε* | *σεβάσου*<br>*σεβαστείτε* |
| **I rest** | *ξεκουράζομαι 14* | *ξεκουραζόμουν* | *ξεκουράστηκα* | *θα ξεκουραστώ*<br>*να ξεκουραστώ* | *έχω ξεκουραστεί*<br>*είχα ξεκουραστεί* | *να ξεκουράζεσαι*<br>*ξεκουράζεστε* | *ξεκουράσου*<br>*ξεκουραστείτε* |
| **I rest** | *αναπαύομαι 14* | *αναπαυόμουν* | *αναπαύθηκα* | *θα αναπαυτώ*<br>*να αναπαυτώ* | *έχω αναπαυτεί*<br>*είχα αναπαυτεί* | *να αναπαύεσαι*<br>*αναπαύεστε* | *αναπαύσου*<br>*αναπαυθείτε* |
| **I restore** | αναστηλώνω 13 | αναστήλωνα | αναστήλωσα | θα αναστηλώσω<br>να αναστηλώσω | έχω αναστηλώσει<br>είχα αναστηλώσει | αναστήλωνε<br>αναστηλώνετε | αναστήλωσε<br>αναστηλώστε |
| **I restrain** | καταστέλλω 13 | κατάστελλα | κατάστειλα | θα καταστείλω<br>να καταστείλω | έχω καταστείλει<br>είχα καταστείλει | κατάστελλε<br>καταστέλλετε | κατάστειλε<br>καταστείλτε |

| English Verb | Present | Imperfect | Past | Simple Future<br>Simple Subjunctive | Present Perfect<br>Past Perfect | Continuous Imperative | Simple Imperative |
|---|---|---|---|---|---|---|---|
| **I restrict** | περιορίζω 13 | περιόριζα | περιόρισα | θα περιορίσω<br>να περιορίσω | έχω περιορίσει<br>είχα περιορίσει | περιόριζε<br>περιορίζετε | περιόρισε<br>περιορίστε |
| **I retire** | αποχωρώ 17 | αποχωρούσα | αποχώρησα | θα αποχωρήσω<br>να αποχωρήσω | έχω αποχωρήσει<br>είχα αποχωρήσει | να αποχωρείς<br>αποχωρείτε | αποχώρησε<br>αποχωρήστε |
| **I retreat** | *αποτραβιέμαι 16* | *αποτραβιόμουν* | *αποτραβήχτηκα* | *θα αποτραβηχτώ*<br>*να αποτραβηχτώ* | *έχω αποτραβηχτεί*<br>*είχα αποτραβηχτεί* | *να αποτραβιέσαι*<br>*αποτραβιέστε* | *αποτραβήξου*<br>*αποτραβηχτείτε* |
| **I retrieve** | αποκατασταίνω 13 | αποκατάσταινα | αποκατάστησα | θα αποκαταστήσω<br>να αποκαταστήσω | έχω αποκαταστήσει<br>είχα αποκαταστήσει | αποκατάσταινε<br>αποκατασταίνετε | αποκατάστησε<br>αποκαταστήστε |
| **I return** | γυρίζω 13 | γύριζα | γύρισα | θα γυρίσω<br>να γυρίσω | έχω γυρίσει<br>είχα γυρίσει | γύρνα<br>γυρνάτε | γύρισε<br>γυρίστε |
| **I return** | *επανέρχομαι 14* | *επανερχόμουν* | *επανήλθα* | *θα επανέλθω*<br>*να επανέλθω* | *έχω επανέλθει*<br>*είχα επανέλθει* | *να επανέρχεσαι*<br>*επανέρχεστε* | *επάνελθε*<br>*επανέλθετε* |
| **I reunite** | ξανασμίγω 13 | ξανάσμιγα | ξανάσμιξα | θα ξανασμίξω<br>να ξανασμίξω | έχω ξανασμίξει<br>είχα ξανασμίξει | ξανάσμιγε<br>ξα νασμίγετε | ξανάσμιξε<br>ξανασμίξτε |
| **I reveal** | αποκαλύπτω 13 | αποκάλυπτα | αποκάλυψα | θα αποκαλύψω<br>να αποκαλύψω | έχω αποκαλύψει<br>είχα αποκαλύψει | αποκάλυπτε<br>αποκαλύπτετε | αποκάλυψε<br>αποκαλύψτε |
| **I revel** | ξεφαντώνω 13 | ξεφάντωνα | ξεφάντωσα | θα ξεφαντώσω<br>να ξεφαντώσω | έχω ξεφαντώσει<br>είχα ξεφαντώσει | ξεφάντωνε<br>ξεφαντώνετε | ξεφάντωσε<br>ξεφαντώστε |
| **I reverse** | αντιστρέφω 13 | αντέστρεφα | αντέστρεψα | θα αντιστρέψω<br>να αντιστρέψω | έχω αντιστρέψει<br>είχα αντιστρέψει | αντίστρεφε<br>αντιστρέφετε | αντίστρεψε<br>αντιστρέψτε |
| **I revise** | αναθεωρώ 17 | αναθεωρούσα | αναθεώρησα | θα αναθεωρήσω<br>να αναθεωρήσω | έχω αναθεωρήσει<br>είχα αναθεωρήσει | να αναθεωρείς<br>αναθεωρείτε | αναθεώρησε<br>αναθεωρήστε |
| **I revive** | αναζωογονώ 17 | αναζωογονούσα | αναζωογόνησα | θα αναζωογονήσω<br>να αναζωογονήσω | έχω αναζωογονήσει<br>είχα αναζωογονήσει | να αναζωογονείς<br>αναζωογονείτε | αναζωογόνησε<br>αναζωογονήστε |

| English Verb | Present | Imperfect | Past | Simple Future<br>Simple Subjunctive | Present Perfect<br>Past Perfect | Continuous Imperative | Simple Imperative |
|---|---|---|---|---|---|---|---|
| **I revive** (enliven) | ζωντανεύω 13 | ζωντάνευα | ζωντάνεψα | θα ζωντανέψω<br>να ζωντανέψω | έχω ζωντανέψει<br>είχα ζωντανέψει | ζωντάνευε<br>ζωντανεύετε | ζωντάνεψε<br>ζωντανέψτε |
| **I revoke** | ανακαλώ 17 | ανακαλούσα | ανακάλεσα | θα ανακαλέσω<br>να ανακαλέσω | έχω ανακαλέσει<br>είχα ανακαλέσει | να ανακαλείς<br>ανακαλείτε | ανακάλεσε<br>ανακαλέστε |
| **I revolt** | επαναστατώ 17 | επαναστατούσα | επαναστάτησα | θα επαναστατήσω<br>να επαναστατήσω | έχω επαναστατήσει<br>είχα επαναστατήσει | να επαναστατείς<br>επαναστατείτε | επαναστάτησε<br>επαναστατήστε |
| **I revolt** | στασιάζω 13 | στασίαζα | στασίασα | θα στασιάσω<br>να στασιάσω | έχω στασιάσει<br>είχα στασιάσει | στασίαζε<br>στασιάζετε | στασίασε<br>στασιάστε |
| **I reward** | ανταμείβω 13 | αντάμειβα | αντάμειψα | θα ανταμείψω<br>να ανταμείψω | έχω ανταμείψει<br>είχα ανταμείψει | αντάμειβε<br>ανταμείβετε | αντάμειψε<br>ανταμείψτε |
| **I ride** | ιππεύω 13 | ίππευα | ίππευσα | θα ιππεύσω<br>να ιππεύσω | έχω ιππεύσει<br>είχα ιππεύσει | ίππευε<br>ιππεύετε | ίππευσε<br>ιππεύστε |
| **I ring** | σημαίνω 13 | σήμαινα | σήμανα | θα σημάνω<br>να σημάνω | έχω σημάνει<br>είχα σημάνει | σήμαινε<br>σημαίνετε | σήμανε<br>σημάντε |
| **It rings** | χτυπάει 15 | χτυπούσε | χτύπησε | θα χτυπήσει<br>να χτυπήσει | έχει χτυπήσει<br>είχε χτυπήσει | χτύπα<br>χτυπάτε | χτύπησε<br>χτυπήστε |
| **I rinse** | ξεπλένω 13 | ξέπλενα | ξέπλυνα | θα ξεπλύνω<br>να ξεπλύνω | έχω ξεπλύνει<br>είχα ξεπλύνει | ξέπλενε<br>ξεπλένετε | ξέπλυνε<br>ξεπλύντε |
| **I ripen** | ωριμάζω 13 | ωρίμαζα | ωρίμασα | θα ωριμάσω<br>να ωριμάσω | έχω ωριμάσει<br>είχα ωριμάσει | ωρίμαζε<br>ωριμάζετε | ωρίμασε<br>ωριμάστε |
| **I rip** | ξεσκίζω 13 | ξέσκιζα | ξέσκισα | θα ξεσκίσω<br>να ξεσκίσω | έχω ξεσκίσει<br>είχα ξεσκίσει | ξέσκιζε<br>ξεσκίζετε | ξέσκισε<br>ξεσκίστε |
| **It rises** (sun) | ανατέλλει 13 | ανάτειλλε | ανάτειλε | θα ανατείλει<br>να ανατείλει | έχει ανατείλει<br>είχε ανατείλει | ανάτειλε<br>ανατείλλετε | ανάτειλε<br>ανατείλτε |

| English Verb | Present | Imperfect | Past | Simple Future<br>Simple Subjunctive | Present Perfect<br>Past Perfect | Continuous Imperative | Simple Imperative |
|---|---|---|---|---|---|---|---|
| **I risk** | ρισκάρω 13 | ρίσκαρα | ρισκάρισα | θα ρισκάρω<br>να ρισκάρω | έχω ρισκάρει<br>είχα ρισκάρει | ρίσκαρε<br>ρισκάρετε | ρισκάρισε<br>ρισκαρίστε |
| **I risk** | αποτολμώ 15 | αποτολμούσα | αποτόλμησα | θα αποτολμήσω<br>να αποτολμήσω | έχω αποτολμήσει<br>είχα αποτολμήσει | αποτόλμα<br>αποτολμάτε | αποτόλμησε<br>αποτολμήστε |
| **I rob** | ληστεύω 13 | λήστευα | λήστεψα | θα ληστέψω<br>να ληστέψω | έχω ληστέψει<br>είχα ληστέψει | λήστευε<br>ληστεύετε | λήστεψε<br>ληστέψτε |
| **I rot** | σαπίζω 13 | σάπιζα | σάπισα | θα σαπίσω<br>να σαπίσω | έχω σαπίσει<br>είχα σαπίσει | σάπιζε<br>σαπίζετε | σάπισε<br>σαπίστε |
| **I rub** | τρίβω 13 | έτριβα | έτριψα | θα τρίψω<br>να τρίψω | έχω τρίψει<br>είχα τρίψει | τρίβε<br>τρίβετε | τρίψε<br>τρίψτε |
| **I ruin** | ρημάζω 13 | ρήμαζα | ρήμαξα | θα ρημάξω<br>να ρημάξω | έχω ρημάξει<br>είχα ρημάξει | ρήμαζε<br>ρημάζετε | ρήμαξε<br>ρημάξτε |
| **I rule** | χαρακώνω 13 | χαράκωνα | χαράκωσα | θα χαρακώσω<br>να χαρακώσω | έχω χαρακώσει<br>είχα χαρακώσει | χαράκωνε<br>χαρακώνετε | χαράκωσε<br>χαρακώστε |
| **I rule**<br>(govern) | εξουσιάζω 13 | εξουσίαζα | εξουσίασα | θα εξουσιάσω<br>να εξουσιάσω | έχω εξουσιάσει<br>είχα εξουσιάσει | εξουσίαζε<br>εξουσιάζετε | εξουσίασε<br>εξουσιάστε |
| **I run** | τρέχω 13 | έτρεχα | έτρεξα | θα τρέξω<br>να τρέξω | έχω τρέξει<br>είχα τρέξει | τρέχα<br>τρέχετε | τρέξε<br>τρέξτε |
| **I rush** | ορμ(ά)ώ 15 | ορμούσα | όρμησα | θα ορμήσω<br>να ορμήσω | έχω ορμήσει<br>είχα ορμήσει | όρμα<br>ορμάτε | όρμησε<br>ορμήστε |
| **I rust** | σκουριάζω 13 | σκούριαζα | σκούριασα | θα σκουριάσω<br>να σκουριάσω | έχω σκουριάσει<br>είχα σκουριάσει | σκούριαζε<br>σκουριάζετε | σκούριασε<br>σκουριάστε |
| **I realise**<br>(materialize) | πραγματώνω 13 | πραγμάτωνα | πραγμάτωσα | θα πραγματώσω<br>να πραγματώσω | έχω πραγματώσει<br>είχα πραγματώσει | πραγμάτωνε<br>πραγματώνετε | πραγμάτωσε<br>πραγματώστε |

| English Verb | Present | Imperfect | Past | Simple Future<br>Simple Subjunctive | Present Perfect<br>Past Perfect | Continuous Imperative | Simple Imperative |
|---|---|---|---|---|---|---|---|
| **I regulate** | ρυθμίζω 13 | ρύθμιζα | ρύθμισα | θα ρυθμίσω<br>να ρυθμίσω | έχω ρυθμίσει<br>είχα ρυθμίσει | ρύθμιζε<br>ρυθμίζετε | ρύθμισε<br>ρυθμίστε |
| **I sabotage** | σαμποτάρω 13 | σαμπόταρα | σαμποτάρησα | θα σαμποτάρω<br>να σαμποτάρω | έχω σαμποτάρει<br>είχα σαμποτάρει | σαμπόταρε<br>σαμποτάρετε | σαμποτάρησε<br>σαμποταρήστε |
| **I sacrifice** | θυσιάζω 13 | θυσίαζα | θυσίασα | θα θυσιάσω<br>να θυσιάσω | έχω θυσιάσει<br>είχα θυσιάσει | θυσίαζε<br>θυσιάζετε | θυσίασε<br>θυσιάστε |
| **I sail** | αποπλέω 13 | απέπλεα | απέπλευσα | θα αποπλεύσω<br>να αποπλεύσω | έχω αποπλεύσει<br>είχα αποπλεύσει | απόπλεε<br>αποπλέετε | απόπλευσε<br>αποπλεύστε |
| **I sallow** | κιτρινίζω 13 | κιτρίνιζα | κιτρίνισα | θα κιτρινίσω<br>να κιτρινίσω | έχω κιτρινίσει<br>είχα κιτρινίσει | κιτρίνιζε<br>κιτρινίζετε | κιτρίνισε<br>κιτρινίστε |
| **I salt** | αλατίζω 13 | αλάτιζα | αλάτισα | θα αλατίσω<br>να αλατίσω | έχω αλατίσει<br>είχα αλατίσει | αλάτιζε<br>αλατίζετε | αλάτισε<br>αλατίστε |
| **I salute** | χαιρετίζω 13 | χαιρέτιζα | χαιρέτισα | θα χαιρετήσω<br>να χαιρετήσω | έχω χαιρετήσει<br>είχα χαιρετήσει | χαιρέτα<br>χαιρετάτε | χαιρέτησε<br>χαιρετήστε |
| **I sanction** | επιδοκιμάζω 13 | επιδοκίμαζα | επιδοκίμασα | θα επιδοκιμάσω<br>να επιδοκιμάσω | έχω επιδοκιμάσει<br>είχα επιδοκιμάσει | επιδοκίμαζε<br>επιδοκιμάζετε | επιδοκίμασε<br>επιδοκιμάστε |
| **I satiate** | μπουχτίζω 13 | μπούχτιζα | μπούχτισα | θα μπουχτίσω<br>να μπουχτίσω | έχω μπουχτίσει<br>είχα μπουχτίσει | μπούχτιζε<br>μπουχτίζετε | μπούχτισε<br>μπουχτίστε |
| **I satirize** | σατιρίζω 13 | σατίριζα | σατίρισα | θα σατιρίσω<br>να σατιρίσω | έχω σατιρίσει<br>είχα σατιρίσει | σατίριζε<br>σατιρίζετε | σατίρισε<br>σατιρίστε |
| **I am satisfied** | *ικανοποιούμαι 18* | *ικανοποιούμουν* | *ικανοποιήθηκα* | *θα ικανοποιηθώ*<br>*να ικανοποιηθώ* | *έχω ικανοποιηθεί*<br>*είχα ικανοποιηθεί* | *να ικανοποιείσαι*<br>*ικανοποιείστε* | *ικανοποιήσου*<br>*ικανοποιηθείτε* |
| **I satisfy** | ικανοποιώ 17 | ικανοποιούσα | ικανοποίησα | θα ικανοποιήσω<br>να ικανοποιήσω | έχω ικανοποιήσει<br>είχα ικανοποιήσει | να ικανοποιείς<br>ικανοποιείτε | ικανοποίησε<br>ικανοποιήστε |

| English Verb | Present | Imperfect | Past | Simple Future<br>Simple Subjunctive | Present Perfect<br>Past Perfect | Continuous Imperative | Simple Imperative |
|---|---|---|---|---|---|---|---|
| **I saunter** (stroll ) | σεριανίζω 13 | σεριάνιζα | σεριάνισα | θα σεριανίσω<br>να σεριανίσω | έχω σεριανίσει<br>είχα σεριανίσει | σεριάνιζε<br>σεριανίζετε | σεριάνισε<br>σεριανίστε |
| **I save** | σώζω 13 | έσωζα | έσωσα | θα σώσω<br>να σώσω | έχω σώσει<br>είχα σώσει | σώζε<br>σώζετε | σώσε<br>σώστε |
| **I save myself** | *σώζομαι 13* | *σωζόμουν* | *σώθηκα* | *θα σωθώ*<br>*να σωθώ* | *έχω σωθεί*<br>*είχα σωθεί* | *να σώζεσαι*<br>*σώζεστε* | *σώσου*<br>*σωθείτε* |
| **I save** | αποταμιεύω 13 | αποταμίευα | αποταμίευσα | θα αποταμιεύσω<br>να αποταμιεύσω | έχω αποταμιεύσει<br>είχα αποταμιεύσει | αποταμίευε<br>αποταμιεύετε | αποταμίευσε<br>αποταμιεύστε |
| **I save up** | εξοικονομώ 15 | εξοικονομούσα | εξοικονόμησα | θα εξοικονομήσω<br>να εξοικονομήσω | έχω εξοικονομήσει<br>είχα εξοικονομήσει | εξοικονόμα<br>εξοικονομάτε | εξοικονόμησε<br>εξοικονομήστε |
| **I saw** | πριονίζω 13 | πριόνιζα | πριόνισα | θα πριονίσω<br>να πριονίσω | έχω πριονίσει<br>είχα πριονίσει | πριόνιζε<br>πριονίζετε | πριόνισε<br>πριονίστε |
| **I say** | λέγω 13 | έλεγα | είπα | θα πω<br>να πω | έχω πει<br>είχα πει | λέγε<br>λέγετε | πες<br>πείτε (πέστε) |
| **I scare** | αγριεύω 13 | αγρίευα | αγρίεψα | θα αγριέψω<br>να αγριέψω | έχω αγριέψει<br>είχα αγριέψει | αγρίευε<br>αγριεύετε | αγρίεψε<br>αγριέψτε |
| **I scandalize** | σκανδαλίζω 13 | σκανδάλιζα | σκανδάλισα | θα σκανδαλίσω<br>να σκανδαλίσω | έχω σκανδαλίσει<br>είχα σκανδαλίσει | σκανδάλιζε<br>σκανδαλίζετε | σκανδάλισε<br>σκανδαλίστε |
| **I schedule** | προγραμματίζω 13 | προγραμμάτιζα | προγραμμάτισα | θα προγραμματίσω<br>να προγραμματίσω | έχω προγραμματίσει<br>είχα προγραμματίσει | προγραμμάτιζε<br>προγραμματίζετε | προγραμμάτισε<br>προγραμματίστε |
| **I scheme** | ραδιουργώ 15 | ραδιουργούσα | ραδιούργησα | θα ραδιουργήσω<br>να ραδιουργήσω | έχω ραδιουργήσει<br>είχα ραδιουργήσει | να ραδιουργείς<br>ραδιουργείτε | ραδιούργησε<br>ραδιουργήστε |
| **I scoff** | σαρκάζω 13 | σάρκαζα | σάρκασα | θα σαρκάσω<br>να σαρκάσω | έχω σαρκάσει<br>είχα σαρκάσει | σάρκαζε<br>σαρκάζετε | σάρκασε<br>σαρκάστε |

| English Verb | Present | Imperfect | Past | Simple Future Simple Subjunctive | Present Perfect Past Perfect | Continuous Imperative | Simple Imperative |
|---|---|---|---|---|---|---|---|
| **I scold** (tell off) | αποπαίρνω 13 | απόπαιρνα | αποπήρα | θα αποπάρω<br>να αποπάρω | έχω αποπάρει<br>είχα αποπάρει | απόπαιρνε<br>αποπέρνετε | να αποπάρεις<br>αποπάρτε |
| **I scrape** | ξύνω 13 | έξυνα | έξυσα | θα ξύσω<br>να ξύσω | έχω ξύσει<br>είχα ξύσει | ξύνε<br>ξύνετε | ξύσε<br>ξύστε |
| **I scratch** | γδέρνω 13 | έγδερνα | έγδειρα | θα γδείρω<br>να γδείρω | έχω γδείρει<br>είχα γδείρει | γδέρνε<br>γδέρνετε | γδείρε<br>γδείρτε |
| **I scream** | κραυγάζω 3 | κραύγαζα | κραύγασα | θα κραυγάσω<br>να κραυγάσω | έχω κραυγάσει<br>είχα κραυγάσει | κραύγαζε<br>κραυγάζετε | κραύγασε<br>κραυγάστε |
| **I seal** | σφραγίζω 13 | σφράγιζα | σφράγισα | θα σφραγίσω<br>να σφραγίσω | έχω σφραγίσει<br>είχα σφραγίσει | σφράγιζε<br>σφραγίζετε | σφράγισε<br>σφραγίστε |
| **I search** | ψάχνω 13 | έψαχνα | έψαξα | θα ψάξω<br>να ψάξω | έχω ψάξει<br>είχα ψάξει | ψάχνε<br>ψάχνετε | ψάξε<br>ψάξτε |
| **I search** | γυρεύω 13 | γύρευα | γύρεψα | θα γυρέψω<br>να γυρέψω | έχω γυρέψει<br>είχα γυρέψει | γύρευε<br>γυρεύτε | γύρεψε<br>γυρέψτε |
| **I season** | καρυκεύω 13 | καρύκευα | καρύκεψα | θα καρυκέψω<br>να καρυκέψω | έχω καρυκέψει<br>είχα καρυκέψει | καρύκευε<br>καρυκεύετε | καρύκεψε<br>καρυκέψτε |
| **I secure** (ensure) | εξασφαλίζω 13 | εξασφάλιζα | εξασφάλισα | θα εξασφαλίσω<br>να εξασφαλίσω | έχω εξασφαλίσει<br>είχα εξασφαλίσει | εξασφάλιζε<br>εξασφαλίζετε | εξασφάλισε<br>εξασφαλίστε |
| **I seduce** | ξελογιάζω 13 | ξελόγιαζα | ξελόγιασα | θα ξελογιάσω<br>να ξελογιάσω | έχω ξελογιάσει<br>είχα ξελογιάσει | ξελόγιαζε<br>ξελογιάζετε | ξελόγιασε<br>ξελογιάστε |
| **I see** | βλέπω 13 | έβλεπα | είδα | θα δω<br>να δω | έχω δει<br>είχα δει | βλέπε<br>βλέπετε | δες<br>δείτε or δέστε |
| **I see off/out** | ξεπροβοδίζω 13 | ξεπροβόδιζα | ξεπροβόδισα | θα ξεπροβοδίσω<br>να ξεπροβοδίσω | έχω ξεπροβοδίσει<br>είχα ξεπροβοδίσει | ξεπροβόδιζε<br>ξεπροβοδίζετε | ξεπροβόδισε<br>ξεπροβοδίστε |

| English Verb | Present | Imperfect | Past | Simple Future<br>Simple Subjunctive | Present Perfect<br>Past Perfect | Continuous Imperative | Simple Imperative |
|---|---|---|---|---|---|---|---|
| **I seek** | αναζητώ 15 | αναζητούσα | αναζήτησα | θα αναζητήσω<br>να αναζητήσω | έχω αναζητήσει<br>είχα αναζητήσει | αναζήτα<br>αναζητάτε | αναζήτησε<br>αναζητήστε |
| **It seems** | *φαίνεται 14* | *φαινόταν* | *φάνηκε* | *θα φανεί*<br>*να φανεί* | *έχει φανεί*<br>*είχε φανεί* | – | – |
| **I seize** | κυριεύω 13 | κυρίευα | κυρίεψα | θα κυριέψω<br>να κυριέψω | έχω κυριέψει<br>είχα κυριέψει | κυρίευε<br>κυριεύετε | κυρίεψε<br>κυριέψτε |
| **I seize**<br>(take/occupy) | μαγκώνω 13 | μάγκωνα | μάγκωσα | θα μαγκώσω<br>να μαγκώσω | έχω μαγκώσει<br>είχα μαγκώσει | μάγκωνε<br>μαγκώνετε | μάγκωσε<br>μαγκώστε |
| **I select** | επιλέγω 13 | επίλεγα | επίλεξα | θα επιλέξω<br>να επιλέξω | έχω επιλέξει<br>είχα επιλέξει | επίλεγε<br>επιλέγετε | επίλεξε<br>επιλέξτε |
| **I sell** | πουλ(ά)ώ 15 | πουλούσα | πούλησα | θα πουλήσω<br>να πουλήσω | έχω πουλήσει<br>είχα πουλήσει | πούλα<br>πουλάτε | πούλησε<br>πουλήστε |
| **I send** | στέλνω 13 | έστελνα | έστειλα | θα στείλω<br>να στείλω | έχω στείλει<br>είχα στείλει | στέλνε<br>στέλνετε | στείλε<br>στείλτε |
| **I sense** | *διαισθάνομαι 14* | *διαισθανόμουν* | *διαισθάνθηκα* | *θα διαισθανθώ*<br>*να διαισθανθώ* | *έχω διαισθανθεί*<br>*είχα διαισθανθεί* | *να διαισθάνεσαι*<br>*διαισθάνεστε* | *διαισθάνσου*<br>*διαισθανθείτε* |
| **I sensitize** | ευαισθητο-<br>ποιώ 17 | ευαισθητο-<br>ποιούσα | ευαισθητο-<br>ποίησα | θα ευαισθητο-<br>ποιήσω<br>να ευαισθητο-<br>ποιήσω | έχω ευαισθητο-<br>ποιήσει<br>είχα ευαισθητο-<br>ποιήσει | να ευαισθητο-<br>ποιείς<br>ευαισθητο-<br>ποιείτε | ευαισθητο-<br>ποίησε<br>ευαισθητο-<br>ποιήστε |
| **I sentence** | καταδικάζω 13 | καταδίκαζα | καταδίκασα | θα καταδικάσω<br>να καταδικάσω | έχω καταδικάσει<br>είχα καταδικάσει | καταδίκαζε<br>καταδικάζετε | καταδίκασε<br>καταδικάστε |
| **I serve** | υπηρετώ 17 | υπηρετούσα | υπηρέτησα | θα υπηρετήσω<br>να υπηρετήσω | έχω υπηρετήσει<br>είχα υπηρετήσει | υπηρέτει<br>υπηρετείτε | υπηρέτησε<br>υπηρετήστε |

| English Verb | Present | Imperfect | Past | Simple Future<br>Simple Subjunctive | Present Perfect<br>Past Perfect | Continuous Imperative | Simple Imperative |
|---|---|---|---|---|---|---|---|
| **I serve** | σερβίρω 13 | σέρβιρα | σερβίρισα | θα σερβίρω<br>να σερβίρω | έχω σερβίρει<br>είχα σερβίρει | σέρβιρε<br>σερβίρετε | σερβίρισε<br>σερβιρίστε |
| **I settle** | διευθετώ 17 | διευθετούσα | διευθέτησα | θα διευθετήσω<br>να διευθετήσω | έχω διευθετήσει<br>είχα διευθετήσει | να διευθετείς<br>διευθετείτε | διευθέτησε<br>διευθετήστε |
| **I settle**<br>(pay up) | ξεχρεώνω 13 | ξεχρέωνα | ξεχρέωσα | θα ξεχρεώσω<br>να ξεχρεώσω | έχω ξεχρεώσει<br>είχα ξεχρεώσει | ξεχρέωνε<br>ξεχρεώνετε | ξεχρέωσε<br>ξεχρεώστε |
| **I settle** | *τακτοποιούμαι 18* | *τακτοποιούμουν* | *τακτοποιήθηκα* | *θα τακτοποιηθώ*<br>*να τακτοποιηθώ* | *έχω τακτοποιηθεί*<br>*είχα τακτοποιηθεί* | *να τακτοποιείσαι*<br>*τακτοποιείστε* | *τακτοποιήσου*<br>*τακτοποιηθείτε* |
| **I set to music** | μελοποιώ 17 | μελοποιούσα | μελοποίησα | θα μελοποιήσω<br>να μελοποιήσω | έχω μελοποιήσει<br>είχα μελοποιήσει | να μελοποιείς<br>μελοπιείτε | μελοποίησε<br>μελοποιήστε |
| **I set up** | στήνω 13 | έστηνα | έστησα | θα στήσω<br>να στήσω | έχω στήσει<br>είχα στήσει | στήνε<br>στήνετε | στήσε<br>στήστε |
| **I sever** | αποκόπτω 13 | απέκοψα | απέκοψα | θα αποκόψω<br>να αποκόψω | έχω αποκόψει<br>είχα αποκόψει | απόκοπτε<br>αποκόπτετε | απόκοψε<br>αποκόψτε |
| **I sew** | ράβω 13 | έραβα | έραψα | θα ράψω<br>να ράψω | έχω ράψει<br>είχα ράψει | ράβε<br>ράβετε | ράψε<br>ράψτε |
| **I shake** | αναταράζω 13 | ανατάραζα | ανατάραξα | θα αναταράξω<br>να αναταράξω | έχω αναταράξει<br>είχα αναταράξει | ανατάραζε<br>αναταράζετε | ανατάραξε<br>αναταράξτε |
| **I shake** | κλονίζω 13 | κλόνιζα | κλόνισα | θα κλονίσω<br>να κλονίσω | έχω κλονίσει<br>είχα κλονίσει | κλόνιζε<br>κλονίζετε | κλόνισε<br>κλονίστε |
| **I shame** | ρεζιλεύω 13 | ρεζίλευα | ρεζίλεψα | θα ρεζιλέψω<br>να ρεζιλέψω | έχω ρεζιλέψει<br>είχα ρεζιλέψει | ρεζίλευε<br>ρεζιλεύετε | ρεζίλεψε<br>ρεζιλέψτε |
| **I shape** | πλάθω 13 | έπλαθα | έπλασα | θα πλάσω<br>να πλάσω | έχω πλάσει<br>είχα πλάσει | πλάθε<br>πλάθετε | πλάσε<br>πλάστε |

| English Verb | Present | Imperfect | Past | Simple Future<br>Simple Subjunctive | Present Perfect<br>Past Perfect | Continuous Imperative | Simple Imperative |
|---|---|---|---|---|---|---|---|
| **I share** | *μοιράζομαι 14* | *μοιραζόμουν* | *μοιράστηκα* | *θα μοιραστώ*<br>*να μοιραστώ* | *έχω μοιραστεί*<br>*είχα μοιραστεί* | *να μοιράζεσαι*<br>*μοιράζεστε* | *μοιράσου*<br>*μοιραστείτε* |
| **I sharpen** | ακονίζω 13 | ακόνιζα | ακόνισα | θα ακονίσω<br>να ακονίσω | έχω ακονίσει<br>είχα ακονίσει | ακόνιζε<br>ακονίζετε | ακόνισε<br>ακονίστε |
| **I shatter** | θραύω 13 | έθραυα | έθραψα | θα θραύσω<br>να θραύσω | έχω θραύσει<br>είχα θραύσει | θραύε<br>θραύετε | θραύσε<br>θραύστε |
| **I shatter** | κομματιάζω 13 | κομμάτιαζα | κομμάτιασα | θα κομματιάσω<br>να κομματιάσω | έχω κομματιάσει<br>είχα κομματιάσει | κομμάτιαζε<br>κομματιάζετε | κομμάτιασε<br>κομματιάστε |
| **I shave** | ξυρίζω 13 | ξύριζα | ξύρισα | θα ξυρίσω<br>να ξυρίσω | έχω ξυρίσει<br>είχα ξυρίσει | ξύριζε<br>ξυρίζετε | ξύρισε<br>ξυρίστε |
| **I shield** | προασπίζω 13 | προάσπιζα | προάσπισα | θα προασπίσω<br>να προασπίσω | έχω προασπίσει<br>είχα προασπίσει | προάσπιζε<br>προασπίζετε | προάσπισε<br>προασπίστε |
| **I shift** | μετακινώ 17 | μετακινούσα | μετακίνησα | θα μετακινήσω<br>να μετακινήσω | έχω μετακινήσει<br>είχα μετακινήσει | να μετακινείς<br>μετακινείτε | μετακίνησε<br>μετακινήστε |
| **I shine** | φέγγω 13 | έφεγγα | έφεξα | θα φέξω<br>να φέξω | έχω φέξει<br>είχα φέξει | φέγγε<br>φέγγετε | φέξε<br>φέξτε |
| **I shine** (furniture/shoes) | γυαλίζω 13 | γυάλιζα | γυάλισα | θα γυαλίσω<br>να γυαλίσω | έχω γυαλίσει<br>είχα γυαλίσει | γυάλιζε<br>γυαλίζετε | γυάλισε<br>γυαλίστε |
| **I shiver** | ριγώ 17 | ριγούσα | ρίγησα | θα ριγήσω<br>να ριγήσω | έχω ριγήσει<br>είχα ριγήσει | να ριγείς<br>ριγείτε | ρίγησε<br>ριγήστε |
| **I shock** | σοκάρω 13 | σόκαρα | σοκάρισα | θα σοκάρω<br>να σοκάρω | έχω σοκάρει<br>είχα σοκάρει | σόκαρε<br>σοκάρετε | σοκάρισε<br>σοκαρίστε |
| **I shoot** | πυροβολώ 17 | πυροβολούσα | πυροβόλησα | θα πυροβολήσω<br>να πυροβολήσω | έχω πυροβολήσει<br>είχα πυροβολήσει | να πυροβολείς<br>πυροβολείτε | πυροβόλησε<br>πυροβολήστε |

| English Verb | Present | Imperfect | Past | Simple Future<br>Simple Subjunctive | Present Perfect<br>Past Perfect | Continuous Imperative | Simple Imperative |
|---|---|---|---|---|---|---|---|
| **I shop** | ψωνίζω 13 | ψώνιζα | ψώνισα | θα ψωνίσω<br>να ψωνίσω | έχω ψωνίσει<br>είχα ψωνίσει | ψώνιζε<br>ψωνίζετε | ψώνισε<br>ψωνίστε |
| **I shout** | φωνάζω 13 | φώναζα | φώναξα | θα φωνάξω<br>να φωνάξω | έχω φωνάξει<br>είχα φωνάξει | φώναζε<br>φωνάζετε | φώναξε<br>φωνάξτε |
| **I shove** | ωθώ 17 | ωθούσα | ώθησα | θα ωθήσω<br>να ωθήσω | έχω ωθήσει<br>είχα ωθήσει | να ωθείς<br>ωθείτε | ώθησε<br>ωθήστε |
| **I show** | δείχνω 13 | έδειχνα | έδειξα | θα δείξω<br>να δείξω | έχω δείξει<br>είχα δείξει | δείχνε<br>δείχνετε | δείξε<br>δείξτε |
| **I shred** | κουρελιάζω 13 | κουρέλιαζα | κουρέλιασα | θα κουρελιάσω<br>να κουρελιάσω | έχω κουρελιάσει<br>είχα κουρελιάσει | κουρέλιαζε<br>κουρελιάζετε | κουρέλιασε<br>κουρελιάστε |
| **I shrink** | *συρρικνώνομαι 14* | *συρρικνωνόμουν* | *συρρικνώθηκα* | *θα συρρικνωθώ*<br>*να συρρικνωθώ* | *έχω συρρικνωθεί*<br>*είχα συρρικνωθεί* | *να συρρικνώνεσαι*<br>*συρρικνώνεστε* | *συρρικνώσου*<br>*συρρικνωθείτε* |
| **I shunt** | μανουβράρω 13 | μανούβραρα | μανουβράρισα | θα μανουβράρω<br>να μανουβράρω | έχω μανουβράρει<br>είχα μανουβράρει | μανούβραρε<br>μανουβράρετε | μανουβράρισε<br>μανουβραρίστε |
| **I sieve** | κοσκινίζω 13 | κοσκίνιζα | κοσκίνισα | θα κοσκινίσω<br>να κοσκινίσω | έχω κοσκινίσει<br>είχα κοσκινίσει | κοσκίνιζε<br>κοσκινίζετε | κοσκίνισε<br>κοσκινίστε |
| **I sigh** | αναστενάζω 13 | αναστέναζα | αναστέναξα | θα αναστενάξω<br>να αναστενάξω | έχω αναστενάξει<br>είχα αναστενάξει | αναστέναζε<br>αναστενάζετε | αναστέναξε<br>αναστενάξτε |
| **I sign** | υπογράφω 13 | υπέγραφα | υπέγραψα | θα υπογράψω<br>να υπογράψω | έχω υπογράψει<br>είχα υπογράψει | υπόγραφε<br>υπογράφετε | υπόγραψε<br>υπογράψτε |
| **I simmer** | κουφοβράζω 13 | κουφόβραζα | κουφόβρασα | θα κουφοβράσω<br>να κουφοβράσω | έχω κουφοβράσει<br>είχα κουφοβράσει | κουφόβραζε<br>κουφοβράζετε | κουφόβρασε<br>κουφοβράστε |
| **I simplify** | απλοποιώ 17 | απλοποιούσα | απλοποίησα | θα απλοποιήσω<br>να απλοποιήσω | έχω απλοποιήσει<br>είχα απλοποιήσει | να απλοποιείς<br>απλοποιείτε | απλοποίησε<br>απλοποιήστε |

| English Verb | Present | Imperfect | Past | Simple Future<br>Simple Subjunctive | Present Perfect<br>Past Perfect | Continuous Imperative | Simple Imperative |
|---|---|---|---|---|---|---|---|
| **I simulate** | *απομιμούμαι 18* | *απομιμούμουν* | *απομιμήθηκα* | *θα απομιμηθώ*<br>*να απομιμηθώ* | *έχω απομιμηθεί*<br>*είχα απομιμηθεί* | *να απομιμίσαι*<br>*απομιμείστε* | *απομιμήσου*<br>*απομιμηθείτε* |
| **I sin** | αμαρτάνω 13 | αμάρτανα | αμάρτησα | θα αμαρτάνω<br>να αμαρτάνω | έχω αμαρτάνει<br>είχα αμαρτάνει | αμάρτανε<br>αμαρτάνετε | αμάρτησε<br>αμαρτήστε |
| **I sing** | τραγουδ(ά)ώ 15 | τραγουδούσα | τραγούδησα | θα τραγουδήσω<br>να τραγουδήσω | έχω τραγουδήσει<br>είχα τραγουδήσει | τραγούδα<br>τραγουδάτε | τραγούδησε<br>τραγουδήστε |
| **I sink** | βουλιάζω 13 | βούλιαζα | βούλιαξα | θα βουλιάξω<br>να βουλιάξω | έχω βουλιάξει<br>είχα βουλιάξει | βούλιαζε<br>βουλιάζετε | βούλιαξε<br>βουλιάξτε |
| **I sit** | *κάθομαι 14* | *καθόμουν* | *κάθησα*<br>*έκατσα* | *θα καθήσω*<br>*να καθήσω* | *έχω καθήσει*<br>*είχα καθήσει* | *να κάθεσαι*<br>*κάθεστε* | *κάθησε (κάτσε)*<br>*καθήστε* |
| **I sit up** | *ανακάθομαι 14* | *ανακαθόμουν* | *ανακάθησα* | *θα ανακαθήσω*<br>*να ανακαθήσω* | *έχω ανακαθήσει*<br>*είχα ανακαθήσει* | *να ανακάθεσαι*<br>*ανακάθεστε* | *ανακάθησε*<br>*ανακαθήστε* |
| **I skim** | ξαφρίζω 13 | ξάφριζα | ξάφρισα | θα ξαφρίσω<br>να ξαφρίσω | έχω ξαφρίσει<br>είχα ξαφρίσει | ξάφριζε<br>ξαφρίζετε | ξάφρισε<br>ξαφρίστε |
| **I slander** | συκοφαντώ 17 | συκοφαντούσα | συκοφάντησα | θα συκοφαντήσω<br>να συκοφαντήσω | έχω συκοφαντήσει<br>είχα συκοφαντήσει | να συκοφαντείς<br>συκοφαντείτε | συκοφάντησε<br>συκοφαντήστε |
| **I slap** | μπατσίζω 13 | μπάτσιζα | μπάτσισα | θα μπατσίσω<br>να μπατσίσω | έχω μπατσίσει<br>είχα μπατσίσει | μπάτσιζε<br>μπατσίζετε | μπάτσισε<br>μπατσίστε |
| **I sleep** | *κοιμάμαι 42* | *κοιμόμουν* | *κοιμήθηκα* | *θα κοιμηθώ*<br>*να κοιμηθώ* | *έχω κοιμηθεί*<br>*είχα κοιμηθεί* | *να κοιμάσαι*<br>*κοιμάστε* | *κοιμήσου*<br>*κοιμηθείτε* |
| **I slide** | ολισθαίνω 13 | ολίσθαινα | ολίσθησα | θα ολισθήσω<br>να ολισθήσω | έχω ολισθήσει<br>είχα ολισθήσει | ολίσθαινε<br>ολισθαίνετε | ολίσθησε<br>ολισθήστε |
| **I slip** | γλιστρ(ά)ώ 15 | γλιστρούσα | γλίστρησα | θα γλιστρήσω<br>να γλιστρήσω | έχω γλιστρήσει<br>είχα γλιστρήσει | γλίστρα<br>γλιστράτε | γλίστρησε<br>γλιστρήστε |

| English Verb | Present | Imperfect | Past | Simple Future<br>Simple Subjunctive | Present Perfect<br>Past Perfect | Continuous Imperative | Simple Imperative |
|---|---|---|---|---|---|---|---|
| **I smash** | συντρίβω 13 | συνέτριβα | συνέτριψα | θα συντρίψω<br>να συντρίψω | έχω συντρίψει<br>είχα συντρίψει | σύντριβε<br>συντρίβετε | σύντριψε<br>συντρίψτε |
| **I smear** | αλείφω 13 | άλειφα | άλειψα | θα αλείψω<br>να αλείψω | έχω αλείψει<br>είχα αλείψει | άλειφε<br>αλείφετε | άλειψε<br>αλείψτε |
| **I smell** | μυρίζω 13 | μύριζα | μύρισα | θα μυρίσω<br>να μυρίσω | έχω μυρίσει<br>είχα μυρίσει | μύριζε<br>μυρίζετε | μύρισε<br>μυρίστε |
| **I smile** | χαμογελ(ά)ώ 15 | χαμογελούσα | χαμογέλασα | θα χαμογελάσω<br>να χαμογελάσω | έχω χαμογελάσει<br>είχα χαμογελάσει | χαμογέλα<br>χαμογελάτε | χαμογέλασε<br>χαμογελάστε |
| **I smoke** | καπνίζω 13 | κάπνιζα | κάπνισα | θα καπνίσω<br>να καπνίσω | έχω καπνίσει<br>είχα καπνίσει | κάπνιζε<br>καπνίζετε | κάπνισε<br>καπνίστε |
| **I smudge** | μουντζουρώνω 13 | μουντζούρωνα | μουντζούρωσα | θα μουντζουρώσω<br>να μουντσουρώσω | έχω μουντζουρώσει<br>είχα μουντζουρώσει | μουντζούρωνε<br>μουντζουρώνετε | μουντσούρωσε<br>μουντσουρώστε |
| **I sneer** | χλευάζω 13 | χλεύαζα | χλεύασα | θα χλευάσω<br>να χλευάσω | έχω χλευάσει<br>είχα χλευάσει | χλεύαζε<br>χλευάζετε | χλεύασε<br>χλευάστε |
| **I sneeze** | *φταρνίζομαι 14* | *φταρνιζόμουν* | *φταρνίστηκα* | *θα φταρνιστώ*<br>*να φταρνιστώ* | *έχω φταρνιστεί*<br>*είχα φταρνιστεί* | *να φταρνίζεσαι*<br>*φταρνίζεστε* | *φταρνίσου*<br>*φταρνιστείτε* |
| **I sniff** | *οσφραίνομαι 14* | *οσφραινόμουν* | *οσφράνθηκα* | *θα οσφρανθώ*<br>*να οσφρανθώ* | *έχω οσφρανθεί*<br>*είχα οσφρανθεί* | *να οσφραίνεσαι*<br>*οσφραίνεστε* | *οσφράνσου*<br>*οσφρανθείτε* |
| **I snore** | ροχαλίζω 13 | ροχάλιζα | ροχάλισα | θα ροχαλίσω<br>να ροχαλίσω | έχω ροχαλίσει<br>είχα ροχαλίσει | ροχάλιζε<br>ροχαλίζετε | ροχάλισε<br>ροχαλίστε |
| **I snort (animal)** | ρουθουνίζω 13 | ρουθούνιζα | ρουθούνισα | θα ρουθουνίσω<br>να ρουθουνίσω | έχω ρουθουνίσει<br>είχα ρουθουνίσει | ρουθούνιζε<br>ρουθουνίζετε | ρουθούνισε<br>ρουθουνίστε |
| **I sober up** | ξεμεθ(ά)ώ 15 | ξεμεθούσα | ξεμέθυσα | θα ξεμεθύσω<br>να ξεμεθύσω | έχω ξεμεθύσει<br>είχα ξεμεθύσει | ξεμέθα<br>ξεμεθάτε | ξεμέθυσε<br>ξεμεθύστε |

| English Verb | Present | Imperfect | Past | Simple Future<br>Simple Subjunctive | Present Perfect<br>Past Perfect | Continuous Imperative | Simple Imperative |
|---|---|---|---|---|---|---|---|
| **I soften** | μαλακώνω 13 | μαλάκωνα | μαλάκωσα | θα μαλακώσω<br>να μαλακώσω | έχω μαλακώσει<br>είχα μαλακώσει | μαλάκωνε<br>μαλακώνετε | μαλάκωσε<br>μαλακώστε |
| **I solve** | λύνω 13 | έλυνα | έλυσα | θα λύσω<br>να λύσω | έχω λύσει<br>είχα λύσει | λύνε<br>λύνετε | λύσε<br>λύστε |
| **I soil** | βρομίζω 13 | βρόμιζα | βρόμισα | θα βρομίσω<br>να βρομίσω | έχω βρομίσει<br>είχα βρομίσει | βρόμιζε<br>βρομίζετε | βρόμισε<br>βρομίστε |
| **I soothe** | γαληνεύω 13 | γαλήνευα | γαλήνεψα | θα γαληνέψω<br>να γαληνέψω | έχω γαληνέψει<br>είχα γαληνέψει | γαλήνευε<br>γαληνεύετε | γαλήνεψε<br>γαληνέψτε |
| **I am sorry** | *λυπάμαι 42* | *λυπόμουν* | *λυπήθηκα* | *θα λυπηθώ*<br>*να λυπηθώ* | *έχω λυπηθεί*<br>*είχα λυπηθεί* | *να λυπάσαι*<br>*λυπάστε* | *λυπήσου*<br>*λυπηθείτε* |
| **I sow** | σπέρνω 13 | έσπερνα | έσπειρα | θα σπείρω<br>να σπείρω | έχω σπείρει<br>είχα σπείρει | σπέρνε<br>σπέρνετε | σπείρε<br>σπείρτε |
| **I sparkle** | σπινθηροβολώ 17 | σπινθηροβολούσα | σπινθηροβόλησα | θα σπινθηροβολήσω<br>να σπινθηροβολήσω | έχω σπινθηροβολήσει<br>είχα σπινθηροβολήσει | να σπινθηροβολείς<br>σπινθηροβολείτε | σπινθηροβόλησε<br>σπινθιροβολήστε |
| **I speak** | μιλ(ά)ώ 15 | μιλούσα | μίλησα | θα μιλήσω<br>να μιλήσω | έχω μιλήσει<br>είχα μιλήσει | μίλα<br>μιλάτε | μίλησε<br>μιλήστε |
| **I speak ill of** | κακολογώ 17 | κακολογούσα | κακολόγησα | θα κακολογήσω<br>να κακολογήσω | έχω κακολογήσει<br>είχα κακολογήσει | να κακολογείς<br>κακολογείτε | κακολόγησε<br>κακολογήστε |
| **I specialize** | *ειδικεύομαι 14* | *ειδικευόμουν* | *ειδικεύτηκα* | *θα ειδικευτώ*<br>*να ειδικευτώ* | *έχω ειδικευτεί*<br>*είχα ειδικευτεί* | *να ειδικεύεσαι*<br>*ειδικεύεστε* | *ειδικεύσου*<br>*ειδικευτείτε* |
| **I spend** | ξοδεύω 13 | ξόδευα | ξόδεψα | θα ξοδέψω<br>να ξοδέψω | έχω ξοδέψει<br>είχα ξοδέψει | ξόδευε<br>ξοδεύετε | ξόδεψε<br>ξοδέψτε |
| **I spend** | δαπαν(ά)ώ 15 | δαπανούσα | δαπάνησα | θα δαπανήσω<br>να δαπανήσω | έχω δαπανήσει<br>είχα δαπανήσει | δαπάνα<br>δαπανάτε | δαπάνησε<br>δαπανήστε |

| English Verb | Present | Imperfect | Past | Simple Future<br>Simple Subjunctive | Present Perfect<br>Past Perfect | Continuous Imperative | Simple Imperative |
|---|---|---|---|---|---|---|---|
| **I spit** | σουβλίζω 13 | σούβλιζα | σούβλισα | θα σουβλίσω<br>να σουβλίσω | έχω σουβλίσει<br>είχα σουβλίσει | σούβλιζε<br>σουβλίζετε | σούβλισε<br>σουβλίστε |
| **I split** | διχάζω 13 | δίχαζα | δίχασα | θα διχάσω<br>να διχάσω | έχω διχάσει<br>είχα διχάσει | δίχαζε<br>διχάζετε | δίχασε<br>διχάστε |
| **I spoil** | χαλ(ά)ώ 15<br>χαλνώ 15 | χαλούσα | χάλασα | θα χαλάσω<br>να χαλάσω | έχω χαλάσει<br>είχα χαλάσει | χάλ(ν)α<br>χαλ(ν)άτε | χάλασε<br>χαλάστε |
| **I sprain** | στραμπουλίζω 13 | στραμπούλιζα | στραμπούλιξα | θα στραμπουλίξω<br>να στραμπουλίξω | έχω στραμπουλίξει<br>είχα στραμπουλίξει | στραμπούλιζε<br>στραμπουλίζετε | στραμπούλιξε<br>στραμπουλίξτε |
| **I spray** | ψεκάζω 13 | ψεκάζω | ψέκασα | θα ψεκάσω<br>να ψεκάσω | έχω ψεκάσει<br>είχα ψεκάσει | ψέκαζε<br>ψεκάζετε | ψέκασε<br>ψεκάστε |
| **I spread** (lay/ cover/set) | στρώνω 13 | έστρωνα | έστρωσα | θα στρώσω<br>να στρώσω | έχω στρώσει<br>είχα στρώσει | στρώνε<br>στρώνετε | στρώσε<br>στρώστε |
| **I spread (out)** | απλώνω 13 | άπλωνα | άπλωσα | θα απλώσω<br>να απλώσω | έχω απλώσει<br>είχα απλώσει | άπλωνε<br>απλώνετε | άπλωσε<br>απλώστε |
| **I spread rumours** | διαδίδω 13 | διέδιδα | διέδωσα | θα διαδώσω<br>να διαδώσω | έχω διαδώσει<br>είχα διαδώσει | διάδιδε<br>διαδίδετε | διάδωσε<br>διαδώστε |
| **I sprinkle** | πασπαλίζω 13 | πασπάλιζα | πασπάλισα | θα πασπαλίσω<br>να πασπαλίσω | έχω πασπαλίσει<br>είχα πασπαλίσει | πασπάλιζε<br>πασπαλίζετε | πασπάλισε<br>πασπαλίστε |
| **I sprout** | βλασταίνω 13 | βλάσταινα | βλάστανα | θα βλαστάνω<br>να βλαστάνω | έχω βλαστάνει<br>είχα βλαστάνει | βλάσταινε<br>βλασταίνετε | βλάστανε<br>βλαστάνετε |
| **I spy** | κατασκοπεύω 13 | κατασκόπευα | κατασκόπευσα | θα κατασκοπεύσω<br>να κατασκοπεύσω | έχω κατασκοπεύσει<br>είχα κατασκοπεύσει | κατασκόπευε<br>κατασκοπεύετε | κατασκόπευσε<br>κατασκοπεύστε |
| **I squabble** | καυγαδίζω 13 | καυγάδιζα | καυγάδισα | θα καυγαδίσω<br>να καυγαδίσω | έχω καυγαδίσει<br>είχα καυγαδίσει | καυγάδιζε<br>καυγαδίζετε | καυγάδισε<br>καυγαδίστε |

| English Verb | Present | Imperfect | Past | Simple Future<br>Simple Subjunctive | Present Perfect<br>Past Perfect | Continuous Imperative | Simple Imperative |
|---|---|---|---|---|---|---|---|
| **I squeeze** | στύβω 13 | έστυβα | έστυψα | θα στύψω<br>να στύψω | έχω στύψει<br>είχα στύψει | στύβε<br>στύβετε | στύψε<br>στύψτε |
| **I stab** | μαχαιρώνω 13 | μαχαίρωνα | μαχαίρωσα | θα μαχαιρώσω<br>να μαχαιρώσω | έχω μαχαιρώσει<br>είχα μαχαιρώσει | μαχαίρωνε<br>μαχαιρώνετε | μαχαίρωσε<br>μαχαιρώστε |
| **I stage** | σκηνοθετώ 17 | σκηνοθετούσα | σκηνοθέτησα | θα σκηνοθετήσω<br>να σκηνοθετήσω | έχω σκηνοθετήσει<br>είχα σκηνοθετήσει | να σκηνοθετείς<br>σκηνοθετείτε | σκηνοθέτησε<br>σκηνοθετήστε |
| **I stagger** | τρικλίζω 13 | τρίκλιζα | τρίκλισα | θα τρικλίσω<br>να τρικλίσω | έχω τρικλίσει<br>είχα τρικλίσει | τρίκλιζε<br>τρικλίζετε | τρίκλισε<br>τρικλίστε |
| **I stagnate** | λιμνάζω 13 | λίμναζα | λίμνασα | θα λιμνάσω<br>να λιμνάσω | έχω λιμνάσει<br>είχα λιμνάσει | λίμναζε<br>λιμνάζετε | λίμνασε<br>λιμνάστε |
| **I stain** | λεκιάζω 13 | λέκιαζα | λέκιασα | θα λεκιάσω<br>να λεκιάσω | έχω λεκιάσει<br>είχα λεκιάσει | λέκιαζε<br>λεκιάζετε | λέκιασε<br>λεκιάστε |
| **I stake** | ποντάρω 13 | πόνταρα | πόνταρα | θα ποντάρω<br>να ποντάρω | έχω ποντάρει<br>είχα ποντάρει | πόνταρε<br>ποντάρετε | πόνταρε<br>ποντάρετε |
| **I stammer** | τραυλίζω 13 | τραύλιζα | τραύλισα | θα τραυλίσω<br>να τραυλίσω | έχω τραυλίσει<br>είχα τραυλίσει | τραύλιζε<br>τραυλίζετε | τραύλισε<br>τραυλίστε |
| **I stand** | *στέκομαι 14* | *στεκόμουν* | *στάθηκα* | *θα σταθώ*<br>*να σταθώ* | *έχω σταθεί*<br>*είχα σταθεί* | *να στέκεσαι*<br>*στέκεστε* | *στάσου*<br>*σταθείτε* |
| **I stare** | θωρώ 17 | θωρούσα | θώρησα | θα θωρήσω<br>να θωρήσω | έχω θωρήσει<br>είχα θωρήσει | να θωρείς<br>θωρείτε | θώρησε<br>θωρήστε |
| **I start** | ξεκιν(ά)ώ 13 | ξεκινούσα | ξεκίνησα | θα ξεκινίσω<br>να ξεκινίσω | έχω ξεκινίσει<br>είχα ξεκινίσει | ξεκίνα<br>ξεκινάτε | ξεκίνησε<br>ξεκινήστε |
| **I startle** | ξαφνιάζω 13 | ξάφνιαζα | ξάφνιασα | θα ξαφνιάσω<br>να ξαφνιάσω | έχω ξαφνιάσει<br>είχα ξαφνιάσει | ξάφνιαζε<br>ξαφνιάζετε | ξάφνιασε<br>ξαφνιάστε |

| English Verb | Present | Imperfect | Past | Simple Future<br>Simple Subjunctive | Present Perfect<br>Past Perfect | Continuous Imperative | Simple Imperative |
|---|---|---|---|---|---|---|---|
| **I starve** | λιμοκτονώ 17 | λιμοκτονούσα | λιμοκτόνησα | θα λιμοκτονήσω<br>να λιμοκτονήσω | έχω λιμοκτονήσει<br>είχα λιμοκτονήσει | να λιμοκτονείς<br>λιμοκτονείτε | λιμοκτόνησε<br>λιμοκτονήστε |
| **I state** | διασαφηνίζω 13 | διασαφήνιζα | διασαφήνισα | θα διασαφηνίσω<br>να διασαφηνίσω | έχω διασαφηνίσει<br>είχα διασαφηνίσει | διασαφήνιζε<br>διασαφηνίζετε | διασαφήνισε<br>διασαφηνίστε |
| **I steal** | κλέβω 13 | έκλεβα | έκλεψα | θα κλέψω<br>να κλέψω | έχω κλέψει<br>είχα κλέψει | κλέβε<br>κλέβετε | κλέψε<br>κλέψτε |
| **I step on** | πατ(ά)ώ 15 | πατούσα | πάτησα | θα πατήσω<br>να πατήσω | έχω πατήσει<br>είχα πατήσει | πάτα<br>πατάτε | πάτησε<br>πατήστε |
| **I sterilize** | αποστειρώνω 13 | αποστείρωνα | αποστείρωσα | θα αποστειρώσω<br>να αποστειρώσω | έχω αποστειρώσει<br>είχα αποστειρώσει | αποστείρωνε<br>αποστειρώνετε | αποστείρωσε<br>αποστειρώστε |
| **I stick** | κολλ(ά)ώ 15 | κολλούσα | κόλλησα | θα κολλήσω<br>να κολλήσω | έχω κολλήσει<br>είχα κολλήσει | κόλλα<br>κολλάτε | κόλλησε<br>κολλήστε |
| **I stimulate** | ερεθίζω 13 | ερέθιζα | ερέθισα | θα ερεθίσω<br>να ερεθίσω | έχω ερεθίσει<br>είχα ερεθίσει | ερέθιζε<br>ερεθίζετε | ερέθισε<br>ερεθίστε |
| **I sting** | κεντρίζω 13 | κέντριζα | κέντρισα | θα κεντρίσω<br>να κεντρίσω | έχω κεντρίσει<br>είχα κεντρίσει | κέντριζε<br>κεντρίζετε | κέντρισε<br>κεντρίστε |
| **I sting** | τσούζω 13 | έτσουζα | έτσουξα | θα τσούξω<br>να τσούξω | έχω τσούξει<br>είχα τσούξει | τσούζε<br>τσούζετε | τσούξε<br>τσούξτε |
| **I stink** | βρωμώ 15 | βρωμούσα | βρώμησα | θα βρωμήσω<br>να βρωμήσω | έχω βρωμήσει<br>είχα βρωμήσει | βρώμα<br>βρωμάτε | βρώμησε<br>βρωμήστε |
| **I stir** | σαλεύω 13 | σάλευα | σάλεψα | θα σαλέψω<br>να σαλέψω | έχω σαλέψει<br>είχα σαλέψει | σάλευε<br>σαλεύετε | σάλεψε<br>σαλέψτε |
| **I stock** | προμηθεύω 13 | προμήθευα | προμήθευσα | θα προμηθεύσω<br>να προμηθεύσω | έχω προμηθεύσει<br>είχα προμηθεύσει | προμήθευε<br>προμηθεύετε | προμήθευσε<br>προμηθεύστε |

| English Verb | Present | Imperfect | Past | Simple Future<br>Simple Subjunctive | Present Perfect<br>Past Perfect | Continuous Imperative | Simple Imperative |
|---|---|---|---|---|---|---|---|
| **I stoop** | σκύβω 13 | έσκυβα | έσκυψα | θα σκύψω<br>να σκύψω | έχω σκύψει<br>είχα σκύψει | σκύβε<br>σκύβετε | σκύψε<br>σκύψτε |
| **I stop** | σταματ(ά)ώ 15 | σταματούσα | σταμάτησα | θα σταματήσω<br>να σταματήσω | έχω σταματήσει<br>είχα σταματήσει | σταμάτα<br>σταματάτε | σταμάτησε<br>σταματήστε |
| **I store** | αποθηκεύω 13 | αποθήκευα | αποθήκευσα | θα αποθηκεύσω<br>να αποθηκεύσω | έχω αποθηκεύσει<br>είχα αποθηκεύσει | αποθήκευε<br>αποθηκεύετε | αποθήκευσε<br>αποθηκεύστε |
| **I strain** | στραγγίζω 13 | στράγγιζα | στράγγισα | θα στραγγίσω<br>να στραγγίσω | έχω στραγγίσει<br>είχα στραγγίσει | στράγγιζε<br>στραγγίζετε | στράγγισε<br>στραγγίστε |
| **I strangle** | στραγγαλίζω 13 | στραγγάλιζα | στραγγάλισα | θα στραγγαλίσω<br>να στραγγαλίσω | έχω στραγγαλίσει<br>είχα στραγγαλίσει | στραγγάλιζε<br>στραγγαλίζετε | στραγγάλισε<br>στραγγαλίστε |
| **I stray** | παραστρατώ 17 | παραστρατούσα | παραστράτησα | θα παραστρατήσω<br>να παραστρατήσω | έχω παραστρατήσει<br>είχα παραστρατήσει | να παραστρατείς<br>παραστρατείτε | παραστράτησε<br>παραστρατήστε |
| **I stream** | ρέω 13 | έρρεα | έρρευσα | θα ρεύσω<br>να ρεύσω | έχω ρεύσει<br>είχα ρεύσει | ρέε<br>ρέετε | ρεύσε<br>ρεύστε |
| **I strengthen** | δυναμώνω 13 | δυνάμωνα | δυνάμωσα | θα δυναμώσω<br>να δυναμώσω | έχω δυναμώσει<br>είχα δυναμώσει | δυνάμωνε<br>δυναμώνετε | δυνάμωσε<br>δυναμώστε |
| **I stretch** | τεντώνω 13 | τέντωνα | τέντωσα | θα τεντώσω<br>να τεντώσω | έχω τεντώσει<br>είχα τεντώσει | τέντωνε<br>τεντώνετε | τέντωσε<br>τεντώστε |
| **I strike** | απεργώ 13 | απεργούσα | απέργησα | θα απεργήσω<br>να απεργήσω | έχω απεργήσει<br>είχα απεργήσει | να απεργείς<br>απεργείτε | απέργησε<br>απεργήστε |
| **I strike** | κεραυνοβολώ 17 | κεραυνοβολούσα | κεραυνοβόλησα | θα κεραυνοβολήσω<br>να κεραυνοβολήσω | έχω κεραυνοβολήσει<br>είχα κεραυνοβολήσει | κεραυνοβόλα<br>κεραυνοβολάτε | κεραυνοβόλησε<br>κεραυνοβολήστε |
| **I strip** | ξεφλουδίζω 13 | ξεφλούδιζα | ξεφλούδισα | θα ξεφλουδίσω<br>να ξεφλουδίσω | έχω ξεφλουδίσει<br>είχα ξεφλουδίσει | ξεφλούδιζε<br>ξεφλουδίζετε | ξεφλούδισε<br>ξεφλουδίστε |

| English Verb | Present | Imperfect | Past | Simple Future<br>Simple Subjunctive | Present Perfect<br>Past Perfect | Continuous Imperative | Simple Imperative |
|---|---|---|---|---|---|---|---|
| **I struggle** | μοχθώ 17 | μοχθούσα | μόχθησα | θα μοχθήσω<br>να μοχθήσω | έχω μοχθήσει<br>είχα μοχθήσει | να μοχθείς<br>μοχθείτε | μόχθησε<br>μοχθήστε |
| **I study** | μελετ(ά)ώ 15 | μελετούσα | μελέτησα | θα μελετήσω<br>να μελετήσω | έχω μελετήσει<br>είχα μελετήσει | μελέτα<br>μελετάτε | μελέτησε<br>μελετήστε |
| **I study** | σπουδάζω 13 | σπούδαζα | σπούδασα | θα σπουδάσω<br>να σπουδάσω | έχω σπουδάσει<br>είχα σπουδάσει | σπούδαζε<br>σπουδάζετε | σπούδασε<br>σπουδάστε |
| **I stumble** | παραπατ(ά)ώ 15 | παραπατούσα | παραπάτησα | θα παραπατήσω<br>να παραπατήσω | έχω παραπατήσει<br>είχα παραπατήσει | παραπάτα<br>παραπατάτε | παραπάτησε<br>παραπατήστε |
| **I stutter** | ψευδίζω 13 | ψεύδιζα | ψεύδισα | θα ψευδίσω<br>να ψευδίσω | έχω ψευδίσει<br>είχα ψευδίσει | ψεύδιζε<br>ψευδίζετε | ψεύδισε<br>ψευδίστε |
| **I subordinate** | *υποτάσσομαι 14* | *υποτασσόμουν* | *υποτάχτηκα* | *θα υποταχτώ*<br>*να υποταχτώ* | *έχω υποταχτεί*<br>*είχα υποταχτεί* | *να υποτάσσεσαι*<br>*υποτάσσεστε* | *υποτάξου*<br>*υποταχτείτε* |
| **I subtract** | αφαιρώ 17 | αφαιρούσα | αφαίρεσα | θα αφαιρέσω<br>να αφαιρέσω | έχω αφαιρέσει<br>είχα αφαιρέσει | να αφαιρείς<br>αφαιρείτε | αφαίρεσε<br>αφαιρέστε |
| **I succeed** | πετυχαίνω 13 | πετύχαινα | πέτυχα | θα πετύχω<br>να πετύχω | έχω πετύχει<br>είχα πετύχει | πετύχαινε<br>πετυχαίνετε | πέτυχε<br>πετύχετε |
| **I succeed** | *διαδέχομαι 14* | *διαδεχόμουν* | *διαδέχτηκα* | *θα διαδεχτώ*<br>*να διαδεχτώ* | *έχω διαδεχτεί*<br>*είχα διαδεχτεί* | *να διαδέχεσαι*<br>*διαδέχεστε* | *διαδέξου*<br>*διαδεχτείτε* |
| **I suck** | θηλάζω 13 | θήλαζα | θήλασα | θα θηλάσω<br>να θηλάσω | έχω θηλάσει<br>είχα θηλάσει | θήλαζε<br>θηλάζετε | θήλασε<br>θηλάστε |
| **I suckle** | βυζαίνω 13 | βύζαινα | βύζαξα | θα βυζάξω<br>να βυζάξω | έχω βυζάξει<br>είχα βυζάξει | βύζαινε<br>βυζαίνετε | βύζαξε<br>βυζάξτε |
| **I suffer** | παθαίνω 13 | πάθαινα | έπαθα | θα πάθω<br>να πάθω | έχω πάθει<br>είχα πάθει | πάθαινε<br>παθαίνετε | πάθε<br>πάθετε |

| English Verb | Present | Imperfect | Past | Simple Future<br>Simple Subjunctive | Present Perfect<br>Past Perfect | Continuous Imperative | Simple Imperative |
|---|---|---|---|---|---|---|---|
| **I suggest** | προτείνω 13 | πρότεινα | πρότεινα | θα προτείνω<br>να προτείνω | έχω προτείνει<br>είχα προτείνει | να προτείνεις<br>προτείνετε | πρότεινε<br>προτείντε |
| **I suit** | βολεύω 13 | βόλευα | βόλεψα | θα βολέψω<br>να βολέψω | έχω βολέψει<br>είχα βολέψει | βόλευε<br>βολεύετε | βόλεψε<br>βολέψτε |
| **I sulk** | σκυθροπιάζω 13 | σκυθρόπιαζα | σκυθρόπιασα | θα σκυθροπιάσω<br>να σκυθροπιάσω | έχω σκυθροπιάσει<br>είχα σκυθροπιάσει | σκυθρόπιαζε<br>σκυθροπιάζετε | σκυθρόπιασε<br>σκυθροπιάστε |
| **I summarize** | συνοψίζω 13 | συνόψιζα | συνόψισα | θα συνοψίσω<br>να συνοψίσω | έχω συνοψίσει<br>είχα συνοψίσει | συνόψιζε<br>συνοψίζετε | συνόψισε<br>συνοψίστε |
| **I summon** | καλώ 17 | καλούσα | κάλεσα | θα καλέσω<br>να καλέσω | έχω καλέσει<br>είχα καλέσει | να καλείς<br>καλείτε | κάλεσε<br>καλέστε |
| **I supply** | εφοδιάζω 13 | εφοδίαζα | εφοδίασα | θα εφοδιάσω<br>να εφοδιάσω | έχω εφοδιάσει<br>είχα εφοδιάσει | εφοδίαζε<br>εφοδιάζετε | εφοδιάστε<br>εφοδιάστε |
| **I support** | υποστηρίζω 13 | υποστήριζα | υποστήριξα | θα υποστηρίξω<br>να υποστηρίξω | έχω υποστηρίξει<br>είχα υποστηρίξει | υποστήριζε<br>υποστηρίζετε | υποστήριξε<br>υποστηρίξτε |
| **I surface** | *αναδύομαι 14* | *αναδυόμουν* | *αναδύθηκα* | *θα αναδυθώ*<br>*να αναδυθώ* | *έχω αναδυθεί*<br>*είχα αναδυθεί* | *να αναδύεσαι*<br>*αναδύεστε* | *αναδύσου*<br>*αναδυθείτε* |
| **I suppose** | υποθέτω 13 | υπέθετα | υπέθεσα | θα υποθέσω<br>να υποθέσω | έχω υποθέσει<br>είχα υποθέσει | υπόθετε<br>υποθέτετε | υπόθεσε<br>υποθέστε |
| **I surmount** | υπερνικώ 15 | υπερνικούσα | υπερνίκησα | θα υπερνικήσω<br>να υπερνικήσω | έχω υπερνικήσει<br>είχα υπερνικήσει | υπερνίκα<br>υπερνικάτε | υπερνίκησε<br>υπερνικήστε |
| **I surpass** | ξεπερνώ 15 | ξεπερνούσα | ξεπέρασα | θα ξεπεράσω<br>να ξεπεράσω | έχω ξεπεράσει<br>είχα ξεπεράσει | ξεπέρνα<br>ξεπερνάτε | ξεπέρασε<br>ξεπεράστε |
| **I surprise** | εκπλήσσω 13 | εξέπλησσα | εξέπληξα | θα εκπλήξω<br>να εκπλήξω | έχω εκπλήξει<br>είχα εκπλήξει | να εκπλήσσεις<br>εκπλήσσετε | έκπληξε<br>εκπλήξτε |

| English Verb | Present | Imperfect | Past | Simple Future Simple Subjunctive | Present Perfect Past Perfect | Continuous Imperative | Simple Imperative |
|---|---|---|---|---|---|---|---|
| **I surrender** | *παραδίδομαι 14* | *παραδιδόμουν* | *παραδόθηκα* | *θα παραδοθώ*<br>*να παραδοθώ* | *έχω παραδοθεί*<br>*είχα παραδοθεί* | *να παραδίδεσαι*<br>*παραδίδεστε* | *παραδόσου*<br>*παραδοθείτε* |
| **I surround** | περιβάλλω 13 | περιέβαλλα | περιέβαλα | θα περιβάλω<br>να περιβάλω | έχω περιβάλει<br>είχα περιβάλει | περίβαλλε<br>περιβάλλετε | περίβαλε<br>περιβάλτε |
| **I surround** (encircle) | περικυκλώνω 13 | περικύκλωνα | περικύκλωσα | θα περικυκλώσω<br>να περικυκλώσω | έχω περικυκλώσει<br>είχα περικυκλώσει | περικύκλωνε<br>περικυκλώνετε | περικύκλωσε<br>περικυκλώστε |
| **I surround** (frame) | πλαισιώνω 13 | πλαισίωνα | πλαισίωσα | θα πλαισιώσω<br>να πλαισιώσω | έχω πλαισιώσει<br>είχα πλαισιώσει | πλαισίωνε<br>πλαισιώνετε | πλαισίωσε<br>πλαισιώστε |
| **I survive** | επιζώ 17 | επιζούσα | επέζησα | θα επιζήσω<br>να επιζήσω | έχω επιζήσει<br>είχα επιζήσει | να επιζείς<br>επιζείτε | επίζησε<br>επιζήστε |
| **I suspect** | *υποπτεύομαι 14* | *υποπτευόμουν* | *υποπτεύθηκα* | *θα υποπτευθώ*<br>*να υποπτευθώ* | *έχω υποπτευθεί*<br>*είχα υποπτευθεί* | *να υποπτεύεσαι*<br>*υποπτεύεστε* | *υποπτεύσου*<br>*υποπτευθείτε* |
| **I suspend** | *κρέμομαι 14* | *κρεμόμουν* | *κρεμάστηκα* | *θα κρεμαστώ*<br>*να κρεμαστώ* | *έχω κρεμαστεί*<br>*είχα κρεμαστεί* | *να κρέμεσαι*<br>*κρέμεστε* | *κρεμάσου*<br>*κρεμαστείτε* |
| **I suspend** (delay / stop) | αναστέλλω 13 | ανάστειλλα | ανάστειλα | θα αναστείλω<br>να αναστείλω | έχω αναστείλει<br>είχα αναστείλει | να αναστέλλεις<br>αναστέλλετε | ανάστειλε<br>αναστείλτε |
| **I swallow** | καταπίνω 13 | κατάπινα | κατάπια | θα καταπιώ<br>να καταπιώ | έχω καταπιεί<br>είχα καταπιεί | κατάπινε<br>καταπίνετε | κατάπιε<br>καταπιείτε |
| **I swallow** | ρουφώ 15 | ρουφούσα | ρούφηξα | θα ρουφήξω<br>να ρουφήξω | έχω ρουφήξει<br>είχα ρουφήξει | ρούφα<br>ρουφάτε | ρούφηξε<br>ρουφήξτε |
| **I sway** | τρεκλίζω 13 | τρέκλιζα | τρέκλισα | θα τρεκλίσω<br>να τρεκλίσω | έχω τρεκλίσει<br>είχα τρεκλίσει | τρέκλιζε<br>τρεκλίζετε | τρέκλισε<br>τρεκλίστε |
| **I swear** (curse) | βρίζω 13 | έβριζα | έβρισα | θα βρίσω<br>να βρίσω | έχω βρίσει<br>είχα βρίσει | βρίζε<br>βρίζετε | βρίσε<br>βρίστε |

| English Verb | Present | Imperfect | Past | Simple Future<br>Simple Subjunctive | Present Perfect<br>Past Perfect | Continuous Imperative | Simple Imperative |
|---|---|---|---|---|---|---|---|
| **I swear** (take an oath) | *ορκίζομαι 14* | *ορκιζόμουν* | *ορκίστηκα* | *θα ορκιστώ*<br>*να ορκιστώ* | *έχω ορκιστεί*<br>*είχα ορκιστεί* | *να ορκίζεσαι*<br>*ορκίζεστε* | *ορκίσου*<br>*ορκιστείτε* |
| **I sweat** | ιδρώνω 13 | ίδρωνα | ίδρωσα | θα ιδρώσω<br>να ιδρώσω | έχω ιδρώσει<br>είχα ιδρώσει | ίδρωνε<br>ιδρώνετε | ίδρωσε<br>ιδρώστε |
| **I sweep** | σκουπίζω 13 | σκούπιζα | σκούπισα | θα σκουπίσω<br>να σκουπίσω | έχω σκουπίσει<br>είχα σκουπίσει | σκούπιζε<br>σκουπίζετε | σκούπισε<br>σκουπίστε |
| **I swell** | *πρήζομαι 14* | *πρηζόμουν* | *πρήστηκα* | *θα πρηστώ*<br>*να πρηστώ* | *έχω πρηστεί*<br>*είχα πρηστεί* | *να πρήζεσαι*<br>*πρήζεστε* | *πρήξου*<br>*πρηστείτε* |
| **I swerve** | λοξοδρομώ 17 | λοξοδρομούσα | λοξοδρόμησα | θα λοξοδρομήσω<br>να λοξοδρομήσω | έχω λοξοδρομήσει<br>είχα λοξοδρομήσει | να λοξοδρομείς<br>λοξοδρομείτε | λοξοδρόμησε<br>λοξοδρομήστε |
| **I swim** | κολυμπ(ά)ώ 15 | κολυμπούσα | κολύμπησα | θα κολυμπήσω<br>να κολυμπήσω | έχω κολυμπήσει<br>είχα κολυμπήσει | κολύμπα<br>κολυμπάτε | κολύμπησε<br>κολυμπήστε |
| **I symbolise** | συμβολίζω 13 | συμβόλιζα | συμβόλισα | θα συμβολίσω<br>να συμβολίσω | έχω συμβολίσει<br>είχα συμβολίσει | συμβόλιζε<br>συμβολίζετε | συμβόλισε<br>συμβολίστε |
| **I sympathise with** | συμπον(ά)ώ 15 | συμπονούσα | συμπόνεσα | θα συμπονέσω<br>να συμπονέσω | έχω συμπονέσει<br>είχα συμπονέσει | συμπόνα<br>συμπονάτε | συμπόνεσε<br>συμπονέστε |
| **I synchronize** | συγχρονίζω 13 | συγχρόνιζα | συγχρόνισα | θα συγχρονίσω<br>να συγχρονίσω | έχω συγχρονίσει<br>είχα συγχρονίσει | συχρόνιζε<br>συχρονίζετε | συχρόνισε<br>συχρονίστε |
| **I taint** | αλλοιώνω 13 | αλλοίωνα | αλλοίωσα | θα αλλοιώσω<br>να αλλοιώσω | έχω αλλοιώσει<br>είχα αλλοιώσει | αλλοίωνε<br>αλλοιώνετε | αλλοίωσε<br>αλλοιώστε |
| **I take** | παίρνω 13 | έπαιρνα | πήρα | θα πάρω<br>να πάρω | έχω πάρει<br>είχα πάρει | παίρνε<br>παίρνετε | πάρε<br>πάρτε |
| **I take a bath** | *λούζομαι 14* | *λουζόμουν* | *λούστηκα* | *θα λουστώ*<br>*να λουστώ* | *έχω λουστεί*<br>*είχα λουστεί* | *να λούζεσαι*<br>*λούζεστε* | *λούσου*<br>*λουστείτε* |

| English Verb | Present | Imperfect | Past | Simple Future<br>Simple Subjunctive | Present Perfect<br>Past Perfect | Continuous Imperative | Simple Imperative |
|---|---|---|---|---|---|---|---|
| **I take off/out** | βγάζω 13 | έβγαζα | έβγαλα | θα βγάλω<br>να βγάλω | έχω βγάλει<br>είχα βγάλει | βγάζε<br>βγάζετε | βγάλε<br>βγάλ(ε)τε |
| **I talk** | ομιλ(ά)ώ 15 | ομιλούσα | ομίλησα | θα ομιλήσω<br>να ομιλήσω | έχω ομιλήσει<br>είχα ομιλήσει | ομίλα<br>ομιλάτε | ομίλησε<br>ομιλήστε |
| **I tame** | δαμάζω 13 | δάμαζα | δάμασα | θα δαμάσω<br>να δαμάσω | έχω δαμάσει<br>είχα δαμάσει | δάμαζε<br>δαμάζετε | δάμασε<br>δαμάστε |
| **I tan** | μαυρίζω 13 | μαύριζα | μαύρισα | θα μαυρίσω<br>να μαυρίσω | έχω μαυρίσει<br>είχα μαυρίσει | μαύριζε<br>μαυρίζετε | μαύρισε<br>μαυρίστε |
| **I taperecord** | μαγνητο-<br>φωνώ 17 | μαγνητο-<br>φωνούσα | μαγνητο-<br>φώνησα | θα μαγνητοφωνήσω<br>να μαγνητοφωνήσω | έχω μαγνητοφωνήσει<br>είχα μαγνητοφωνήσει | να μαγνητοφωνείς<br>μαγνητοφωνείτε | μαγνητοφώνησε<br>μαγνητοφωνήστε |
| **I taste** | δοκιμάζω 13 | δοκίμαζα | δοκίμασα | θα δοκιμάσω<br>να δοκιμάσω | έχω δοκιμάσει<br>είχα δοκιμάσει | δοκίμαζε<br>δοκιμάζετε | δοκίμασε<br>δοκιμάστε |
| **I taste** | *γεύομαι 14* | *γευόμουν* | *γεύτηκα* | *θα γευτώ*<br>*να γευτώ* | *έχω γευτεί*<br>*είχα γευτεί* | *να γεύεσαι*<br>*γεύεστε* | *γεύσου*<br>*γευτείτε* |
| **I teach** | διδάσκω 13 | δίδασκα | δίδαξα | θα διδάξω<br>να διδάξω | έχω διδάξει<br>είχα διδάξει | δίδασκε<br>διδάσκετε | δίδαξε<br>διδάξτε |
| **I teach** | δασκαλεύω 13 | δασκάλευα | δασκάλεψα | θα δασκαλέψω<br>να δασκαλέψω | έχω δασκαλέψει<br>είχα δασκαλέψει | δασκάλευε<br>δασκαλεύετε | δασκάλεψε<br>δασκαλέψτε |
| **I tear** | σκίζω 13 | έσκιζα | έσκισα | θα σκίσω<br>να σκίσω | έχω σκίσει<br>είχα σκίσει | σκίζε<br>σκίζετε | σκίσε<br>σκίστε |
| **I tease** | πειράζω 13 | πείραζα | πείραξα | θα πειράξω<br>να πειράξω | έχω πειράξει<br>είχα πειράξει | πείραζε<br>πειράζετε | πείραξε<br>πειράξτε |
| **I telephone** | τηλεφωνώ 17 | τηλεφωνούσα | τηλεφώνησα | θα τηλεφωνήσω<br>να τηλεφωνήσω | έχω τηλεφωνήσει<br>είχα τηλεφωνήσει | να τηλεφωνείς<br>τηλεφωνείτε | τηλεφώνησε<br>τηλεφωνήστε |

| English Verb | Present | Imperfect | Past | Simple Future<br>Simple Subjunctive | Present Perfect<br>Past Perfect | Continuous Imperative | Simple Imperative |
|---|---|---|---|---|---|---|---|
| **I tell** | λέω 20 | έλεγα | είπα | θα πω<br>να πω | έχω πει<br>είχα πει | λέγε<br>λέγετε | πες<br>πέστε |
| **I tempt** | δελεάζω 13 | δελέαζα | δελέασα | θα δελεάσω<br>να δελεάσω | έχω δελεάσει<br>είχα δελεάσει | δελέαζε<br>δελεάζετε | δελέασε<br>δελεάστε |
| **I terminate** | τερματίζω 13 | τερμάτιζα | τερμάτισα | θα τερματίσω<br>να τερματίσω | έχω τερματίσει<br>είχα τερματίσει | τερμάτιζε<br>τερματίζετε | τερμάτισε<br>τερματίστε |
| **I terrorize** | τρομοκρατώ 15 | τρομοκρατούσα | τρομοκράτησα | θα τρομοκρατήσω<br>να τρομοκρατήσω | έχω τρομοκρατήσει<br>είχα τρομοκρατήσει | τρομοκράτα<br>τρομοκρατάτε | τρομοκράτησε<br>τρομοκρατήστε |
| **I testify** | καταθέτω 13 | κατέθετα | κατέθεσα | θα καταθέσω<br>να καταθέσω | έχω καταθέσει<br>είχα καταθέσει | κατάθετε<br>καταθέτετε | κατάθεσε<br>καταθέστε |
| **I thank** | ευχαριστώ 17 | ευχαριστούσα | ευχαρίστησα | θα ευχαριστήσω<br>να ευχαριστήσω | έχω ευχαριστήσει<br>είχα ευχαριστήσει | να ευχαριστείς<br>ευχαριστείτε | ευχαρίστησε<br>ευχαριστήστε |
| **I think** | νομίζω 13 | νόμιζα | νόμισα | θα νομίσω<br>να νομίσω | έχω νομίσει<br>είχα νομίσει | νόμιζε<br>νομίζετε | νόμισε<br>νομίστε |
| **I think**<br>(about s'g) | *σκέφτομαι 14* | *σκεφτόμουν* | *σκέφτηκα* | *θα σκεφτώ*<br>*να σκεφτώ* | *έχω σκεφτεί*<br>*είχα σκεφτεί* | *να σκέφτεσαι*<br>*σκέφτεστε* | *σκέψου*<br>*σκεφτείτε* |
| **I am thirsty** | διψώ 15 | διψούσα | δίψασα | θα διψάσω<br>να διψάσω | έχω διψάσει<br>είχα διψάσει | δίψα<br>διψάτε | δίψασε<br>διψάστε |
| **I thrash** | κατατροπώνω 13 | κατατρόπωνα | κατατρόπωσα | θα κατατροπώσω<br>να κατατροπώσω | έχω κατατροπώσει<br>είχα κατατροπώσει | κατατρόπωνε<br>κατατροπώνετε | κατατρόπωσε<br>κατατροπώστε |
| **I threaten** | απειλώ 17 | απειλούσα | απείλησα | θα απειλήσω<br>να απειλήσω | έχω απειλήσει<br>είχα απειλήσει | να απειλείς<br>απειλείτε | απείλησε<br>απειλήστε |
| **I thrive** | προκόβω 13 | πρόκοβα | πρόκοψα | θα προκόψω<br>να προκόψω | έχω προκόψει<br>είχα προκόψει | πρόκοβε<br>προκόβετε | πρόκοψε<br>προκόψτε |

| English Verb | Present | Imperfect | Past | Simple Future<br>Simple Subjunctive | Present Perfect<br>Past Perfect | Continuous Imperative | Simple Imperative |
|---|---|---|---|---|---|---|---|
| **I throw** | πετ(ά)ώ 15 | πετούσα | πέταξα | θα πετάξω<br>να πετάξω | έχω πετάξει<br>είχα πετάξει | πέτα<br>πετάτε | πέταξε<br>πετάξτε |
| **I tickle** | γαργαλ(ά)ώ 15 | γαργαλούσα | γαργάλησα | θα γαργαλήσω<br>να γαργαλήσω | έχω γαργαλήσει<br>είχα γαργαλήσει | γαργάλα<br>γαργαλάτε | γαργάλησε<br>γαργαλήστε |
| **I tie** | δένω 13 | έδενα | έδεσα | θα δέσω<br>να δέσω | έχω δέσει<br>είχα δέσει | δένε<br>δένετε | δέσε<br>δέστε |
| **I tilt** | γέρνω 13 | έγερνα | έγειρα | θα γείρω<br>να γείρω | έχω γείρει<br>είχα γείρει | γέρνε<br>γέρνετε | γείρε<br>γείρτε |
| **I time** | χρονομετρώ 15 | χρονομετρούσα | χρονομέτρησα | θα χρονομετρήσω<br>να χρονομετρήσω | έχω χρονομετρήσει<br>είχα χρονομετρήσει | χρονομέτρα<br>χρονομετράτε | χρονομέτρησε<br>χρονομετρήστε |
| **I tire** | κουράζω 13 | κούραζα | κούρασα | θα κουράσω<br>να κουράσω | έχω κουράσει<br>είχα κουράσει | κούραζε<br>κουράζετε | κούρασε<br>κουράστε |
| **I am tired** | *κουράζομαι 14* | *κουραζόμουν* | *κουράστηκα* | *θα κουραστώ*<br>*να κουραστώ* | *έχω κουραστεί*<br>*είχα κουραστεί* | *να κουράζεσαι*<br>*κουράζεστε* | *κουράσου*<br>*κουραστείτε* |
| **I torment** | τυραννώ(ά)ώ 15 | τυραννούσα | τυράννησα | θα τυραννήσω<br>να τυραννήσω | έχω τυραννήσει<br>είχα τυραννήσει | τυράννα<br>τυραννάτε | τυράννησε<br>τυραννήστε |
| **I torture** | βασανίζω 13 | βασάνιζα | βασάνισα | θα βασανίζω<br>να βασανίζω | έχω βασανίζει<br>είχα βασανίζει | βασάνιζε<br>βασανίζετε | βασάνισε<br>βασανίστε |
| **I touch** | αγγίζω 13 | άγγιζα | άγγιξα | θα αγγίξω<br>να αγγίξω | έχω αγγίξει<br>είχα αγγίξει | άγγιζε<br>αγγίζετε | άγγιξε<br>αγγίξτε |
| **I touch** | ψηλαφίζω 13 | ψηλάφιζα | ψηλάφισα | θα ψηλαφίσω<br>να ψηλαφίσω | έχω ψηλαφίσει<br>είχα ψηλαφίσει | ψηλάφιζε<br>ψηλαφίζετε | ψηλάφισε<br>ψηλαφίστε |
| **I am touched** (moved) | *συγκινούμαι 18* | *συγκινούμουν* | *συγκινήθηκα* | *θα συγκινηθώ*<br>*να συγκινηθώ* | *έχω συγκινηθεί*<br>*είχα συγκινηθεί* | *να συγκινείσαι*<br>*συγκινείστε* | *συγκινήσου*<br>*συγκινηθείτε* |

| English Verb | Present | Imperfect | Past | Simple Future<br>Simple Subjunctive | Present Perfect<br>Past Perfect | Continuous Imperative | Simple Imperative |
|---|---|---|---|---|---|---|---|
| **I tour** | περιοδεύω 13 | περιόδευα | περιόδευσα | θα περιοδεύσω<br>να περιοδεύσω | έχω περιοδεύσει<br>είχα περιοδεύσει | περιόδευε<br>περιοδεύετε | περιόδευσε<br>περιοδεύστε |
| **I tow** | ρυμουλκώ 17 | ρυμουλκούσα | ρυμούλκησα | θα ρυμουλκήσω<br>να ρυμουλκήσω | έχω ρυμουλκήσει<br>είχα ρυμουλκήσει | να ρυμουλκείς<br>ρυμουλκείτε | ρυμούλκησε<br>ρυμουλκήστε |
| **I trace** | εξιχνιάζω 13 | εξιχνίαζα | εξιχνίασα | θα εξιχνιάσω<br>να εξιχνιάσω | έχω εξιχνιάσει<br>είχα εξιχνιάσει | εξιχνίαζε<br>εξιχνιάζετε | εξιχνίασε<br>εξιχνιάστε |
| **I trade** | *εμπορεύομαι 14* | *εμπορευόμουν* | *εμπορεύτηκα* | *θα εμπορευτώ*<br>*να εμπορευτώ* | *έχω εμπορευτεί*<br>*είχα εμπορευτεί* | *να εμπορεύεσαι*<br>*εμπορεύεστε* | *εμπορεύσου*<br>*εμπορευτείτε* |
| **I am trained** | *εκπαιδεύομαι 14* | *εκπαιδευόμουν* | *εκπαιδεύτηκα* | *θα εκπαιδευτώ*<br>*να εκπαιδευτώ* | *έχω εκπαιδευτεί*<br>*είχα εκπαιδευτεί* | *να εκπαιδεύεσαι*<br>*εκπαιδεύεστε* | *εκπαιδεύσου*<br>*εκπαιδευτείτε* |
| **I transfer** | μεταφέρω 13 | μετέφερα | μετέφερα | θα μεταφέρω<br>να μεταφέρω | έχω μεταφέρει<br>είχα μεταφέρει | να μεταφέρεις<br>μεταφέρετε | μετάφερε<br>μεταφέρτε |
| **I transform** | μεταμορφώνω 13 | μεταμόρφωνα | μεταμόρφωσα | θα μεταμορφώσω<br>να μεταμορφώσω | έχω μεταμορφώσει<br>είχα μεταμορφώσει | μεταμόρφωνε<br>μεταμορφώνετε | μεταμόρφωσε<br>μεταμορφώστε |
| **I transgress** | παραβαίνω 13 | παρέβαινα | παρέβηκα | θα παραβώ<br>να παραβώ | έχω παραβεί<br>είχα παραβεί | παράβαινε<br>παραβαίνετε | να παραβείς<br>παραβείτε |
| **I am in transit** | *μετακινούμαι 18* | *μετακινούμουν* | *μετακινήθηκα* | *θα μετακινηθώ*<br>*να μετακινηθώ* | *έχω μετακινηθεί*<br>*είχα μετακινηθεί* | *να μετακινείσαι*<br>*μετακινείστε* | *μετακινήσου*<br>*μετακινηθείτε* |
| **I translate** | μεταφράζω 13 | μετάφραζα | μετέφρασα | θα μεταφράσω<br>να μεταφράσω | έχω μεταφράσει<br>είχα μεταφράσει | μετάφραζε<br>μεταφράζετε | μετάφρασε<br>μεταφράστε |
| **I transmit** | μεταδίδω 13 | μετέδιδα | μετέδωσα | θα μεταδώσω<br>να μεταδώσω | έχω μεταδώσει<br>είχα μεταδώσει | μετάδιδε<br>μεταδίδετε | μετάδωσε<br>μεταδώστε |
| **I transpire** | διαπνέω 13 | διέπνεα | διέπνευσα | θα διαπνεύσω<br>να διαπνεύσω | έχω διαπνεύσει<br>είχα διαπνεύσει | διάπνεε<br>διαπνέετε | διάπνευσε<br>διαπνεύστε |

| English Verb | Present | Imperfect | Past | Simple Future<br>Simple Subjunctive | Present Perfect<br>Past Perfect | Continuous Imperative | Simple Imperative |
|---|---|---|---|---|---|---|---|
| **I transport** | μετακομίζω 13 | ματακόμιζα | μετακόμισα | θα μετακομίσω<br>να μετακομίσω | έχω μετακομίσει<br>είχα μετακομίσει | μετακόμιζε<br>μετακομίζετε | μετακόμισε<br>μετακομίστε |
| **I trap** | παγιδεύω 13 | παγίδευα | παγίδεψα | θα παγιδέψω<br>να παγιδέψω | έχω παγιδέψει<br>είχα παγιδέψει | παγίδευε<br>παγιδεύετε | παγίδεψε<br>παγιδέψτε |
| **I travel** | ταξιδεύω 13 | ταξίδευα | ταξίδεψα | θα ταξιδέψω<br>να ταξιδέψω | έχω ταξιδέψει<br>είχα ταξιδέψει | ταξίδευε<br>ταξιδεύετε | ταξίδεψε<br>ταξιδέψτε |
| **I tread on** | τσαλαπατώ 15 | τσαλαπατούσα | τσαλαπάτησα | θα τσαλαπατήσω<br>να τσαλαπατήσω | έχω τσαλαπατήσει<br>είχα τσαλαπατήσει | τσαλαπάτα<br>τσαλαπατάτε | τσαλαπάτησε<br>τσαλαπατήστε |
| **I treat** | κερν(ά)ώ 15 | κερνούσα | κέρασα | θα κεράσω<br>να κεράσω | έχω κεράσει<br>είχα κεράσει | κέρνα<br>κερνάτε | κέρασε<br>κεράστε |
| **I treat**<br>(use / handle) | *μεταχειρίζομαι 14* | *μεταχειριζόμουν* | *μεταχειρίστηκα* | *θα μεταχειριστώ*<br>*να μεταχειριστώ* | *έχω μεταχειριστεί*<br>*είχα μεταχειριστεί* | *να μεταχειρίζεσαι*<br>*μεταχειρίζεστε* | *μεταχειρίσου*<br>*μεταχειριστείτε* |
| **I treble** | τριπλασιάζω 13 | τραπλασίαζα | τριπλασίασα | θα τριπλασιάσω<br>να τριπλασιάσω | έχω τριπλασιάσει<br>είχα τριπλασιάσει | τριπλασίαζε<br>τριπλασιάζετε | τριπλασίασε<br>τριπλασιάστε |
| **I tremble** | τρέμω 13 | έτρεμα | έτρεμα | θα τρέμω<br>να τρέμω | – | να τρέμεις<br>τρέμετε | τρέμε<br>τρέμετε |
| **I triumph** | θριαμβεύω 13 | θριάμβευα | θριάμβευσα | θα θριαμβεύσω<br>να θριαμβεύσω | έχω θριαμβεύσει<br>είχα θριαμβεύσει | θριάμβευε<br>θριαμβεύετε | θριάμευσε<br>θριαμβεύστε |
| **I try** | δικάζω 13 | δίκαζα | δίκασα | θα δικάσω<br>να δικάσω | έχω δικάσει<br>είχα δικάσει | δίκαζε<br>δικάζετε | δίκασε<br>δικάστε |
| **I turn**<br>(page/key) | γυρν(ά)ώ 15<br>γυρίζω 13 | γυρνούσα | γύρισα | θα γυρίσω<br>να γυρίσω | έχω γυρίσει<br>είχα γυρίσει | γύρνα<br>γυρνάτε | γύρισε<br>γυρίστε |
| **I twist** | στρίβω 13 | έστριβα | έστριψα | θα στρίψω<br>να στρίψω | έχω στρίψει<br>είχα στρίψει | στρίβε<br>στρίβετε | στρίψε<br>στίψτε |

| English Verb | Present | Imperfect | Past | Simple Future<br>Simple Subjunctive | Present Perfect<br>Past Perfect | Continuous Imperative | Simple Imperative |
|---|---|---|---|---|---|---|---|
| **I twist** | διαστρεβλώνω 13 | διαστρέβλωνα | διαστρέβλωσα | θα διαστρεβλώσω<br>να διαστρεβλώσω | έχω διαστρεβλώσει<br>είχα διαστρεβλώσει | διαστρέβλωνε<br>διαστρεβλώνετε | διαστρέβλωσε<br>διαστρεβλώστε |
| **I type** | δακτυλο-<br>γραφώ 17 | δακτυλο-<br>γραφούσα | δακτυλο-<br>γράφησα | θα δακτυλογραφήσω<br>να δακτυλογραφήσω | έχω δακτυλογραφήσει<br>είχα δακτυλογραφήσει | να δακτυλογραφείς<br>δακτυλογραφείτε | δακτυλογράφησε<br>δακτυλογραφήστε |
| **I underline** | υπογραμμίζω 13 | υπογράμμιζα | υπογράμμισα | θα υπογραμμίσω<br>να υπογραμμίσω | έχω υπογραμμίσει<br>είχα υπογραμμίσει | υπογράμμιζε<br>υπογραμμίζετε | υπογράμμισε<br>υπογραμμίστε |
| **I underrate** | υποτιμ(ά)ώ 15 | υποτιμούσα | υποτίμησα | θα υποτιμήσω<br>να υποτιμήσω | έχω υποτιμήσει<br>είχα υποτιμήσει | υποτίμα<br>υποτιμάτε | υποτίμησε<br>υποτιμήστε |
| **I understand** | καταλαβαίνω 13 | καταλάβαινα | κατάλαβα | θα καταλάβω<br>να καταλάβω | έχω καταλάβει<br>είχα καταλάβει | καταλάβαινε<br>καταλαβαίνετε | κατάλαβε<br>καταλάβετε |
| **I undertake** | αναλαμβάνω 13 | αναλάμβανα | ανέλαβα | θα αναλάβω<br>να αναλάβω | έχω αναλάβει<br>είχα αναλάβει | αναλάμβανε<br>αναλαμβάνετε | ανάλαβε<br>αναλάβετε |
| **I undress** | γδύνω 13 | έγδυνα | έγδυσα | θα γδύσω<br>να γδύσω | έχω γδύσει<br>είχα γδύσει | γδύνε<br>γδύνετε | γδύσε<br>γδύστε |
| **I am unfair** | αδικώ 17 | αδικούσα | αδίκησα | θα αδικήσω<br>να αδικήσω | έχω αδικήσει<br>είχα αδικήσει | να αδικείς<br>αδικείτε | αδίκησε<br>αδικήστε |
| **I unfasten** | ξεκουμπώνω 13 | ξεκούμπωνα | ξεκούμπωσα | θα ξεκουμπώσω<br>να ξεκουμπώσω | έχω ξεκουμπώσει<br>είχα ξεκουμπώσει | ξεκούμπωνε<br>ξεκουμπώνετε | ξεκούμπωσε<br>ξεκουμπώστε |
| **I unfold** | ξετυλίγω 13 | ξετύλιγα | ξετύλιξα | θα ξετυλίξω<br>να ξετυλίξω | έχω ξετυλίξει<br>είχα ξετυλίξει | ξετύλιγε<br>ξετυλίγετε | ξετύλιξε<br>ξετυλίξτε |
| **I unglue** | ξεκολλώ 15 | ξεκολλούσα | ξεκόλλησα | θα ξεκολλήσω<br>να ξεκολλήσω | έχω ξεκολλήσει<br>είχα ξεκολλήσει | ξεκόλλα<br>ξεκολλάτε | ξεκόλλησε<br>ξεκολλήστε |
| **I unite** | ενώνω 13 | ένωνα | ένωσα | θα ενώσω<br>να ενώσω | έχω ενώσει<br>είχα ενώσει | ένωνε<br>ενώνετε | ένωσε<br>ενώστε |

| English Verb | Present | Imperfect | Past | Simple Future<br>Simple Subjunctive | Present Perfect<br>Past Perfect | Continuous Imperative | Simple Imperative |
|---|---|---|---|---|---|---|---|
| **I unleash** | ξαμολ(ά)ώ 15 | ξαμολούσα | ξαμόλησα | θα ξαμολήσω<br>να ξαμολήσω | έχω ξαμολήσει<br>είχα ξαμολήσει | ξαμόλα<br>ξαμολάτε | ξαμόλησε<br>ξαμολήστε |
| **I unload** | ξεφορτώνω 13 | ξεφόρτωνα | ξεφόρτωσα | θα ξεφορτώσω<br>να ξεφορτώσω | έχω ξεφορτώσει<br>είχα ξεφορτώσει | ξεφόρτωνε<br>ξεφορτώνετε | ξεφόρτωσε<br>ξεφορτώστε |
| **I unlock** | ξεκλειδώνω 13 | ξεκλείδωνα | ξεκλείδωσα | θα ξεκλειδώσω<br>να ξεκλειδώσω | έχω ξεκλειδώσει<br>είχα ξεκλειδώσει | ξεκλείδωνε<br>ξεκλειδώνετε | ξεκλείδωσε<br>ξεκλειδώστε |
| **I unpack** | ξεπακετάρω 13 | ξεπακέταρα | ξεπακετάρησα | θα ξεπακετάρω<br>να ξεπακετάρω | έχω ξεπακετάρει<br>είχα ξεπακετάρει | ξεπακέταρε<br>ξεπακετάρετε | ξεπακετάρησε<br>ξεπακετάρήστε |
| **I unravel** | διαλευκαίνω 13 | διαλεύκαινα | διαλεύκανα | θα διαλευκάνω<br>να διαλευκώνω | έχω διαλευκάνει<br>είχα διαλευκάνει | διαλεύκαινε<br>διαλευκαίνετε | διαλεύκανε<br>διαλευκάντε |
| **I unstitch** | ξηλώνω 13 | ξήλωνα | ξήλωσα | θα ξηλώσω<br>να ξηλώσω | έχω ξηλώσει<br>είχα ξηλώσει | ξήλωνε<br>ξηλώνετε | ξήλωσε<br>ξηλώστε |
| **I untie** | ξεδένω 13 | ξέδενα | ξέδεσα | θα ξεδέσω<br>να ξεδέσω | έχω ξεδέσει<br>είχα ξεδέσει | ξέδενε<br>ξεδένετε | ξέδεσε<br>ξεδέστε |
| **I unwind** | ξεσκάζω 13 | ξέσκαζα | ξέσκασα | θα ξεσκάσω<br>να ξεσκάσω | έχω ξεσκάσει<br>είχα ξεσκάσει | ξέσκαζε<br>ξεσκάζετε | ξέσκασε<br>ξεσκάστε |
| **I update** | εκσυγχρονίζω 13 | εκσυγχρόνιζα | εκσυγχρόνισα | θα εκσυγχρονίσω<br>να εκσυγχρονίσω | έχω εκσυγχρονίσει<br>είχα εκσυγχρονίσει | εκσυγχρόνιζε<br>εκσυγχρονίζετε | εκσυγχρόνισε<br>εκσυγχρονίστε |
| **I upset** | στενοχωρώ 17 | στενοχωρούσα | στενοχώρησα | θα στενοχωρήσω<br>να στενοχωρήσω | έχω στενοχωρήσει<br>είχα στενοχωρήσει | να στενοχωρείς<br>στενοχωρείτε | στενοχώρησε<br>στενοχωρήστε |
| **I urge** | παρακινώ 17 | παρακινούσα | παρακίνησα | θα παρακινήσω<br>να παρακινήσω | έχω παρακινήσει<br>είχα παρακινήσει | να παρακινείς<br>παρακινείτε | παρακίνησε<br>παρακινήστε |
| **I urge** | προτρέπω 13 | πρότρεπα | πρότρεψα | θα προτρέψω<br>να προτρέψω | έχω προτρέψει<br>είχα προτρέψει | πρότρεπε<br>προτρέπετε | πρότρεψε<br>προτρέψτε |

| English Verb | Present | Imperfect | Past | Simple Future<br>Simple Subjunctive | Present Perfect<br>Past Perfect | Continuous Imperative | Simple Imperative |
|---|---|---|---|---|---|---|---|
| **I urinate** | κατουρ(ά)ώ 15 | κατουρούσα | κατούρησα | θα κατουρήσω<br>να κατουρήσω | έχω κατουρήσει<br>είχα κατουρήσει | κατούρα<br>κατουράτε | κατούρησε<br>κατουρήστε |
| **I use** | χρησιμοποιώ 17 | χρησιμοποιούσα | χρησιμοποίησα | θα χρησιμοποιήσω<br>να χρησιμοποιήσω | έχω χρησιμοποιήσει<br>είχα χρησιμοποιήσει | να χρησιμοποιείς<br>χρησιμοποιείτε | χρησιμοποίησε<br>χρησιμοποιήστε |
| **I utilize** | αξιοποιώ 17 | αξιοποιούσα | αξιοποίησα | θα αξιοποιήσω<br>να αξιοποιήσω | έχω αξιοποιήσει<br>είχα αξιοποιήσει | να αξιοποιείς<br>αξιοποιείτε | αξιοποίησε<br>αξιοποιήστε |
| **I vacate** | εκκενώνω 13 | εκκένωνα | εκκένωσα | θα εκκενώσω<br>να εκκενώσω | έχω εκκενώσει<br>είχα εκκενώσει | εκκένωνε<br>εκκενώνετε | εκκένωσε<br>εκκενώστε |
| **I vaccinate** | εμβολιάζω 13 | εμβολίαζα | εμβολίασα | θα εμβολιάσω<br>να εμβολιάσω | έχω εμβολιάσει<br>είχα εμβολιάσει | εμβολίαζε<br>εμβολιάζετε | εμβολίασε<br>εμβολιάστε |
| **I vacillate** | *ταλλαντεύομαι 14* | *ταλλαντευόμουν* | *ταλλαντεύτηκα* | *θα ταλλαντευτώ*<br>*να ταλλαντευτώ* | *έχω ταλλαντευτεί*<br>*είχα ταλλαντευτεί* | *να ταλλαντεύεσαι*<br>*ταλλαντεύεστε* | *ταλλαντεύσου*<br>*ταλλαντευτείτε* |
| **I validate** | επικυρώνω 13 | επικύρωνα | επικύρωσα | θα επικυρώσω<br>να επικυρώσω | έχω επικυρώσει<br>είχα επικυρώσει | επικύρωνε<br>επικυρώνετε | επικύρωσε<br>επικυρώστε |
| **I value** | εκτιμ(ά)ώ 15 | εκτιμούσα | εκτίμησα | θα εκτιμήσω<br>να εκτιμήσω | έχω εκτιμήσει<br>είχα εκτιμήσει | εκτίμα<br>εκτιμάτε | εκτίμησε<br>εκτιμήστε |
| **I vaporize** | *εξατμίζομαι 14* | *εξατμιζόμουν* | *εξατμίστηκα* | *θα εξατμιστώ*<br>*να εξατμιστώ* | *έχω εξατμιστεί*<br>*είχα εξατμιστεί* | *να εξατμίζεσαι*<br>*εξατμίζεστε* | *εξατμίσου*<br>*εξατμιστείτε* |
| **I vary** | ποικίλλω 13 | ποίκιλλα | ποίκιλα | θα ποικίλω<br>να ποικίλω | έχω ποικίλει<br>είχα ποικίλει | ποίκιλλε<br>ποικίλλετε | ποίκιλε<br>ποικίλτε |
| **I vegetate** | φυτοζωώ 17 | φυτοζωούσα | φυτοζώησα | θα φυτοζωήσω<br>να φυτοζωήσω | έχω φυτοζωήσει<br>είχα φυτοζωήσει | να φυτοζωείς<br>φυτοζωείτε | φυτοζώησε<br>φυτοζωήστε |
| **I vent** (emotions) | ξαλαφρώνω 13 | ξαλάφρωνα | ξαλάφρωσα | θα ξαλαφρώσω<br>να ξαλαφρώσω | έχω ξαλαφρώσει<br>είχα ξαλαφρώσει | ξαλάφρωνε<br>ξαλαφρώνετε | ξαλάφρωσε<br>ξαλαφρώστε |

| English Verb | Present | Imperfect | Past | Simple Future<br>Simple Subjunctive | Present Perfect<br>Past Perfect | Continuous Imperative | Simple Imperative |
|---|---|---|---|---|---|---|---|
| **I ventilate** | εξαερίζω 13 | εξαέριζα | εξαέρισα | θα εξαερίσω<br>να εξαερίσω | έχω εξαερίσει<br>είχα εξαερίσει | εξαέριζε<br>εξαερίζετε | εξαέρισε<br>εξαερίστε |
| **I verify** | επαληθεύω 13 | επαλήθευα | επαλήθευσα | θα επαληθεύσω<br>να επαληθεύσω | έχω επαληθεύσει<br>είχα επαληθεύσει | επαλήθευε<br>επαληθεύετε | επαλήθευσε<br>επαληθεύστε |
| **I vex** | τσατίζω 13 | τσάτιζα | τσάτισα | θα τσατίσω<br>να τσατίσω | έχω τσατίσει<br>είχα τσατίσει | τσάτιζε<br>τσατίζετε | τσάτισε<br>τσατίστε |
| **I vibrate** | δονώ 17 | δονούσα | δόνησα | θα δονήσω<br>να δονήσω | έχω δονήσει<br>είχα δονήσει | να δονείς<br>δονείτε | δόνησε<br>δονήστε |
| **I victimize** | κατατρέχω 13 | κατέτρεχα | κατέτρεξα | θα κατατρέξω<br>να κατατρέξω | έχω κατατρέξει<br>είχα κατατρέξει | κατάτρεχε<br>κατατρέχετε | κατάτρεξε<br>κατατρέξτε |
| **I vindicate** | δικαιώνω 13 | δικαίωνα | δικαίωσα | θα δικαιώσω<br>να δικαιώσω | έχω δικαιώσει<br>είχα δικαιώσει | δικαίωνε<br>δικαιώνετε | δικαίωσε<br>δικαιώστε |
| **I violate** | παραβιάζω 13 | παραβίαζα | παραβίασα | θα παραβιάσω<br>να παραβιάσω | έχω παραβιάσει<br>είχα παραβιάσει | παραβίαζε<br>παραβιάζετε | παραβίασε<br>παραβιάστε |
| **I visit** | *επισκέπτομαι 14* | *επισκεπτόμουν* | *επισκέφτηκα* | *θα επισκεφτώ*<br>*να επισκεφτώ* | *έχω επισκεφτεί*<br>*είχα επισκεφτεί* | *να επισκέπτεσαι*<br>*επισκέπτεστε* | *επισκέψου*<br>*επισκεφτείτε* |
| **I vitalize** | τονώνω 13 | τόνωνα | τόνωσα | θα τονώσω<br>να τονώσω | έχω τονώσει<br>είχα τονώσει | τόνωνε<br>τονώνετε | τόνωσε<br>τονώστε |
| **I volunteer** | *προσφέρομαι 14* | *προσφερόμουν* | *προσφέρθηκα* | *θα προσφερθώ*<br>*να προσφερθώ* | *έχω προσφερθεί*<br>*είχα προσφερθεί* | *να προσφέρεσαι*<br>*προσφέρεστε* | *προσφέρσου*<br>*προσφερθείτε* |
| **I vomit** | ξερν(ά)ώ 15 | ξερνούσα | ξέρασα | θα ξεράσω | έχω ξεράσει<br>είχα ξεράσει | ξέρνα<br>ξερνάτε | ξέρασε<br>ξεράστε |
| **I vote** | ψηφίζω 13 | ψήφιζα | ψήφισα | θα ψηφίσω<br>να ψηφίσω | έχω ψηφίσει<br>είχα ψηφίσει | ψήφιζε<br>ψηφίζετε | ψήφισε<br>ψηφίστε |

| English Verb | Present | Imperfect | Past | Simple Future<br>Simple Subjunctive | Present Perfect<br>Past Perfect | Continuous Imperative | Simple Imperative |
|---|---|---|---|---|---|---|---|
| **I vouch** | βεβαιώ 17 | βεβαιούσα | βεβαίωσα | θα βεβαιώσω<br>να βεβαιώσω | έχω βεβαιώσει<br>είχα βεβαιώσει | βεβαίωνε<br>βεβαιώνετε | βεβαίωσε<br>βεβαιώστε |
| **I vulgarize** | εκχυδαΐζω 13 | εκχυδάϊζα | εκχυδάϊσα | θα εκχυδαίσω<br>να εκχυδαίσω | έχω εκχυδαΐσει<br>είχα εκχυδαΐσει | εκχυδάϊζε<br>εκχυδαΐζετε | εκχυδάϊσε<br>εκχυδαΐστε |
| **I wait** | περιμένω 13 | περίμενα | περίμενα | θα περιμένω<br>να περιμένω | έχω περιμένει<br>είχα περιμένει | να περιμένεις<br>περιμένετε | περίμενε<br>περιμέντε |
| **I wake up** | ξυπν(ά)ώ 15 | ξυπνούσα | ξύπνησα | θα ξυπνήσω<br>να ξυπνήσω | έχω ξυπνήσει<br>είχα ξυπνήσει | ξύπνα<br>ξυπνάτε | ξύπνησε<br>ξυπνήστε |
| **I walk** | περπατ(ά)ώ 15 | περπατούσα | περπάτησα | θα περπατήσω<br>να περπατήσω | έχω περπατήσει<br>είχα περπατήσει | περπάτα<br>περπατάτε | περπάτησε<br>περπατήστε |
| **I wander** | *περιπλανώμαι 42* | *περιπλανόμουν* | *περιπλανήθηκα* | *θα περιπλανηθώ*<br>*να περιπλανηθώ* | *έχω περιπλανηθεί*<br>*είχα περιπλανηθεί* | *να περιπλανάσαι*<br>*περιπλανάστε* | *περιπλανήσου*<br>*περιπλανηθείτε* |
| **I want** | θέλω 13 | ήθελα | θέλησα | θα θελήσω<br>να θελήσω | έχω θελήσει<br>είχα θελήσει | θέλε<br>θέλετε | θέλησε<br>θελήστε |
| **I warn** | προειδοποιώ 17 | προειδοποιούσα | προειδοποίησα | θα προειδοποιήσω<br>να προειδοποιήσω | έχω προειδοποιήσει<br>είχα προειδοποιήσει | να προειδοποιείς<br>προειδοποιείτε | προειδοποίησε<br>προειδοποιήστε |
| **I warrant** | εξουσιοδοτώ 17 | εξιουσιοδοτούσα | εξουσιοδότησα | θα εξουσιοδοτήσω<br>να εξουσιοδοτήσω | έχω εξουσιοδοτήσει<br>είχα εξουσιοδοτήσει | να εξουσιοδοτείς<br>εξουσιοδοτείτε | εξουσιοδότησε<br>εξουσιοδοτήστε |
| **I wash** | πλένω 14 | έπλενα | έπλεινα | θα πλείνω<br>να πλείνω | έχω πλείνει<br>είχα πλείνει | πλένε<br>πλένετε | πλείνε<br>πλείντε |
| **I waste** | σπαταλ(ά)ώ 15 | σπαταλούσα | σπατάλησα | θα σπαταλήσω<br>να σπαταλήσω | έχω σπαταλήσει<br>είχα σπαταλήσει | σπατάλα<br>σπαταλάτε | σπατάλησε<br>σπαταλήστε |
| **I waste** | χαραμίζω 13 | χαράμιζα | χαράμισα | θα χαραμίσω<br>να χαραμίσω | έχω χαραμίσει<br>είχα χαραμίσει | χαράμιζε<br>χαραμίζετε | χαράμισε<br>χαραμίστε |

| English Verb | Present | Imperfect | Past | Simple Future<br>Simple Subjunctive | Present Perfect<br>Past Perfect | Continuous Imperative | Simple Imperative |
|---|---|---|---|---|---|---|---|
| **I watch** | επαγρυπνώ 15 | επαγρυπνούσα | επαγρύπνησα | θα επαγρυπνήσω<br>να επαγρυπνήσω | έχω επαγρυπνήσει<br>είχα επαγρυπνήσει | επαγρύπνα<br>επαγρυπνάτε | επαγρύπνησε<br>επαγρυπνήστε |
| **I wave** | κυματίζω 13 | κυμάτιζα | κυμάτισα | θα κυματίσω<br>να κυματίσω | έχω κυματίσει<br>είχα κυματίσει | κυμάτιζε<br>κυματίζετε | κυμάτισε<br>κυματίστε |
| **I wax** | κερώνω 13 | κέρωνα | κέρωσα | θα κερώσω<br>να κερώσω | έχω κερώσει<br>είχα κερώσει | κέρωνε<br>κερώνετε | κέρωσε<br>κερώστε |
| **I wear** | φορ(ά)ώ 15 | φορούσα | φόρεσα | θα φορέσω<br>να φορέσω | έχω φορέσει<br>είχα φορέσει | φόρα<br>φοράτε | φόρεσε<br>φορέστε |
| **I weather** | *μαραίνομαι 14* | *μαραινόμουν* | *μαράθηκα* | *θα μαραθώ*<br>*να μαραθώ* | *έχω μαραθεί*<br>*είχα μαραθεί* | *να μαραίνεσαι*<br>*μαραίνεστε* | *να μαραθείς*<br>*μαραθείτε* |
| **I weave** | υφαίνω 13 | ύφαινα | ύφανα | θα υφάνω<br>να υφάνω | έχω υφάνει<br>είχα υφάνει | ύφαινε<br>υφαίνετε | ύφανε<br>υφάντε |
| **I wed** | *στεφανώνομαι 14* | *στεφανωνόμουν* | *στεφανώθηκα* | *θα στεφανωθώ*<br>*να στεφανωθώ* | *έχω στεφανωθεί*<br>*είχα στεφανωθεί* | *να στεφανώνεσαι*<br>*στεφανώνεστε* | *στεφανώσου*<br>*στεφανωθείτε* |
| **I weep** | δακρύζω 13 | δάκρυζα | δάκρυσα | θα δακρύσω<br>να δακρύσω | έχω δακρύσει<br>είχα δακρύσει | δάκρυζε<br>δακρύζετε | δάκρυσε<br>δακρύστε |
| **I weigh** | ζυγίζω 13 | ζύγιζα | ζύγισα | θα ζυγίσω<br>να ζυγίσω | έχω ζυγίσει<br>είχα ζυγίσει | ζύγιζε<br>ζυγίζετε | ζύγισε<br>ζυγίστε |
| **I welcome** | καλωσορίζω 13 | καλωσώριζα | καλωσώρισα | θα καλωσορίσω<br>να καλωσορίσω | έχω καλωσορίσει<br>είχα καλωσορίσει | καλωσόριζε<br>καλωσορίζετε | καλωσόρισε<br>καλωσορίστε |
| **I whack** | κτυπ(ά)ώ 15 | κτυπούσα | κτύπησα | θα κτυπήσω<br>να κτυπήσω | έχω κτυπήσει<br>είχα κτυπήσει | κτύπα<br>κτυπάτε | κτύπησε<br>κτυπήστε |
| **I wheeze** | *ασθμαίνω 13* | *άσθμαινα* | – | – | – | – | – |

| English Verb | Present | Imperfect | Past | Simple Future<br>Simple Subjunctive | Present Perfect<br>Past Perfect | Continuous Imperative | Simple Imperative |
|---|---|---|---|---|---|---|---|
| **I whip** | μαστιγώνω 13 | μαστίγωνα | μαστίγωσα | θα μαστιγώσω<br>να μαστιγώσω | έχω μαστιγώσει<br>είχα μαστιγώσει | μαστίγωνε<br>μαστιγώνετε | μαστίγωσε<br>μαστιγώστε |
| **I whisper** | ψιθυρίζω 13 | ψιθύριζα | ψιθύρισα | θα ψιθυρίσω<br>να ψιθυρίσω | έχω ψιθυρίσει<br>είχα ψιθυρίσει | ψιθύριζε<br>ψιθυρίζετε | ψιθύρισε<br>ψιθυρίστε |
| **I whistle** | σφυρίζω 13 | σφύριζα | σφύριξα | θα σφυρίξω<br>να σφυρίξω | έχω σφυρίξει<br>είχα σφυρίξει | σφύριζε<br>σφυρίζετε | σφύριξε<br>σφυρίξτε |
| **I whitewash** | ασπρίζω 13 | άσπριζα | άσπρισα | θα ασπρίσω<br>να ασπρίσω | έχω ασπρίσει<br>είχα ασπρίσει | άσπριζε<br>ασπρίζετε | άσπρισε<br>ασπρίστε |
| **I widen** | φαρδαίνω 13 | φάρδαινα | φάρδυνα | θα φαρδύνω<br>να φαρδύνω | έχω φαρδύνει<br>είχα φαρδύνει | φάρδαινε<br>φαρδαίνετε | φάρδυνε<br>φαρδύντε |
| **I wiggle** | *κουνιέμαι 16* | *κουνιόμουν* | *κουνήθηκα* | *θα κουνηθώ*<br>*να κουνηθώ* | *έχω κουνηθεί*<br>*είχα κουνηθεί* | *να κουνιέσαι*<br>*κουνιέστε* | *κουνήσου*<br>*κουνηθείτε* |
| **I win** | νικ(ά)ώ 15 | νικούσα | νίκησα | θα νικήσω<br>να νικήσω | έχω νικήσει<br>είχα νικήσει | νίκα<br>νικάτε | νίκησε<br>νικήστε |
| **I wince** | *συσπώμαι 42* | *συσπόμουν* | *συσπάστηκα* | *θα συσπαστώ*<br>*να συσπαστώ* | *έχω συσπαστεί*<br>*είχα συσπαστεί* | *να συσπάσαι*<br>*συσπάστε* | *συσπάσου*<br>*συσπαστείτε* |
| **I wink** | τρεμοσβήνω 13 | τρεμόσβηνα | τρεμόσβησα | θα τρεμοσβήσω<br>να τρεμοσβήσω | έχω τρεμοσβήσει<br>είχα τρεμοσβήσει | τρεμόσβηνε<br>τρεμοσβήνετε | τρεμόσβησε<br>τρεμοσβήστε |
| **I wind** | κουρδίζω 13 | κούρδιζα | κούρδισα | θα κουρδίσω<br>να κουρδίσω | έχω κουρδίσει<br>είχα κουρδίσει | κούρδιζε<br>κουρδίζετε | κούρδισε<br>κουρδίστε |
| **I wipe** | σφουγγίζω 13 | σφούγγιζα | σφούγγισα | θα σφουγγίσω<br>να σφουγγίσω | έχω σφουγγίσει<br>είχα σφουγγίσει | σφούγγιζε<br>σφουγγίζετε | σφούγγισε<br>σφουγγίστε |
| **I wish** | *εύχομαι 14* | *ευχόμουν* | *ευχήθηκα* | *θα ευχηθώ*<br>*να ευχηθώ* | *έχω ευχηθεί*<br>*είχα ευχηθεί* | *να εύχεσαι*<br>*εύχεστε* | *ευχήσου*<br>*ευχηθείτε* |

| English Verb | Present | Imperfect | Past | Simple Future<br>Simple Subjunctive | Present Perfect<br>Past Perfect | Continuous Imperative | Simple Imperative |
|---|---|---|---|---|---|---|---|
| **I withdraw** | *αποσύρομαι 14* | *αποσυρόμουν* | *αποσύρθηκα* | *θα αποσυρθώ*<br>*να αποσυρθώ* | *έχω αποσυρθεί*<br>*είχα αποσυρθεί* | *να αποσύρεσαι*<br>*αποσύρεστε* | *αποσύρσου*<br>*αποσυρθείτε* |
| **I withhold** | κατακρατ(ά)ώ 15 | κατακρατούσα | κατακράτησα | θα κατακρατήσω<br>να κατακρατήσω | έχω κατακρατήσει<br>είχα κατακρατήσει | κατακράτα<br>καταρατάτε | κατακράτησε<br>κατακρατήστε |
| **I withstand** | αντέχω 13 | άντεχα | άντεξα | θα αντέξω<br>να αντέξω | έχω αντέξει<br>είχα αντέξει | άντεχε<br>αντέχετε | άντεξε<br>αντέξτε |
| **I witness** | μαρτυρώ 17 | μαρτυρούσα | μαρτύρησα | θα μαρτυρήσω<br>να μαρτυρήσω | έχω μαρτυρήσει<br>είχα μαρτυρήσει | μαρτύρα<br>μαρτυράτε | μαρτύρησε<br>μαρτυρήστε |
| **I wobble** | τρεμουλιάζω 13 | τρεμούλιαζα | τρεμούλιασα | θα τρεμουλιάσω<br>να τρεμουλιάσω | έχω τρεμουλιάσει<br>είχα τρεμουλιάσει | τρεμούλιαζε<br>τρεμουλιάζετε | τρεμούλιασε<br>τρεμουλιάστε |
| **I wolf** | χάφτω 13 | έχαφτα | έχαψα | θα χάψω<br>να χάψω | έχω χάψει<br>είχα χάψει | χάφτε<br>χάφτετε | χάψε<br>χάψτε |
| **I wonder** | *αναρωτιέμαι 16* | *αναρωτιόμουν* | *αναρωτήθηκα* | *θα αναρωτηθώ*<br>*να αναρωτηθώ* | *έχω αναρωτηθεί*<br>*είχα αναρωτηθεί* | *να αναρωτιέσαι*<br>*αναρωτιέστε* | *αναρωτήσου*<br>*αναρωτηθείτε* |
| **I wonder** | *διερωτώμαι 42* | *διερωτόμουν* | *διερωτήθηκα* | *θα διερωτηθώ*<br>*να διερωτηθώ* | *έχω διερωτηθεί*<br>*είχα διερωτηθεί* | *να διερωτάσαι*<br>*διερωτάστε* | *διερωτήσου*<br>*διερωτηθείτε* |
| **I am worried** | *στενοχωριέμαι 16* | *στενοχωριόμουν* | *στενοχωρέθηκα* | *θα στενοχωρηθώ*<br>*να στενοχωρηθώ* | *έχω στενοχωρηθεί*<br>*είχα στενοχωρηθεί* | *να στενοχωριέσαι*<br>*στενοχωριέστε* | *στενοχωρήσου*<br>*στενοχωρηθείτε* |
| **I work** | δουλεύω 13 | δούλευα | δούλεψα | θα δουλέψω<br>να δουλέψω | έχω δουλέψει<br>είχα δουλέψει | δούλευε<br>δουλεύετε | δούλεψε<br>δουλέψτε |
| **I worry** | ανησυχώ 17 | ανησυχούσα | ανησύχησα | θα ανησυχήσω<br>να ανησυχήσω | έχω ανησυχήσει<br>είχα ανησυχήσει | να ανησυχείς<br>ανησυχείτε | ανησύχησε<br>ανησυχήστε |
| **I worsen** | χειροτερεύω 13 | χειροτέρευα | χειροτέρεψα | θα χειροτερέψω<br>να χειροτερέψω | έχω χειροτερέψει<br>είχα χειροτερέψει | χειροτέρευε<br>χειροτερεύετε | χειροτέρεψε<br>χειροτερέψτε |

| English Verb | Present | Imperfect | Past | Simple Future<br>Simple Subjunctive | Present Perfect<br>Past Perfect | Continuous Imperative | Simple Imperative |
|---|---|---|---|---|---|---|---|
| **I worship** | λατρεύω 13 | λάτρευα | λάτρεψα | θα λατρέψω<br>να λατρέψω | έχω λατρέψει<br>είχα λατρέψει | λάτρευε<br>λατρεύετε | λάτρεψε<br>λατρέψτε |
| **I wrap** | περιτυλίγω 13 | περιτύλιγα | περιτύλιξα | θα περιτυλίξω<br>να περιτυλίξω | έχω περιτυλίξει<br>είχα περιτυλίξει | περιτύλιγε<br>περιτυλίγετε | περιτύλιξε<br>περιτυλίξτε |
| **I wreck** | ναυαγώ 17 | ναυαγούσα | ναυάγησα | θα ναυαγήσω<br>να ναυαγήσω | έχω ναυαγήσει<br>είχα ναυαγήσει | να ναυαγείς<br>ναυαγείτε | ναυάγησε<br>ναυαγήστε |
| **I wrestle** | παλεύω 13 | πάλευα | πάλεψα | θα παλέψω<br>να παλέψω | έχω παλέψει<br>είχα παλέψει | πάλευε<br>παλεύετε | πάλεψε<br>παλέψτε |
| **I wriggle** | *συστρέφομαι 14* | *συστρεφόμουν* | *συστράφηκα* | *θα συστραφώ*<br>*να συστραφώ* | *έχω συστραφεί*<br>*είχα συστραφεί* | *να συστρέφεσαι*<br>*συστρέφεστε* | *να συστραφείς*<br>*συστραφείτε* |
| **I write** | γράφω 13 | έγραφα | έγραψα | θα γράψω<br>να γράψω | έχω γράψει<br>είχα γράψει | γράφε<br>γράφετε | γράψε<br>γράψτε |
| **I x-ray** | ακτινογραφώ 17 | ακτινογραφούσα | ακτινογράφησα | θα ακτινογραφήσω<br>να ακτινογραφήσω | έχω ακτινογραφήσει<br>είχα ακτινογραφήσει | να ακτινογραφείς<br>ακτινογραφείτε | ακτινογράφησε<br>ακτινογραφήστε |
| **I yawn** | *χασμουριέμαι 16* | *χασμουριόμουν* | *χασμουρήθηκα* | *θα χασμουρηθώ*<br>*να χασμουρηθώ* | *έχω χασμουρηθεί*<br>*είχα χασμουρηθεί* | *να χασμουριέσαι*<br>*χασμουριέστε* | *χασμουρήσου*<br>*χασμουρηθείτε* |
| **I yelp** | σκούζω 13 | έσκουζα | έσκουξα | θα σκούξω<br>να σκούξω | έχω σκούξει<br>είχα σκούξει | σκούζε<br>σκούζετε | σκούξε<br>σκούξτε |
| **I yield** | αποφέρω 13<br>αποφέρνω 13 | απέφερνα | απέφερα | θα αποφέρω<br>να αποφέρω | έχω αποφέρει<br>είχα αποφέρει | απόφερνε<br>αποφέρνετε | απόφερε<br>αποφέρτε |

# B. PAGE INDEX OF VERBS IN GREEK ALPHABETICAL ORDER

| | |
|---|---|
| ανακόπτω 94 | I check |
| ανακουφίζω 181 | I relieve |
| ανακρίνω 177 | I question |
| ανακύπτω 74 | I arise (difficulty) |
| αναλαμβάνω 201 | I undertake |
| *αναλογίζομαι 87* | I brood (person) |
| αναλύω 72 | I analyse |
| αναλώνω 105 | I consume |
| αναμένω 77 | I await |
| αναμορφώνω 180 | I reform |
| ανανεώνω 181 | I renew |
| αναπαρασταίνω 67 | I act out |
| *αναπαύομαι 183* | I rest |
| αναπηδώ 155 | I leap |
| αναπληρώνω 182 | I replace |
| αναπνέω 86 | I breathe |
| αναποδογυρίζω 167 | I overturn |
| αναπολώ 179 | I recollect |
| αναπτερώνω 178 | I raise |
| *αναπτύσσομαι 160* | I mature |
| αναπτύσσω 119 | I develop |
| *αναρωτιέμαι 217* | I wonder |
| ανασκαλεύω 178 | I rake |
| αναστατώνω 121 | I disturb |
| αναστέλλω 203 | I suspend /delay/ stop |
| αναστενάζω 193 | I sigh |
| αναστηλώνω 183 | I restore |
| αναταράζω 191 | I shake |
| ανατέλλει 185 | It rises (sun) |
| ανατιμ(ά)ώ 74 | I appreciate |
| ανατινάζω 130 | I explode |
| ανατρέπω 166 | I overrule |

| | |
|---|---|
| ανατρέφω 87 | I bring up |
| αναθρέφω 87 | I bring up |
| *αναφέρομαι 100* | I come up (in conversation) |
| αναφέρω 182 | I report |
| αναφωνώ 128 | I exclaim |
| αναχαιτίζω 149 | I inhibit |
| αναχωρώ 117 | I depart |
| ανεβαίνω 141 | I go up |
| *ανέρχεται 72* | It amounts to |
| *ανέρχομαι 75* | I ascend |
| *ανέχομαι 75* | I bear (tolerate) |
| ανήκω 80 | I belong |
| ανησυχώ 217 | I worry |
| ανθίζω 82 | I bloom |
| ανιχνεύω 118 | I detect |
| ανοίγω 165 | I open |
| ανορθώνω 178 | I raise |
| *ανταγωνίζομαι 101* | I compete |
| ανταλλάζω 128 | I exchange |
| ανταμείβω 185 | I reward |
| ανταμώνω 160 | I meet |
| αντανακλώ 180 | I reflect |
| ανταποδίδω 181 | I render |
| *ανταποκρίνομαι 73* | I answer to |
| *αντεπιτίθεμαι 108* | I coun-terattack |
| αντέχω 217 | I withstand |
| αντηχώ 124 | I echo |
| αντιγράφω 108 | I copy |
| αντιδρώ 178 | I react |
| αντικαθιστώ 182 | I replace |
| αντικρούω 106 | I contest (decision) |
| *αντιλαμβάνομαι 178* | I realise |

| | |
|---|---|
| αντιμετωπίζω 104 | I confront |
| αντιπαθώ 122 | I dislike |
| αντιπαραβάλλω 106 | I contrast |
| αντιπροσωπεύω 182 | I represent |
| *αντιστέκομαι 183* | I resist |
| αντιστρέφω 184 | I reverse |
| *αντιτάσσομαι 115* | I defy |
| *αντιτίθεμαι 164* | I object |
| αντιφάσκω 106 | I contradict |
| αντλώ 176 | I pump |
| ανυψώνω 84 | I boost |
| αξιοποιώ 202 | I utilize |
| αξιώ 150 | I insist |
| απαγάγω 153 | I kidnap |
| απαγορεύω 174 | I prohibit |
| απαιτώ 116 | I demand |
| *απαλάσσομαι 139* | I get rid of |
| απαλλάσσω 129 | I exempt |
| απαντ(ά)ώ 73 | I answer |
| *απαρνούμαι 117* | I deny |
| απαστράφτω 134 | I flash |
| απασχολώ 125 | I employ |
| απατώ 94 | I cheat |
| *απατώμαι 161* | I am mistaken |
| απειθώ 71 | I am disobedient |
| απεικονίζω 171 | I portray |
| απειλώ 206 | I threaten |
| απεργώ 200 | I strike |
| *απευθύνομαι 68* | I address |
| *απεχθάνομαι 119* | I detest |
| απλοποιώ 193 | I simplify |
| απλώνω 197 | I spread (out) |
| αποβάλλω 129 | I expel |

| | |
|---|---|
| *αποβιβάζομαι 70* | I alight |
| αποβλέπω 75 | I aspire |
| απογοητεύω 121 | I disappoint |
| αποδεικνύω 175 | I prove |
| αποδεκατίζω 162 | I mow down (decimate) |
| *αποδέχομαι 68* | I admit |
| αποδοκιμάζω 103 | I condemn |
| αποζημιώνω 101 | I compensate |
| αποθαρρύνω 120 | I discourage |
| αποθηκεύω 200 | I store |
| αποθυσαυρίζω 145 | I hoard (money/food) |
| αποκαλώ 90 | I call |
| *αποκαλύπτομαι 100* | I come out |
| αποκαλύπτω 184 | I reveal |
| αποκαρδιώνω 116 | I demoralize |
| αποκατασταίνω 184 | I retrieve |
| αποκεντρώνω 114 | I decentralise |
| αποκεφαλίζω 80 | I behead |
| αποκλείω 128 | I exclude |
| *αποκοιμιέμαι 163* | I nod off |
| αποκόπτω 191 | I sever |
| αποκρατικοποιώ 117 | I denationalize |
| *αποκρίνομαι 182* | I reply |
| αποκρούω 180 | I reject |
| αποκρύβω 102 | I conceal |
| αποκρυπτογραφώ 114 | I decipher |
| αποκρυσταλλώνω 111 | I crystalise |
| απολαμβάνω 125 | I enjoy |
| *απολογούμαι 74* | I apologize |
| απολυμαίνω 120 | I disinfect |
| απομακρύνω 181 | I remove |
| *απομιμούμαι 194* | I simulate |
| απομονώνω 152 | I isolate |

| | |
|---|---|
| απονέμω 77 | I award |
| αποξενώνω 70 | I alienate |
| αποπαίρνω 189 | I scold |
| αποπλέω 187 | I sail |
| απορρίπτω 180 | I reject |
| *αποσαρθρώνομαι 114* | I decay |
| αποσαφηνίζω 96 | I clear |
| αποσβήνω 127 | I erase |
| αποσιωπώ 146 | I hush up |
| αποσπώ 121 | I distract |
| αποστάζω 86 | I brew |
| αποστειρώνω 199 | I sterilize |
| αποστέλλω 104 | I consign |
| αποστηθίζω 160 | I memorize |
| αποσυνδέω 120 | I disconnect |
| *αποσύρομαι 217* | I withdraw |
| αποταμιεύω 188 | I save |
| *αποτελείται 104* | It consists |
| αποτιμ(ά)ώ 76 | I assess |
| αποτολμώ 186 | I risk |
| *αποτραβιέμαι 184* | I retreat |
| αποτρέπω 77 | I avert |
| αποτυγχάνω 131 | I fail |
| απουσιάζω 70 | I am absent |
| αποφασίζω 114 | I decide |
| αποφέρω 218 | I yield |
| αποφέρνω 218 | I yield |
| αποφεύγω 77 | I avoid |
| αποχτώ 67 | I acquire |
| αποχωρώ 184 | I retire |
| απωθώ 182 | I repulse |
| αργώ 155 | I am late |
| αρδεύω 152 | I irrigate |

| | |
|---|---|
| *αρκούμαι 105* | I content myself |
| αρματώνω 127 | I equip |
| αρμέγω 160 | I milk |
| *αρνούμαι 180* | I refuse |
| αρπάζω 92 | I catch |
| αρρωσταίνω 72 | I am taken ill |
| αρχειοθετώ 133 | I file |
| αρχίζω 80 | I begin |
| *ασθμαίνω 205* | I wheeze |
| ασκώ 129 | I exert |
| ασπρίζω 216 | I whitewash |
| *αστειεύομαι 153* | I joke |
| αστοχώ 161 | I misfire |
| αστράφτω 157 | I lighten |
| ασφαλίζω 151 | I insure |
| *ασχολούμαι 125* | I engage |
| ατακτώ 161 | I misbehave |
| ατενίζω 180 | I regard (consider) |
| αυξάνω 148 | I increase |
| αυξαίνω 148 | I increase |
| αυτοκτονώ 101 | I commit suicide |
| αυτοσχεδιάζω 147 | I improvise |
| αφαιρώ 201 | I subtract |
| *αφανίζομαι 169* | I perish |
| *αφηγούμαι 162* | I narrate |
| αφήνω 156 | I leave (abandon) |
| αφιερώνω 115 | I dedicate |
| αφομοιώνω 76 | I assimilate |
| αφοπλίζω 119 | I disarm |
| αφορά 103 | It concerns |
| αφυπνίζω 75 | I arouse |
| αχριστεύω 148 | I incapacitate |
| αψηφώ 115 | I defy |

| | |
|---|---|
| βαδίζω 159 | I march |
| βάζω 176 | I put |
| βαθαίνω 115 | I deepen |
| βαθμολογώ 159 | I mark |
| βαραίνω 89 | I burden |
| βαράω 145 | I hit |
| *βαριέμαι 132* | I am fed up |
| βασανίζω 207 | I torture |
| *βασίζομαι 181* | I rely |
| βασίζω 78 | I base |
| βαστώ 145 | I hold (support/bear) |
| βαφτίζω 78 | I baptise |
| βάφω 99 | I colour (dye) |
| βγάζω 205 | I take off/out |
| βγαίνω 140 | I go out |
| βεβαιώ 214 | I vouch |
| *βεβαιώνομαι 159* | I make certain |
| βεβαιώνω 69 | I affirm |
| βεβηλώνω 115 | I defile |
| *βελτιώνομαι 87* | I brighten up |
| βελτιώνω 147 | I improve |
| βηματίζω 167 | I pace |
| βήχω 108 | I cough |
| *βιάζομαι 146* | I hurry |
| βιάζω 178 | I rape |
| βλάπτω 112 | I damage |
| βλασταίνω 197 | I sprout |
| βλαστημώ 82 | I blaspheme |
| βλέπω 189 | I see |
| βογκώ 161 | I moan |
| βοηθ(ά)ώ 144 | I help |
| βολεύω 202 | I suit |
| βομβαρδίζω 84 | I bomb |

| | |
|---|---|
| βόσκω 141 | I graze |
| βουίζω 90 | I buzz |
| βουλιάζω 194 | I sink |
| βουλώνω 82 | I block up |
| βουρκώνω 83 | I blur |
| βουρλίζω 149 | I infuriate |
| βουρτσίζω 88 | I brush |
| βουτυρώνω 90 | I butter |
| βουτώ 122 | I dive |
| βράζω 83 | I boil |
| βρέχει 177 | It rains |
| βρίζω 203 | I swear (curse) |
| *βρίσκομαι 71* | I am found |
| βρίσκω 134 | I find |
| βρομίζω 196 | I soil |
| βρωμώ 199 | I stink |
| βυζαίνω 201 | I suckle |
| βυθίζω 171 | I plunge |
| βυθομετρώ 132 | I fathom |
| γαληνεύω 196 | I soothe |
| γαλουχώ 164 | I nurture |
| γαντζώνω 145 | I hook |
| γαργαλ(ά)ώ 207 | I tickle |
| γαυγίζω 78 | I bark |
| γδέρνω 189 | I scratch |
| γδύνω 210 | I undress |
| γελ(ά)ώ 155 | I laugh |
| *γελιέμαι 116* | I delude myself |
| γελοιοποιώ 154 | I lampoon |
| γεμίζω 133 | I fill |
| γενικεύω 138 | I generalise |
| γεννάω 90 | I give birth to |
| γερν(ά)ώ 69 | I age |

| | |
|---|---|
| γέρνω 207 | I tilt |
| γευματίζω 158 | I lunch |
| *γεύομαι 205* | I taste |
| γεφυρώνω 87 | I bridge |
| γιατρεύω 144 | I heal |
| *γίνομαι 79* | I become |
| γιορτάζω 92 | I celebrate |
| γιουχαΐζω 84 | I boo |
| γκαρίζω 86 | I bray |
| γκρεμίζω 154 | I knock down (building) |
| γκρινιάζω 142 | I grumble |
| γλείφω 156 | I lick |
| γλεντώ 143 | I have fun |
| γλιστρ(ά)ώ 194 | I slip |
| γλυτώνω 127 | I escape |
| γλωσσοτρώγω 162 | I nag |
| γνέφω 163 | I nod ( head) |
| *γνωρίζομαι 71* | I am acquainted |
| γνωρίζω 154 | I know |
| γογγύζω 141 | I groan |
| γοητεύω 77 | I attract |
| γονατίζω 154 | I kneel |
| γουργουρίζω 142 | I gurgle |
| γουστάρω 132 | I fancy |
| γραπώνω 141 | I grab |
| *γράφομαι 126* | I enrol myself |
| γράφω 218 | I write |
| γριπιάζω 143 | I have flu |
| γρονθοκοπώ 176 | I punch |
| γρυλίζω 142 | I grunt |
| γυαλίζω 192 | I shine (furniture/ shoes) |

| | |
|---|---|
| γυμνώνω 78 | I bare (reveal) |
| γυρεύω 189 | I search |
| γυρίζω 184 | I return |
| γυρν(ά)ώ 209 | I turn |
| δαγκώνω 81 | I bite |
| δακρύζω 215 | I weep |
| δακτυλογραφώ 210 | I type |
| δαμάζω 205 | I tame |
| *δανείζομαι 84* | I borrow |
| δανείζω 156 | I lend |
| δαπαν(ά)ώ 196 | I spend |
| δασκαλεύω 205 | I teach |
| δειλιάζω 158 | I hesitate |
| δειπνώ 119 | I dine |
| δείχνω 193 | I show |
| δελεάζω 206 | I tempt |
| δένω 207 | I tie |
| *δεξιώνομαι 126* | I entertain |
| δέρνω 79 | I batter |
| *δεσμεύομαι 101* | I commit myself |
| δεσμεύω 81 | I bind |
| δηλητηριάζω 171 | I poison |
| δηλώνω 114 | I declare |
| δημιουργώ 109 | I create |
| δημοσιεύω 176 | I publish |
| δημοσιοποιώ 114 | I declassify |
| διαβάζω 178 | I read |
| διαβεβαιώνω 76 | I assure (convince) |
| *διαβρώνομαι 108* | I corrode (metal) |
| διαγράφω 116 | I delete |
| *διαγωνίζομαι 106* | I contest |
| *διαδέχομαι 201* | I succeed |
| διαδηλώνω 116 | I demonstrate (protest) |

| | |
|---|---|
| διαδίδω 197 | I spread rumours |
| διαθέτω 69 | I afford (time) |
| διαιρώ 122 | I divide |
| *διαισθάνομαι 190* | I sense |
| διαιωνίζω 169 | I perpetuate |
| διακινδυνεύω 93 | I chance |
| *διακλαδίζομαι 136* | I fork |
| διακόπτω 151 | I interrupt |
| διακοσμώ 68 | I adorn (with objects) |
| διακρίνω 120 | I discriminate |
| διαλέγω 95 | I choose |
| διαλευκαίνω 211 | I unravel |
| *διαλογίζομαι 171* | I ponder |
| *διαλύομαι 100* | I come apart |
| διαλύω 121 | I dissolve |
| *διαμαρτύρομαι 175* | I protest |
| διαμένω 183 | I reside |
| διαμορφώνω 136 | I form |
| διανέμω 116 | I deliver |
| *διανοούμαι 103* | I conceive |
| διανυκτερεύω 166 | I overnight |
| διαπιστώνω 75 | I ascertain (details/facts) |
| *διαπληκτίζομαι 86* | I brawl |
| διαπνέω 208 | I transpire |
| διαπομπεύω 170 | I pillory |
| *διαπραγματεύομαι 163* | I negotiate (contract) |
| διαπράττω 101 | I commit (crime) |
| διαρκώ 155 | I last (keep going) |
| διαρρέω 135 | I flow |
| διαρρηγνύω 86 | I breach |
| διασαφηνίζω 199 | I state |
| διασκεδάζω 135 | I enjoy myself |

| | |
|---|---|
| διασκευάζω 67 | I adapt |
| διασκορπίζω 121 | I disperse |
| διασπώ 121 | I disrupt |
| *διασταυρώνομαι 151* | I intersect (roads) |
| διασταυρώνω 110 | I cross-check |
| διαστρεβλώνω 210 | I twist |
| διασύρω 120 | I disparage |
| διασχίζω 110 | I cross (street) |
| διασώζω 183 | I rescue |
| διατάζω 100 | I command |
| *διατείνομαι 105* | I contend |
| *διατηρούμαι 153* | I keep |
| διατηρώ 104 | I conserve (preserve) |
| διατρυπώ 84 | I bore |
| διατυπώνω 169 | I phrase (verbally) |
| διαφεύγω 135 | I flee |
| διαφημίζω 69 | I advertise |
| διαφθείρω 108 | I corrupt (someone) |
| διαφοροποιώ 119 | I differentiate |
| διαφυλάττω 159 | I maintain |
| διαφωνώ 119 | I disagree |
| διαφωτίζω 126 | I enlighten |
| *διαχειρίζομαι 68* | I administer |
| διαψεύδω 80 | I belie (disprove) |
| διδάσκω 205 | I teach |
| διεκδικώ 96 | I claim |
| διερευν(ά)ώ 150 | I inquire into |
| διερμηνεύω 151 | I interpret |
| *διερωτώμαι 217* | I wonder |
| διευθετώ 191 | I settle |
| διευκολύνω 131 | I facilitate |
| διευκρινίζω 96 | I clarify |
| διευρύνω 87 | I broaden |

| | |
|---|---|
| *διηγούμαι 162* | I narrate |
| δικάζω 209 | I try |
| δικαιολογώ 128 | I excuse |
| *δικαιούμαι 124* | I earn |
| δικαιώνω 213 | I vindicate |
| δίνω 139 | I give |
| διοικώ 100 | I command |
| διορθώνω 108 | I correct |
| διορίζω 74 | I appoint |
| διπλασιάζω 122 | I double |
| διπλώνω 136 | I fold |
| διστάζω 144 | I hesitate |
| διχάζω 197 | I split |
| διχοτομώ 81 | I bisect |
| διψώ 206 | I am thirsty |
| δογματίζω 122 | I dogmatize |
| δοκιμάζω 205 | I taste |
| δολοφονώ 75 | I assassinate |
| δονώ 17 | I vibrate |
| δοξάζω 140 | I glorify |
| δουλεύω 217 | I work |
| δραματοποιώ 122 | I dramatize |
| δραπετεύω 127 | I escape (from prison) |
| δροσίζω 107 | I cool |
| δυναμώνω 200 | I strengthen |
| δυσαρεστώ 121 | I displease |
| *δυσκολεύομαι 134* | I find difficult |
| δυσκολεύω 102 | I complicate |
| δυσφημώ 117 | I denigrate |
| δωροδοκώ 86 | I bribe |
| *εγγυώμαι 142* | I guarantee |
| εγκαθιστώ 150 | I install |
| εγκαινιάζω 148 | I inaugurate |

| | |
|---|---|
| εγκαλώ 96 | I cite (legal action) |
| εγκρίνω 74 | I approve |
| εγκωμιάζω 100 | I commend (praise) |
| εδραιώνω 127 | I establish |
| εθίζω 68 | I addict |
| *ειδικεύομαι 196* | I specialize |
| ειδοποιώ 164 | I notify |
| *ειρωνεύομαι 161* | I ridicule |
| εισάγω 147 | I import |
| εισβάλλω 151 | I invade |
| εισδύω 170 | I pierce |
| *εισηγούμαι 175* | I propose |
| εισπνέω 86 | I breathe in |
| εισπράττω 99 | I collect (debts) |
| εισχωρώ 169 | I permeate |
| εκβιάζω 81 | I blackmail |
| εκδηλώνω 116 | I demonstrate |
| εκδίδω 176 | I publish |
| εκθαμβώνω 72 | I amaze |
| εκθέτω 129 | I exhibit |
| εκθρονίζω 117 | I depose |
| εκκαθαρίζω 96 | I clear |
| εκκενώνω 212 | I vacate |
| εκκολάπτω 148 | I incubate |
| εκλέγω 124 | I elect |
| *εκμεταλλεύομαι 130* | I exploit |
| εκμηδενίζω 73 | I annihilate |
| εκμισθώνω 156 | I let |
| *εκνευρίζομαι 139* | I get nervous |
| εκνευρίζω 73 | I annoy |
| *εκπαιδεύομαι 208* | I am trained |
| εκπέμπω 87 | I broadcast |

| | |
|---|---|
| εκπληρώνω 137 | I fulfil |
| εκπλήσσω 202 | I surprise |
| εκπνέω 129, 86 | I expire |
| εκπονώ 124 | I elaborate |
| εκπυρσοκροτώ 140 | I go off (gun) |
| *εκρήγνυμαι 127* | I erupt (volcano) |
| εκστρατεύω 90 | I campaign |
| εκσυγχρονίζω 211 | I update |
| εκσφενδονίζω 135 | I fling |
| εκτείνω 178 | I reach |
| εκτελώ 128 | I execute |
| εκτιμ(ά)ώ 212 | I value |
| *εκτονώνομαι 181* | I relax |
| εκτονώνω 115 | I defuse (crisis) |
| *εκτοξεύομαι 82* | I blast off (rocket) |
| εκτοξεύω 155 | I launch |
| εκτοπίζω 121 | I displace |
| *εκτρέπομαι 119* | I deviate |
| εκτρέφω 86 | I breed (animals) |
| εκτυφλώνω 113 | I dazzle |
| εκφοβίζω 88 | I browbeat |
| *εκφράζομαι 130* | I express myself |
| εκφράζω 130 | I express |
| εκφωνώ 75 | I articulate |
| εκχυδαΐζω 214 | I vulgarize |
| ελαττώνω 179 | I reduce |
| ελέγχω 94 | I check |
| ελευθερώνω 137 | I free |
| ελπίζω 145 | I hope |
| εμβολιάζω 212 | I vaccinate |
| εμπλέκω 152 | I involve |
| *εμπνέομαι 148* | I am inspired |
| εμπνέω 150 | I inspire |

| | |
|---|---|
| εμποδίζω 144 | I hinder |
| *εμπορεύομαι 208* | I trade |
| *εμφανίζομαι 73* | I appear |
| εμφανίζω 159 | I manifest |
| εμφιαλώνω 84 | I bottle |
| εμψυχώνω 73 | I animate |
| εναλλάσσω 70 | I alternate |
| *ενδιαφέρομαι 151* | I interest |
| ενεργοποιώ 67 | I activate |
| ενεργώ 67 | I act |
| ενημερώνω 87 | I brief |
| ενθαρρύνω 125 | I encourage |
| *ενθουσιάζομαι 71* | I am enthusiastic |
| ενισχύω 72 | I amplify |
| εννοώ 160 | I mean |
| ενοχλώ 84 | I bother (disturb) |
| ενσαρκώνω 148 | I incarnate |
| ενσωματώνω 125 | I embody |
| εντείνω 151 | I intensify |
| εντοπίζω 157 | I locate |
| εντυπωσιάζω 147 | I impress |
| ενώνω 210 | I unite |
| εξαγνίζω 96 | I cleanse (purify) |
| εξαγοράζω 87 | I bribe |
| εξαγριώνω 152 | I irritate |
| εξάγω 130 | I export |
| εξαερίζω 213 | I ventilate |
| *εξαιρούμαι 123* | I am exempted |
| εξαίρω 144 | I highlight |
| εξαιρώ 128 | I except |
| εξακοντίζω 92 | I catapult |
| εξακριβώνω 134 | I find out |
| εξαλείφω 124 | I eliminate |

| | |
|---|---|
| εξαναγκάζω 136 | I force |
| *εξαντλούμαι 89* | I burn out (by overworking) |
| εξαπατώ 94 | I cheat (at cards) |
| εξάπτω 128 | I excite |
| εξαργυρώνω 91 | I cash (cheque) |
| εξαρθρώνω 120 | I dislocate |
| *εξαρτώμαι 117* | I depend on |
| εξασφαλίζω 189 | I secure (ensure) |
| *εξατμίζομαι 212* | I vaporize |
| *εξαφανίζομαι 119* | I disappear |
| εξερευνώ 130 | I explore |
| *εξέρχομαι 129* | I exit |
| εξετάζω 128 | I examine |
| εξευτελίζω 115 | I degrade |
| εξηγώ 129 | I explain |
| εξιχνιάζω 208 | I trace |
| εξογκώνω 88 | I bulge |
| *εξοικιώνομαι 131* | I familiarize myself |
| εξοικονομώ 188 | I save up |
| εξολοθρεύω 130 | I exterminate |
| εξοπλίζω 74 | I arm |
| εξοργίζω 72 | I anger (someone) |
| εξορίζω 129 | I exile |
| εξουδετερώνω 163 | I neutralize |
| εξουσιάζω 186 | I rule (govern) |
| εξουσιοδοτώ 17 | I warrant |
| εξοφλώ 182 | I repay |
| εξυψώνω 124 | I elevate |
| εξωθώ 147 | I impel |
| εξωρύσσω 130 | I extract |
| επαγρυπνώ 215 | I watch |
| επαινώ 172 | I praise |

| | |
|---|---|
| επαιτώ 80 | I beg |
| επαληθεύω 213 | I verify |
| επαναλαμβάνω 182 | I repeat |
| επαναστατώ 185 | I revolt |
| επαναφέρω 87 | I bring back (restore) |
| επανεξετάζω 179 | I reconsider |
| *επανέρχομαι 184* | I return |
| *επεκτείνομαι 85* | I branch out expand) |
| επενδύω 152 | I invest |
| επεξηγώ 124 | I elucidate |
| επηρεάζω 149 | I influence |
| επιβάλλω 147 | I impose |
| επιβαραίνω 89 | I burden (with problems) |
| επιβεβαιώνω 103 | I confirm |
| *επιβιβάζομαι 83* | I board |
| επιβλέπω 167 | I oversee |
| επιβραδύνω 113 | I deaden |
| επιδεικνύω 135 | I flaunt |
| επιδεινώνω 69 | I aggravate (situation) |
| επιδιώκω 176 | I pursue |
| επιδοκιμάζω 187 | I sanction |
| επιζώ 203 | I survive |
| επιθεωρώ 150 | I inspect |
| επιθυμώ 118 | I desire |
| *επικαλούμαι 152* | I invoke |
| επικοινωνώ 101 | I communicate |
| επικρατώ 173 | I prevail |
| επικρίνω 93 | I censure |
| επικυρώνω 212 | I validate |
| επιλέγω 190 | I select |
| *επιμελούμαι 124* | I edit |
| επιμένω 150 | I insist |

| | |
|---|---|
| επινοώ 131 | I fabricate |
| επιπλέω 135 | I float |
| επιπλήττω 179 | I rebuke |
| επιπλώνω 138 | I furnish |
| επισημαίνω 171 | I point out |
| *επισκέπτομαι 213* | I visit |
| επισκευάζω 182 | I repair |
| επισκιάζω 166 | I outshine (surpass) |
| επισυνάπτω 69 | I affix |
| επιτελώ 169 | I perform |
| *επιτίθεμαι 76* | I attack |
| επιτρέπω 226 | I permit |
| επιτυγχάνω 67 | I achieve |
| επιτυχαίνω 67 | I achieve |
| επιφέρει 138 | It generates |
| επιχειρηματολογώ 74 | I argue (reason) |
| *επωφελούμαι 174* | I profit by |
| *ερεθίζομαι 149* | I am inflamed |
| ερεθίζω 199 | I stimulate |
| ερευνώ 183 | I research |
| ερμηνεύω 130 | I explain |
| *έρχομαι 99* | I come |
| εστιάζω 93 | I centre on |
| ετοιμάζω 172 | I prepare |
| ευαισθητοποιώ 190 | I sensitize |
| ευημερώ 175 | I prosper |
| ευλογώ 82 | I bless |
| ευνοώ 132 | I favour |
| *ευχαριστιέμαι 171* | I am pleased |
| ευχαριστώ 206 | I thank |
| *εύχομαι 216* | I wish |
| *εφάπτομαι 107* | I contact |
| εφαρμόζω 134 | I fit |

| | |
|---|---|
| εφευρίσκω 151 | I invent |
| εφοδιάζω 202 | I supply |
| έχω 143 | I have |
| *ζαλίζομαι 133* | I feel dizzy |
| ζαρώνω 110 | I cringe |
| ζαυλακώνω 113 | I daze |
| ζεσταίνω 144 | I heat |
| ζηλεύω 126 | I envy |
| ζημιώνω 112 | I damage |
| ζητ(ά)ώ 75 | I ask (request) |
| ζητιανεύω 80 | I beg |
| ζητωκραυγάζω 95 | I cheer |
| ζυγίζω 215 | I weigh |
| ζυγώνω 74 | I approach |
| ζυμώνω 153 | I knead |
| ζω 157 | I live (am alive) |
| ζωγραφίζω 167 | I paint |
| ζωηρεύω 126 | I enliven |
| ζωντανεύω 185 | I revive (enliven) |
| ζώνω 80 | I belt |
| *ηγούμαι 155* | I lead |
| ηρεμώ 90 | I calm |
| | I calm down |
| ησυχάζω 177 | I quieten (down) |
| ηχογραφώ 179 | I record |
| θάβω 89 | I bury |
| θαλασσώνω 162 | I muddle |
| θαμπώνω 113 | I dazzle |
| *θαυμάζομαι 71* | I am admired |
| θαυμάζω 68 | I admire |
| θέλγω 94 | I charm |
| θέλω 214 | I want |
| θεοποιώ 226 | I idolize |

| | |
|---|---|
| θεραπεύω 111 | I cure |
| θερίζω 143 | I harvest |
| θέτω 155 | I lay |
| *θεωρούμαι 71* | I am considered |
| θεωρώ 104 | I consider |
| θηλάζω 201 | I suck |
| θίγω 165 | I offend |
| θλίβω 121 | I distress |
| θολώνω 97 | I cloud |
| θραύω 192 | I shatter |
| θρηνώ 81 | I bemoan |
| θριαμβεύω 209 | I triumph |
| θρυμματίζω 111 | I crush (ice) |
| *θυμάμαι 181* | I remember |
| θυμίζω 181 | I remind |
| θυμώνω 71 | I am angry |
| θυσιάζω 187 | I sacrifice |
| θωρώ 198 | I stare |
| ιδιωτικοποιώ 173 | I privatise |
| ιδρύω 136 | I found |
| ιδρώνω 204 | I sweat |
| *ικανοποιούμαι 187* | I am satisfied |
| ικανοποιώ 187 | I satisfy |
| ικετεύω 147 | I implore |
| ιππεύω 185 | I ride |
| ισιώνω 85 | I brace (shoulders) |
| ισοπεδώνω 134 | I flatten |
| ισορροπώ 78 | I balance |
| ισοσταθμίζω 165 | I offset |
| ισοφαρίζω 127 | I equalize |
| *ισχυρίζομαι 70* | I allege |
| ισχυροποιώ 125 | I enforce |
| καγχάζω 152 | I jeer |

| | |
|---|---|
| καθαρίζω 96 | I clean |
| καθελκύω 155 | I launch (ship) |
| καθιερώνω 150 | I institute |
| καθοδηγώ 150 | I instruct |
| *κάθομαι 194* | I sit |
| καθορίζω 115 | I define |
| καθρεφτίζω 160 | I mirror |
| καθυστερώ 116 | I delay |
| καί(γ)ω 89 | I burn |
| κακαρίζω 98 | I cluck |
| κακολογώ 196 | I speak ill of |
| κακομαθαίνω 167 | I pamper |
| κακομεταχειρίζομαι 89 | I bully |
| κακοποιώ 143 | I harm |
| καλλιεργώ 111 | I cultivate |
| καλοπιάνω 98 | I coax |
| καλπάζω 138 | I gallop |
| καλύπτω 98 | I coat |
| καλώ 202 | I summon |
| καλωσορίζω 215 | I welcome |
| καμαρώνω 85 | I brag |
| καμουφλάρω 90 | I camouflage |
| κανακεύω 168 | I pamper |
| κανονίζω 75 | I arrange |
| κάνω 122 | I do |
| καπνίζω 195 | I smoke |
| καρπαζώνω 97 | I clout |
| καρποφορώ 137 | I fruit |
| καρυκεύω 189 | I season |
| καρφιτσώνω 97 | I clip (fasten to) |
| καρφώνω 162 | I nail |
| καταβάλλω 166 | I overpower |
| καταβροχθίζω 142 | I gulp |

| | |
|---|---|
| καταγγέλλω 117 | I denounce |
| καταγράφω 94 | I chart |
| καταδίδω 149 | I inform |
| καταδικάζω 190 | I sentence |
| καταδιώκω 94 | I chase |
| καταθέτω 206 | I testify |
| καταθλίβω 117 | I depress |
| κατακλύζω 148 | I inundate |
| κατακρατ(ά)ώ 217 | I withhold |
| κατακρίνω 115 | I decry |
| κατακτώ 104 | I conquer |
| καταλαβαίνω 210 | I understand |
| καταλαμβάνω 165 | I occupy |
| καταλήγω 103 | I conclude |
| καταλογίζω 75 | I ascribe |
| καταμερίζω 70 | I allocate |
| καταναγκάζω 98 | I coerce |
| καταναλώνω 105 | I consume |
| κατανοώ 102 | I comprehend |
| καταπίνω 203 | I swallow |
| καταπλήττω 76 | I astonish |
| καταπολεμώ 99 | I combat |
| *καταριέμαι 112* | I curse |
| καταρρέω 86 | I break down |
| κατασκευάζω 105 | I construct |
| κατασκηνώνω 90 | I camp |
| κατασκοπεύω 197 | I spy |
| καταστέλλω 183 | I restrain |
| καταστρέφω 118 | I destroy |
| κατάσχω 103 | I confiscate |
| κατατάσσω 96 | I class |
| κατατοπίζω 87 | I brief (prime/inform) |
| κατατρέχω 213 | I victimize |

| | |
|---|---|
| κατατροπώνω 206 | I thrash |
| καταφέρνω 159 | I manage |
| *καταχρώμαι 124* | I embezzle |
| καταχωρώ 126 | I enrol |
| *καταψηφίζομαι 166* | I am outvoted |
| καταψύχω 95 | I chill |
| κατεβαίνω 118 | I descend |
| κατεδαφίζω 116 | I demolish |
| κατευθύνω 70 | I aim |
| κατηγορώ 67 | I accuse |
| κατοικώ 149 | I inhabit |
| κατορθώνω 106 | I contrive |
| κατουρ(ά)ώ 212 | I urinate |
| κατοχυρώνω 76 | I assure (success) |
| κατρακυλ(ά)ώ 91 | I cascade (water) |
| κατσαδιάζω 95 | I chide |
| κατσαρώνω 111 | I curl |
| κατσουφιάζω 137 | I frown |
| καυγαδίζω 197 | I squabble |
| καυτηριάζω 92 | I cauterize |
| καυχιέμαι 83 | I boast |
| καψαλίζω 141 | I grill |
| κεντ(ά)ώ 125 | I embroider |
| κεντράρω 93 | I centralize |
| κεντρίζω 199 | I sting |
| κερατώνω 111 | I cuckold |
| κεραυνοβολώ 200 | I strike |
| κερδίζω 138 | I gain |
| κερν(ά)ώ 209 | I treat |
| κερώνω 215 | I wax |
| κεφαλαιοποιώ 91 | I capitalize |
| κηρύττω 73 | I announce |
| κινδυνεύω 112 | I am in danger |

| | |
|---|---|
| κινηματογραφώ 134 | I film |
| κιτρινίζω 187 | I sallow |
| κλαί(γ)ω 111 | I cry |
| κλέβω 199 | I steal |
| κλειδώνω 157 | I lock |
| κλείνω 97 | I close |
| κληροδοτώ 81 | I bequeath |
| κληρονομώ 149 | I inherit |
| κλιμακώνω 127 | I escalate |
| κλονίζω 191 | I shake |
| κλωσσάω 87 | I brood (hen) |
| κλωτσώ 153 | I kick |
| κοάζω 110 | I croak |
| κόβω 112 | I cut |
| κοιλαίνω 117 | I dent |
| *κοιμάμαι 194* | I sleep |
| κοιτάζω 157 | I look at |
| κοκκινίζω 83 | I blush |
| *κοκορεύομαι 85* | I brag |
| κολακεύω 135 | I flatter |
| κολλ(ά)ώ 199 | I stick |
| κολυμπ(ά)ώ 204 | I swim |
| κομματιάζω 192 | I shatter |
| κομπάζω 83 | I boast |
| κομπιάζω 131 | I falter |
| *κοντοστέκομαι 168* | I pause |
| κοπανάω 79 | I bash |
| κοπλιμεντάρω 102 | I compliment |
| κορνάρω 145 | I hoot (car horn) |
| κορνιζώνω 137 | I frame (picture) |
| κοροϊδεύω 161 | I mock |
| κοσκινίζω 193 | I sieve |
| κοστίζω 108 | I cost |

| | |
|---|---|
| κουβαλώ 91 | I carry |
| κουβαριάζω 109 | I cower |
| κουβεντιάζω 94 | I chat |
| κουδουνίζω 152 | I jingle |
| κουκουλώνω 146 | I hush up (scandal) |
| *κουλουριάζομαι 112* | I curl up |
| κουμαντάρω 84 | I boss |
| κουμπώνω 88 | I buckle |
| *κουνιέμαι 216* | I wiggle |
| *κουράζομαι 207* | I am tired |
| κουράζω 207 | I tire |
| κουρδίζω 216 | I wind |
| κουρελιάζω 193 | I shred |
| κουρσεύω 158 | I loot (plunder) |
| κουτσομπολεύω 141 | I gossip |
| κουφοβράζω 193 | I simmer |
| κρατώ 145 | I hold |
| κραυγάζω 189 | I scream |
| *κρέμομαι 203* | I suspend |
| κρεμώ 143 | I hang (execute) |
| κρίνω 153 | I judge |
| κριτικάρω 110 | I criticize |
| κρούω 154 | I knock |
| κρύβω 144 | I hide |
| κρυολογώ 92 | I catch cold |
| κρυφακούω 166 | I overhear |
| κρυφοκοιτάζω 169 | I peep |
| κρυώνω 71 | I am cold |
| κτυπ(ά)ώ 215 | I whack |
| κυβερνώ 141 | I govern |
| κυκλοφορώ 95 | I circulate |
| *κυμαίνομαι 135* | I fluctuate |
| κυματίζω 215 | I wave |

| | |
|---|---|
| κυνηγώ 146 | I hunt |
| κυριαρχώ 122 | I dominate |
| κυριεύω 190 | I seize |
| κυρώνω 178 | I ratify |
| κωδικοποιώ 98 | I codify |
| κωλυσιεργώ 133 | I filibuster |
| *λαγοκοιμάμαι 122* | I doze |
| λαδώνω 141 | I grease (lubricate) |
| λαθεύω 161 | I am mistaken |
| λαμβάνω 179 | I receive |
| λαμποκοπώ 140 | I glare |
| λάμπω 140 | I glitter |
| λαξεύω 91 | I carve |
| λατρεύω 218 | I worship |
| λαχανιάζω 168 | I pant |
| λαχταρ(ά)ώ 109 | I crave |
| λέ(γ)ω 188 | I say |
| λεηλατώ 170 | I pillage |
| λείπω 70 | I am absent (missing) |
| λειτουργώ 138 | I function |
| λεκιάζω 198 | I stain |
| λεπτολογώ 177 | I quibble |
| λέω 20 | I tell |
| ληστεύω 186 | I rob |
| *λιάζομαι 79* | I bask |
| λιγοστεύω 156 | I lessen |
| λιμνάζω 198 | I stagnate |
| λιμοκτονώ 199 | I starve |
| λιντσάρω 159 | I lynch |
| λιπαίνω 158 | I lubricate |
| λιποθυμώ 131 | I faint |
| λιποτακτώ 118 | I desert |
| λιώνω 160 | I melt |

| | |
|---|---|
| λογαριάζω 179 | I reckon |
| *λογικεύομαι 178* | I reason |
| λογοκρίνω 93 | I censor |
| λογομαχώ 121 | I dispute |
| λοξοδρομώ 204 | I swerve |
| λούζω 79 | I bathe |
| λουστράρω 171 | I polish |
| λυγίζω 81 | I bend |
| λύνω 196 | I solve |
| *λυπάμαι 196* | I am sorry |
| λυτρώνω 156 | I liberate |
| μαγειρεύω 107 | I cook |
| μαγεύω 132 | I fascinate |
| μαγκώνω 190 | I seize (take/occupy) |
| μαγνητοφωνώ 205 | I taperecord |
| μαζεύω 99 | I collect |
| μαθαίνω 155 | I learn |
| *μαίνομαι 179* | I rage |
| μακραίνω 156 | I lengthen |
| μαλακώνω 196 | I soften |
| μαλώνω 177 | I quarrel |
| μανιάζω 126 | I enrage |
| μανουβράρω 193 | I shunt |
| μαντάρω 113 | I darn |
| μαντεύω 142 | I guess |
| μαντρώνω 107 | I coop up |
| μαραζώνω 154 | I languish |
| *μαραίνομαι 215* | I weather |
| μαρτυρώ 217 | I witness |
| μασ(ά)ώ 95 | I chew |
| μαστιγώνω 216 | I whip |
| ματαιώνω 91 | I cancel |
| ματώνω 82 | I bleed (nose) |

| | |
|---|---|
| μαυρίζω 205 | I tan |
| μαχαιρώνω 198 | I stab |
| μεγαλοποιώ 128 | I exaggerate |
| μεγαλώνω 142 | I grow (business) |
| μεγεθύνω 126 | I enlarge |
| μεθ(ά)ώ 139 | I get drunk |
| μεθοκοπάω 84 | I booze |
| μελανιάζω 88 | I bruise |
| μελετ(ά)ώ 201 | I study |
| μελοποιώ 191 | I set to music |
| μένω 181 | I remain |
| μεσολαβώ 151 | I intervene |
| μεταβάλλω 93 | I change |
| μεταδίδω 208 | I transmit |
| *μετακινούμαι 208* | I am in transit |
| μετακινώ 192 | I shift |
| μετακομίζω 209 | I transport |
| μεταμορφώνω 208 | I transform |
| μεταναστεύω 125 | I emigrate |
| μεταναστεύω 147 | I immigrate |
| μετανιώνω 180 | I regret |
| μετανοώ 182 | I repent |
| μεταποιώ 70 | I alter |
| μετατρέπω 107 | I convert |
| μεταφέρω 208 | I transfer |
| μεταφράζω 208 | I translate |
| *μεταχειρίζομαι 209* | I treat (use / handle) |
| μετρ(ά)ώ 160 | I measure |
| *μηχανεύομαι 103* | I concoct |
| μηχανορραφώ 171 | I plot |
| μιαίνω 149 | I infect |
| μιλ(ά)ώ 196 | I speak |
| *μιμούμαι 146* | I imitate |

| | |
|---|---|
| *μισοκοιμάμαι 122* | I doze |
| μισώ 143 | I hate |
| μνημονεύω 96 | I cite |
| μνημονεύω 100 | I commemorate |
| μοιάζω 183 | I resemble |
| *μοιράζομαι 192* | I share |
| μοιράζω 121 | I distribute |
| μολύνω 171 | I pollute |
| μονώνω 150 | I insulate |
| μορφώνω 124 | I educate |
| μουγκρίζω 80 | I bellow |
| μουντζουρώνω 195 | I smudge |
| μουρμουρίζω 162 | I murmur |
| μοχθώ 201 | I struggle |
| μπαίνω 126 | I enter |
| μπατσίζω 194 | I slap |
| μπερδεύω 126 | I entangle |
| *μπλέκομαι 148* | I am involved |
| μπλοκάρω 82 | I block |
| μπλοφάρω 83 | I bluff |
| μπογιατίζω 123 | I dye |
| μπορώ 91 | I can |
| μπουγαδιάζω 155 | I launder |
| μποϊκοτάρω 85 | I boycott |
| μπουσουλάω 109 | I crawl |
| μπουχτίζω 187 | I satiate |
| μυρίζω 195 | I smell |
| μυώ 149 | I initiate |
| μωλοπίζω 88 | I bruise |
| ναρκώνω 72 | I anaesthetize |
| ναυαγώ 218 | I wreck |
| ναυλώνω 137 | I freight |
| νευριάζω 133 | I fidget |

| | |
|---|---|
| νεύω 79 | I beckon |
| νεωτερίζω 149 | I innovate |
| νηστεύω 132 | I fast |
| νικ(ά)ώ 216 | I win |
| νιώθω 133 | I feel (consider) |
| νοθεύω 68 | I adulterate |
| *νοιάζομαι 84* | I bother (about something) |
| νοικιάζω 144 | I hire |
| νοικιάζω 181 | I rent |
| νομίζω 206 | I think |
| νομιμοποιώ 156 | I legalize |
| νομοθετώ 156 | I legislate |
| *ντρέπομαι 71* | I am ashamed |
| ντροπιάζω 120 | I disgrace |
| *ντύνομαι 139* | I get dressed |
| ντύνω 123 | I dress |
| νυστάζω 133 | I feel sleepy |
| ξαλαφρώνω 212 | I vent (emotions) |
| ξαμολ(α)ώ 211 | I unleash |
| ξαναβρίσκω 179 | I recover |
| ξανακυλώ 78 | I backslide |
| *ξανάρχομαι 100* | I come back |
| ξανασμίγω 184 | I reunite |
| ξαπλώνω 156 | I lie down |
| ξαφνιάζω 198 | I startle |
| ξαφρίζω 194 | I skim |
| ξεγελώ 136 | I fool |
| ξεδένω 211 | I untie |
| ξεκιν(ά)ώ 198 | I start |
| ξεκλειδώνω 211 | I unlock |
| ξεκοκαλίζω 84 | I bone |

| | |
|---|---|
| ξεκολλώ 210 | I unglue |
| ξεκουμπώνω 210 | I unfasten |
| *ξεκουράζομαι 183* | I rest |
| (ξε)κουφαίνω 114 | I deafen |
| ξελογιάζω 189 | I seduce |
| ξεμακραίνω 179 | I recede |
| ξεμεθ(ά)ώ 195 | I sober up |
| ξεμπερδεύω 120 | I disentangle |
| ξεναγώ 142 | I guide |
| *ξενιτεύομαι 129* | I expatriate |
| ξεπακετάρω 211 | I unpack |
| ξεπερνώ 202 | I surpass |
| ξεπέφτω 94 | I cheapen |
| ξεπλένω 185 | I rinse |
| ξεπληρώνω 182 | I repay |
| ξεπροβοδίζω 189 | I see off/out |
| ξερν(ά)ώ 213 | I vomit |
| ξεροβήχω 97 | I clear my throat |
| ξέρω 154 | I know |
| ξεσηκώνω 148 | I incite |
| ξεσκάζω 211 | I unwind |
| ξεσκαλίζω 84 | I burrow |
| ξεσκεπάζω 130 | I expose |
| ξεσκίζω 185 | I rip |
| ξεσκονίζω 123 | I dust |
| ξεσπ(ά)ώ 127 | I erupt (riots/war) |
| ξεσφίγγω 158 | I loosen (clothing) |
| ξετυλίγω 210 | I unfold |
| ξεφαντώνω 184 | I revel |
| ξεφεύγω 127 | I escape |
| ξεφλουδίζω 200 | I strip |
| *ξεφορτώνομαι 123* | I dump |
| ξεφορτώνω 211 | I unload |

| | |
|---|---|
| ξεφουρνίζω 83 | I blurt out |
| ξεφυλλίζω 88 | I browse |
| ξεφυσώ 176 | I puff |
| ξεφυτρώνω 110 | I crop up |
| ξεφωνίζω 81 | I belt out |
| ξεχνώ 136 | I forget |
| ξεχρεώνω 191 | I settle (pay up) |
| ξηλώνω 211 | I unstitch |
| ξημερώνει 113 | It dawns |
| ξοδεύω 196 | I spend |
| ξύνω 189 | I scrape |
| ξυπν(ά)ώ 214 | I wake up |
| ξυρίζω 192 | I shave |
| οδηγώ 123 | I drive |
| οικτίρω 170 | I pity |
| ολισθαίνω 194 | I slide |
| ολοκληρώνω 101 | I complete (task) |
| ομιλ(ά)ώ 205 | I talk |
| ομολογώ 103 | I confess |
| *ονειρεύομαι 123* | I dream |
| ονειροπολώ 113 | I daydream |
| ονομάζω 162 | I name |
| οπλίζω 98 | I cock (rifle/gun) |
| οργανώνω 165 | I organise |
| ορίζω 118 | I designate |
| οριστοικοποιώ 97 | I clinch (a deal) |
| *ορκίζομαι 204* | I swear (take an oath) |
| ορμ(ά)ώ 186 | I rush |
| οροθετώ 118 | I determine |
| *οσφραίνομαι 195* | I sniff |
| ουρλιάζω 145 | I howl (wind/animal) |
| οφείλω 164 | I am obliged |
| οχυρώνω 136 | I fortify |

| παγιδεύω 209 | I trap |
|---|---|
| παγιώνω 134 | I fix |
| παγώνω 137 | I freeze |
| παζαρεύω 78 | I bargain |
| παθαίνω 201 | I suffer |
| *παιδεύομαι 154* | I labour |
| παίζω 170 | I play |
| παίρνω 204 | I take |
| πακετάρω 167 | I pack |
| παλεύω 218 | I wrestle |
| *πανικοβάλλομαι 168* | I panic |
| *παντρεύομαι 160* | I marry |
| παντρεύω 159 | I marry (join together) |
| παραβαίνω 208 | I transgress |
| παραβιάζω 213 | I violate |
| παραβλέπω 166 | I overlook |
| παραγγέλλω 165 | I order |
| παραγεμίζω 109 | I cram |
| παράγω 174 | I produce |
| *παραδέχομαι 67* | I acknowledge (fact/situation) |
| *παραδίδομαι 203* | I surrender |
| παραδίδω 116 | I deliver (hand over) |
| παραθέτω 177 | I quote (politician/poet) |
| *παραιτούμαι 183* | I resign |
| παρακάμπτω 96 | I circumvent |
| παρακινώ 211 | I urge |
| παρακμάζω 114 | I decline |
| *παρακοιμάμαι 167* | I oversleep |
| παρακολουθώ 77 | I attend |
| παρακούω 120 | I disobey |
| παρακωλύω 173 | I prevent |
| παραλείπω 165 | I omit |
| παραλύω 168 | I paralyse |
| παραμελώ 163 | I neglect |
| παραμένω 157 | I linger |
| παραμερίζω 92 | I cast aside |
| παραμονεύω 158 | I lurk |
| παραπατ(ά)ώ 201 | I stumble |
| παραπλανώ 116 | I delude |
| παραποιώ 131 | I falsify |
| *παραπονούμαι 101* | I complain |
| *παραπονιέμαι 101* | I complain |
| παρασέρνω 158 | I lure (entice) |
| παρασταίνω 117 | I depict |
| παραστρατώ 200 | I stray |
| παρατ(ά)ώ 177 | I quit |
| παρατείνω 130 | I extend |
| παρατηρώ 164 | I observe |
| παραφορτώνω 98 | I clutter |
| παραχαράσσω 108 | I counterfeit |
| παραχωρώ 70 | I allot |
| παρεκλίνω 154 | I lapse |
| παρελαύνω 168 | I parade |
| παρεμβαίνω 151 | I intervene |
| παρεμβάλλω 150 | I insert |
| παρεμποδίζω 164 | I obstruct |
| παρενοχλώ 143 | I harass |
| παρεξηγώ 161 | I misunderstand |
| παρέχω 175 | I provide |
| παρηγορώ 100 | I comfort |
| παριστάνω 147 | I impersonate |
| παρκάρω 168 | I park |
| παροτρύνω 174 | I prompt |
| *παρουσιάζομαι 159* | I make an appearance |
| παρουσιάζω 173 | I present (introduce) |
| πασαλείβω 113 | I daub |
| πασπαλίζω 197 | I sprinkle |
| πασπατεύω 133 | I fiddle |
| πατ(ά)ώ 199 | I step on |
| παφλάζω 154 | I lap |
| παχαίνω 80 | I become fat |
| πεθαίνω 119 | I die |
| πείθω 107 | I convince |
| πειν(ά)ώ 71 | I am hungry |
| πειράζω 205 | I tease |
| *πειραματίζομαι 129* | I experiment |
| πελεκώ 95 | I chop down/off |
| πενθώ 161 | I mourn |
| *περηφανεύομαι 175* | I am proud |
| περιβάλλω 203 | I surround |
| περιγελώ 118 | I deride |
| περιγράφω 118 | I describe |
| περιέχω 105 | I contain |
| περικόβω 180 | I reduce |
| περικυκλώνω 203 | I surround (encircle) |
| περιλαμβάνω 148 | I include |
| περιμένω 214 | I wait |
| περιοδεύω 208 | I tour |
| *περιορίζομαι 103* | I am confined |
| περιορίζω 184 | I restrict |
| *περιπλανώμαι 214* | I wander |
| περιπλέκω 102 | I complicate |
| *περιποιούμαι 77* | I attend to |
| περιπολώ 168 | I patrol |
| περιτυλίγω 218 | I wrap |
| περιφρονώ 118 | I despise |

| | |
|---|---|
| περιφρουρώ 175 | I protect |
| περν(ά)ώ 168 | I pass by |
| περπατ(ά)ώ 214 | I walk |
| πετ(ά)ώ 207 | I throw |
| πετυχαίνω 201 | I succeed |
| πετώ 136 | I fly |
| πέφτω 131 | I fall |
| πηγαίνω, πάω 140 | I go |
| πηδώ 153 | I jump |
| *πιάνομαι 139* | I get caught |
| πιάνω 92 | I catch |
| πιέζω 173 | I press |
| πιλοτάρω 163 | I navigate |
| πίνω 123 | I drink |
| πιστεύω 80 | I believe |
| πιστοποιώ 93 | I certify |
| πιστώνω 109 | I credit (finance) |
| πλάθω 191 | I shape |
| πλαισιώνω 203 | I surround (frame) |
| πλαστογραφώ 143 | I fake (documents) |
| πλαταίνω 87 | I broaden |
| πλατσουλίζω 167 | I paddle |
| πλέκω 154 | I knit |
| πλένω 214 | I wash |
| πληγώνω 146 | I hurt |
| πλημμυρίζω 135 | I flood |
| πληροφορώ 149 | I inform |
| πληρώνω 168 | I pay |
| πλησιάζω 74 | I approach |
| πλήττω 71 | I am bored |
| *πνίγομαι 95* | I choke (on food) |
| πνίγω 123 | I drown |
| ποζάρω 172 | I pose |

| | |
|---|---|
| ποθώ 158 | I lust |
| ποικίλλω 212 | I vary |
| πολεμώ 133 | I fight |
| πολιορκώ 81 | I besiege |
| *πολιτεύομαι 140* | I go in for politics |
| πολιτογραφώ 162 | I naturalize |
| πολλαπλασιάζω 162 | I multiply |
| πον(ά)ώ 67 | I ache |
| ποντάρω 198 | I stake |
| πουλ(ά)ώ 190 | I sell |
| *πραγματεύομαι 114* | I deal with |
| πραγματοποιώ 76 | I attain (realize) |
| πραγματώνω 186 | I realise |
| *πρήζομαι 204* | I swell |
| πριονίζω 188 | I saw |
| *προάγομαι 68* | I advance |
| προάγω 174 | I promote |
| προαναγγέλλω 144 | I herald |
| προασπίζω 192 | I shield |
| προβάλλω 174 | I project |
| προβάρω 180 | I rehearse |
| προβιβάζω 174 | I promote |
| προβλέπω 172 | I predict |
| προβληματίζω 177 | I puzzle |
| προγραμματίζω 188 | I schedule |
| προγυμνάζω 98 | I coach (student) |
| προδίδω 81 | I betray |
| προδικάζω 172 | I prejudge |
| προεδρεύω 173 | I preside |
| προειδοποιώ 214 | I warn |
| προεξέχω 175 | I protrude |
| *προέρχομαι 100* | I come from |
| *προετοιμάζομαι 139* | I get ready |

| | |
|---|---|
| προκαλώ 176 | I provoke |
| προκαταβάλλω 117 | I deposit |
| προκαταλαμβάνω 172 | I prejudice |
| προκηρύσσω 174 | I proclaim |
| προκηρύττω 174 | I proclaim |
| προκόβω 206 | I thrive |
| προλαβαίνω 92 | I catch up |
| *προμηθεύομαι 165* | I obtain |
| προμηθεύω 199 | I stock |
| προξενώ 92 | I cause |
| προοδεύω 174 | I progress |
| *προπονούμαι 172* | I practice |
| *προπονιέμαι 172* | I practise |
| προπονώ 98 | I coach (athlete) |
| προσανατολίζω 166 | I orientate |
| *προσαρμόζομαι 68* | I adjust (rules) |
| προσαρτώ 73 | I annex |
| προσβάλλω 150 | I insult |
| προσδένω 132 | I fasten |
| προσδίδω 76 | I attach (importance) |
| προσδοκώ 129 | I expect |
| προσελκύω 77 | I attract (attention) |
| *προσεύχομαι 172* | I pray |
| προσέχω 164 | I notice |
| προσηλυτίζω 107 | I convert (religion) |
| προσθέτω 67 | I add |
| προσκαλώ 152 | I invite |
| προσκολλ(ά)ώ 76 | I attach |
| προσλαμβάνω 145 | I hire (employ) |
| προσπαθώ 77 | I attempt |
| προσπερνώ 167 | I overtake |
| *προσποιούμαι 173* | I pretend |
| προστατεύω 175 | I protect |

| | |
|---|---|
| προσυπογράφω 108 | I countersign |
| προσφέρ(ν)ω 165 | I offer |
| *προσφέρομαι 213* | I volunteer |
| προτείνω 202 | I suggest |
| προτιμώ 172 | I prefer |
| προτρέπω 211 | I urge |
| προϋποθέτω 173 | I presume |
| προϋπολογίζω 88 | I budget |
| *προφασίζομαι 171* | I plead |
| προφέρω 174 | I pronounce |
| προφητεύω 175 | I prophesy |
| προχωρώ 173 | I proceed |
| πτοώ 113 | I daunt |
| πυγμαχώ 85 | I box (sport) |
| πυροβολώ 192 | I shoot |
| ράβω 191 | I sew |
| ραγίζω 95 | I chip |
| ραδιουργώ 188 | I scheme |
| ρεζιλεύω 191 | I shame |
| *ρεύομαι 89* | I burp |
| ρευστοποιώ 157 | I liquefy |
| ρέω 200 | I stream |
| ρημάζω 186 | I ruin |
| ριγώ 192 | I shiver |
| ρισκάρω 186 | I risk |
| ρίχνω 158 | I lower (price) |
| ριψοκινυνεύω 144 | I hazard (guess) |
| ροκανίζω 170 | I plane |
| ρουθουνίζω 195 | I snort(animal) |
| ρουφώ 203 | I swallow |
| ροχαλίζω 195 | I snore |
| ρυθμίζω 187 | I regulate |
| ρυμουλκώ 208 | I tow |

| | |
|---|---|
| ρωτ(ά)ώ 75 | I ask (a question) |
| σαγηνεύω 91 | I captivate |
| σακατεύω 110 | I cripple |
| σαλεύω 199 | I stir |
| σαλπάρω 92 | I cast off (from shore) |
| σαμποτάρω 187 | I sabotage |
| σαπίζω 186 | I rot |
| σαρκάζω 188 | I scoff |
| σαστίζω 104 | I confuse |
| σατιρίζω 187 | I satirize |
| σβήνω 130 | I extinguish |
| σβωλιάζω 97 | I clot |
| *σέβομαι 183* | I respect |
| σείω 85 | I brandish |
| σερβίρω 191 | I serve |
| σεριανίζω 188 | I saunter (stroll ) |
| *σέρνομαι 110* | I creep |
| σέρνω 176 | I pull |
| *σηκώνομαι 139* | I get up |
| σηκώνω 156 | I lift (up) |
| σημαίνω 185 | I ring |
| σημειώνω 159 | I mark (indicate) |
| σιγοτραγουδώ 145 | I hum (tune) |
| *σιγουρεύομαι 159* | I make sure |
| σιδερώνω 152 | I iron |
| σιμώνω 140 | I go near |
| *σιχαίνομαι 157* | I loathe |
| σιωπώ 81 | I am silent |
| σκάβω 119 | I dig |
| σκάζω 89 | I burst (tyre/pipe) |
| σκανδαλίζω 188 | I scandalize |
| σκαρφαλώνω 97 | I climb |

| | |
|---|---|
| *σκαρφίζομαι 123* | I dream up (contrive) |
| σκαρώνω 107 | I cook up (make up) |
| σκεπάζω 109 | I cover |
| *σκέφτομαι 206* | I think (about s'g) |
| σκηνοθετώ 198 | I stage |
| σκίζω 205 | I tear |
| σκιρτώ 85 | I bound |
| σκιτσάρω 123 | I draw |
| σκοπεύω 69 | I aim |
| σκοτίζω 169 | I pester |
| σκοτώνω 153 | I kill |
| σκούζω 218 | I yelp |
| σκουντ(ά)ώ 152 | I jog (someone) |
| σκουπίζω 204 | I sweep |
| σκουριάζω 186 | I rust |
| σκύβω 200 | I stoop |
| σκυθρωπιάζω 202 | I sulk |
| σοκάρω 192 | I shock |
| σουβλίζω 197 | I spit |
| σουφρώνω 170 | I pilfer |
| σπάζω 86 | I break |
| σπαταλ(ά)ώ 214 | I waste |
| σπέρνω 196 | I sow |
| σπεύδω 143 | I hasten |
| σπινθηροβολώ 196 | I sparkle |
| σπουδάζω 201 | I study |
| σπρώχνω 176 | I push |
| σταθεροποιώ 104 | I consolidate |
| σταματ(ά)ώ 200 | I stop |
| στασιάζω 185 | I revolt |
| *σταυροκοπιέμαι 110* | I cross myself |
| σταυρώνω 111 | I crucify |

| | |
|---|---|
| στεγνώνω 123 | I dry |
| *στέκομαι 198* | I stand |
| στέλνω 190 | I send |
| στενεύω 162 | I narrow |
| *στενοχωριέμαι 217* | I am worried |
| στενοχωρώ 211 | I upset |
| στερεώνω 175 | I prop up |
| *στερούμαι 154* | I lack |
| στερώ 118 | I deprive |
| *στεφανώνομαι 215* | I wed |
| στέφω 110 | I crown |
| στήνω 191 | I set up |
| *στηρίζομαι 108* | I count on |
| στηρίζω 78 | I back |
| στοιβάζω 167 | I cram |
| στοιχειώνω 143 | I haunt |
| στοιχηματίζω 81 | I bet |
| στολίζω 115 | I decorate (adorn with) |
| *στοχάζομαι 105* | I contemplate |
| στραβοκοιτάζω 137 | I frown on |
| στραβώνω 82 | I blind |
| στραγγαλίζω 200 | I strangle |
| στραγγίζω 200 | I strain |
| στραμπουλίζω 197 | I sprain |
| στρατολογώ 179 | I recruit |
| στρίβω 209 | I twist |
| *στριμώχνομαι 110* | I crowd |
| στριμώχνω 108 | I corner |
| στρώνω 197 | I spread (lay/cover/set) |
| στύβω 198 | I squeeze |
| στυπώνω 83 | I blot |
| συγκαλύπτω 109 | I cover up |

| | |
|---|---|
| συγκαλώ 107 | I convene |
| *συγκατατίθεμαι 104* | I consent |
| *συγκεντρώνομαι 103* | I concentrate |
| *συγκινούμαι 207* | I am touched (moved) |
| συγκινώ 57 | I affect (move deeply) |
| συγκλίνω 107 | I converge |
| *συγκρατούμαι 105* | I contain myself |
| *συγκρατιέμαι 105* | I contain myself |
| συγκρατώ 106 | I control (inflation) |
| συγκρίνω 101 | I compare |
| *συγκρούομαι 109* | I crash (collide) |
| συγυρίζω 97 | I clear up |
| συγχαίρω 104 | I congratulate |
| συγχρονίζω 204 | I synchronize |
| *συγχύζομαι 139* | I get upset |
| συγχωρώ 136 | I forgive |
| συζητώ 120 | I discuss |
| συζώ 98 | I cohabit |
| συκοφαντώ 194 | I slander |
| συλλαμβάνω 75 | I arrest |
| συλλέγω 99 | I collect (as hobby) |
| *συλλογίζομαι 104* | I consider |
| συμβαίνει 143 | It happens |
| συμβάλλω 106 | I contribute |
| *συμβιβάζομαι 102* | I compromise |
| συμβολίζω 204 | I symbolise |
| *συμβουλεύομαι 105* | I consult |
| συμβουλεύω 69 | I advise |
| *συμμερίζομαι 133* | I feel for (sympathise with) |
| συμμετέχω 168 | I participate |
| *συμμορφώνομαι 104* | I conform |
| συμπεραίνω 103 | I conclude (deduce) |

| | |
|---|---|
| συμπιέζω 102 | I compress |
| συμπίπτω 99 | I coincide |
| συμπληρώνω 102 | I complete (form) |
| συμπον(ά)ώ 204 | I sympathise with |
| συμπράττω 99 | I collaborate |
| συμφωνώ 69 | I agree |
| συναθροίζω 138 | I gather |
| *συναισθάνομαι 133* | I feel for (emotionally) |
| συναντ(ά)ώ 160 | I meet |
| συνάπτω 153 | I join |
| *συνδέομαι 157* | I log on (computer) |
| συνδέω 104 | I connect |
| συνδυάζω 99 | I combine |
| συνεισφέρω 106 | I contribute |
| *συνεργάζομαι 107* | I cooperate |
| *συνέρχομαι 100* | I come round |
| συνεχίζω 106 | I continue |
| συνηγορώ 69 | I advocate |
| συνηθίζω 139 | I get used to |
| συνθέτω 102 | I compose (music) |
| συνιστώ 105 | I constitute |
| συννεφιάζει 97 | It clouds over |
| συνοδεύω 127 | I escort |
| συνομιλώ 107 | I converse |
| συνορεύω 84 | I border |
| συνοψίζω 202 | I summarize |
| συνταξιοδοτώ 169 | I pension off |
| συντάσσω 102 | I compose (letter) |
| συντηρώ 173 | I preserve |
| συντονίζω 107 | I coordinate |
| συντρέχω 76 | I assist |
| συντρίβω 195 | I smash |
| συνωμοτώ 105 | I conspire |

| | |
|---|---|
| *συρρικνώνομαι 193* | I shrink |
| *συσκέπτομαι 103* | I confer (jury/panel) |
| συσκοτίζω 164 | I obscure |
| *συσπώμαι 216* | I wince |
| *συστέλλομαι 106* | I contract |
| συστήνω 151 | I introduce |
| *συστρέφομαι 218* | I wriggle |
| συστρέφω 106 | I contort (face) |
| συσφίγγω 105 | I constrict |
| συχνάζω 137 | I frequent |
| σφάλλω 127 | I am in error |
| σφίγγω 98 | I clutch |
| σφουγγαρίζω 161 | I mop |
| σφουγγίζω 216 | I wipe |
| σφραγίζω 189 | I seal |
| σφυρίζω 216 | I whistle |
| σχεδιάζω 118 | I design |
| *σχετίζομαι 76* | I associate (link/connect) |
| σχετίζω 180 | I relate |
| σχηματίζω 90 | I form |
| σχολιάζω 101 | I comment |
| *σώζομαι 188* | I save myself |
| σώζω 188 | I save |
| σωπαίνω 153 | I keep silent |
| *σωριάζομαι 99* | I collapse |
| ταΐζω 132 | I feed |
| ταιριάζω 160 | I match (materials) |
| *τακτοποιούμαι 191* | I settle |
| τακτοποιώ 177 | I put in order |
| ταλαιπωρώ 169 | I pester |
| ταλαντεύω 112 | I dangle |
| *ταλλαντεύομαι 212* | I vacillate |

| | |
|---|---|
| *ταμπουρώνομαι 78* | I barricade |
| ταξιδεύω 209 | I travel |
| ταξινομώ 96 | I classify |
| ταπεινώνω 146 | I humiliate |
| ταράζω 70 | I alarm |
| ταυτίζω 146 | I identify (distinguish) |
| ταχυδρομώ 172 | I post |
| τελειοποιώ 169 | I perfect |
| τελειώνω 134 | I finish |
| τεμπελιάζω 155 | I laze |
| τεντώνω 200 | I stretch |
| τερματίζω 206 | I terminate |
| τηγανίζω 137 | I fry |
| τηλεγραφώ 90 | I cable |
| τηλεφωνώ 205 | I telephone |
| τηρώ 68 | I adhere |
| τιμώ 145 | I honour |
| τιμωρώ 176 | I punish |
| τινάζω 135 | I flick |
| τιτιβίζω 95 | I chirp |
| τολμώ 113 | I dare |
| τονίζω 125 | I emphasize |
| τονώνω 213 | I vitalize |
| τοποθετώ 170 | I place |
| τουμπάρω 90 | I cajole |
| τραβ(ά)ώ 176 | I pull |
| τραγανίζω 111 | I crunch |
| τραγουδ(ά)ώ 194 | I sing |
| *τραντάζομαι 89* | I bump |
| τραυλίζω 198 | I stammer |
| τραυματίζω 149 | I injure |
| τρεκλίζω 203 | I sway |
| τρεμοπαίζω 135 | I flicker (eyelids) |

| | |
|---|---|
| τρεμοσβήνω 216 | I wink |
| τρεμουλιάζω 217 | I wobble |
| τρέμω 209 | I tremble |
| τρέφω 164 | I nourish |
| τρέχω 186 | I run |
| τρίβω 186 | I rub |
| τριγυρίζω 125 | I encircle |
| τριγυρν(ά)ώ 125 | I encircle |
| τριζοβολάω 109 | I crackle |
| τρίζω 109 | I creak |
| τρικλίζω 198 | I stagger |
| τριπλασιάζω 209 | I treble |
| τρομάζω 137 | I frighten |
| τρομοκρατώ 206 | I terrorize |
| τροποποιώ 72 | I amend (text/laws) |
| τροφοδοτώ 92 | I cater for |
| τρυπάω 170 | I pierce |
| τρώ(γ)ω 124 | I eat |
| τσακίζω 111 | I crush |
| *τσακώνομαι 79* | I battle |
| *τσακώνομαι 79* | I quarrel |
| τσακώνω 74 | I apprehend |
| τσαλακώνω 112 | I crinkle |
| τσαλαπατώ 209 | I tread on |
| τσατίζω 213 | I vex |
| τσεκάρω 94 | I check |
| τσιμεντάρω 92 | I cement |
| τσιμπολογώ 163 | I nibble |
| τσιμπώ 170 | I pinch (filch/pilfer) |
| τσοντάρω 95 | I chip in |
| τσουγκρίζω 97 | I clink |
| τσούζω 199 | I sting |
| τσουλάω 109 | I crawl (traffic) |

| | |
|---|---|
| τυλίγω 98 | I coil |
| τυποποιώ 136 | I formulate |
| τυπώνω 173 | I print |
| τυραννάω 207 | I torment |
| τυφλώνω 82 | I blind |
| υγραίνω 112 | I dampen |
| υιοθετώ 68 | I adopt |
| *υπάγομαι 100* | I come under |
| υπαγορεύω 119 | I dictate |
| *υπαινίσσομαι 147* | I imply |
| υπακούω 164 | I obey |
| υπαναχωρώ 102 | I compromise |
| υπάρχω 129 | I exist |
| υπεραγαπώ 68 | I adore |
| *υπερασπίζομαι 115* | I defend |
| υπερβαίνω 128 | I exceed |
| υπερβάλλω 128 | I exaggerate |
| υπερεκτιμώ 166 | I overestimate |
| *υπερθερμαίνομαι 166* | I overheat |
| υπερισχύω 171 | I predominate |
| υπερνικώ 202 | I surmount |
| υπερπηδώ 166 | I override |
| υπερτιμώ 166 | I overprice |
| υπηρετώ 190 | I serve |
| υπνωτίζω 160 | I mesmerize |
| υποβαθμίζω 120 | I discredit |
| υποβάλλω 73 | I apply for (job/permit) |
| υποβιβάζω 114 | I debase |
| υπογραμμίζω 210 | I underline |
| υπογράφω 193 | I sign |
| υποδεικνύω 148 | I indicate |
| *υποδέχομαι 179* | I receive |

| | |
|---|---|
| υποδηλώνω 144 | I hint |
| υποδουλώνω 126 | I enslave |
| *υποδύομαι 147* | I impersonate (mimic) |
| υποθέτω 202 | I suppose |
| υποθηκεύω 161 | I mortgage |
| υποκινώ 150 | I instigate |
| *υποκλίνομαι 85* | I bow |
| *υποκρίνομαι 170* | I play-act |
| υποκύπτω 85 | I bow (yield) |
| υπολογίζω 128 | I estimate |
| υπομένω 143 | I have patience |
| *υποπτεύομαι 203* | I suspect |
| υποστηρίζω 202 | I support |
| *υπόσχομαι 171* | I promise |
| *υποτάσσομαι 201* | I subordinate |
| υποτιμ(ά)ώ 210 | I underrate |
| *υποχρεώνομαι 164* | I am obliged |
| υποχρεώνω 164 | I oblige |
| υποχωρώ 78 | I backtrack |
| υφαίνω 215 | I weave |
| υψώνω 178 | I raise (elevate) |
| *φαίνεται 190* | It seems |
| *φαίνομαι 73* | I appear |
| φαλιρίζω 140 | I go broke |
| *φαντάζομαι 146* | I imagine |
| φαντασιοκοπώ 132 | I fantasize |
| φαρδαίνω 216 | I widen |
| φέγγω 192 | I shine |
| φέρνω 87 | I bring |
| *φέρομαι 80* | I behave |
| φεύγω 155 | I leave |
| φθάνω 77 | I attain (reach) |

| | |
|---|---|
| φιλοδοξώ 71 | I am ambitious |
| φιλονικώ 74 | I argue (quarrel) |
| φιλοφρονώ 101 | I complement |
| φιλώ 153 | I kiss |
| φιμώνω 138 | I gag |
| *φλέγομαι 70* | I am ablaze |
| φλερτάρω 135 | I flirt |
| φλυαρώ 94 | I chatter |
| *φοβάμαι 132* | I fear |
| φονεύω 162 | I murder |
| φορ(ά)ώ 215 | I wear |
| *φορολογούμαι 168* | I am taxed |
| φορτώνω 157 | I load |
| φορώ 177 | I put on (wear) |
| φουσκαλιάζω 82 | I blister |
| φουσκώνω 133 | I fill |
| φράζω 78 | I bar |
| φρακάρω 152 | I jam |
| φρενάρω 85 | I brake (slow down) |
| *φρεσκάρομαι 137* | I freshen up |
| φρεσκάρω 88 | I brush up |
| φροντίζω 91 | I care for |
| φρονώ 115 | I deem |
| φρουρώ 142 | I guard |
| φταίω 72 | I am to blame |
| φτάνω 75 | I arrive |
| *φταρνίζομαι 195* | I sneeze |
| φτιάχνω 159 | I make |
| φυλακίζω 147 | I imprison |
| φυλάω 142 | I guard |
| φυσάω 83 | I blow |
| φυτεύω 170 | I plant |
| φυτοζωώ 212 | I vegetate |

| | |
|---|---|
| φωλιάζω 163 | I nest |
| φωνάζω 193 | I shout |
| φωταγωγώ 135 | I floodlight |
| φωτίζω 146 | I illuminate |
| φωτογραφίζω 169 | I photograph |
| χαζεύω 88 | I browse |
| χαϊδεύω 91 | I caress |
| χαιρετίζω 187 | I salute |
| χαιρετώ 141 | I greet |
| *χαίρομαι 139* | I am glad |
| χαλ(ά)ώ χαλνώ 197 | I spoil |
| χαλαρώνω 181 | I relax |
| χαλιναγωγώ 111 | I curb |
| χαλώ 86 | I break down (machine) |
| χαμηλώνω 119 | I dip |
| χαμογελ(ά)ώ 195 | I smile |
| *χάνομαι 158* | I am lost |
| χάνω 158 | I lose |
| χαράζω 125 | I engrave |
| χαρακτηρίζω 93 | I characterize |
| χαρακώνω 186 | I rule |
| χαραμίζω 214 | I waste |
| χαρίζω 122 | I donate |
| χαρτογραφώ 94 | I chart |
| χαρτοπαίζω 138 | I gamble |
| *χασμουριέμαι 218* | I yawn |
| χασομερώ 113 | I dawdle |
| χάφτω 217 | I wolf |
| χαχανίζω 139 | I giggle |
| *χειρίζομαι 142* | I handle |
| χειροκροτώ 96 | I clap |
| χειρονομώ 138 | I gesticulate |
| χειροτερεύω 217 | I worsen |
| χειρουργώ 165 | I operate |
| χλευάζω 195 | I sneer |
| χλωμιάζω 167 | I pale |
| χορεύω 112 | I dance |
| χορηγώ 141 | I grant |
| χοροπηδώ 85 | I bounce |
| χοροστατώ 165 | I officiate |
| χοχλάζω 88 | I bubble |
| *χρειάζομαι 163* | I need |
| χρεοκοπώ 140 | I go bankrupt |
| χρεώνω 93 | I charge |
| χρηματοδοτώ 134 | I finance |
| χρησιμοποιώ 212 | I use |
| χρονολογώ 113 | I date (object) |
| χρονομετρώ 207 | I time |
| χρονοτριβώ 197 | I linger |
| χρωματίζω 99 | I colour in |
| χρωστ(ά)ώ 167 | I owe |
| χτενίζω 99 | I comb |
| χτίζω 88 | I build |
| χτυπ(ά)ώ 79 | I beat |
| χτυπάει 185 | It rings |
| χύνω 172 | I pour |
| χωρίζω 122 | I divorce |
| ψαλιδίζω 97 | I clip (hedges) |
| ψάλλω / ψέλνω 93 | I chant |
| ψαρεύω 134 | I fish |
| ψάχνω 189 | I search |
| ψαχουλεύω 138 | I fumble |
| ψέγω 82 | I blame |
| ψεκάζω 197 | I spray |
| ψελλίζω 77 | I babble |
| ψευδίζω 201 | I stutter |
| *ψεύδομαι 156* | I lie |
| ψηλαφίζω 207 | I touch |
| ψηλώνω 142 | I grow |
| ψήνω 78 | I bake |
| ψηφίζω 213 | I vote |
| ψιθυρίζω 216 | I whisper |
| ψωνίζω 193 | I shop |
| ωθώ 193 | I shove |
| ωραιοποιώ 79 | I beautify |
| ωριμάζω 185 | I ripen |
| *ωφελούμαι 174* | I profit |

**Στοιχειοθεσία – Εκτύπωση**

UNIVERSITY STUDIO PRESS

Αρμενοπούλου 32 – 546 35 Θεσσαλονίκη
Τηλ. 2310 208 731, 209 837 – Fax 2310 216 647

**Βιβλιοδεσία**

Γ. Δεληδημητρίου

ΒΙΒΛΙΟΔΕΤΙΚΗ

Αγ. Δημητρίου 190 – Τηλ. 2310 216 888